HUNTSMAN'S QUARRY
KEMERTON

HUNTSMAN'S QUARRY, KEMERTON

A Late Bronze Age settlement and landscape in Worcestershire

Robin Jackson

With contributions by Alex Bayliss, Peter Bellamy, Christopher Bronk Ramsey, Roger C. P. Doonan, James Greig, Derek Hurst, Andrew Moss, Mike Napthan, Elizabeth Pearson, Stephanie Pinter-Bellows, Ian Tyers, David F. Williams and Ann Woodward

Illustrated by Laura Templeton, Carolyn Hunt and Steve Rigby

Oxbow Books
Oxford & Philadelphia

Published in the United Kingdom in 2015 by
OXBOW BOOKS
10 Hythe Bridge Street, Oxford OX1 2EW

and in the United States by
OXBOW BOOKS
1950 Lawrence Road, Havertown, PA 19083

© Oxbow Books and the individual authors 2015

Hardcover Edition: ISBN 978-1-78297-994-4
Digital Edition: ISBN 978-1-78297-995-1

A CIP record for this book is available from the British Library

Library of Congress Cataloging-in-Publication Data

Names: Jackson, Robin (Robin Andrew) | Bayliss, Alexandra.
Title: Huntsman's Quarry, Kemerton : a late Bronze Age settlement and
    landscape in Worcestershire / Robin Jackson ; with contributions by Alex
    Bayliss, Peter Bellamy, Christopher Bronk Ramsey, Roger C.P. Doonan, James
    Greig, Derek Hurst, Andrew Moss, Mike Napthan, Elizabeth Pearson,
    Stephanie Pinter-Bellows, Ian Tyers, David F. Williams and Ann Woodward ;
    illustrated by Laura Templeton, Carolyn Hunt and Steve Rigby.
Description: Oxford : Oxbow Books, 2015. | Includes bibliographical
    references and index.
Identifiers: LCCN 2015024856| ISBN 9781782979944 (hardcover) | ISBN
    9781782979951 (digital)
Subjects: LCSH: Huntsman's Quarry Site (Kemerton, England) | Quarries and
    quarrying--England--Worcestershire. | Bronze age--England--Worcestershire.
    | Human settlements--England--Worcestershire. | Landscape
    archaeology--England--Worcestershire. | Excavations
    (Archaeology)--England--Worcestershire. | Excavations
    (Archaeology)--England--Kemerton. | Worcestershire (England)--Antiquities.
    | Kemerton (England)--Antiquities.
Classification: LCC DA600.K24 J33 2015 | DDC 936.2/449--dc23 LC record available at http://
lccn.loc.gov/2015024856

Printed in Malta by Gutenberg Press

For a complete list of Oxbow titles, please contact:

UNITED KINGDOM
Oxbow Books
Telephone (01865) 241249, Fax (01865) 794449
Email: oxbow@oxbowbooks.com
www.oxbowbooks.com

UNITED STATES OF AMERICA
Oxbow Books
Telephone (800) 791-9354, Fax (610) 853-9146
Email: queries@casemateacademic.com
www.casemateacademic.com/oxbow

Oxbow Books is part of the Casemate Group

Front cover: Reconstruction of the Late Bronze Age settlement (by Steve Rigby)
Back cover: Late Bronze Age ceramic weights and pottery

Contents

Contents

List of Figures and Tables

List of Tables

Contributors

ALEX BAYLISS
Scientific Dating Team
Historic England
1 Waterhouse Square
138–142 Holborn
London EC1N 2ST

PETER S. BELLAMY
Terrain Archaeology
The Granary
Ilsington Farm House
Tincleton
Dorchester
Dorset DT2 8QW

CHRIS BRONK RAMSEY
Scientific Dating Team
Historic England
1 Waterhouse Square
138–142 Holborn
London EC1N 2ST

GORDON COOK
Scientific Dating Team
Historic England
1 Waterhouse Square
138–142 Holborn
London EC1N 2ST

ROGER C. P. DOONAN
Department of Archaeology
University of Sheffield
Northgate House
West Street
Sheffield S1 4ET

JAMES GREIG
7 Southwold Avenue,
King's Norton
Birmingham B30 3RJ

CAROLYN HUNT
Worcestershire County Council
Archive and Archaeology Service
The Hive
Sawmill Walk
The Butts
Worcester WR1 3PB

DEREK HURST
Worcestershire County Council
Archive and Archaeology Service
The Hive
Sawmill Walk
The Butts
Worcester WR1 3PB

ROBIN JACKSON
Worcestershire County Council
Archive and Archaeology Service
The Hive
Sawmill Walk
The Butts
Worcester WR1 3PB

JOHN MEADOWS,
Scientific Dating Team
Historic England
1 Waterhouse Square
138–142 Holborn
London EC1N 2ST

ANDREW MOSS
School of Geography, Earth and Environmental Sciences
University of Birmingham
Edgbaston
Birmingham B15 2TT

MIKE NAPTHAN
Mike Napthan Archaeology
3 Hamilton Road,
Worcester WR5 1AG

ELIZABETH PEARSON
Worcestershire County Council
Archive and Archaeology Service
The Hive
Sawmill Walk
The Butts
Worcester WR1 3PB

STEPHANIE PINTER BELLOWS
19 Butts Paddock
Canewdon
Rochford
Essex SS4 3QT

STEVE RIGBY
Worcestershire County Council
Archive and Archaeology Service
The Hive
Sawmill Walk
The Butts
Worcester WR1 3PB

LAURA TEMPLETON
Worcestershire County Council
Archive and Archaeology Service
The Hive
Sawmill Walk
The Butts
Worcester WR1 3PB

IAN TYERS
Dendrochronological Consultancy Ltd
65 Crimcar Drive
Sheffield S10 4EF

DAVID F WILLIAMS
Faculty of Humanities
University of Southampton
Avenue Campus
Highfield
Southampton SO17 1BF

ANN WOODWARD
17 Great Western Road
Dorchester
Dorset DT1 1UF

Project Summary

Archaeological investigations undertaken at Huntsman's Quarry, Kemerton in south Worcestershire during 1995–1996 recorded significant Late Bronze Age occupation areas and field systems spreading across more than 8 hectares.

Waterholes and associated roundhouses, structures and pits were set within landscape of fields and droveways, elements of which probably pre-dated the settlement. Substantial artefactual and ecofactual assemblages were recovered from the upper fills of the waterholes and larger pits. The settlement had a predominantly pastoral economy supported by some textile and bronze production. Ceramics included a notable proportion of non-local fabrics demonstrating that the local population enjoyed a wide range of regional contacts. Wider ranging, national exchange networks were also indicated by the presence of shale objects as well as the supply of bronze for metalworking, perhaps indicative of a site of some social status. Together the evidence indicates a settlement which can be compared favourably to those known along the Thames Valley but until now not recognised in this part of the country.

Based upon an extensive programme of radiocarbon dating, it is evident that some of the waterholes and elements of the field systems were laid out during the 12th century cal BC with areas of unenclosed settlement being subsequently established within this bounded landscape. Dating of charred residues from a substantial plainware assemblage indicates that occupation was focused in the 11th century cal BC, perhaps spanning as little as four or five generations. It is argued that, rather than all areas having been contemporaneously occupied, occupation of individual areas was short-lived with the focus of the settlement shifting on a regular basis. It is proposed that this occurred on a generational basis, with each generation setting up a new 'homestead' with an associated waterhole. Possibly at the same time, the settlement of the previous generation was formally abandoned, a process marked by the closure of the waterholes. Slight variations in the composition of the ceramic assemblages across the site provide some support for this model of settlement shift.

Cropmark evidence and limited other investigations indicate that the fields and droveways recorded represent a small fragment of a widespread system of boundaries established across the gravel terraces lying between Bredon Hill and the Carrant Brook. This managed and organised landscape appears to have been established for the maintenance of an economy primarily based on relatively intensive livestock farming; the trackways facilitating seasonal movement of stock between meadows alongside the Carrant Brook, the adjacent terraces and the higher land on Bredon Hill.

Limited evidence for Upper Palaeolithic, Mesolithic and Neolithic activity was also recovered. Three closely spaced Beaker pits, along with a scatter of other similarly dated features and residual finds provided the first certain evidence of occupation, while Early Bronze funerary activity was represented by a ring-ditch. Together with features and finds from the nearby Aston Mill Quarry, these provide important evidence of early prehistoric activity in this area.

Résumé

Des investigations archéologiques entreprises à Huntsman's Quary Kemerton, dans le sud du comté de Worcestershire pendant les années 1995–1996 ont relevé/répertorié des zones d'occupation et des systèmes de champs de l'âge du bronze final qui s'étendaient sur plus de 8 hectares.

Des mares/trous d'eau et des maisons rondes, structures et fosses associées se situaient/nichaient dans un paysage de champs et de chemins de bouvier s'inséraient, dont certains éléments semblent prédater l'occupation. Des assemblages substantiels relatifs aux objets manufacturés et à l'écologie furent recouvrés dans les parties supérieures du comblement des trous d' eau et des grandes fosses. L'économie de l'occupation était essentiellement pastorale soutenue par la production d'un peu de textile et de bronze. Les céramiques comprenaient une proportion importante dont le matériau ne provenait pas de la région ce qui démontre que la population locale jouissait d'une vaste gamme de contacts dans une région plus étendue. Des réseaux d'échange nationaux sont indiqués/suggérés par la présence d'objets en shiste ainsi que par la présence de bronze pour la métallurgie, ce qui pointe peut-être vers un site d'un certain statut social. Ensemble, les témoignages indiquent une occupation qu'on peut comparer favorablement avec celles que l'on connaît le long de la vallée de la Tamise mais qui jusqu'à présent n'a pas été reconnue dans cette partie du pays.

Reposant sur un vaste programme de datation au radiocarbone, il s'avère que certains des trous d'eau et des éléments des systèmes de champs furent établis/créés au cours du XIIe siècle av.J.-C. cal, des aires d'occupation non encloses s'établissant par la suite à l'intérieur de ce paysage clos/limité. La datation de résidus carbonisés d'un assemblage substantiel de poterie grossière indique que l'occupation se concentrait au XIe siècle av.J.-C., ne couvrant peut-être pas plus de quatre ou cinq générations. Nous argumentons que, plutôt que d'avoir toutes les aires occupées en même temps, l'occupation de chaque aire était de courte durée et le centre/foyer de l'occupation se déplaçait à intervalles réguliers. Nous suggérons que cela se passait sur une base générationnelle, chaque génération établissant une nouvelle 'ferme' avec un trou d'eau associé. Il se peut qu'en même temps, l'occupation/le campement de la précédente génération soit officiellement/formellement abandonné, un processus/une action marquée par la fermeture des trous d'eau. De légères variations dans la composition des assemblages de céramique à travers le site viennent soutenir ce modèle de transfert/d'évolution/ changement d'occupation.

Des témoignages d'anomalies dans les cultures et d'autres investigations limitées indiquent que les champs et les chemins de bouviers répertoriés représentent un petit fragment d'un système largement répandu de limites établies à travers les terrasses de gravier situées entre Bredon Hill et Carrant Brook. Ce paysage géré et organisé semble avoir été établi pour entretenir une économie reposant essentiellement sur des fermes pratiquant un élevage relativement extensif ; les chemins facilitant un mouvement saisonnier du bétail entre les prairies le long de Carrant Brook, les terrasses adjacentes et les terres plus élevées de Bredon Hill. On a également découvert des témoignages limités d'activité au paléolithique supérieur , mésolithiqu et néolithique. Trois fosses campaniformes très rapprochées, à côté d'autres indices de dates similaires et des trouvailles résiduelles ont fourni la première preuve certaine d'occupation, tandis qu'une activité funéraire du bronze était représentée par un fossé circulaire.

Traduction: Annie Pritchard

Zusammenfassung

Im Rahmen von 1995–1996 durchgeführten archäologischen Untersuchungen in der Huntsmans Kiesgrube bei Kemerton im Süden der Grafschaft Worcestershire wurde ein bedeutendes spätbronzezeitliches Siedlungsareal und eine Feldflur dokumentiert, die sich über mehr als 8 Hektar erstreckte.

Wasserlöcher und angegliederte Rundhäuser, Strukturen und Gruben lagen in einer von Feldern und Weidewegen geprägten Landschaft mit Elementen, die wahrscheinlich teilweise älter als die Siedlung sind. Aus den oberen Verfüllungsschichten der Wasserlöcher und größeren Gruben wurden beträchtliche Mengen an Funden und paläobotanischen Resten geborgen. Die Siedlung war vorwiegend weidewirtschaftlich geprägt, daneben wurde aber auch Textil- und Bronzeverarbeitung betrieben. Das keramische Fundmaterial umfasst einen bedeutenden Anteil nicht-lokaler Warenarten, was zeigt, dass die ortsansässige Bevölkerung über umfangreiche regionale Kontakte verfügte. Auf weiterreichende, nationale Austauschnetzwerke lassen Funde von Gegenständen aus Schieferton sowie die Versorgung mit Bronze für die Metallverarbeitung schließen, was vielleicht einen Fundplatz einer höheren sozialen Stellung andeutet. In der Zusammenschau vermitteln die Funde und Befunde das Bild einer Siedlung, die einen Vergleich mit jenen entlang des Themse-Tals nicht zu scheuen braucht, die aber in diesem Teil Englands bislang noch nicht erkannt worden sind.

Auf Grundlage umfangreicher Radiokarbon-Datierungen zeigt sich, dass einige Wasserlöcher und Elemente des Flursystems während des 12. Jhs. v.Chr. angelegt wurden, während offene Siedlungsbereiche in dieser parzellierten Landschaft später hinzu kamen.

Datierungen verkohlter Reste, die sich an Gefäßen der umfangreichen Grobkeramik fanden, zeigen, dass sich die Besiedlung auf das 11. Jh. v. Chr. konzentrierte und vielleicht nicht mehr als vier oder fünf Generationen umfasste. Statt einer gleichzeitigen Besiedlung aller Bereiche gehen die Autoren eher von einer kurzlebigen Besiedlung einzelner Bereiche und einer regelmäßigen Verlagerung dieser Siedlungsbereiche aus. Es wird vorgeschlagen, dass dies einmal pro Generation erfolgte, wobei jede Generation ein neues „Gehöft" mit dazugehörigem Wasserloch errichtete. Möglicherweise wurde zur gleichen Zeit das Gehöft der vorangehenden Generation formell aufgegeben, ein Prozess, der durch die Verfüllung der Wasserlöcher markiert wurde. Geringe Unterschiede in der Zusammensetzung des keramischen Fundmaterials von unterschiedlichen Bereichen des Fundplatzes unterstützen dieses Modell der Siedlungsverlagerung.

Bewuchsmerkmale und weitere kleinräumige Untersuchungen deuten an, dass die hier dokumentierten Felder und Weidewege Teil eines ausgedehnten Flursystems sind, dass auf den Schotterterrassen zwischen Bredon Hill und dem Carrant Brook angelegt wurde. Diese bewirtschaftete und organisierte Landschaft scheint mit Hinblick auf den Unterhalt einer auf relativ intensive Viehhaltung ausgerichteten Wirtschaftsweise angelegt worden zu sein; die Weidewege ermöglichten saisonalen Viehtrieb zwischen den Weiden entlang des Carrant Brook, den benachbarten Terrassen und dem höher gelegenen Land auf dem Bredon Hill.

Vereinzelt fanden sich auch Indizien für jungpaläolithische, mesolithische und neolithische Aktivitäten. Drei eng beieinanderliegende becherzeitliche Gruben sowie Streuungen von weiteren Befunden und Einzelfunden ähnlicher Zeitstellung liefern die ersten sicheren Hinweise auf Besiedlung, wohingegen ein Kreisgraben frühbronzezeitliche Bestattungsaktivitäten repräsentiert. Zusammen mit Befunden und Funden aus der nahegelegenen Aston Mill Kiesgrube liefern diese Ergebnisse wichtige Hinweise auf die urgeschichtliche Besiedlung dieser Region.

Übersetzung: Jörn Schuster

Acknowledgements

Worcestershire Archive and Archaeology Service would like to thank the quarry operators Huntsman's Quarries Ltd for all their kind cooperation and help in ensuring the successful completion of the fieldwork. In particular John Milner (Managing Director), Nick Hanks (Director), and Ian Thomas (Production Manager) are thanked for their help in the setting up and running of the project. Steve Davis and Dave Whitcomb (Ackerman 360° excavator and dumper drivers) deserve particular mention for their skilful operation of plant without which the level of fieldwork record produced would not have been possible.

Andy Josephs of Wardell Armstrong, the Archaeological Consultant for Huntsman's Quarries, is thanked for his part in setting up and co-ordinating the project and helping to maintain successful liaison between Huntsman's and both the Planning Advisory Section and the Field Section of the Service.

The project was initiated, designed and co-ordinated by Robin Jackson (Senior Project Manager) with the advice and guidance of Simon Woodiwiss (Principal Field Archaeologist). Malcolm Atkin (County Archaeology Officer at the time) helped with the overall development and progress of the fieldwork.

The post-excavation analysis and publication programme was funded by Historic England through the Historic Environment Enabling Programme and Helen Keeley, Kathy Perrin, Alex Gibson, Tony Wilmott and Tim Williams are thanked for their useful comments and support in progressing this project, along with the anonymous referee appointed by Historic England whose input did much to refine the report.

The successful completion of the fieldwork was due largely to the hard work and professionalism of Mike Napthan (Assistant Archaeological Field Officer) who led the salvage recording and Dave Wichbold (Archaeological Assistant) who provided invaluable assistance throughout. Further assistance on site was provided by other staff of the Service: Martin Cook, Luke Fagan, Paul Godbehere, Suzanne Hartley, Helena Kelly, Dale Rouse and Nigel Topping.

Volunteer assistance was provided by Judith Bannerman, Frances Champion, Felicity Clarke, Pam Craven, Vanessa Constant, Mike Glyde, Gordon Rae, Stephanie Smith and Mick Wilkes.

During post-excavation many colleagues have provided advice and encouragement and in particular I would like to thank Hal Dalwood, Derek Hurst and Simon Woodiwiss. In addition Stephanie Ratkai and Annette Hancocks are thanked for their help in the initial co-ordination and assessment of the artefacts and the late Leyland Shawe for his tireless voluntary work processing and marking finds. Mike Glyde is thanked for making available aerial photographic plots from his ongoing work.

Lastly, many thanks must go to all of the post-excavation team who have contributed to the production of this report. Individual text sections have been attributed to author where relevant with the remainder of the report having been produced by Robin Jackson.

Illustrations were undertaken by the members of the Services' Illustration Team of whom Laura Templeton completed the bulk of the work assisted by Carolyn Hunt and Steve Rigby.

Part 1.
Introduction

Background

A programme of archaeological fieldwork was undertaken at Huntsman's Quarry, Kemerton, Worcestershire between September 1994 and May 1996 in response to extension of an existing quarry. The work was carried out by the Field Section of Hereford and Worcester County Archaeological Service (now Worcestershire Archive and Archaeology Service) on behalf of Huntsman's Quarries Limited.

The subsequent programme of assessment and analysis was completed with support from English Heritage between 1997 and 2005. The report is structured in five parts. The first section provides the background to the project and this is followed by three sections covering the results of the fieldwork (structural, artefactual and environmental). The fifth and final section presents a discussion of the results and considers the site in both its regional and national context.

Location, geology and topography

Huntsman's Quarry lies to the southwest of the village of Kemerton which is situated towards the centre of a long narrow parish on the south side of Bredon Hill towards the southern end of Worcestershire.

The site includes parts of the parishes of Kemerton and Bredon and is centred on NGR SO 939 363 (Fig. 1). The local landscape is dominated by Bredon Hill, a massive Jurassic outlier of the Cotswolds which lies about 2km north of the site and overlooks much of the surrounding Vale of Evesham and the Lower Avon Valley (Fig. 2). The site is almost flat, with only a slight slope downwards to the south and east providing drainage to one of a series of small watercourses feeding the Carrant Brook, a tributary of the River Avon. Prior to gravel extraction the site area comprised two fields used as agricultural land but now occupied by a lake and nature reserve.

The solid geology of the valley consists of grey mudstones and clays of the Lower Lias, while Oolitic limestone forms the top of the hill (Whittaker 1972, 3–5). The drift geology is rather complex (Briggs *et al.* 1975), owing to the interaction of glacial gravel terraces (which equate to the Avon 2nd Terrace) and fan gravels. The site lies towards the southern edge of the latter which are the product of solifluction and decalcification of the underlying limestone gravels on the lower slopes of Bredon Hill (Worssam 1982, 1, 8).

Archaeological and historical background

Kemerton has one of the most comprehensive sequences of evidence for human activity of any parish in Worcestershire (Fig. 2). Material evidence dates from as early as the Palaeolithic while *in situ* deposits have been recorded dating from the Neolithic onwards. This extensive record results from a relatively high level of archaeological investigation within the area. In the main, sites have originally been identified through cropmarks and have been investigated in advance of destruction by quarrying for sand and gravel.

The earliest evidence of human activity from Kemerton is represented by the discovery of a significant assemblage of Palaeolithic material during quarrying in the 1980s at Aston Mill Quarry, Kemerton (Whitehead 1988). Fifteen hand-axes along with other broadly contemporary material were recorded and on typological grounds appear related to a Lavallois industry. A further Palaeolithic handaxe was found in the parish during the making of a television programme for the Channel Four production, *Time Team* in 1998 and may also be of similar date (Terrain Archaeology 2001). This represents a significant grouping and, though not *in situ*, represents the most extensive collection of Palaeolithic material recovered from the county.

The most extensive previous archaeological project in Kemerton was the salvage recording undertaken in advance of quarrying at Aston Mill, on the southern edge of the parish (Fig. 2). This produced widespread evidence of former occupation dating from the Mesolithic onwards (Hillson 1975; Dinn and Evans 1990). This included a thin scatter of Mesolithic flint, possible Late Neolithic occupation, an Early Bronze Age ring-ditch with secondary cremations of Middle to Late Bronze Age date, Middle Iron Age pits and enclosure ditches, Late Iron Age and early Roman ditches and an Anglo-Saxon period *grubenhaus*.

Elsewhere within the area covered by the modern parish, small-scale projects over the years have recorded further evidence of former activity. In 1963, a Beaker period barrow with two interments was recorded on the slopes of Bredon Hill at the north end of the parish (Thomas 1965; Fig. 2:2). The *Time Team* programme made in 1998 investigated cropmark sites to the north of Huntsman's Quarry, dating a small enclosure to the Middle Iron Age and a larger series of enclosures to the Late Iron Age and Roman periods (Terrain Archaeology 2001; Fig. 2:5 and 2:9). Of later date, Anglo-Saxon period domestic occupation has been recorded at two locations beyond Aston Mill and includes two further *grubenhauser* dating from the 6th to 7th centuries AD (Fagan *et al.* 1994; Terrain Archaeology 2001; Fig. 2:5 and 2:16).

Subsequent occupation appears to have been focused around the two surviving settlements of Kinsham and Kemerton, the current locations of which have medieval origins. Earthworks and cropmarks in the surrounding fields, allied to extensive evidence from the excavated areas, show widespread areas of medieval ridge and furrow systems within the surrounding fields. The excavated evidence is supported by some limited documentary research. This has included study of the Anglo-Saxon Charter bounds for the parish, while cartographic analysis has enabled the hypothetical reconstruction of the medieval open field system (Sachse nd.). Most recently, research associated with the production of a further television programme (BBC2; Talking Landscapes) has drawn upon existing evidence to produce a model of landscape change and development.

Apart from the investigated sites, the parish includes numerous cropmark sites occupying the gravel terraces north of the Carrant Brook. These provide evidence for several enclosures and associated field systems and trackways including a scheduled and well-defined enclosure and ditched trackway to the south of the quarry (Fig. 2:12), which surface finds suggest is of Iron Age or Roman date. These cropmark complexes extend east and west of the parish along the Carrant Valley. These include pit alignments, ring-ditches and extensive field systems of apparently Bronze Age, Iron Age and Roman date. Dotted throughout these, there are contemporary settlement enclosures. Several of these sites have been investigated in varying levels of detail. Small-scale trial investigations were carried out in 2004 of a small hengiform cropmark

site at Bredon's Norton by the Department of Applied Science, Geography and Archaeology of University College Worcester (Fig. 2:1). This recorded cremations inserted into the top of a large infilled ditch which has produced pottery provisionally dated to the Bronze Age (Jodie Lewis pers. comm.). Large-scale excavations were undertaken in advance of quarrying at Beckford in the 1970s and 1980s. Although not yet published, interim reports record extensive evidence of Middle Iron Age settlement and of a major Bronze Age boundary ditch pre-dating it (Britnell 1975; Fig. 2:8). Late Iron Age and earlier Roman activity were also present, but these do not appear to represent occupation and a major settlement shift at the onset of the Late Iron Age seems to be represented. Two Anglo-Saxon cemeteries were also excavated in advance of quarrying to the west of Beckford in the 1950s (Evison and Hill 1996; Fig. 2:17 and 2:18). As at Aston Mill Quarry, Palaeolithic hand-axes have been discovered during the course of the quarrying at Beckford.

Above the river valley, the southern slopes of Bredon Hill have produced many chance finds of prehistoric to Roman date, indicating extensive occupation and activity. A small hillfort, Conderton Camp, lies on these slopes and appears to have been occupied throughout the Middle Iron Age (Thomas 2005), while the hilltop itself is the focus of a major Iron Age promontory fort, Kemerton Camp, that was partially excavated in the 1930s producing extensive evidence of occupation and other activity of this period (Cruso Henken 1938). Finally the medieval castle at Elmley Castle is believed to overlie a further Iron Age hillfort.

Project history

Quarrying at Huntsman's Quarry, Kemerton commenced in 1988 with extraction completed across a permitted area lying immediately to the south of that covered by this report (Fig. 2). This work was undertaken subject only to an access condition permitting the County Archaeology Officer or their representative to visit the quarry. No provision was made for investigation and funding of any remains to be disturbed and with the exception of a couple of unfruitful visits the whole area was quarried without archaeological input.

In 1993 submission of an application to extend the quarry to the north prompted a programme of evaluation and investigation of this area. Pre-determination evaluation was recommended by the County Archaeology Officer; however, contrary to this advice, permission was granted subject to an agreed programme of archaeological works. Huntsman's, advised by Mr Andrew Josephs of Wardell Armstrong (their consultants) and in consultation with the Field and Planning Advisory Sections of the Service, agreed a staged programme of archaeological work to be undertaken both prior to, and, if necessary, during subsequent quarrying operations.

The resultant programme of works commenced with a staged evaluation, comprising geophysical survey, fieldwalking and trial trenching. This resulted in the definition of a 'core area' of prehistoric settlement and adjacent, but peripheral, activity extending beyond it. This resulted in the preservation of the defined 'core area' and a further stage of archaeological work comprising salvage recording in advance of quarrying of the remainder. This was anticipated to record low levels of occupation-related activity and field systems associated with settlement in the 'core area'. In the event, extensive and significant deposits of Beaker through to Late Bronze Age date were recorded across most of the area of salvage recording and these far exceeded the reasonable expectations of the evaluation programme. The extent and significance of the discoveries was such that it was recognised before fieldwork was completed that the developer funding would not be able to cover the costs of maintaining a level of fieldwork recording commensurate with the importance and potential of the site. In addition, it was clear that the established post-excavation analysis and publication funding would not support the level of analysis which the results warranted. English Heritage was therefore approached with a request for funding to support the project.

Following discussions and a brief presentation it was agreed in principle, given the exceptional and unexpected extent and significance of the site, that English Heritage would support the post-excavation analysis and publication programme required. Existing funds were then used to maintain an adequate record in the field, to prepare a site archive and to prepare an assessment and updated project design for the post-fieldwork analysis (Napthan *et al.* 1997). Following approval, a programme of analysis was completed between 1998 and 2005. The resultant report was externally refereed and the report edited leading to production of this publication.

Aims

Evaluation

The evaluation aimed, through a staged programme of work, to determine the presence or absence of archaeological deposits within the proposed quarrying area and where present to assess their extent, character, state of preservation, date and potential archaeological significance.

Salvage recording

The aims of the salvage recording were defined in an archaeological brief which formed part of the agreed planning conditions for the site. These were based upon the evaluation results and were incorporated and expanded in the resultant Project Design. These documents recognised the high significance of the site and highlighted the rarity of Bronze Age occupation sites at both a national and more particularly a regional level. The importance of the ceramic assemblage from the evaluation was also emphasised as was the potential value of the site as part of a 'varied

archaeological landscape…with both temporal and spatial relationships between successive Bronze Age, Iron Age, Roman and Saxon settlement sites'.

The site was divided into three zones, two of which were identified as covering the well-preserved remains of the 'core' of the Bronze Age settlement. These were assessed to be of national significance and, following discussions with Huntsman's, this area was omitted from the quarry ensuring preservation *in situ* of significant deposits. Beyond this 'core', a third zone was defined as also including prehistoric deposits but the evaluation had indicated that these tailed off towards the west and suggested that they were peripheral to the main settlement. Salvage recording was therefore identified as an appropriate mitigation strategy for this zone. The objectives of the salvage recording were therefore primarily to identify the extent and nature of the deposits by means of excavation of a sample and rapid planning of the remainder of the features.

Post-excavation

As result of the post-fieldwork assessment ten research themes were identified for the project, focusing upon the extensive evidence for Late Bronze Age settlement and associated field systems recorded. These were:

- Structures and settlement patterns;
- Linear boundary patterns (drove/trackways and field systems);
- Funerary features;
- Hearths/burnt features;
- Waste disposal patterns;
- Local environment;
- Craft and technology;
- Food resources cultivation and diet;
- The settlement in a regional and national framework;
- Methodological implications.

Methodology (by Robin Jackson and Mike Napthan)

The evaluation

A geophysical survey was undertaken in June 1994 by Stratascan and consisted of a magnetic susceptibility survey of the whole area based on a 20m grid. This was undertaken with the aim of testing an area known to contain faint cropmarks. This was followed by a targeted intensive magnetometer and resistance meter survey in the area indicated by the magnetic susceptibility survey as having the highest archaeological potential. A number of anomalies were identified, plotted in detail and interpreted as part of a circular bank and ditch, enclosure boundaries, possible hearths, a buried metal object and ridge and furrow (Barker 1994). The focus of site activity was suggested to be close to the southern boundary in the centre of the eastern field, around the area identified by the initial cropmark evidence.

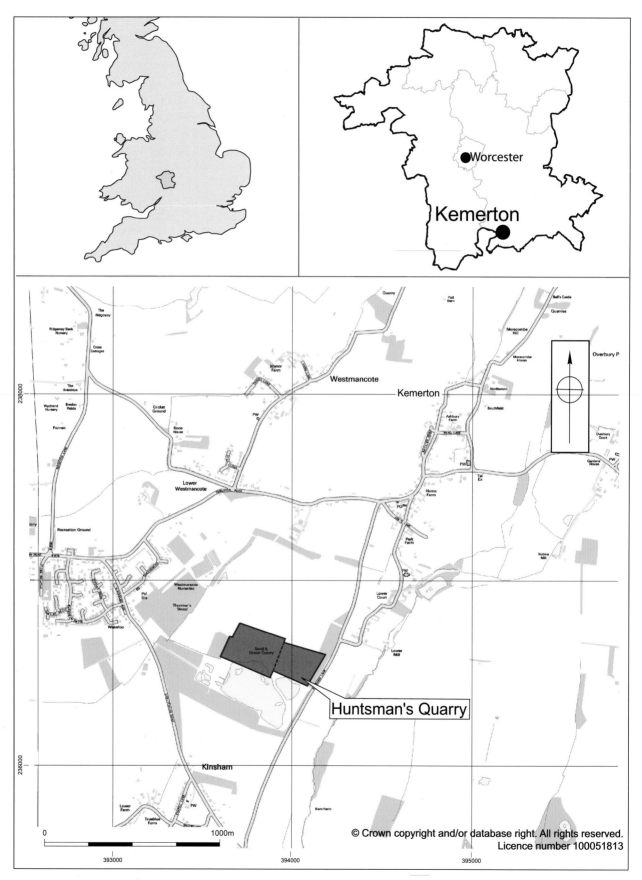

Figure 1. Location of site.

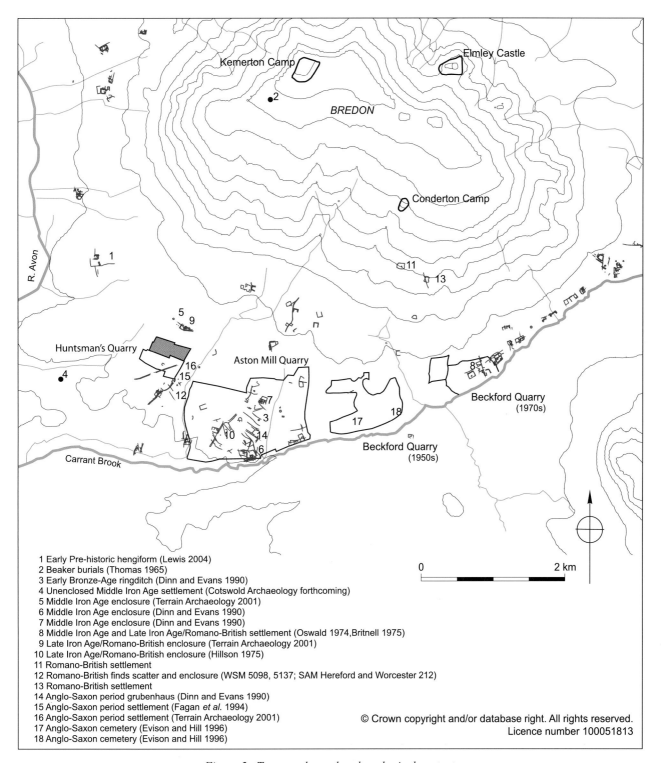

1 Early Pre-historic hengiform (Lewis 2004)
2 Beaker burials (Thomas 1965)
3 Early Bronze-Age ringditch (Dinn and Evans 1990)
4 Unenclosed Middle Iron Age settlement (Cotswold Archaeology forthcoming)
5 Middle Iron Age enclosure (Terrain Archaeology 2001)
6 Middle Iron Age enclosure (Dinn and Evans 1990)
7 Middle Iron Age enclosure (Dinn and Evans 1990)
8 Middle Iron Age and Late Iron Age/Romano-British settlement (Oswald 1974,Britnell 1975)
9 Late Iron Age/Romano-British enclosure (Terrain Archaeology 2001)
10 Late Iron Age/Romano-British enclosure (Hillson 1975)
11 Romano-British settlement
12 Romano-British finds scatter and enclosure (WSM 5098, 5137; SAM Hereford and Worcester 212)
13 Romano-British settlement
14 Anglo-Saxon period grubenhaus (Dinn and Evans 1990)
15 Anglo-Saxon period settlement (Fagan *et al.* 1994)
16 Anglo-Saxon period settlement (Terrain Archaeology 2001)
17 Anglo-Saxon cemetery (Evison and Hill 1996)
18 Anglo-Saxon cemetery (Evison and Hill 1996)

Figure 2. Topography and archaeological context.

Subsequent to the geophysical survey the entire area was fieldwalked (based on transects and stints at 20m intervals) in September 1994 with the aim of identifying any surface artefact concentrations, which might reflect areas of activity or provide date indicators (Cook and Hurst 1994). The density of material recovered was low; a total of only 30 worked flints were recovered from an area of approximately 8ha and no prehistoric ceramics were recovered. The Roman and medieval finds also indicated a low level of activity, without distinct clusters.

The results of the geophysical survey and fieldwalking were not conclusive and no specific target areas could be defined; thus evaluation trenching was undertaken of the whole area of the proposed quarry extension in

October–November 1994. Ten trenches (Trenches 1–10; Fig. 3) totalling 1000m in length were excavated and selected deposits were then excavated by hand. Recording followed standard practice (County Archaeological Service Recording System 1993, as amended). An additional area of 300m² (Trench 11; Figs 3 and 4) was opened in order to provide a wider view where the features seemed to be concentrated. In total 2150m² were investigated for the evaluation which comprised slightly over 2% of the proposed extraction area.

A low density of features was identified over much of the site with the exception of a concentration towards the eastern boundary. Here, a cluster of stake and postholes in the southeast corner were cut through the subsoil and contained a small number of Bronze Age sherds. Further investigation of an expanded area at this location (Trench 11) revealed two very substantial features containing large assemblages of Late Bronze Age pottery, bone and flint (Fig. 4). One pit contained anaerobically preserved timber and other environmental remains.

As a result of the evaluation, an area of significant Late Bronze Age deposits was defined concentrated in the eastern part of the proposed development. At a site meeting it was agreed that preservation *in situ* was the preferred option for this 'core' area. Huntsman's Quarries explored the possibility of preservation by record of these deposits; this option was not taken up, however, and the area was excluded from the quarry extension and returned to agricultural use. For the remaining area, where only a thin scatter of small and largely sterile features had been identified, it was agreed that salvage recording was an appropriate response. This anticipated a low level of occupation activity on the periphery of the settlement, allied perhaps to field systems. A further archaeological brief was then prepared for this recording by the Planning Advisory Section and the Field Section was commissioned to undertake the work which commenced in November 1994 and continued until September 1996.

Salvage recording

Fieldwork occurred in response to each new area stripped of topsoil (Fig. 3). The broad aim throughout was to identify, record and sample any archaeological features revealed. Each phase of fieldwork was allocated an area number (Areas 12–21) and a discrete group of context numbers. The latter extended the evaluation sequence which had used trench numbers as a prefix (*e.g.* Trench 10 used context numbers 1000, 10001, 1002, etc.) except now the area number formed the prefix.

Two small parts of the excluded 'core' area were brought into the extraction area during the course of the project following negotiations with the Service; Area 13 being added for operational reasons as a haul road for the quarry, and part of Area 16 which needed to be 'rounded off' for landscaping purposes. As part of Area 13 lay within the previous extraction area for which there was

no archaeological constraint, a 50% level of recording was considered appropriate. Area 16 was subject to 100% salvage excavation as it was fully within that part of the current extraction area defined as being of archaeological significance.

The eastern field was stripped using a 360° Ackerman tracked excavator and 20 ton Volvo dumper. The methodology varied according to ground conditions but generally every effort was made to avoid driving across areas until they had been fully recorded. The nature of the subsoil resulted in rapid wheel rutting in all but the driest conditions. Selected small areas were hand cleaned wherever possible immediately following the stripping; for considerable areas of the site, however, this proved to be unnecessary since the plant operators were highly efficient and produced a 'finished surface' on which archaeological features were generally readily identifiable (Figs 4 and 5).

Within the western field, Area 18 was stripped of topsoil using a D30 Kommatsu tracked tractor towing a box scraper, and cleaned up using the 360° excavator and dumper as before. Where it proved impractical to excavate two large pits (contexts 1833 and 1835) by hand, the majority of the fill was transferred to an 8m³ skip, using the Ackerman, for later finds retrieval by volunteers at the unit offices. Areas 20 and 21 were stripped as before using the Ackerman 360° and two Volvo dumper trucks. The northwest corner of this field was not investigated since mineral reserves were considered insufficient to warrant extraction.

Across the site, the entire stripped area was planned at 1:100, with excavated detail and sections drawn at 1:20. The plans were tied into a single site grid aligned with the southern field boundary and extended as the stripping progressed. The percentage of features excavated was as determined in the brief and reflected the expectation that Bronze Age activity reduced from east to the west across the investigated area. Consequently, Areas 12, 14, 15, 17 and 19 were 10% sampled, Area 13 was 50% sampled and the excavated part of Area 16 was 100% sampled. Areas 18, 20 and 21 were 5% sampled.

Whilst only a small proportion of features were excavated, exposure of the whole 70,000m² of the area allied to the results from the areas of higher sampling (Areas 13 and part of 16) facilitated selection of 'key' features (in terms of those few which had stratigraphic relationships), identifiable structures and artefact-rich features for examination. This enabled a very high artefact recovery rate in relation to the minimal levels of resources employed. Wherever possible the entire fills of artefact-rich features were excavated while those features which, when half-sectioned, were found to be devoid of artefacts were not explored further.

As a consistent approach to excavation and recording was necessary to enable direct comparisons to be drawn between different parts of the site, it was decided to retain a core team of two staff to undertake all of the field work. An Assistant Archaeological Field Officer (Mike

Napthan) undertook most of the monitoring of machine stripping and the pre-excavation planning at 1:100, whilst an Archaeological Assistant (Dave Wichbold) undertook the majority of excavation. One or other was present on site during all phases of fieldwork. This maintained consistent cover even during necessary absences for leave and operational requirements of the Service. Additional staff and volunteers provided assistance when available.

Full access to the site during stripping and extraction operations was granted by the quarry operators Huntsman's Quarries Ltd. and the landowner Adrian Darby. No reinstatement of archaeological trenches or features was required since quarrying followed immediately. The site has now been fully worked out and has been landscaped to include a lake and a wildlife habitat.

Conditions of preservation

Within the site as a whole a number of observations were made regarding the level of preservation of prehistoric features.

Firstly, the formation of medieval ridge and furrow had had a major impact on deposit survival. Although no longer visible as earthworks, furrows were evident across the whole area and, as is commonly the case, had truncated deposits along their entire length. As far as possible the furrow fills were removed during machining but generally it was observed that only deeper deposits had survived truncation by the formation of these features.

Conditions of preservation were better on the areas which had been beneath ridges; however, plough truncation since the medieval period had not only levelled the ridges but had also to an extent truncated deposits beneath them. Deposit survival was best towards the southern and northern field boundaries, possibly as a result of protection by deeper soil depths on plough headlands formed at the ends of the ridge and furrow. More severe truncation was present in the central part of the field. Here only deeper cut features survived in any quantity; this may also, however, partially reflect the original character of the settlement activity which appears to have been less intense in this area.

Pottery and other artefacts were mostly well-preserved although some ceramic fabrics had suffered leaching of inclusions, and consequently tended to be more fragmented and abraded. Overall, the condition of animal bone was poor as is commonly the case on gravel sites. One exception was within larger, deeper features that penetrated the watertable and here preservation was generally very good, especially of bone. This may reflect more alkaline conditions resulting from drainage of the nearby limestone outcrop of Bredon Hill. Waterlogged conditions in several cases had also led to the survival of organic material but otherwise organic survival was restricted to charred remains typical of dry site conditions.

Post-excavation methods

Morphological analysis

Plan analysis formed the principal tool for identification of structures and other components of the settlement. Context descriptions were considered along with more detailed artefactual and ecofactual data which particularly contributed to the development of broad phasing and characterisation of the settlement components. Analysis has not been exhaustive but has focussed on major cut features, linear features, clearly defined structures and areas of more intense activity.

Site plans within the report covering the entire investigated area show only assigned and other archaeological features within any given phase but omit uncertain features of possibly natural origin, as well as later ridge and furrow where it obscures information. Detailed plans of individual structures or structure groups show all features, both certain and uncertain.

Identification, characterisation and dating of deposits

Analysis has been based on feature and/or deposit type. Any distinct structures which could be identified (*e.g.* roundhouses and fencelines) have been allocated a context group number and type (*e.g.* Roundhouse: Context Group 34). Other settlement components such as waterholes, individual pits, funerary features and hearths/burnt features have been similarly allocated context group numbers and types (*e.g.* Waterhole: Context Group 3). Table 1 summarises all context groups allocated against type. Linear features such as trackways, enclosures and field boundaries have been considered on a cross-site basis as well as within individual areas.

Within individual features, fills have been considered as either primary (relating to initial use of feature – *e.g.* a silting fill in the base of a waterhole or packing in a posthole), secondary (relating to subsequent use of a feature once its primary function was no longer active – *e.g.* dumped deposits in the upper part of a waterhole) or tertiary fills (relating to final stages of use/life of feature – *e.g.* ploughsoil/weathered fills in the uppermost part of a pit which has been otherwise infilled).

Some limitations in dating, identification and characterisation of context groups and settlement components were predicted from the outset. These limitations reflect the restricted numbers of features from which artefacts have been derived and the limited instances where relationships were present between features. Dating has therefore often relied on association of context groups, components and unassigned features with the better dated elements of the settlement within a given area. In the light of the widespread evidence for Late Bronze Age activity, it is clear that this represents the main period of site activity and, as a result, undated or poorly dated features have been assumed to be

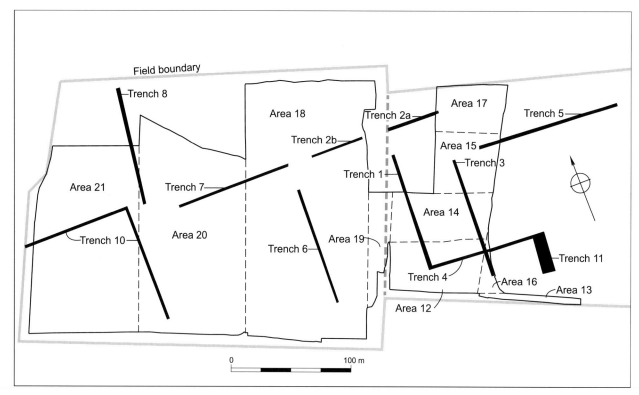

Figure 3. Evaluation trenches and excavation areas.

Figure 4. Area 11 during evaluation.

Figure 5. View showing typical conditions following topsoil stripping.

of this date. It is, however, recognised that this assumption has its own limitations and that other interpretations of the patterning and phasing of activity could be reached.

The density of features in many of the clusters (allied to the variety of structure plans potentially present in any given area) has restricted the number of clearly identifiable structures and therefore groups. Consequently in many cases unexcavated or poorly dated postholes, lesser pits and other anomalous deposits have remained unassigned. These have, however, been assessed to some extent on the basis of their fill characteristics and general appearance and divided between those felt liable to represent genuine archaeological features and those believed to be natural in origin (*e.g.* root

holes, animal burrows or geological anomalies). In addition, although simple characterisation has been possible in the majority of cases (pit, posthole, ditch, etc.), higher levels of functional interpretation of many features and feature groupings (domestic building, agricultural structure, rubbish pit, etc.) have not proved possible.

The range and character of activities represented in any given area has been considered (*e.g.* occupation, waste disposal, agricultural, craft/production, etc.) and the relationship between these areas across the site has been discussed. Consideration has also been made of any evidence for the changing morphology and development of the site throughout the period of occupation, and several zones of settlement have been identified. These possibly represent different types of site activity within a settlement, but are considered more likely to reflect several phases of occupation, although as outlined above detailed dating has not been possible.

Archiving

The project archive has been deposited at the Worcestershire County Museum at Hartlebury.

Table 1. Context Groups.

Context Group	Type	Context Group	Type
CG1	Bowl-shaped pit	CG50	Curvilinear gully structure
CG2	Basin-shaped pit	CG51	Curvilinear gully structure
CG3	Waterhole	CG52	Pond
CG4	Waterhole	CG53	Fence/drafting gate
CG5	Basin-shaped pit	CG54	Roundhouse
CG6	Waterhole	CG55	Roundhouse
CG7	Waterhole	CG56	Roundhouse
CG8	Waterhole	CG57	Roundhouse
CG9	Basin-shaped pit	CG58	Roundhouse
CG10	Bowl-shaped pit	CG59	Roundhouse
CG11	Bowl-shaped pit	CG60	Roundhouse
CG12	Bowl-shaped pit	CG61	Rectilinear structure
CG13	Bowl-shaped pit	CG62	Rectilinear structure
CG14	Waterhole	CG63	Rectilinear structure
CG15	Basin-shaped pit	CG64	Rectilinear structure
CG16	Bowl-shaped pit	CG65	Rectilinear structure
CG17	Basin-shaped pit	CG66	Post-defined enclosure
CG18	Waterhole	CG67	Post-defined enclosure
CG19	Pit/post	CG68	Post-defined enclosure
CG20	Basin-shaped pit	CG69	Semi-circular post structure
CG21	Bowl-shaped pit	CG70	Four-post structure
CG22	Bowl-shaped pit	CG71	Four-post structure
CG23	Pit/post	CG72	Four-post structure
CG24	Pit/post	CG73	Four-post structure
CG25	Pit/post	CG74	Four-post structure
CG26	Basin-shaped pit	CG75	T-shaped structure
CG27	Bowl-shaped pit	CG76	T-shaped structure
CG28	Hearth pit	CG77	Hearth pit
CG29	Isolated posthole	CG78	Roundhouse
CG30	Hearth pit	CG79	Ring-ditch
CG31	Basin-shaped pit	CG80	Bowl-shaped pit
CG32	Isolated posthole	CG81	Bowl-shaped pit
CG33	Isolated posthole	CG82	U-shaped pit
CG34	Isolated posthole	CG83	Irregular pit
CG35	Isolated posthole	CG84	Pit
CG36	Basin-shaped pit	CG85	Bowl-shaped pit
CG37	Bowl-shaped pit	CG86	Post and gully structure
CG38	Bowl-shaped pit	CG87	Post and gully structure
CG39	Basin-shaped pit	CG88	Post and gully structure
CG40	Bowl-shaped pit	CG89	Semi-circular post structure
CG41	Hearth pit	CG90	Isolated posthole
CG42	Bowl-shaped pit	CG91	Pit/post
CG43	Hearth pit	CG92	Pit/post
CG44	Hearth pit	CG93	Bowl-shaped pit
CG45	Hearth pit	CG94	Pit
CG46	Hearth pit	CG95	Irregular pit
CG47	Boundary/fence	CG96	Cremated bone deposit
CG48	Boundary/fence	CG97	Hearth pit
CG49	Boundary/fence	CG98	Pit

Part 2.
Dating and structural evidence

Radiocarbon dating (by Alex Bayliss, Robin Jackson and Christopher Bronk Ramsey)

Introduction

Thirty radiocarbon age determinations were obtained on samples from pits excavated in 1994–6. Another eight samples of animal bone were submitted for analysis, but failed to produce sufficient collagen for reliable dating.

The samples were processed by the Oxford Radiocarbon Accelerator Unit, and were prepared using the methods outlined in Hedges et al. (1989) and measured using Accelerator Mass Spectrometry (Bronk Ramsey and Hedges 1997).

The laboratory maintains a continual programme of quality assurance procedures, in addition to participation in international inter-comparisons (Scott et al. 1990; Rozanski et al. 1992; Scott et al. 1998). At the time when the first set of samples from this site was measured, these tests identified an intermittent problem with the graphitisation process at Oxford. However, the consistency of the results from this site suggests that all measurements are accurate (see below), and relevant quality assurance data for these samples are provided in Bronk Ramsey et al. (2002).

Results

The results are given in Table 2, and are quoted in accordance with the international standard known as the Trondheim convention (Stuiver and Kra 1986). They are conventional radiocarbon ages (Stuiver and Polach 1977).

Calibration

The calibrations of these results, relating the radiocarbon measurements directly to calendar dates, are given in Table 2 and in outline in Figures 6–10. All have been calculated using the calibration curve of Stuiver et al. (1998) and the computer program OxCal (v3.5) (Bronk Ramsey 1995; 1998; 2001). The calibrated date ranges cited in the text are those for 95% confidence. They are quoted in the form recommended by Mook (1986), with the end points rounded outwards to 10 years. The ranges quoted in italics are posterior density estimates derived from mathematical modelling of archaeological problems (see below). The ranges in plain type in Table 2 have been calculated according to the maximum intercept method (Stuiver and Reimer 1986). All other ranges are derived from the probability method (Stuiver and Reimer 1993).

Methodological approach

A Bayesian approach has been adopted for the interpretation of the chronology from this site (Buck et al. 1996). Although the simple calibrated dates are accurate estimates of the dates of the samples, this is usually not what archaeologists really wish to know. It is the dates of the archaeological events represented by those samples which are of interest. In the case of Kemerton, it is the chronology of the use of the settlement and ceramics that is under consideration, not the dates of individual pieces of pottery or macrofossils. The dates of this activity can be estimated not only using the absolute dating information from the radiocarbon measurements on the samples, but also by using the relative dating information provided by stratigraphy.

Fortunately methodology is now available which allows the combination of these different types of information explicitly, to produce realistic estimates of the dates of archaeological interest. It should be emphasised that the *posterior density estimates* produced by this modelling are

Table 2. Radiocarbon determinations.

Laboratory Number	Sample Reference	Material	Radiocarbon Age (BP)	δ¹³C (‰)	Calibrated date range (95% confidence)	Posterior density estimate (95% probability; Fig. 7)
OxA-10776	CG1 1830A	refitting pottery, charred residue	2852±36	-24.6	1190–900 cal BC	*1090–980 cal BC*
OxA-10777	CG1 1830B	refitting pottery, charred residue	2840±37	-25.8	1190–900 cal BC	*1080–980 cal BC*
OxA-9483	CG4 2032A	refitting pottery, charred residue	2970±40	-24.8	1380–1040 cal BC	*1100–1000 cal BC*
OxA-9484	CG4 2032B	refitting pottery, charred residue	2890±45	-26.0	1260–920 cal BC	*1100–990 cal BC*
OxA-10778	CG4 2032C	refitting pottery, charred residue	2861±37	-28.1	1210–910 cal BC	*1090–980 cal BC*
OxA-10779	CG4 2032D	refitting pottery, charred residue	2850±37	-24.1	1190–900 cal BC	*1090–980 cal BC*
OxA-10780	CG4 2032E	refitting pottery, charred residue	2868±37	-25.8	1210–910 cal BC	*1090–980 cal BC*
OxA-9490	CG4 2050A	wood, *Corylus/Alnus* roundwood	2895±45	-28.4	1260–920 cal BC	-
OxA-9424	CG4 2050B	wood, *Corylus* roundwood	2992±36	-28.1	1380–1120 cal BC	-
OxA-10781	CG6 1836A	refitting pottery, charred residue	2865±40	-23.2	1210–910 cal BC	*1090–980 cal BC*
OxA-10782	CG6 1836B	refitting pottery, charred residue	2812±37	-26.6	1050–830 cal BC	*1080–970 cal BC*
OxA-9486	CG7 1834A	refitting pottery, charred residue	2938±40	-27.0	1300–1000 cal BC	*1070–1000 cal BC*
OxA-9559	CG7 1834B	refitting pottery, charred residue	2950±80	-29.5	1410–910 cal BC	*1070–980 cal BC*
OxA-10783	CG7 1834C	refitting pottery, charred residue	2860±38	-24.2	1210–910 cal BC	*1070–980 cal BC*
OxA-10784	CG7 1838	refitting pottery, charred residue	2916±38	-27.2	1260–990 cal BC	*1090–1000 cal BC*
OxA-9435	CG7 1855B	refitting pottery, charred residue	2968±39	-23.3	1380–1040 cal BC	*1120–1010 cal BC*
OxA-10785	CG7 1855C	refitting pottery, charred residue	2862±37	-22.6	1210–910 cal BC	*1110–1010 cal BC*
OxA-10786	CG8 1103A	refitting pottery, charred residue	2882±37	-25.0	1220–920 cal BC	*1100–990 cal BC*
OxA-9488	CG8 1115A	wood, *Prunus Spinosa*	3122±39	-27.1	1430–1260 cal BC	-
OxA-10375	CG8 1115A	replicate of OxA-9488	3077±34	-26.5		
OxA-9489	CG8 1115B	wood, *Salix/Populus* sp. 1-2 years growth	2980±40	-26.5	1380–1040 cal BC	-
OxA-10787	CG9 1111A	refitting pottery, charred residue	2860±40	-25.4	1210–900 cal BC	*1090–980 cal BC*
OxA-10788	CG9 1111B	refitting pottery, charred residue	2823±35	-24.9	1050–890 cal BC	*1080–970 cal BC*
OxA-10789	CG9 1111C	refitting pottery, charred residue	2894±37	-25.7	1260–930 cal BC	*1100–990 cal BC*
OxA-9485	CG10 2010B	refitting pottery, charred residue	2950±40	-28.1	1370–1000 cal BC	*1100–1000 cal BC*
OxA-9923	CG10 2010C	refitting pottery, charred residue	2910±60	-26.9	1370–910 cal BC	*1100–990 cal BC*
OxA-10790	CG10 2010D	refitting pottery, charred residue	2886±36	-25.7	1220–930 cal BC	*1100–990 cal BC*
OxA-10842	CG10 2010E	refitting pottery, charred residue	2810±50	-24.2	1130–830 cal BC	*1090–970 cal BC*
OxA-10791	CG19 1601A	charred seed, *Triticum* sp.	2885±40	-23.3	1260–920 cal BC	*1100–990 cal BC*
OxA-10792	CG19 1601B	charred seed, *Triticum* sp.	2891±36	-22.6	1260–930 cal BC	*1100–990 cal BC*

not absolute. They are interpretative *estimates*, which can and will change as further data become available and as other researchers choose to model the existing data from different perspectives.

The technique used is a form of Markov Chain Monte Carlo sampling, and has been applied using the program OxCal v3.5 (http://www.rlaha.ox.ac.uk/), which uses a mixture of the Metropolis-Hastings algorithm and the more specific Gibbs sampler (Gilks *et al.* 1996; Gelfand and Smith 1990). Details of the algorithms employed by this program are available from the on-line manual or in Bronk Ramsey (1995; 1998; 2001), and fully worked examples are given in the series of papers by Buck *et al.* (1991; 1992; 1994a; 1994b). The algorithm used in the models described below can be derived from the structures shown in Figures 6–10.

This section concentrates on describing the archaeological evidence which has been incorporated into the chronological model, explaining the reasoning behind the interpretative choices made in producing the models presented. These archaeological decisions fundamentally underpin the choice of statistical model.

Objectives of dating programme

The radiocarbon programme was designed to achieve the following objectives:

- to provide absolute dating for the important Late Bronze Age ceramic assemblage;
- to determine whether the characteristic forms in this assemblage are early in the Plain Ware tradition;
- to provide absolute dating for later prehistoric activity on the site.

No suitable material could be obtained from the rectangular post-built structures on the site, and insufficient material was available for dating from the circular structures. It is therefore impossible to confirm directly whether these are contemporary with the ceramic assemblage. Dating the latest element of the ceramic assemblage, including finger-tip and incised geometric decoration (CG91), was also considered, but suitable samples could not be found.

Two cremated bone deposits were identified but could not be dated as the material had unfortunately been mislaid. When it was recovered, late in the analytical programme, it was found to consist of cremated bone only, with no fragments of fuel debris.

Datable material was available from a series of Beaker pits, but mathematical simulations suggested that, in the absence of sufficient stratigraphic relationships to constrain the calibration of the radiocarbon results, the dates produced would not refine the chronology of the features provided by the ceramic typology.

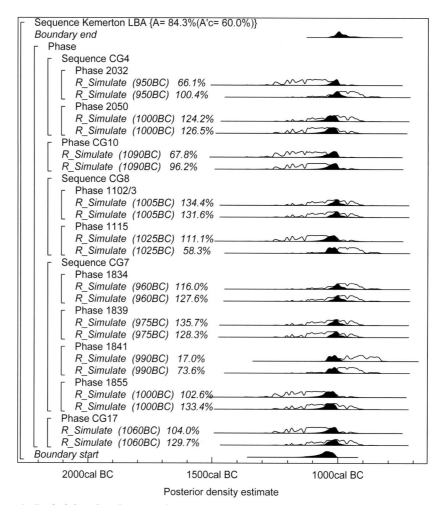

Figure 6. Probability distributions of simulated dates from the sequence at Huntsman's Quarry.

Sampling strategy

Initially a simulation of the dating problems from Kemerton was built using the R_Simulate function of OxCal, the earliest and latest estimated dates for the ceramic assemblage, and the stratigraphic relationships between potential samples (*e.g.* Fig. 6). This modelling suggested that, depending on the duration of the site and its actual date (and hence the part of the calibration curve on which it would fall), between 15 and 30 radiocarbon measurements would be required to provide a sufficiently precise chronology to be archaeologically useful.

For this reason, a sequential sampling strategy was adopted and, initially, a series of 18 samples was submitted for dating. All samples were from pits and waterholes containing large Late Bronze Age ceramic assemblages. Samples were selected from features in every area of the site. Preference was given to pits or waterholes where a sequence of samples could be found from stratigraphically related contexts since the preliminary statistical modelling had shown that the constraints on the simple calibrated dates provided by such relative dating would produce considerably more precision in the chronological estimates provided by the eventual model.

Stratigraphic relationships occur between contexts, not between samples, however. It is therefore critical that the samples which are dated were fresh when deposited in the contexts from which they were recovered. In this case, this is thought to be probable because the ceramic assemblage consisted of large, unabraded sherds and the bone appeared to be 'fresh'. In addition there were concentrations of charcoal in the fills. All in all, the pit and waterhole fills appear to incorporate refuse in primary contexts from the nearby settlement structures, or possibly refuse derived directly from short-term middens in these settlement areas. Nevertheless, datable material from these deposits still had to meet an extremely rigorous set of criteria before it was selected for dating. These were chosen to minimise the risk of submitting residual samples.

These criteria were:

- articulated animal bone deposits – these must have been buried with tendons attached or they would not have remained in articulation, and so were almost certainly less than six months old when buried (Mant 1987, 71);
- waterlogged plant macrofossils – to be residual these would have had to have been redeposited from

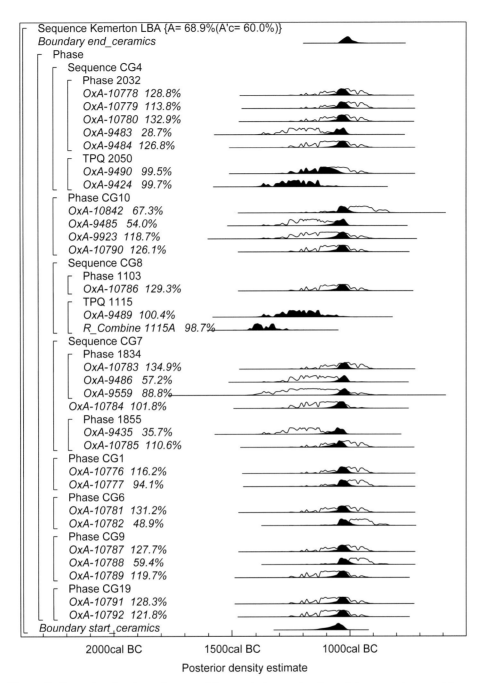

Figure 7. Posterior density estimates of dates relating to the date of the ceramic assemblage.

another context where conditions were suitable for their preservation (generally unlikely, particularly in a discrete context such as a pit);

• refitting sherds with internal carbonised residues – the presence of more than one sherd from the same vessel in a context suggests that the primary disposal of the broken vessel was in that context; internal residues are likely to consist of food remains rather than, for example, sooting from a fire;

• butchered animal bone, from contexts containing re-fitting sherds where articulated bone was not available.

Unfortunately only 11 results were obtained from the first series of samples, as all the bone samples contained insufficient collagen for dating. However, the consistency of these results is such that it appears that the hypothesis that this material was refuse dumped in what were effectively primary contexts is true. This being so, a second set of samples was submitted. This consisted of 16 further samples of carbonised residues on the internal surfaces of refitting pottery sherds, and two samples of charred cereal grains. All these samples were from contexts where refitting sherds or articulated animal bone was present.

OxA-10375 was a replicate measurement of sample

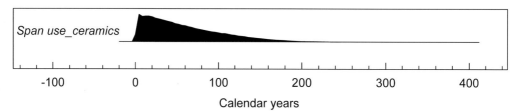

Figure 8. Probability distribution of the period during which dated ceramic assemblage was in use.

CG8 1115A (OxA-9488), measured as part of the internal quality assurance procedures of the Oxford Radiocarbon Accelerator Unit.

Archaeological interpretation

The interpretative model for the chronology of the Late Bronze Age ceramic assemblage at Huntsman's Quarry is shown in Figure 7.

The relative order of the dated contexts, known from stratigraphy, is included in the model. This means that, in CG7, the samples from context 1855 (OxA-9435 and OxA-10785) are earlier than that from context 1838 (OxA-10784), which is earlier than those from context 1834 (OxA-9486, OxA-9559, and OxA-10783). In CG8, the samples from context 1115 (OxA-9488, OxA-10375, and OxA-9489) are earlier than that from context 1103. A weighted mean has been taken of the two measurements on *Prunus spinosa* twig 1115A before calibration (OxA-9488 and OxA-10375; T'=0.8; T'(5%)=3.8; v=1; 3097±26BP; Ward and Wilson 1978). In CG4 the two results from context 2050 (OxA-9424 and OxA-9490) are earlier than those from context 2032 (OxA-9483–4 and OxA-10778–80).

The radiocarbon measurements are in good agreement with the incorporation of this relative dating information in the model (A=68.9%; Bronk Ramsey 1995). This suggests that there is little residual material among the dated samples, supporting our archaeological interpretation of the taphonomy of this material (see above). The freshness of the samples when deposited in the contexts from which they were recovered is also supported by the consistency of the radiocarbon measurements from each context. Twenty-eight samples have been dated from ten contexts on the site which have more than one radiocarbon measurement. Only from two of these contexts, CG7 1855 and CG8 1115, are the measurements statistically significantly different (at 95% confidence), and in both cases the measurements are consistent at 99% confidence. This variation is no more than would be expected by the quoted statistical scatter on the measurements if all the material from each context was actually of exactly the same date.

In the model shown in Figure 7, the samples from primary fills of the pits and waterholes have been used to constrain the dates of the ceramic-bearing deposits above. These secondary deposits in the pits and waterholes are

believed to represent infilling with fresh domestic rubbish. The samples from the crop processing debris dumped along with many sherds from a highly fragmented vessel in CG19 are considered equivalent to this material.

This model suggests that the ceramics from this site were used and deposited between *1130–1010 cal BC (95% probability)* or *1090–1020 cal BC (68% probability)* and *1050–960 cal BC (95% probability)* or *1040–990 cal BC (68% probability*; Fig. 7). They were used for between *1 and 160 years (95% probability)* or *1 and 80 years (68% probability*; Fig. 8).

The dated features come from across the site, so it appears that there is no discernable difference in date for the disuse of the waterholes and, presumably, the occupation of the roundhouses from which the rubbish used to backfill them was derived.

It is possible, however, that the waterholes themselves were actually dug and in use rather earlier. A model which includes the samples from the primary fills of the waterholes as part of the phase of Bronze Age activity on the site is shown in Figure 9. Sample 1115A is a statistical outlier and has been excluded from the analysis (A=16.0%; Bronk Ramsey 1995). This model suggests that the Bronze Age activity started in *1210–1040 cal BC* and ended in *1050–920 cal BC (95% probability)* or started in *1170–1120 cal BC* or *1110–1050 cal BC* and ended in *1020–960 cal BC (68% probability)*. The waterholes were in use for between *10 and 250 years (95% probability)* or *50 and 190 years (68% probability*; Fig. 10).

Conclusions

The absolute dating programme at Huntsman's Quarry has achieved its objectives. It seems that the waterholes, and presumably the field system with which they were associated, were dug and laid out in *1210–1040 cal BC (95% probability*; Fig. 9). This activity may have been contemporary with the roundhouses excavated on the site, although, as these are undated, this cannot be proven. Between *1130–1010 cal BC* and *1050–960 cal BC (95% probability*; Fig. 7), the waterholes fell into disuse, and were infilled. These fills incorporated large quantities of fresh domestic debris containing a substantial ceramic assemblage. This material may have come from the inhabitants of the roundhouses.

The waterholes and associated field system were probably

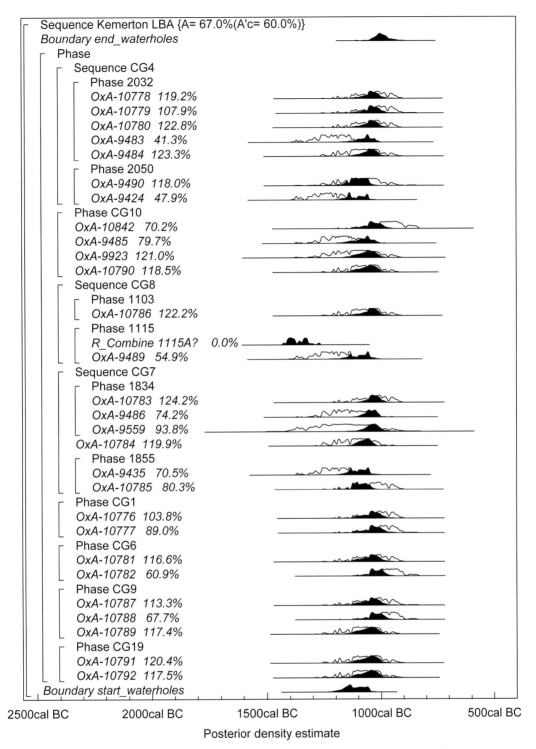

Figure 9. Posterior density estimates of dates relating to the use of the waterholes.

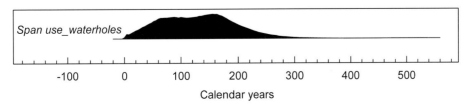

Figure 10. Probability distribution of the period during which the waterholes were in use.

in use for between *10 and 250 years* (*95% probability*; Fig. 10). The dated ceramic assemblage, which derives from the disuse of this system, spans a shorter period of between *1 and 160 years* (*95% probability*; Fig. 8). Centering on the 11th century cal BC, the Plain Ware assemblage from Kemerton is early in the development of this tradition.

Earlier prehistoric activity (by Robin Jackson and Mike Napthan)

Upper Palaeolithic and Mesolithic activity

A limited amount of activity during the Upper Palaeolithic

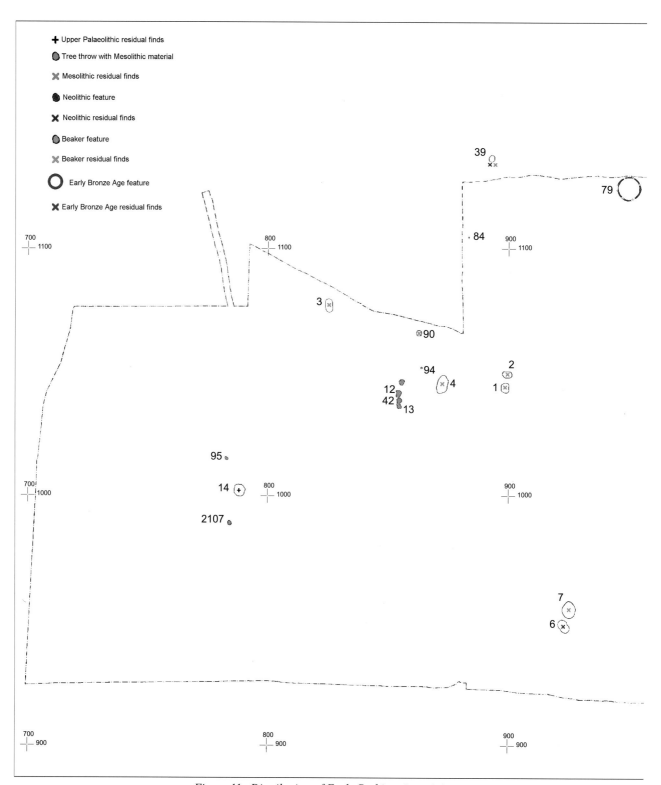

Figure 11. Distribution of Early Prehistoric activity.

was indicated by the presence of two residual flint tools in a Late Bronze Age waterhole (context 2102; CG14; Bellamy, this volume). It is uncertain whether these indicate the presence of occupation of this date, or whether they represent casual losses, although the latter appears more probable.

Mesolithic activity was better represented with a focus of activity in the northeastern part of the site (Fig. 11). Here, diagnostic Mesolithic artefacts were recovered from a tree-throw (context 1722) and as residual material in the fill of a later field boundary (context 212). Further material of probable Mesolithic date was centered on Area 17 and

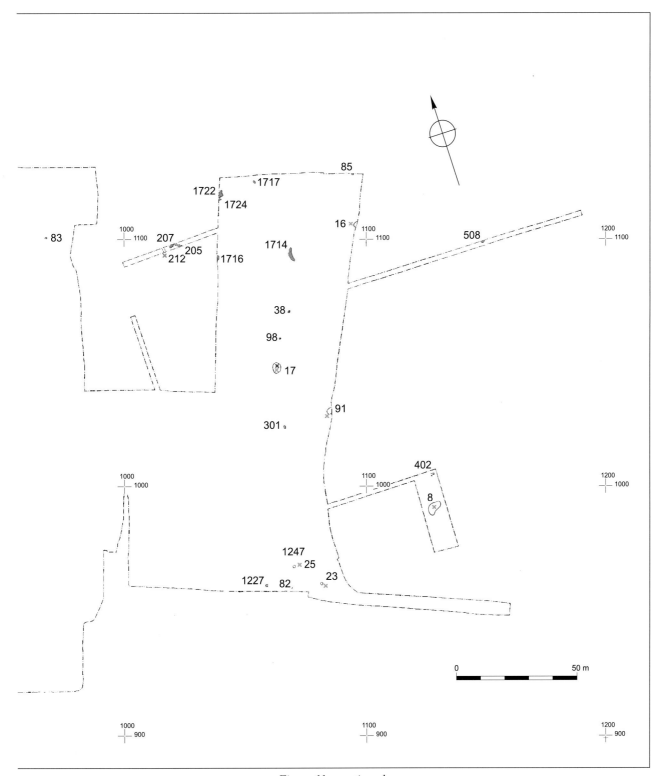

Figure 11. continued

included blade debitage, blade cores and two retouched pieces (Bellamy, this volume). These were recovered from further tree-throws of probable Mesolithic date (contexts 206/207, 1714, 1716 and 1717) as well as residual material in a Late Bronze Age posthole which appears to have disturbed another tree-throw (context 1724). Some of the flint was burnt and, together with the presence of tools and working waste concentrated into this part of the site, this is understood to reflect Mesolithic settlement in this vicinity.

A sparse scatter of blade debitage across the remainder of the site may reflect casual losses around such an occupation focus.

Neolithic activity

Summary

Two pits of probable Middle Neolithic date were recorded. The first (CG38; Figs 11 and 12) contained a single fill and has been dated by material tentatively identified as from a Peterborough Ware bowl (Woodward and Jackson, this volume). At least two other vessels were represented but were not sufficiently diagnostic to enable any greater certainty about the date of the feature. To the south, a further pit (CG98) may be broadly contemporary. This contained eight flints including a core. Both pits had a single fill and no evidence of silting or weathering of the sides indicating that they had been dug and infilled within a short period of time. In the same area a narrow, broken blade recovered from a Late Bronze Age pit (CG17) may be a residual item dating from this period (Bellamy, this volume).

Other certain evidence of Neolithic activity derives from sherds from a Grooved Ware vessel recovered as residual material from a Late Bronze Age pit (context 1801; CG39; Woodward and Jackson). This supports the presence of at least a low level of activity during this period.

Further Neolithic features may have been present but none has been firmly identified owing to the absence of securely dateable material.

Detailed descriptions

Pit: Context Group 38 (Fig. 12)

Grid	1067/1070
Fill/cut	1520
Plan	Sub-circular
Profile	Bowl-shaped
Dimensions	0.90 × 0.20m

Shallow, bowl-shaped pit with a single reddish-brown silt sand fill. This included a moderate pottery assemblage (18 sherds plus crumbs, weighing 261g), occasional charcoal flecks and rare bone fragments (15, including cow and sheep/goat).

Pit: Context Group 98 (Fig. 12)

Grid	1061/1058
Fill/cut	1515
Plan	Sub-oval
Profile	Concave
Dimensions	1.32 × 1.05 × 0.21m

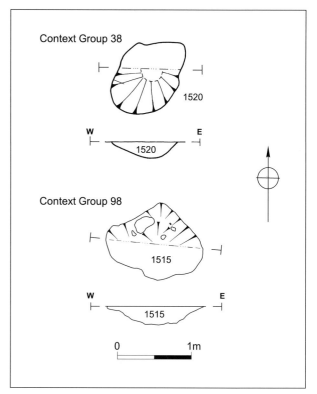

Figure 12. Neolithic pits (CG38 and CG98).

Shallow pit with single charcoal-flecked fill. This produced a small assemblage of flint (19, including a core).

Beaker activity

Summary

Beaker period activity was represented by a group of three closely spaced pits (CG12, 13 and 42; Fig. 13). Several isolated pits and other features were also identified, of which one lay to the north of the pit group (CG94), the remainder being widely dispersed (CG82, 83, 84, 85 and 95; Fig. 11). All were dated on the basis of Beaker ceramics.

Naturally derived lower fills distinguished the three closely spaced pits. These probably reflect weathering or collapse of the unstable sand and gravel deposits through which the pits had been excavated. The upper fills were darker and produced assemblages of Beaker ceramics, flint and other finds. One pit (CG12) contained notably more material than the other two (Table 3). The ceramics indicated that these episodes of filling probably dated from the second half of the third millennium BC.

In contrast to the Neolithic pit described earlier, these pits appear to have been left open for some time before backfilling; the basal fills indicating a period of weathering of an open feature prior to deposition of the upper fills. The upper fills, representing disuse of the features, had distinct assemblages incorporated within them. One pit (CG12) included a considerable quantity of material including 98 sherds representing no less than eight different fineware

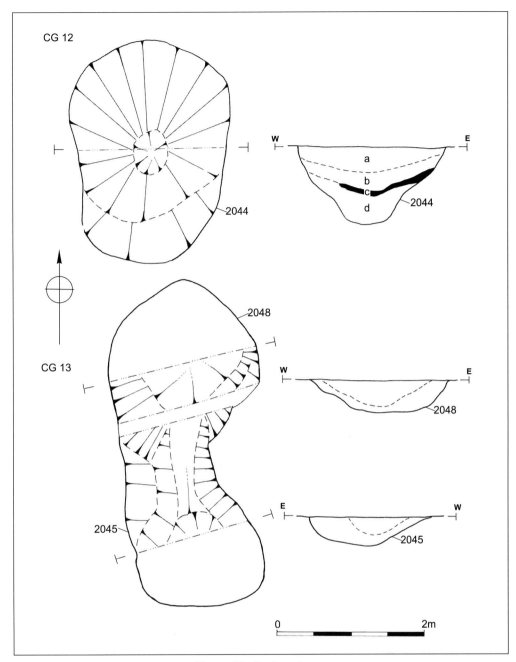

Figure 13. Beaker pit group.

vessels as well 28 of the 29 flint items recovered from the pit group. A further posthole or small pit (CG94) situated to the north may also have been associated, while the appearance of the fill and the dimensions of an unexcavated pit in this area indicate that it is liable to represent a further element of this feature group.

The remaining certain Beaker period features were widely dispersed. These included one further pit (CG85), three large postholes or small pits (CG83, CG94 and CG95) and two isolated postholes (CG82 and CG84). Of these, two were of particular interest (CG82 and CG83) in that each contained quantities of pottery (9 and 24 sherds respectively) indicative of deposition of substantial chunks

Table 3. Summary of Beaker pit contents.

Context Group	Pottery	Flint	Other finds
12	98	28	Bone, burnt stone
13	17	1	Bone, burnt stone
42	19	0	Bone, burnt stone

from single vessels or possibly, since both pits/postholes were truncated, entire vessels. Burnt stone, fired clay and flint were also present in some features.

It is considered probable that further activity of this date is represented amongst the large number of unassigned features, which were poorly dated, undated or unexcavated.

Several of these contained only flint, and occasionally daub or burnt stone. Since the majority of the flint assemblage has been identified as representative of a flake industry of Late Neolithic/Early Bronze Age date (Bellamy, this volume) it seems likely that at least some of these features may be broadly contemporaneous with the Beaker activity or possibly the Early Bronze Age ring-ditch. These include a gully containing five worked flints including a chisel arrowhead (context 204/205), a pit (302/301) and several isolated postholes (contexts 401/402, 507/508, 1227, 1247 and 2106/2107), one of which (2106/7) contained a fine plano-convex knife.

These indications of more widespread Beaker activity are supported by the presence of residual Beaker pottery and flint in a range of Late Bronze Age features and especially from the substantial waterholes (context 1828, CG1; context 709, CG2; context 2039, CG3; contexts 2032 & 2060, CG4; context 1848, CG7; context 1102 & 1103, CG8; context 1708, CG16; context 1517, CG17; context 1604, CG23; context 1216, CG25; context 1801, CG39; context 2042, CG90; contexts 1438 & 1439, CG91; and context 1856). Of these, the waterhole (CG4) lying closest to the Beaker pit group contained the most material, including decorated sherds, plain sherds and one of the largest flint assemblages from the site (49, including several diagnostically characteristic Late Neolithic/Beaker tools).

Taken together these dispersed features and residual material suggest that, apart from the clearly defined focus in the vicinity of the Beaker pit group, further areas of activity were present across the site.

Detailed descriptions

PIT: CONTEXT GROUP 12 (FIG. 13)

Grid	0855/1039
Fill/cut	2043/2044
Plan	Sub-oval
Profile	Bowl-shaped
Dimensions	2.80 × 2.00 × 1.00m

Relatively deep pit with sloping sides and a concave base. Although only a single fill (context 2043) was recorded, an annotated sketch section shows four phases of fill deposition.

The lowest fill was primarily slumped gravel derived from weathering of the sides (2043d). One small bone fragment was recovered. A shallow deposit of dark grey, charcoal-rich, sandy loam (2043c) overlaid this and contained occasional bone (2 calcined fragments), burnt limestone, worked flint and a considerable quantity of Beaker pottery. The upper fills, although charcoal-flecked only contained a few undecorated sherds of Beaker pottery and worked flint (including a scraper) in a tan brown clay (2043b) and a clean brown loam (2043a). A total of 98 sherds of pottery, 28 worked flints and 130 fragments of bone were recovered from this fill sequence

PIT: CONTEXT GROUP 13 (FIG. 13)

Grid	0855/1034
Fill/cut	2046/2045
Plan	Sub-oval?
Profile	Bowl-shaped
Dimensions	2.00 × 1.60 × 0.38m

A shallow pit, probably sub-oval in plan but linked by a short gully to an adjacent pit CG42 and thus of uncertain original shape. The relationship of the gully to this pit and CG42 was not determined but the features are believed to have been contemporaneous.

The fill (2046) was recorded as a single sandy loam; however, upper and lower elements of this were distinguished by colour. The lower part was a tan brown deposit and was very hard to distinguish from the surrounding natural sand. The upper part was greyer in colour and both burnt limestone and charcoal were present along with a small quantity of Beaker pottery (17 sherds), flint (1) and animal bone (4 fragments).

PIT: CONTEXT GROUP 42 (FIG. 13)

Grid	0855/1038
Fill/cut	2047/2048
Plan	Sub-oval?
Profile	Bowl-shaped
Dimensions	2.30 × 1.90 × 0.40m

A shallow pit, probably sub-oval in plan but linked by a short gully to an adjacent pit CG13 and thus of uncertain original shape. The relationship of the gully to this pit and CG13 was not determined but the features are believed to have been contemporaneous.

The fill (2047) was recorded as a single sandy loam, however, upper and lower elements of this were distinguished by colour. The lower part was a sandy brown loam while the upper part was greyer in colour. Burnt limestone and charcoal were present along with a small quantity of Beaker pottery (19 sherds) and animal bone (5 fragments). This feature is apparently contemporary with both CG12 and CG13.

POSTHOLE: CONTEXT GROUP 82 (FIG. 11)

Grid	1069/0961
Fill/cut	1210/1211
Plan	Sub-oval
Profile	U-shaped
Dimensions	0.57 × 0.31 × 0.12m

Small sub-oval feature, probably a posthole. This had a single, grey brown, fine sandy loam fill, which was heavily flecked with charcoal. Produced 9 sherds of Beaker pottery (apparently all from same vessel), fired clay (3 fragments) and a single heat-cracked pebble.

POSTHOLE/PIT: CONTEXT GROUP 83 (FIG. 11)

Grid	0969/1102
Fill/cut	1823
Plan	Sub-oval
Profile	Irregular
Dimensions	0.80 × 0.50 × 0.12m

Shallow rather irregular hollow with depression at one end – possibly a post setting. Single fill of very dark grey brown, silty loam with occasional to moderate quantities of charcoal flecking. This produced 24 sherds of Beaker pottery, most of which derived from a single vessel.

POSTHOLE: CONTEXT GROUP 84 (FIG. 11)

Grid	0883/1105
Fill/cut	1816
Plan	Sub-oval
Profile	Concave
Dimensions	0.43 × 0.35 × 0.10m

Posthole with single fill of mid grey brown, compact, silty loam with occasional charcoal flecking and burnt stone. Contained 5 sherds of Beaker pottery.

PIT: CONTEXT GROUP 85 (FIG. 11)

Grid	1092/1128
Fill/cut	1705
Plan	Sub-circular
Profile	Bowl-shaped
Dimensions	1.10 × 0.90+ × 0.25m

Small pit with a single fill of mid grey brown, sandy clay silt with occasional charcoal flecking and burnt limestone. Contained a single sherd of Beaker pottery and a fragment of burnt limestone.

55565

POSTHOLE/PIT: CONTEXT GROUP 94 (FIG. 11)

Grid	0872/1068
Fill/cut	2055
Plan	Sub-oval
Profile	Bowl/U-shaped
Dimensions	0.90 × 0.80 × 0.42m

Steep-sided, large posthole or small pit located just over 10m from the pit group described above. Although excavated as a single fill, the section shows a sequence of four fills. A charcoal flecked base fill was overlain by a paler, loamy clay deposit itself overlain by a greyer clay loam. A mid grey clay loam formed the uppermost fill. Charcoal fleck and burnt limestone were both noted and a single sherd of Beaker pottery and a flint were recovered.

POSTHOLE/PIT: CONTEXT GROUP 95 (FIG. 11)

Grid	0782/1015
Fill/cut	2110/2111
Plan	Sub-oval
Profile	Irregular
Dimensions	1.00 × 0.80 × 0.23m

Irregular feature which probably represents the remains of a disturbed posthole. A charcoal flecked, compact sandy fill produced a single sherd of Beaker pottery.

Early Bronze Age activity

Summary

Early Bronze Age activity was represented by a small ring-ditch located on the north side of the site (Figs 14 and 15). The ring-ditch almost certainly marks the position of a former burial mound although no trace of any barrow mound survived, probably as a result of extensive plough truncation. No primary burial was identified, again probably owing to truncation. Dating of the construction of the original monument is uncertain.

A length of the southeastern side of the ditch had been recut (1814). This contained cremated bone and an accessory cup (Woodward and Jackson, this volume), and is understood to represent the insertion of a secondary burial into the monument during the Early Bronze Age.

The feature had been disturbed by two phases of later activity; a pair of later Bronze Age boundary or trackway ditches and a medieval furrow which had disturbed the accessory cup and cremated bone within 1814.

Further Early Bronze Age material was identified in the form of fragments from a large urn, recovered as residual material within a Late Bronze Age waterhole (CG6; Fig. 11).

Other activity of this date may be represented among the large number of poorly dated, undated and uninvestigated features present.

Detailed descriptions

RING-DITCH: CONTEXT GROUP 79 (FIGS 14 AND 15)

Grid	0950/1125
Fill/cut	1812, 1813
Recut	1814
Dimensions	10.00 dia

Ring-ditch, 10m in diameter (1812/1813 cut), with a short recut section (1814) on its southeastern side. Both the ring-ditch and re-cut had been disturbed by later prehistoric boundary features (1810 and 1859) and a medieval furrow. No central feature survived, however, a number of undated but sterile features around and within the ring-ditch may have been related.

The ring-ditch was approximately circular having a slightly flattened northern side. Its fill was a mid to dark grey brown silty clay loam with burnt stone and daub inclusions. Charcoal flecking was also noted and concentrated on the southern and eastern sides of the feature. No artefacts or bone were recovered.

The re-cut section (1814), although not having clearly defined limits was distinctly wider, deeper and straighter than the main ring-ditch. Its fill, a very dark grey sandy loam, was characterised by the presence of abundant charcoal along with a quantity of burnt limestone and daub flecks. Pottery (97 sherds) representing at least five vessels was recovered and included an Early Bronze Age accessory cup. Flint (4) and animal bone (47 fragments) was also recovered.

A small quantity of heavily calcined bone was also present. The fragment size made it impossible (Pinter Bellows, this volume) to determine whether this was human or animal bone, however, the association with an accessory cup and its placement in a re-cut within a ring-ditch strongly suggest that this represents a partial, dispersed cremation.

Late Bronze Age activity (by Robin Jackson and Mike Napthan)

Late Bronze Age activity was widely dispersed across the whole site and included waterholes, substantial pits, lesser pits, hearths/ovens and very large numbers of structural features (Fig. 16). The latter mainly comprised post and stakeholes but there were also some post and trench constructions. In addition the site was traversed by a series of boundary features, some paired to form track or droveways, others clearly defining fields. A pond and an isolated and unaccompanied deposit of cremated bone may also be of this date.

Few stratigraphic relationships were present and dating evidence was limited, being mainly confined to waterholes, larger pits and a limited number of lesser features. However, features containing material assemblages were well dated and produced substantial quantities of diagnostic Late Bronze Age pottery. Supported by the extensive programme of radiocarbon dating discussed above, this has allowed this main phase of activity at the site to be closely dated. It seems that at least some of the waterholes and presumably the associated field system were excavated and laid out in *1210–1040 cal BC (95% probability)*. The early period of use of these waterholes and field systems does not appear to have been accompanied by occupation within the excavated site, though settlement areas must have lain in the vicinity.

Settlement activity subsequently spreading across the area appears to have been located within these field systems and has for the most part been dated by the deposition of substantial ceramic assemblages and other occupation debris into the waterholes between *1130–1010 cal BC and 1050–960 cal BC (95% probability)*.

Many smaller features were either not excavated or were excavated but produced no dating evidence. As noted previously, some of these may relate to earlier

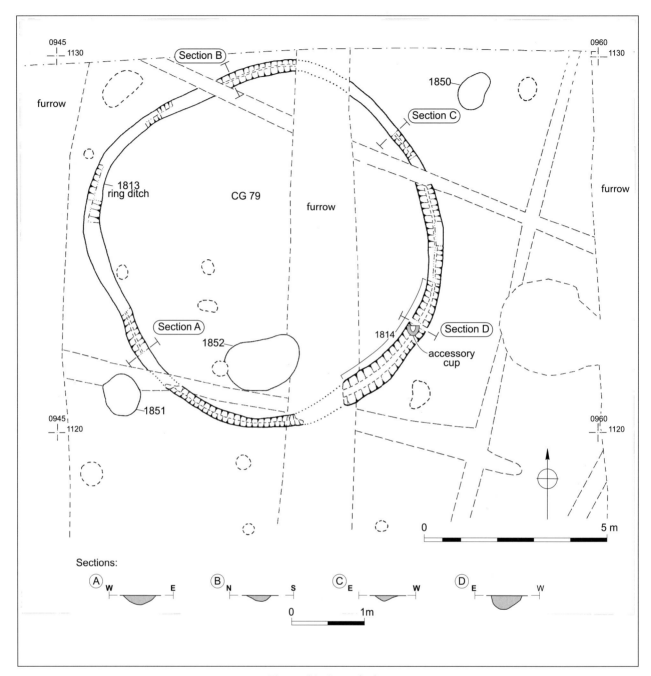

Figure 14. Ring-ditch.

phases of activity; however, for analytical purposes they are considered here as the majority are liable to have been Late Bronze Age in date, this being the main period of occupation and material deposition at the site.

Fields and tracks/droves

Summary

Although poorly dated owing to the lack of artefactual evidence and stratigraphic relationships, examination of the ditches and gullies present has allowed identification of two principal alignments of field boundaries and droves which can be associated with later prehistoric activity at the site and particularly with the large pits interpreted as waterholes (see below).

The earliest boundaries, and the most commonly present, are those based on a west-north-west to east-south-east alignment and those at approximately right-angles to them. These form a grid-like pattern of fields and two apparent droves (FS1; Fig. 17).

They can be associated with at least one of the major waterholes (CG14) which was sited directly on one of these boundaries allowing access from fields to both

Figure 15. Ring-ditch during excavation.

sides of the ditch. A minor alteration or kink in alignment of this boundary allied to the fact that it clearly did not cut the waterhole demonstrates that the two were almost certainly contemporary; the slight kink indicating that the boundary had been created to meet an existing waterhole. Projection of the alignments of two other ditches indicates that these would also probably have had similarly located waterholes (CG4 and CG8), while overall the projected pattern of the field system indicates either the presence of, or access to, a waterhole in most land-parcels. Some reworking and sub-division of these fields is indicated within the overall pattern by slightly discrepant but broadly parallel alignments and blocking or modification of tracks/ droves; however, overall the pattern is consistent with a single system used, maintained and adapted as required over a period of time.

Dating of the primary silting fills in two of the waterholes (CG4 and CG8) indicates that these, and therefore presumably the field system, were established up to 100 years prior to the main period of settlement of the site. The function of the waterholes may therefore have changed from provision of water for stock to a wider range of uses including water for human consumption and craft and agricultural processing related activities as well as for animals. This change in use, or in range of uses, seen for the waterholes may be reflected in a changed layout of the landscape since a second field system can be identified (FS2; Fig. 17). This was based on, and at right-angles to, a well defined northeast to southwest aligned ditched drove or track. This reorganisation formed a less intensively bounded landscape. The establishment of this more open

system may have been accompanied by the construction of one or more of the large post-defined enclosures which may have been used to manage stock in this less heavily bounded landscape (CG66, 67 and 68; see below).

Detailed descriptions

FIELD SYSTEM: FS1 (FIG. 17)

Field system comprising heavily truncated ditches/gullies running on broadly west-north-west to east-south-east alignments and at right-angles to them. Best defined in the northern and western parts of the excavated area but heavily truncated throughout especially within the central part of the site.

Few stratigraphic relationships could be established either between the ditches or with other site features. One notable exception was where one of the ditches (context 2073) met a waterhole (CG14). This appeared to neither cut the waterhole nor be truncated by it; rather it had a slight but distinct kink in its alignment at this point indicating that it had probably been excavated up to and then beyond an existing waterhole (see Fig. 25). The projected alignment of another ditch (context 2076) would similarly intersect a waterhole (CG4), as possibly would a third example (context 1414 with CG8). This indicates a close relationship with the waterholes and suggests that the date of the establishment of this field system was the same as that of the digging of these waterholes; namely sometime during the period *1210–1040 cal BC* as established by radiocarbon dating of material from the base fills of two of these waterholes. Another key stratigraphic relationship was the cutting through of the Early Bronze Age ring-ditch (CG79; by contexts 1810 and 1859) and the truncation by elements of Field System 2. Notably, although several ditches forming the later system (FS2) included Late Bronze Age pottery, securely datable material was not recovered from any of the features forming this earlier field system perhaps indicating that its main period of use fell before the establishment of settlement areas.

Some reworking and sub-division of these fields is indicated within the overall pattern by slightly discrepant but broadly parallel alignments and blocking or modification of tracks/droves; however, overall the

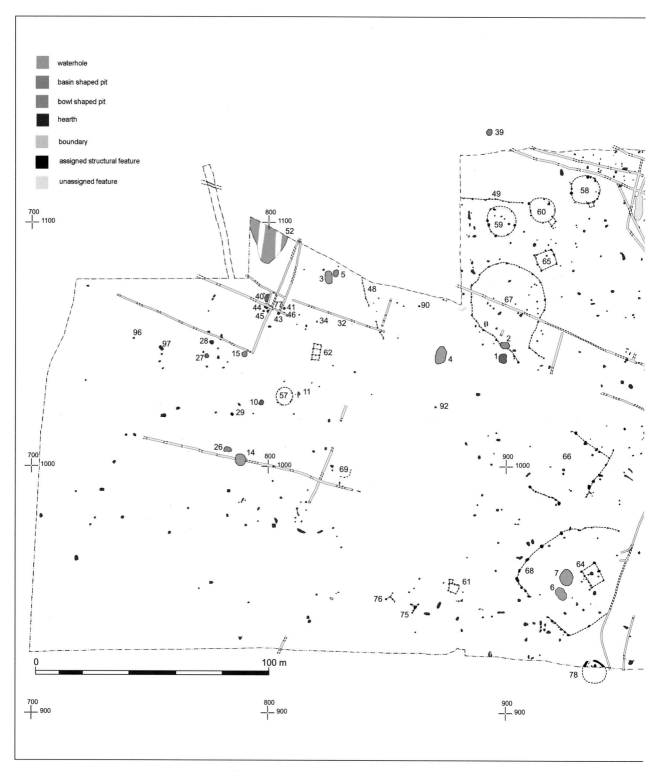

waterhole

basin shaped pit

bowl shaped pit

hearth

boundary

assigned structural feature

unassigned feature

Figure 16. Late Bronze Age activity.

pattern is consistent with a single system used, maintained and adapted as required over a period of time, prior to the complete reorganisation reflected by Field System 2.

FIELD SYSTEM: FS2 (FIG. 17)

Field system comprising heavily truncated ditches/gullies. These ran on broadly northeast to southwest alignments and had several other elements apparently running off them. These were all located in the eastern half

of the site while the western half appeared to be open, comprising a single large land unit.

The most distinct feature of the system was a trackway or drove defined by parallel ditch/gullies crossing the southwest corner of the excavated area. To its north, a more broadly spaced pair of ditches/gullies ran parallel to each other and may have been used to funnel stock from a north or northwesterly direction towards where the ditches/gullies opened out into the large land parcel to the west. A potential gate in the

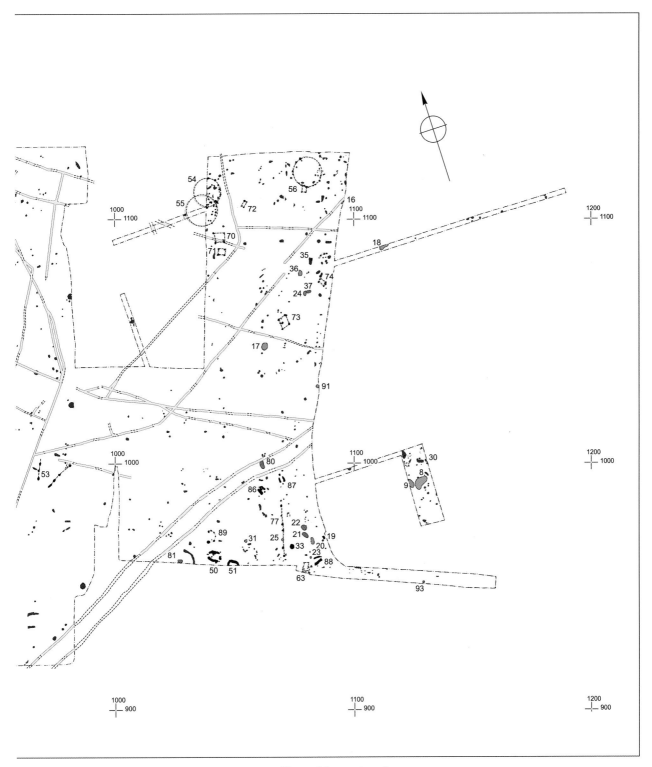

Figure 16. continued

south side of this 'funnel-like' arrangement would have allowed access to land to the southeast.

Within the large land parcel, as noted above there was no evidence for any ditch/gully defined sub-divisions; however, three large post-defined enclosures (CG66, 67 and 68; see below) may have acted to constrain stock within the area. Only the eastern side of the large land parcel was defined, formed in part by a reworked and slightly realigned element of the earlier field system and in part by retention of part of that earlier

system. The latter seems to have had a gate inserted into it, either to allow access into the large land parcel or into one of the aforementioned post-defined enclosures (CG68; see Fig. 16).

As in the case of the earlier field system, some relationship between the land units and the waterholes seems likely but stratigraphic relationships between the ditches/gullies and other features were very limited and only a few sherds of Late Bronze Age pottery were retrieved from elements of this second system. Overall, the impression is that this system may

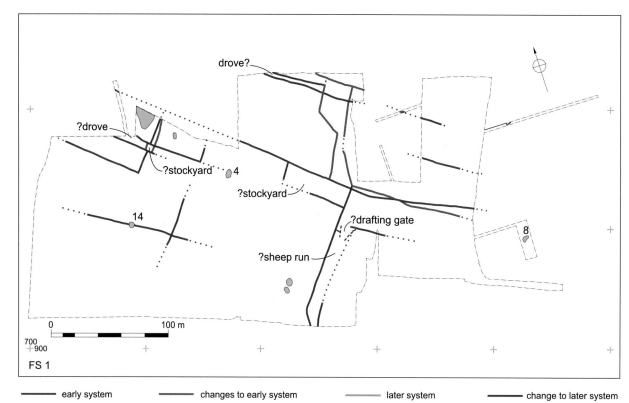

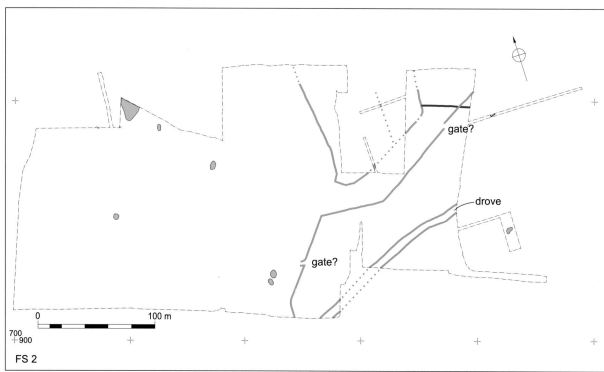

Figure 17. Late Bronze Age field systems.

correspond with the later stages of occupation and activity at the site or possibly even slightly post-date it.

The waterholes

Summary

Seven substantial features were scattered across the site (Figs 16 and 18–27) and are interpreted as waterholes.

These were investigated in varying levels of detail ranging from total excavation to half sectioning. In some cases, excavation included machining out of lower fills to recover finds and samples and also to allow the base level to be established and full sections to be exposed.

The fill characteristics, overall dimensions and profiles of these features, and the fact that they had been excavated through sand and gravel into underlying clay deposits, enabled interpretation as waterholes. Such features have been regularly identified on Late Bronze Age sites, as at Shorncote (Hearne and Heaton 1994; Hearne and Adam 1999; Brossler *et al.* 2002) and Reading Business Park (Moore and Jennings 1992; Brossler, Early and Allen 2004).

The waterholes typically contained two distinct phases of fill. At the base, fine sand and silt deposits interleaved with tipping and slumped layers of coarser sand and gravel. These probably derived from weathering and collapse of the sides of the features, which for the most part had been excavated through relatively unstable sand and gravel. These processes had also undoubtedly contributed to the irregular, rather Y-shaped profiles of four of the seven examples identified.

Given the investment of effort required to dig these features, it seems likely that they would have been cleaned out on occasion prior to being allowed to silt up for a final time. Consequently, these fills are considered to have principally developed during the final periods of use of the waterholes.

In a couple of cases there were indications that the shallow, damp, silted up hollows of the upper cones of these features had then been left open for a while, since soily accumulations had developed in them. Overlying these silting deposits and slumped lower fills were dumps of material, including horizons containing large quantities of burnt stone, charcoal and a wide range of artefacts and ecofacts. Apart from large quantities of pottery, flint and animal bone, ceramic weights, metal working debris from the manufacture of bronze weapons, bone pins and shale armlets fragments were recovered as a was a single human bone (a vertebra). One (CG4) contained the remains of a wooden ladder.

The artefact rich horizons were interleaved with soily dumps. Similar upper fill sequences were present in each of the waterholes. These appear to have been deposited over a relatively short period of time, clearly reflecting abandonment and deliberate infilling (closure) of the features. Subsidence over the softer lower silt fills had caused these horizons to tip towards the centre of the waterholes and in several cases had led to the formation of a depression over the centre of the feature. The resultant hollows had filled with relatively loamy and sterile soils that probably derived from the slow accumulation of topsoil or ploughsoil within them.

In two instances (CG3 and CG8), waterholes were paired with substantial basin-shaped pits which were clay-lined, making them suitable for holding water. These

may therefore have been associated, at least in part, with a specialist production/craft activity. Other uses of the waterholes probably included supply of drinking water (for both humans and stock) as well as for other domestic and craft uses.

Two waterholes (CG6 and 7) were located immediately adjacent to each other within an enclosure (CG66), and it seems probable that one replaced the other. However, the possibility should not be excluded that one was used to extract water and the other to store it, or even allow disturbed silt to settle out and thereby improve the quality of the water for drinking.

Three further waterholes were identified. Two of these (CG4 and CG14) lay within relatively open areas of the site and may primarily have functioned to provide water for stock. The location of one of these, CG14, was particularly suited to this function being located on the line of field boundary and therefore being accessible from two fields. The final waterhole (CG18) was identified within an evaluation trench in an area subsequently excluded from quarrying and therefore remains of uncertain association.

Detailed descriptions

WATERHOLE: CONTEXT GROUP 3 (FIG. 18)

Grid	0825/1078
Cut	2038
Fills	2039, 2040
Plan	Sub-oval
Profile	Basin-shaped
Dimensions	5.40 × 2.90 × 1.53m+

Substantial pit, with steeply sloping/near vertical sides cutting through thin sand and gravel deposits to clay. Initially only clearly defined fills in the northwest quadrant were excavated and drawn. The corresponding fills in the northeast quadrant were later rapidly removed and the section cut further to the south, however, no detailed records were made. Natural was not certainly identified at the base of these excavated portions and further lower fills may have been present. The recorded fills were excavated as two separate contexts, a base fill (2040) and an upper fill (2039). However, the drawn section shows considerable sub-division of these.

The base fill (2040) can be divided into seven separate deposits the lowest of which was a mixed grey/orangey brown clay with gravel, rare burnt limestone and charcoal (2040g). This was sealed by a layer of fairly clean grey clay (2040f) over which sand (2040e) had slumped. A deposit of orange brown mottled clay (2040d) overlaid this and was in turn sealed by a thin lens of charcoal flecked grey clay (2040c). Lastly orange mottled brown clay (2040b) and a mid grey brown clay had been deposited (2040a). These deposits appear to represent several episodes of silting and weathering of the sides of the feature. Few finds were present within this basal fill which only produced 6 sherds of pottery, 2 fragments of daub, a flint and 7 fragments of animal bone.

Overlying this was the upper fill (2039) which could be divided into three separate events. These upper deposits were clearly distinguishable from the lower ones in section and there is some suggestion that the pit had been partially recut. A band of grey sandy clay (2039c) may have represented a stabilisation horizon which developed at a time when the waterhole had largely silted up and was not being used. This was sealed by a mottled brown clay with occasional burnt limestone fragments (2039b). Only the final fill (2039a), a dumped deposit, was markedly different as it contained abundant charcoal and burnt stone in a dark grey clayey matrix. Pottery and other finds were more abundant in this upper fill comprising 29 sherds of pottery, 10 pieces of fired clay/daub, a fragment of a shale armlet, 2 flints, and 53 fragments of animal bone.

Despite the small proportion excavated, it would seem likely that this

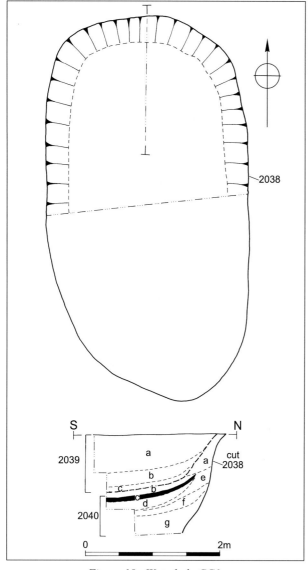

Figure 18. Waterhole CG3.

feature was a waterhole or at least may have been used to hold or store water. Evidence of slumping was limited, the sides probably remaining stable since the pit had been primarily excavated through clay. However, considerable quantities of silt had accumulated probably reflecting gradual weathering and decay of the feature edges. Less than 1.00m separated the waterhole from the lined pit CG5 and it is felt that the function of these was related. The most probable interpretation is that CG3 served as a waterhole/water storage facility with the adjacent feature using some of the water within an industrial/craft process. Upon abandonment the feature had been infilled with a dumped deposit containing domestic refuse and other debris (charcoal and burnt stone).

WATERHOLE: CONTEXT GROUP 4 (FIGS 19 AND 20)

Grid	0872/1048
Cut	2031
Fills	2032, 2033, 2034, 2049, 2050, 2060 (cleaning finds probably from 2032)
Plan	Sub-oval
Profile	Irregular
Dimensions	7.08 × 4.20 × 2.00m+

A very large (*c.* 30m³) and steep sided, sub-oval cut, having irregular steeply sloping sides to the east and west, a stepped northern side

and a more gently sloping south side. The feature penetrated into the underlying clay but the base was not certainly defined and it may have been considerably deeper. Several distinct phases of infilling could be defined from the complex set of fills recorded in section.

The earliest excavated fills consisted of a sequence of slumped sand, gravel and organic rich silt/clay deposits consistent with a large, open, water-filled feature (contexts 2033, 2034, 2049 and 2050). These occupied the deep central part of the feature. The profile, with a wide, cone-shaped upper part and narrow base, allied to the interleaving lower deposits representing both organic rich silts and slumped or weathered sandy/gravel deposits suggest that this feature was open for a long period of time and it is likely that it was recut or cleaned out on several occasions. This suggestion is supported by radiocarbon dating of organic material from context 2050 which indicates that the waterhole was probably established in the 12th century cal BC but that its abandonment was approximately 100 years later (compare OxA-9490 and OxA-9424 from 2050 with OxA-9483, OxA-9484, OxA-10778, OxA-10779 and OxA-10780 from 2032; Table 2).

The feature appears to have been sufficiently deep to hold water year round resulting in the preservation of timbers and other organic material in the lower fills. A worked timber embedded in context 2050, and extending into context 2034, formed the remains of a ladder placed at an angle within the lower silts in a position where it could have assisted access. Apart from this and a small quantity of animal bone (23 fragments), these deposits produced no finds and were only occasionally charcoal flecked.

After a long period of use and a final silting phase, a sequence of deposits infilled the surviving upper part of the feature. Although excavated as one context (2032), the drawn section indicates that this was a complex deposit. The lowest part (2032a) contained moderate quantities of charcoal and burnt stone as well as some organic material and this may reflect a period of trample and occasional dumping into the base of the surviving upper cone of an otherwise silted up waterhole. Overlying this, were two distinct horizons of charcoal-rich material each sealed by a dump of dark grey-brown sandy clay (2032b). Large quantities of burnt limestone and charcoal were present in these dumped deposits which also included significant assemblages of pottery, bone and other finds. A slumped deposit on the north side appears to have occurred at this time, possibly resulting from collapse of the steeper, unstable sides of the pit during dumping into the feature from this direction. Although variable in composition, the deposition of 3032b appears to have been fairly rapidly completed since the associated Late Bronze Age material assemblage was mostly in a fresh, unabraded condition with little evidence of gnawing of bones or fragmentation of pottery. The final uppermost fills (2032c and d) were paler in colour and contained fewer artefacts and are considered to represent weathering or sporadic dumping into a shallow hollow resulting from settling of the contents of the infilled waterhole.

As described above, finds were present in variable quantities throughout this fill with particularly high concentrations in 2032b; however, since 2032 was excavated as a single context quantifications cannot be broken down into individual elements. A total of 565 sherds of pottery weighing 6.778kg was recovered and included many Late Bronze Age form sherds. A small quantity of residual Beaker material was included (11 sherds) while most of the 49 flint items recovered from this fill were also probably of Beaker date. Apart from pottery and flint, the finds assemblage included bronze working waste (12 mould pieces, 15 wrap pieces and 6 fragments of hearth material), part of a shale armlet, a bone pin, a bead, clay weight fragments (21 fragments including both cylindrical and pyramidal forms), numerous fired clay fragments and a relatively large quantity of highly fragmented animal bone (669 fragments weighing 4.631kg). A human vertebra was also present.

Lastly, the cleaning layer (2060) from the initial investigation of this feature produced a further 33 sherds of pottery along with small amounts of fired clay, flint and animal bone.

WATERHOLE: CONTEXT GROUP 6 (FIG. 21)

Grid	0923/0950
Cut	1835
Fills	1836, 1837 (cleaning), 1840, 1842
Plan	Irregular
Profile	Basin-shaped
Dimensions	4.00 × 3.00 × 1.50m+

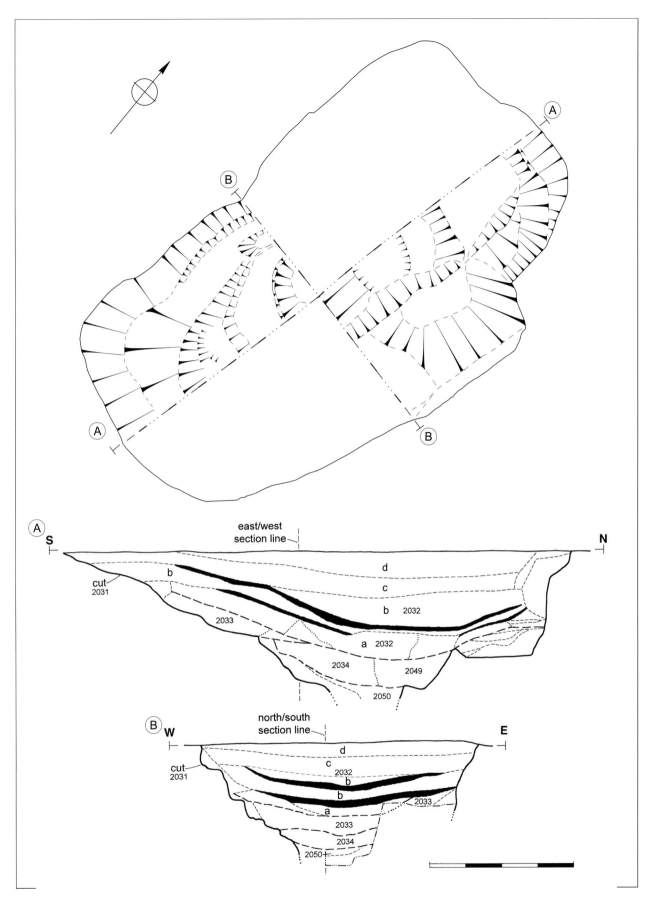

Figure 19. Waterhole CG4.

Figure 20. East facing section of Waterhole CG4 during excavation.

Large irregular cut, with a bi-lobed appearance suggesting that this possibly represented two intercutting features, an earlier sub-circular one, to the south, and an irregular later one, to the north. The sides were steeply sloping to near vertical and the feature was cut through relatively thin gravel deposits into the underlying clay. A complex sequence of fills included evidence of silting, weathering, slumping and dumping. Initial investigation comprised excavation of a central slot and recording of the resultant section. The north side was then excavated, although the high water table and unstable sides precluded excavation to base in any part of the feature. Subsequently, machine excavation was undertaken (context 1842) of most of the remainder of the feature. This largely derived from the south side and base and was placed in a skip and subsequently sorted for finds.

The lower fills (not fully excavated) consisted primarily of silting and slumped material (context 1840b and c) overlaid by a grey silty sand deposit (context 1840a). Tip or slump lines on the eastern side of the feature indicated that these fills had been deposited in several episodes or over some period of time. Only limited quantities of pottery (39 sherds), flint (1), charcoal, burnt stone and animal bone (9 fragments) were recovered; large conjoining base sherds indicating that several large vessels may have been present possibly having served to scoop up water.

More than one phase of deposition was also evident in the upper fill (context 1836). The base horizon comprised a layer of charcoal and domestic waste. This was overlain by a layer containing abundant small burnt stones and moderate charcoal (1836c), a tipping deposit of comparatively clean gravel (1836b) and a final layer of charcoal-rich material with abundant burnt limestone (1836a). This phase of fill deposition contrasts with that of the base, and is consistent with deliberate infilling with dumped material. Material recovered included a substantial ceramic assemblage (369 sherds, weighing 4.013kg; mostly from 1836d), bronze working waste (25 mould pieces, 14 wrap pieces and a fragment of hearth material), flint (4), a ceramic weight (of pyramidal form) and animal bone (147 fragments). The large unabraded sherd size of pottery and lack of gnawed bones suggest that deposition may have occurred over a short period of time. A 'cleaning' layer (context 1837) from the top of the pit contained a further 32 sherds of pottery, 2 flints and 24 fragments of animal bone. This may include some contamination from a medieval furrow which had partially truncated the pit. Although representing a substantial portion of the feature, and including a mixture of 1836 and 1840, the machined out southern side of the feature (context 2042) produced a surprisingly small assemblage (8 sherds of pottery, 2 flints and 11 fragments of bone). This suggests that material was deposited from the northern side of the feature and thus concentrated there, or alternatively may support the suggestion (made above) that two intercutting features were represented.

The depth and sequence of deposits indicated that the feature lay open and partially waterfilled for a considerable period, slowly silting up (context 1840b and c). This would be compatible with use as a waterhole or perhaps as a pit for holding water. Possible uses include soaking, water storage or flax retting; however, in view of the quantities of burnt limestone present (in context 1840a as well as 1836a, c and d), water heating is also a possibility. Domestic and other waste was only deposited on a large scale later in its life, reflecting deliberate infilling and abandonment.

WATERHOLE: CONTEXT GROUP 7 (FIGS 22 AND 23)

Grid	0925/0955
Cut	1833
Fills	1834, 1838, 1839, 1841, 1843, 1848, 1853, 1855
Plan	Sub-circular
Profile	Irregular
Dimensions	5.5 × 3.3m

Large, sub-circular feature immediately to the northeast of CG6 excavated through natural sand and gravel into the clay below. A sub-circular weathering cone was distinct from the near vertical sides towards the base giving the feature a Y-shaped profile. The northern half was largely hand-excavated to a depth of up to 2.00m. Depth, and the level of the water-table, precluded further hand-excavation; however, subsequently upper elements of the southern half were excavated by mechanical excavator and placed in a skip. Some finds were collected during machining (1848) while the skip material was hand-excavated for finds at a later date (context 1843). The lower part of the feature was only recorded in section following gravel extraction, finds again being collected during this process (1853 and 1855).

The lower, largely machine excavated, fills comprised silting and slumping deposits probably derived from weathering and/or collapse of the upper sides of the feature, thus creating the Y-shaped profile. The lowest elements (contexts 1841 and 1855) contained quantities of burnt limestone and finds including 97 sherds of pottery, a fragment of a pyramidal clay weight, a flint and 71 fragments of animal bone. Some contamination from upper fills may be present but these included some large chunks of vessel bases which may have served to scoop water from the feature.

These basal fills were sealed by a further silting/slumping horizon (context 1839), within which bands of stony gravel clearly suggested weathering from the sides. Finds included pottery (4 sherds), a daub fragment and animal bone (16 fragments).

Above these silting deposits a thin layer of yellowy brown silty clay had formed (context 1838), the lower part of which included small quantities of charcoal flecks, burnt limestone slabs, bone (26 fragments), pottery (4 sherds) and a single flint. This may represent a phase when the sides of the feature had stabilised and the feature formed a muddy hollow.

The upper part of the pit was filled by dumped deposits, recorded as a single context (1834) but clearly representing several phases of deposition. A lower dumped deposit (1834b) included ash and charcoal-rich lenses along with large quantities of artefacts and burnt stone. This was overlain by a further dump of very dark grey brown silty loam (1834a) containing occasional burnt limestone, charcoal, pot and bone. A total of 157 sherds of pottery (weighing 1.268kg) were recovered along with fragments of pyramidal ceramic weights (24 fragments, representing 6 pyramidal weights), daub/fired clay (7), metal working waste (4 mould pieces), flint (13) and animal bone (208 fragments). The generally unabraded condition of the artefacts recovered allied to the similarly fresh condition of the animal bone (which also showed little evidence of gnawing) suggests that this may all have been dumped in a relatively short space of time.

Finally a shallow pit-like depression in the top of the waterhole was filled by a gravel-rich deposit. The depth, profile and fill characteristics of this feature all argue in favour of it having functioned as a waterhole, possibly at the same time as the adjacent feature CG6 or, alternatively, having replaced or pre-dated it. A relatively long period of use is indicated by radiocarbon dating of charred residues on pottery from the primary fill 1855 which provided somewhat earlier dates than those taken from pottery within the upper abandonment fill (1834; compare OxA-9435 and OxA-10785 from 1855 with OxA-9486, OxA-9559 and OxA-10783 from 1834; Table 2). Some periodic cleaning out of silts may therefore have occurred prior to the time when it finally silted up (1838) and was rapidly infilled with dumped deposits rich in cultural material (1834).

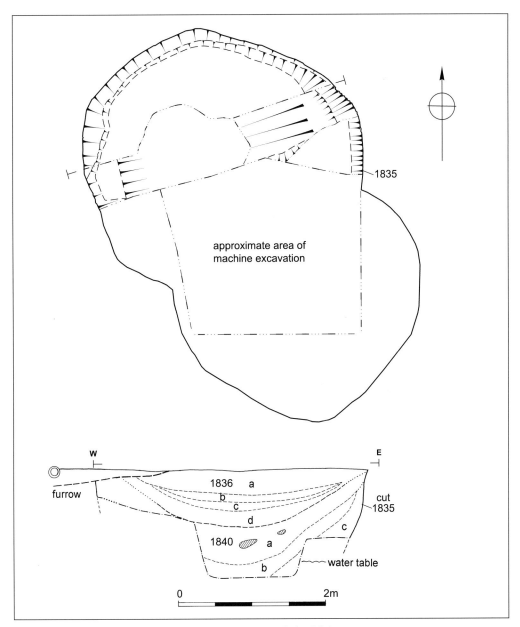

Figure 21. Waterhole CG6.

WATERHOLE: CONTEXT GROUP 8 (FIG. 24)

Grid	1120/0999
Cut	1105
Fills	1102 (possibly contaminated), 1103, 1104, 1110, 1112, 1113, 1114, 1115
Plan	Sub-oval
Profile	Irregular
Dimensions	6.00 × 4.20 × 1.40m+

A large sub-oval pit with an upper weathering cone and steepening sides towards the base which lay below the current watertable, suggesting that this probably held water year round. The feature was only investigated during the evaluation and lay within the area later excluded from extraction; thus only a narrow section was excavated and the base was not observed. The upper fills had been truncated along the western edge by a medieval furrow (context 1108).

The lowest observed fills consisted primarily of fine silty deposits and stonier material much of which is likely to have weathered or slumped from the sides (contexts 1112, 1113, 1114 and 1115). Worked timbers had been dumped into one deposit as the silting progressed (at interface

of 1114 and 1115); however, otherwise these deposits were sterile with the exception of burnt stone and rare charcoal flecking. At the top of these deposits, separating them from the upper fills was a dump of burnt limestone fragments (context 1110). Again no artefacts were present.

The upper fills (contexts 1102, 1103 and 1104) were characterised by the presence of significant quantities of domestic waste. Pottery was most abundant within context 1103 which provided 74 of the 92 sherds recovered from these deposits. Flint (14 pieces), ceramic weights (16 fragments, including cylindrical and possible pyramidal forms), a fine bone pin and animal bone (131 fragments) were also recovered from these upper fills. These are interpreted as dumped horizons associated with the disuse of the feature and deposited once the lower half had filled with silt. The fresh condition of the pottery and animal bone, and lack of gnawing on the latter, indicated that deposition was over a relatively short space of time.

The feature almost certainly functioned as a waterhole and can be related to the immediately adjacent CG9, a possible soaking/boiling pit. The formation of a large weathering cone and evidence for slumping/ silting indicate that this remained open for a considerable period of time and occasional cleaning out of silts would seem likely. This suggestion

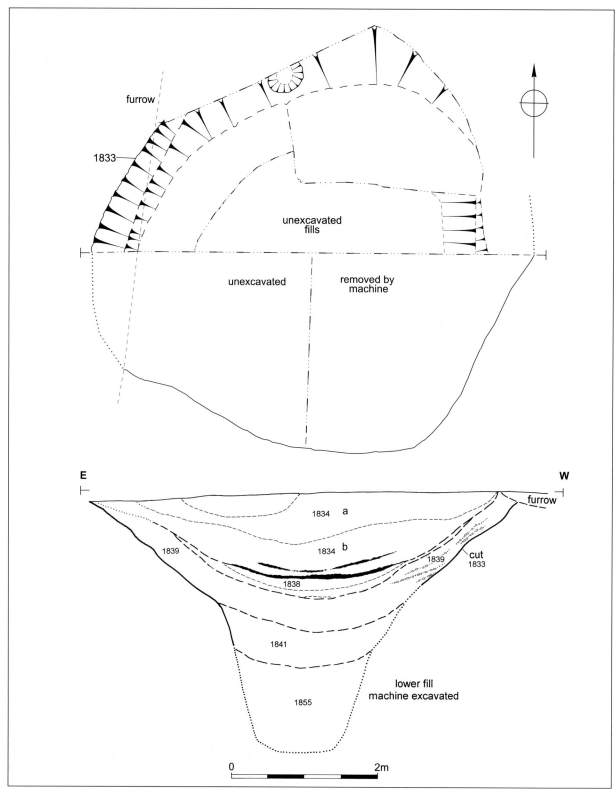

Figure 22. Waterhole CG7.

is supported by radiocarbon dating of organic material from 1115 which provided earlier dates than those taken from a charred residue present on pottery from the upper abandonment fill (1103; compare OxA-9488, OxA-9489 and OxA-10375 from 1115 with OxA-10786 from 1103; Table 2).

WATERHOLE: CONTEXT GROUP 14 (FIGS 25 AND 26)

Grid	0787/1002
Cut	2102
Fill	2101
Plan	Sub-circular

Figure 23. North facing section of Waterhole CG7 prior to machine excavation of lower fills.

Profile   Bowl-shaped
Dimensions   4.50 × 1.90m

A very large, sub-circular, irregular bowl-shaped cut in which extensive weathering and slumping was evident. This had clearly altered the profile which may originally have been fairly steep-sided. The feature penetrated gravel and sand to the underlying clay. A possible stakehole was visible in section, and it would seem likely that the soft edges of the feature had been revetted. Initially, only a small section was hand-excavated across the east side; however, this was subsequently extended using a mechanical excavator to allow recording of a complete section. Although the fills were removed and recorded as one context, the resultant section showed a complex series of fills which appear to reflect several phases of use/disuse.

The initial phase (2101e) is represented by a series of deposits of sand, gravel and clay. These contained only a few artefacts, occasional fragments of burnt stone and slight charcoal flecking, and principally appear to have resulted from weathering and slumping of the gravel and clay sides. The feature may have been in use for some period of time prior to this; if it had been revetted as suggested above, the revetment must

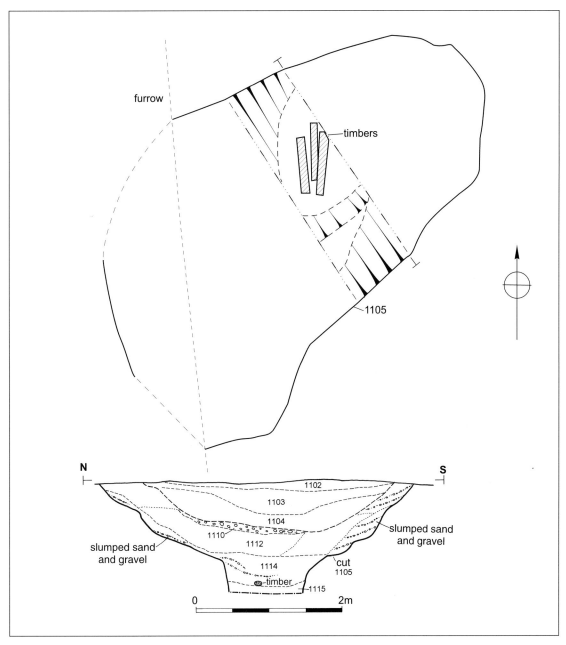

Figure 24. Waterhole CG8.

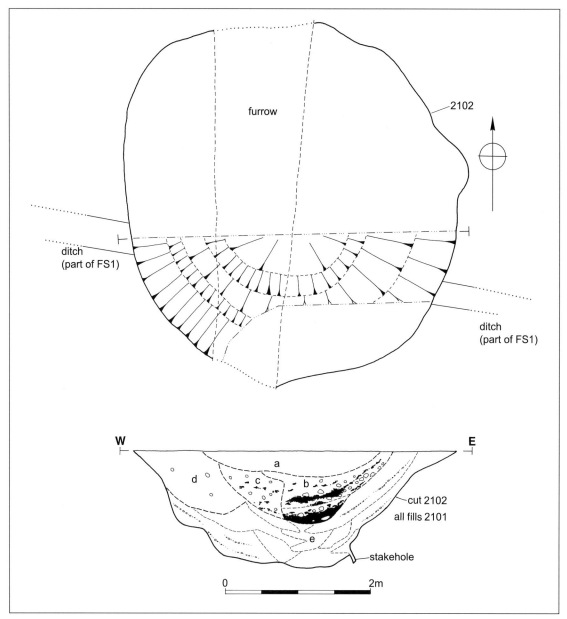

Figure 25. Waterhole CG14.

Figure 26. North facing section of Waterhole CG14 during excavation.

have either been removed or decayed leading to collapse and erosion of the sides. Subsequently material was deposited or accumulated in a recut section of the western side of the feature (2101d). This mainly comprised naturally derived gravel, sand and clay and may reflect further slumping and weathering. A second apparent recut contained dumped deposits, one very charcoal-rich with some burnt stone (2101c), the other including charcoal, burnt limestone and artefacts in abundant quantities (2101b). These potentially recut sections are felt to represent some reworking of the feature prior to a deliberate abandonment and infilling with artefact rich dumps.

Finally a light brown sandy loam, almost devoid of artefacts and charcoal, filled a hollow at the top of the feature (2101a). This may reflect settling of the lower fills and subsequent deposition or weathering of material into it, but may also in part represent the fill of a medieval furrow.

Variable quantities of artefacts were noted on the section drawings for each fill as described above; however, they were not separated on site, the whole fill sequence including pottery (132 sherds, weighing 0.512kg), flint (17), ceramic weight fragments (4, from a ?cylindrical weight) and animal bone (83 fragments)

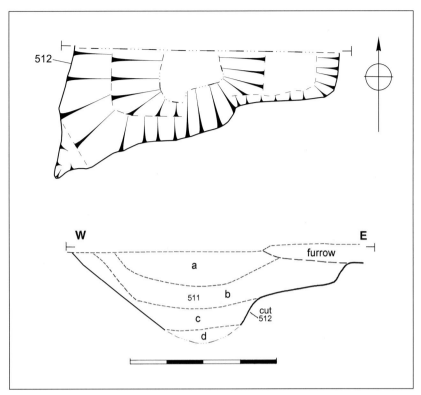

Figure 27. Waterhole CG18.

As described above the feature may initially have had revetted sides. Owing to its depth and the fact that it cut into the clay, this feature is liable to have held water and is interpreted as a waterhole. This interpretation is strengthened by its apparent association with a field boundary (FS1), since it would have been accessible from both fields and thus represents an ideal location for such a feature.

WATERHOLE: CONTEXT GROUP 18 (FIG. 27)

Grid	1112/1090
Fill/cut	511, 512
Plan	Not defined but probably sub-oval
Profile	Irregular
Dimensions	3.00 × 1.50+ × 1.24m+

A large, rather irregular pit with a stepped eastern side. This was only recorded during the evaluation (Trench 5) since it was situated beyond the later agreed quarrying area. As a result only the southern part of this substantial feature was recorded. The base was not observed.

The investigated portion was excavated as a single fill; however, four separate phases of infill are visible in the drawn section. At the base was a dark sticky clay loam (511d) representing silting. This was overlain by two dumped deposits, the first a clay loam containing abundant burnt limestone and charcoal (511c), the second a sandy loam with moderate quantities of charcoal and burnt limestone (511b). The uppermost fill was a loamy deposit with occasional charcoal flecks (511a), probably representing ploughsoil or weathering deposits occupying the hollow formed over the settling contents of this feature. Although only large quantities of burnt material were recorded along with animal bone (54 fragments) and a small ceramic assemblage (9 sherds), the unexcavated portion may contain a rich material assemblage in common with the other waterholes.

Pond: CG52 (Fig. 16)

A large spread of dark grey brown silty loam, with occasional gravel patches was located on the north margin of the site (0800E/1095N). This measured at least 17.00 × 14.00m in plan and although not investigated in any detail, was revealed to be some 0.30m deep. No finds were recovered and the feature therefore remains undated.

This part of the site was revealed to contain no sand and gravel and the feature was cut into clay, making it seem probable that this represents a shallow pond. This perhaps fulfilled a similar function as the waterholes, providing water for stock, human consumption and/or craft industries. The presence of a group of six hearths (CG 41, 43–6 and 77) associated with burnt stone and lying to the south of the pond would be consistent with the latter of these functions.

Pits

Pits of variable size and character were present across the whole of the recorded area (Fig. 16). These were sample excavated, the more extensive sampling focussing on those which in plan were most substantial or appeared to have the most artefact or ecofact rich fills.

Since these pits contained the majority of the artefactual and ecofactual evidence, and were liable to have had a range of uses, they have warranted a higher level of interpretation than simply being described as pits. Consequently they have been classified according to their profile as follows:

- Basin-shaped: a steep to vertical sided feature with sharp break to flattish or gently concave base;
- Bowl-shaped: a steep to sloping sided feature with

clear break in slope to concave base;
- Irregular – pit with complex profile

This approach has been taken at comparable Late Bronze Age settlement sites and, in conjunction with analysis of fill characteristics and associated artefactual and ecofactual assemblages, facilitates functional interpretation and consideration of distribution patterns (see for instance Bradley *et al.* 1980, 221–4; Brossler, Early and Allen 2004, 30–9).

Several further pits are liable to be represented among the larger-sized but uninvestigated features scattered across the site.

The basin-shaped pits

Ten basin-shaped pits were identified (Figs 28–30). No particular concentrations could be identified, although a slightly higher number were located towards the eastern side of the investigated area. A number of observations about their associations and potential functions can be made.

Two pits appeared to have a direct relationship with the waterholes described above (CG5 and 9 can be paired with CG3 and 8 respectively). Both had clay-linings suggesting that they had a use which required either containment or exclusion of liquids. They may have functioned as grain storage pits, where excluding groundwater is important to control germination; however, dry storage on the site seems more probably to have been above ground (for instance in the 4-post structures). It seems most probable therefore, especially in the light of their proximity to waterholes, that these two pits had a function associated with water storage or holding water as part of an industrial or domestic process. In both cases, the lower (primary) fills contained large quantities of burnt limestone suggesting that the pits were probably used to heat water or another liquid. Similar features elsewhere have been postulated to be boiling pits for cooking (O'Kelly 1956, 615–18), while alternatively industrial uses can be suggested including use in tanning or the felting, fulling and dyeing of woollen cloth (Jeffery 1991, 97–107). Burnt stone has even been associated with saunas (Barfield and Hodder 1977, 370–9; Barfield 1991, 59–67). Alternatively, the burnt stone may simply have been dumped into these features when they fell into disuse and derived from localised activities where they were used in other ways; for instance in cooking by placing hot stones in pottery or leather containers or using hot stones as roasting plates or griddles.

Of the remaining eight basin-shaped pits, only four (CG2, 15, 17 and 39) could be dated with any certainty to the Late Bronze Age. These were all associated with quantities of burnt stone and charcoal and contained varying quantities of other settlement debris including pottery. Variations in the quantities of material culture present may reflect the proximity of the pits to areas of domestic settlement or that they had different uses. For example, both CG2 and CG39 were sited close to a group of roundhouses (CG58, 59 and 60) but had contrasting fills and were of very different sizes. Of these, CG39, although much the smaller feature (measuring 1.50 × 0.42m), contained a considerable quantity of pottery (94 sherds) in relation to its size. Unusually for the site, this material was all present in the primary fill indicating that this pit was probably dug specifically for waste disposal. Also unusual was that none of this pottery had burnt internal residues which were commonly present in the larger assemblages at the site. In contrast, CG2, the other basin-shaped pit close to these roundhouses, was a substantial feature (4.00 × 3.50 × 1.20m). This had very large quantities of charcoal and burnt limestone in its upper fill; however, only contained a small quantity of pottery and other finds. This may have been closely functionally related to an adjacent bowl-shaped pit (CG1) which was similarly very large and contained abundant charcoal and burnt stone, but also included numerous finds. These may have been associated with cooking as discussed below (see Bowl-shaped pits).

The remaining basin-shaped pits (CG20, 26, 31 and 36) are of less certain function. In the absence of domestic waste, craft-related or agricultural processing functions are considered likely. Alternatively, they could have been excavated for the extraction of sand and gravel for use as consolidating material across the settlement; for instance on paths, around waterholes and as house floors. It should also be noted that these four features produced no firm dating evidence but are considered liable to be of Late Bronze Age date, on the basis of their location within areas of activity of this date and since this represented the main phase of human occupation at the site. Despite this, the possibility that some of these features were associated with earlier phases of occupation should not be excluded.

Pit: Context Group 2 (Fig. 28)

Grid	0900/1050
Cut	710, 1844
Fills	709, 1845, 1846, 1847
Plan	Sub-circular
Profile	Basin-shaped
Dimensions	4.00 × 3.50 × 1.20m

A large sub-circular pit (710 and 1844) cut through sand and gravel and into the underlying clay indicating that it would potentially have been water-filled, at least during winter months. Although only partially excavated, this was shown to be basin-shaped and had three distinct phases of infill similar to those in the adjacent bowl-shaped pit (CG1) but, in contrast to the latter, this only contained a very small quantity of material culture.

The primary fill was a charcoal-flecked, yellowish grey-brown, silty clay deposit intermixed with abundant sand and gravel (1847) slumped from the sides. This filled the lower third of the pit and is strongly suggestive of a period of weathering and slumping over a considerable period of time. A small quantity of pottery (4 sherds) and animal bone (15 fragments) was recovered from this deposit.

The primary fill was sealed by a very charcoal-rich horizon occupying the base of a layer of mid to dark grey brown sandy loam (context 1846). The charcoal-rich horizon contained burnt limestone and daub but no finds.

The uppermost fill, which possibly represents levelling of a disused feature, consisted of material derived from the topsoil with moderate charcoal flecks, a single sherd of pottery, 2 flints and 11 fragments of animal bone (contexts 709 and 1845).

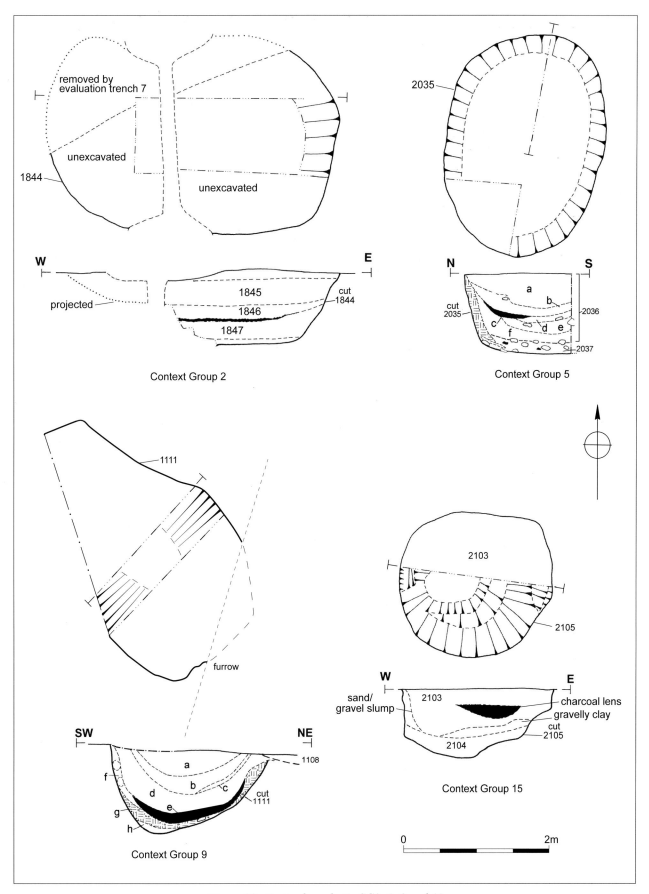

Figure 28. Basin shaped pits CG2, 5, 9 and 15.

Figure 29. Basin shaped pit CG5 (showing clay-lining).

PIT: CONTEXT GROUP 5 (FIGS 28 AND 29)

Grid	0827/1080
Cut	2035
Fills	2036, 2037
Plan	Sub-oval
Profile	Basin-shaped
Dimensions	3.00 × 2.60 × 1.10m

A sub-oval, basin-shaped pit having very steeply-sloping sides and a flattish base. The northwest quadrant was excavated and recorded in detail, with only rapid excavation and recording of the eastern half, leaving the southwest quadrant unexcavated. The pit had been cut through sand and gravel at its very base where it penetrated the underlying (gleyed) clay. Above the interface between the gravel and clay, the pit was lined with a brown sandy clay. Two distinct fills were recorded.

The base fill (context 2037) comprised a 0.25m deep dump of burnt limestone (over 60kg were recorded) in a matrix of silty clay intermixed with sandy gravels. Quantities of charcoal were noted adhering to the stones which had been deposited over a small scatter of large pot sherds (13, weighing 0.354kg) and animal bone (14 fragments) at the base of the pit.

Overlying this was a secondary fill (context 2036) that, although recorded as one context, has been divided (from an annotated section drawing) to reflect what were clearly several stages of deposition. Initially a greyish tan brown clay loam was deposited (2036f) containing small charcoal lumps. This was overlain by two similar but slightly greyer deposits containing burnt limestone fragments (2036d and 2036e). A lens of very charcoal-rich material (2036c) and a dump of charcoal-flecked gravely material (2036b) followed, and the feature was finally levelled off with a thick dump of rather sterile dark grey material (2036a). A moderate-sized pottery assemblage was recovered from this fill, mostly from towards the eastern side of the feature (108 sherds, weighing 0.374kg). Ceramic weight fragments (45 from a single weight of indeterminate form), daub (6 fragments), flint (3) and animal bone (110 fragments) were also present. The animal bone assemblage included a partial dog skeleton. The characteristics of this fill suggest that this represented a deliberate backfilling with material dumped from the eastern side of the pit.

PIT: CONTEXT GROUP 9 (FIG. 28)

Grid	1115/0998
Fill/cut	1111
Plan	Sub-oval
Profile	Basin-shaped
Dimensions	4.00 × 2.00 × 1.10m+

Large sub-oval, basin-shaped pit which was only partially exposed and investigated during evaluation. Its eastern side had been partially truncated by a medieval furrow (context 1108). The feature was excavated as a single context (fill/cut 1111); however, the section drawing has allowed fills to be sub-divided in post-excavation (1111a–1111h; Fig CG9). The base of the pit slightly penetrated the clays underlying the natural gravel.

The recorded fills can be divided into primary and secondary phases of use. At the base was a deposit of greyish clay (1111h) overlain by a yellowish slightly gravely clay (1111g). The latter extended up the eastern side of the pit. A similar less clayey deposit (1111f) extended up the west side. Together these are interpreted as the remnants of a clay-lining. The comparative absence of silting and slumping may reflect the protective and consolidating qualities of the clay-lining rather than rapid disuse. The lower fill (1111e) was characterised by the presence of heavy charcoal-flecking and several large chunks of burnt limestone at its base. This deposit may be associated with use as a soaking or boiling pit.

The second phase of use is characterised by deliberate backfilling of the pit with a series of fills. Initially a dark grey charcoal-rich loam (1111d) was deposited. This was noted to contain only a few finds and was overlain by a dump of gravel (1111c) on the east side of the pit. Above these a layer with abundant burnt limestone was deposited (1111b). This dump of material was noted as including the majority of the artefacts recovered. The latter comprised a substantial ceramic assemblage (404 sherds, weighing 3.809kg), flint (7), fired clay/daub (1), a worked and burnt bone fragment (the point of an awl or chisel) and animal bone (164 fragments, weighing 1.801kg).

Lastly, some settling of the contents of the pit appears to have occurred, probably as a result of decaying organic material; the resultant hollow being levelled with a mid grey clayey loam with occasional gravel and charcoal flecks (1111a). Three radiocarbon dates on charred residues from refitting groups of pottery sherds recovered from this fill were obtained (OxA-10787–9; Table 2).

The feature would have been suitable for a number of functions. Possible uses include soaking, water storage or flax retting; however, in view of the quantities of burnt limestone present (in context 1111e and 1111b) water heating/boiling is a strong possibility. Domestic and other waste was only deposited within the feature on a large-scale later in its life, possibly reflecting deliberate abandonment.

PIT: CONTEXT GROUP 15 (FIG. 28)

Grid	0789/1045
Cut	2105
Fills	2103, 2104
Plan	Sub-circular
Profile	Basin-shaped
Dimensions	2.10 × 1.90 × 0.90m

A sub circular, basin-shaped pit with a near vertical western side and a steep, but irregularly cut, eastern one. Two fills were recorded, the lower of which (2104) consisted primarily of slumped sand and gravel, with very occasional charcoal and burnt limestone. The upper fill (2103) was of yellowish dark grey brown silty clay and contained a distinct lens of charcoal-rich material. Small quantities of burnt limestone, pottery (6 sherds), animal bone (9 fragments) and a single flint flake were also present. Although some slumping was evident, the near vertical sides suggest that this may initially have been revetted in some way as the natural gravel rapidly erodes if exposed to the elements. The sterile nature of the lower fills suggests that the primary function was not waste disposal and the feature may have provided storage or had some specialist function.

PIT: CONTEXT GROUP 17 (FIG. 30)

Grid	1061/1049
Cut	1514
Fills	1517, 1519
Plan	Sub-circular
Profile	Basin-shaped
Dimensions	2.20 × 0.55m

Pit extensively damaged by dumper wheel-rut. Surviving elements indicated that this had two fills. The base fill (1519) was a mixed grey gravely clay with occasional charcoal lumps. This may represent the remnant of a lining. The upper fill (1517) contained a substantial assemblage of pottery (198 sherds) along with a considerable quantity of bone and antler (100+), burnt limestone, flint (1) and ceramic weight (1 fragment of indeterminate form).

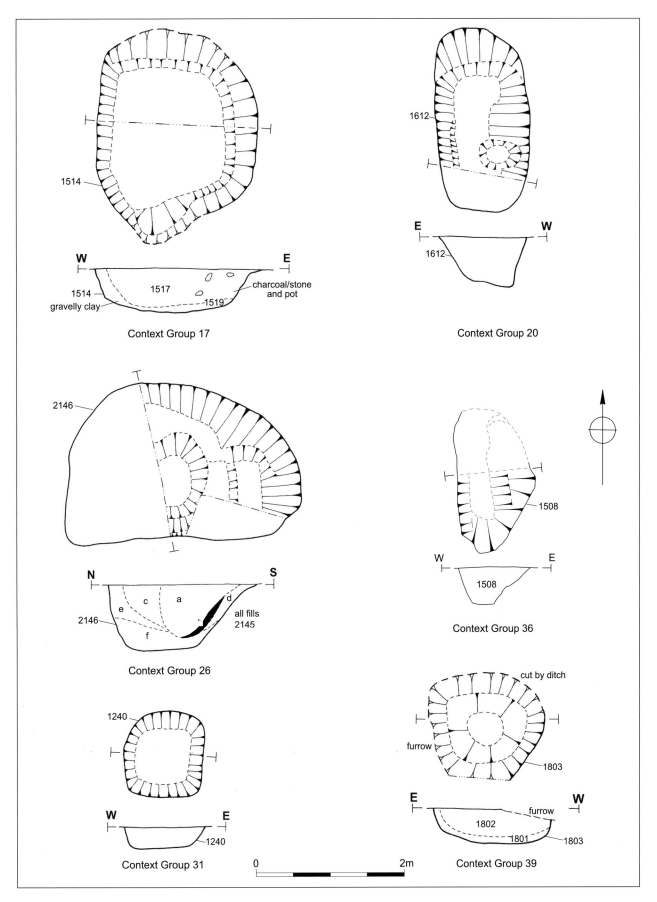

Figure 30. Basin shaped pits CG17, 20, 26, 31, 36 and 39.

PIT: CONTEXT GROUP 20 (FIG. 30)

Grid   1083/0970
Fill/cut   1612
Plan   Sub-oval
Profile   Basin-shaped
Dimensions   2.50 × 1.40 × 0.65m

Pit with a shallow sub-circular depression in its base. The latter may represent a setting for an associated post or a feature pre-dating the pit. The single fill was a lightly charcoal flecked, dark grey brown silty loam with only rare charcoal, flint (1) and bone (the latter recorded only in the field). The absence of domestic waste contrasts strongly with another feature (CG19) only 2m away. The primary function is unclear, however, a wicker (or similar) lining might have been present since there was no evidence of slumping which would be expected in the loose gravel into which the pit was cut.

PIT: CONTEXT GROUP 26 (FIG. 30)

Grid   0781/1007
Fill/cut   2145, 2146
Plan   Sub-oval
Profile   Basin-shaped
Dimensions   3.23 × 2.03 × 0.86m

Fairly substantial pit. The bulk of the fill sequence (recorded as a single context) comprised comparatively clean sand and gravel deposits representing silting of the base, and weathering and slumping of the sides (2145c, d, e and f). An upper charcoal stained fill and a charcoal-rich lens (2145a and b) overlaid these and are interpreted as deliberate infilling deposits. The latter contained a small quantity of animal bone (30 fragments), the latter being the only finds recovered, although pottery was noted as a 'very rare' inclusion on site. The feature lies within 5m of a major waterhole (CG14); however, it is uncertain whether they were contemporary. No evidence for a lining was recorded and the presence of slumped fills suggests that either none existed or that if one had been present a considerable time had elapsed between its removal or decay and the subsequent infilling of the pit. The feature is without clear evidence for function.

PIT: CONTEXT GROUP 31 (FIG. 30)

Grid   1055/0969
Fill/cut   1240
Plan   Sub-square
Profile   Basin-shaped
Dimensions   1.05 × 1.10 × 0.28m

A sub-square pit with a flat base. The fill was a mid to dark brown sandy loam containing charcoal flecks, burnt limestone and burnt daub. No artefacts were recorded and function remains undetermined.

PIT: CONTEXT GROUP 36 (FIG. 30)

Grid   1077/1078
Fill/cut   1508
Plan   Sub-oval
Profile   Basin-shaped
Dimensions   1.90 x1.00 × 0.50m

Pit, with stepped east side. Partially obscured by disturbed area at north end (possibly a further feature). The fill contained quantities of burnt daub and charcoal but no other finds. The function remains undetermined.

PIT: CONTEXT GROUP 39 (FIG. 30)

Grid   0890/1137
Cut   1803
Fills   1801, 1802
Plan   Sub-circular
Profile   Basin-shaped
Dimensions   1.50 × 0.42m

Pit, recorded to the north of the main investigated area when revealed in the side of a newly excavated drainage ditch. Truncated by the latter to the north and disturbed on the west side by a medieval furrow. Two fills were recorded. The lower fill (1801) was a dark grey brown coarse sandy clay loam with moderate charcoal flecks, a considerable quantity of pottery (94 sherds, including 19 sherds from a Late Neolithic Grooved Ware vessel), fired clay (4), charcoal, burnt limestone, heat-cracked pebbles, flint (2) and animal bone (6 fragments). The upper fill (1802) was lighter in colour and contained a small amount of burnt stone, a single flint and animal bone (2 fragments).

The profile of the base fill suggests that this may originally have had an organic content and been compressed as the organic material decomposed. Several of the pottery sherds had been crushed *in situ*. This feature, which was the most northerly excavated, was unusual in that the initial fill was rich in domestic waste but had an almost sterile upper fill. It is possible that it originated as a waste disposal feature or as a cooking pit.

The bowl-shaped pits

Twelve examples of bowl-shaped pits were recorded and, as with the basin-shaped pits, these were distributed across the investigated area. These varied widely in size and in the complexity and content of their fills (Figs. 31–3). A range of potential functions and associations can be identified.

Of these, one in particular (CG1) stood out. This was both of considerable size and also contained a substantial artefactual and ecofactual assemblage. Since it only penetrated sand and gravel, the feature seems unlikely to have functioned as a waterhole. Another substantial, but basin-shaped pit (CG2), was located only a couple of metres to its north and a related function would seem likely. Both pits included silting deposits towards their bases and both included charcoal and burnt, stone-rich deposits overlying these. However, whilst the bowl-shaped example (CG1) was rich in artefacts, as noted above the adjacent pit (CG2) contained very few. An association with heating is indicated by the large volumes of charcoal and burnt limestone present in both instances, perhaps with a clear division being made between processes of use and discard being represented across the two features. One suggestion is that these were associated with the preparation and cooking of food since the large pottery assemblage recovered from CG1 was notable for the large numbers of vessels with charred internal residues (303 of 627 sherds, representing 48% of the assemblage in comparison with a site average of 25%). Another possibility is that the burnt residues were associated with metalworking since over half of the mould and wrap pieces from the manufacture of bronze weapons recovered from the site derived from within this pit.

Other bowl-shaped pits also contained large volumes of burnt limestone and charcoal as well as artefacts, the latter including pottery with a high proportion of sherds having charred internal residues. For instance, CG10 produced a relatively large assemblage of pottery (60% with charred internal residues) and animal bone, including articulated cattle thoracic vertebrae (?meat joint) which might indicate cooking or domestic waste disposal; a suggestion supported by the proximity of a roundhouse (CG57). A second pit (CG11) in this vicinity also contained a high proportion of pottery sherds with charred internal residues (67%) as well as animal bone and, in the absence of any notable quantities of burnt limestone or charcoal, domestic waste disposal may be indicated.

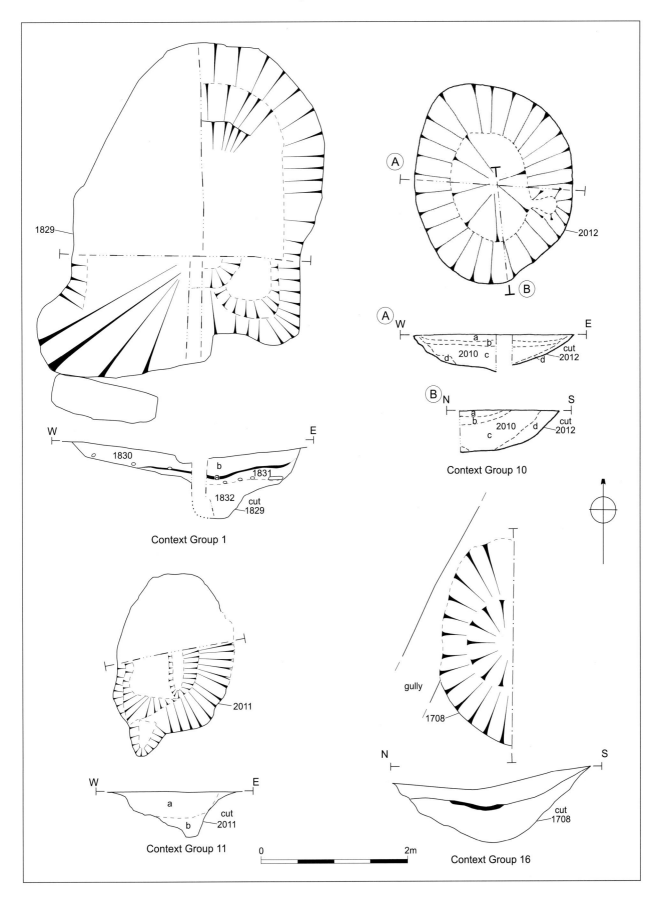

Context Group 1

Context Group 10

Context Group 11

Context Group 16

Figure 31. Bowl shaped pits CG1, 10, 11 and 16.

Another of the bowl-shaped pits (CG16) was also sited close to a roundhouse (CG56). This contained a small quantity of pottery and other finds, burnt limestone and charcoal, and may have been associated with cooking or waste disposal.

The remaining bowl-shaped pits which could not be so readily associated with buildings were mostly sterile with few or no finds, although burnt limestone, charcoal and fired clay or daub were present in some instances. Cooking or disposal functions seem likely but other, craft related or agricultural processing functions should also be considered. Alternatively, as with the basin-shaped pits of uncertain associations, they could have been excavated for the extraction of sand and gravel for use as consolidating material across the settlement.

PIT: CONTEXT GROUP 1 (FIG. 31)

Grid	0898/1033
Cut	1829
Fills	1828 (cleaning), 1830, 1831, 1832, 1854 (material recovered after gravel extraction)
Plan	Sub-circular
Profile	Bowl-shaped
Dimensions	4.00 × 3.20 × 1.04m

A substantial feature, having a distinct lobe or re-cut to the southwest and a deeper area to the east. This was only partially investigated but appeared not to have been excavated sufficiently deeply originally to have penetrated the underlying clay. The pit had a distinct, stepped, profile breaking from a shallow upper slope to a near vertical slope in the deeper portion. The sequence of fills indicated that it was probably open for a considerable period of time with three broad phases of use/infill identified.

Charcoal flecked, pale yellow grey-brown silt sand filled the bottom half, approximately to the level of the break in slope in the pit sides (context 1832). This probably resulted from weathering over a period of time, with some slumping as well accounting for the irregular plan and profile. Some re-cutting or re-working of the upper edges may, however, also have occurred. The base deposit was virtually sterile although small quantities of limestone were present, several fragments of which exhibited signs of burning.

The next phase was represented by two fills occupying a shallow bowl-shaped depression or slumped area over the earlier fills. Context 1831 occupied the base of the depression and was a mid-brown silty loam containing a single sherd of pottery, a fragment of animal bone, 2 fragments from a ceramic weight (?cylindrical), charcoal and burnt limestone fragments. This possibly derived from localised topsoil deposits scraped up and dumped into the pit. This was sealed by a thin band of charcoal-rich material intermixing with a very dark grey brown silty

loam (context 1830a). This contained a significant quantity of material concentrated towards the charcoal-rich base of the fill, and including burnt limestone, pottery (607 sherds, weighing 2.225kg), worked flint (49 items), a complete cylindrical ceramic weight and animal bone (293 fragments, weighing 1.294kg) along with a quantity of metalworking debris (comprising 64 mould pieces, 26 wrap pieces and a fragment of hearth material). Two radiocarbon determinations were obtained from charred residues on the pottery (OxA-10776 and OxA-10777; Table 2). A significant quantity of residual Beaker period flint (49 items) and pottery (14 sherds) were present suggesting that this had disturbed an area of activity of this date. Further finds were recovered during cleaning of the pit (1828) and from the unexcavated part of the feature during and after gravel extraction (context 1854). These included pottery (31 sherds), flint (2 pieces) and metalworking waste (3 mould pieces and 2 wrap pieces).

A final phase of deposition within the pit (context 1830b) comprised material derived from the topsoil. This was largely sterile and infilled the uppermost part of a shallow slumped hollow over the earlier deposits. This was in turn truncated by both a furrow and two land drains.

PIT: CONTEXT GROUP 10 (FIGS 31 AND 32)

Grid	0795/1025
Fill/cut	2010/2012
Plan	Sub-circular
Profile	Bowl-shaped
Dimensions	2.80 × 2.20 × 0.45m

A regular and well-defined pit. Several fills were present, the lowest of which (2010d) was a greyish brown sand devoid of artefacts. This appeared to be primarily the product of mixing of the base fill with the soft sandy natural sides of the feature. The earliest genuine fill was a very dark grey sandy loam containing frequent pottery, burnt limestone and large animal bone, some partially articulated (2010c). This layer was sealed by a dump of burnt limestone fragments with occasional pot sherds (2010b). The whole feature was sealed by a thin layer of mid brown sand with very rare charcoal flecks (2010a).

The material assemblage was relatively rich, including pottery (130 sherds, 60% of which had charred internal residues), flint (5), ceramic weight (2 fragments, representing an extended cylindrical form and a ?pyramidal form) and relatively large fragments of animal bone (95 fragments, some partially articulated, weighing 1.726kg). This pit was located immediately adjacent to a roundhouse (CG57) with which it may have been associated, the contents perhaps being domestic waste primarily derived from food preparation.

Four radiocarbon dates on charred internal residues from four different groups of refitting pottery sherds were obtained from these deposits (from 2010; OxA-9485, OxA-9923, OxA-10790, and OxA-10842; Table 2).

PIT: CONTEXT GROUP 11 (FIG. 31)

Grid	0811/1030
Fill/cut	2011
Plan	Sub-oval
Profile	Bowl-shaped
Dimensions	2.44 × 1.60 × 0.60m

A bowl-shaped pit with a deeper shallow gully cut along the east side of its base. A dark grey brown silty loam filled the upper, more regularly cut part of the pit (2011a), while the deeper element was filled with a compact gravel and sand loam (2011b).

A moderate quantity of pottery (58 sherds) was recovered, of which a significant proportion had burnt internal residues (67%). Other finds comprised animal bone (11 fragments), a lump of fired clay and flint (4) from the upper part of the fill. This pit was located immediately adjacent to a roundhouse (CG57) with which it may have been closely associated.

PIT: CONTEXT GROUP 16 (FIG. 31)

Grid	1095/1105
Fill/Cut	1708
Plan	?Sub-circular
Profile	Bowl-shaped
Dimensions	1.70 × 1.10+ × 0.80m+

Well-defined pit on eastern limit of excavated area. Not fully excavated.

Figure 32. Bowl shaped pit CG10 during excavation.

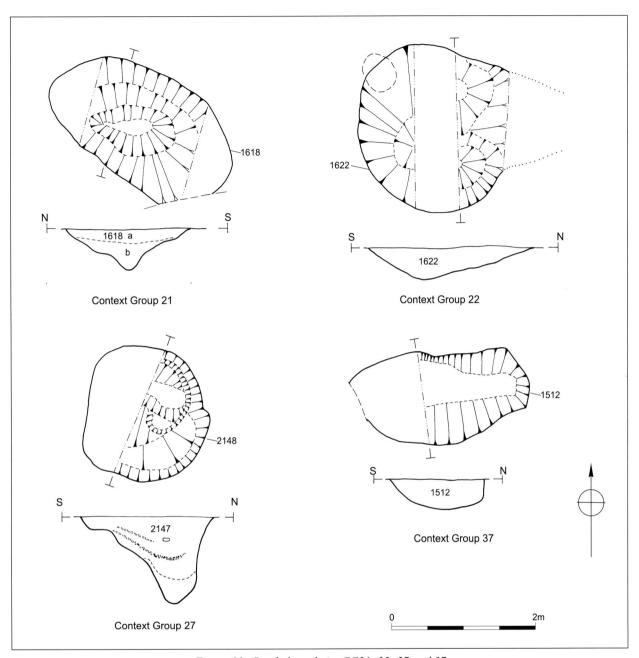

Figure 33. Bowl shaped pits CG21, 22, 27 and 37.

Cut by field boundary (FS2). Fill recorded as single context along with the cut, but section shows a base fill with burnt limestone and charcoal, overlain by a charcoal-rich lens and sealed by a deposit of dark grey silty clay loam. Fifteen sherds of pottery were recovered, including Late Bronze Age material but also several sherds of Beaker of early-mid Bronze Age date. A small quantity of fired clay/daub (2), animal bone (15) and flint (2) was also present.

PIT: CONTEXT GROUP 21 (FIG. 33)

Grid	1080/0972
Fill/cut	1618
Plan	Sub-oval
Profile	Stepped, bowl-shaped
Dimensions	2.50 × 1.20 × 0.72m

Pit, with a stepped profile. A single fill was recorded, a very compact, mid greyish-brown sandy clay loam; however, the section shows this to

have a paler upper element (1618a) and a darker lower element (1618b). The latter was characterised by quantities of very fine charcoal flecks, especially towards its base. No pottery was present but burnt stone and daub flecks were recorded and small quantities of flint (2) and animal bone (6) were recovered.

PIT: CONTEXT GROUP 22 (FIG. 33)

Grid	1079/0975
Fill/cut	1622
Plan	Sub-circular
Profile	Bowl-shaped
Dimensions	2.30 × 0.52m

Pit with an irregular base. The east side merged with an adjacent feature (context 1623) interpreted as representing an area of tree disturbance. The relationship between these features was somewhat ambiguous; however, it appears likely that the tree has disturbed the pit thus accounting for the latter's somewhat irregular appearance. A compact, mid greyish-brown sandy clay loam fill contained occasional charcoal flecks, small flecks of daub and a few fragments of burnt limestone.

PIT: CONTEXT GROUP 27 (FIG. 33)

Grid   0772/1041
Fill/cut   2147, 2148
Plan   Sub-circular
Profile   Bowl-shaped
Dimensions   1.82 × 1.70 × 1.12m

A relatively deep feature with a near vertical northern edge and a stepped southern one. The lowest fill, a slightly silty sand and gravel, derived from weathering and slumping (probably from the southern side). A secondary fill comprised a dark grey brown silty clay deposit with lenses of burnt limestone and gravel and a small quantity of animal bone (2). This may represent a deliberate infilling of the feature. The function of the pit remains undetermined.

PIT: CONTEXT GROUP 37 (FIG. 33)

Grid   1080/1069
Fill/cut   1512
Plan   Sub-oval
Profile   Bowl-shaped
Dimensions   2.65 × 1.25 × 0.40m

Sloping sided, sub-oval feature with slightly flattened north edge and near vertical sides. Its west end was truncated by a later pit/posthole (CG24). The fill contained only rare charcoal flecks and occasional very small burnt stone fragments. The function of the pit is indeterminate.

PIT: CONTEXT GROUP 40 (FIG. 36)

Grid   0798/1069
Fill/cut   2027
Plan   Sub-oval
Profile   Bowl-shaped
Dimensions   3.40 × 1.90 × 0.42m

Shallow pit with a single fill of grey brown clay which was intermixed with gravels to its base. Sterile except for light charcoal flecking, a single flint, a fire-cracked pebble and some burnt limestone. The feature lay close to a group of features containing large quantities of burnt stone (CG41, 43, 44, 45, 46 and 77). These have been interpreted as hearths and CG40 may therefore represent an associated pit or small pond for storage of water. Although it had been cut into gravel and no certain lining was present, the gravely clay at the base of the feature may have served to make it watertight.

PIT: CONTEXT GROUP 80 (LOCATED ON FIG. 16)

Grid   1062/0999
Fill/cut   1254, 1255
Plan   Sub-oval
Profile   Bowl-shaped
Dimensions   2.50+ × 1.20 × 0.70m

Fairly substantial, pit observed on junction between two extraction areas and mainly recorded from section and disturbed site surface. Sloping sided and concave based with a single, dark grey brown fill. Charcoal flecking and daub/fired clay were both present but the feature was otherwise sterile.

PIT: CONTEXT GROUP 81 (LOCATED ON FIG. 16)

Grid   1028/0961
Fill/cut   1204
Plan   Sub-oval
Profile   Bowl-shaped
Dimensions   1.60 × 1.20 × 0.60m+

Pit recorded after machine excavation of furrow. Single fill observed comprising a very dark grey, compact, sandy loam. No finds were recovered.

PIT: CONTEXT GROUP 93 (LOCATED ON FIG. 16)

Grid   1131/0955

Fill/cut   1338
Plan   Sub-oval
Profile   Bowl-shaped
Dimensions   2.00 × 1.10 × 0.35m

Relatively shallow pit with a single dark fill containing daub and charcoal flecks but no finds.

Small pits/postholes

Several features could not be readily defined as either pits or postholes (Fig. 34). They were rather small and were not comparable with any of the pits described above. Although potentially representing large postholes, for the most part they could not readily be associated with any structures. Other functions are therefore considered.

In the light of their relatively limited dimensions, a number of these features were notable for having contained larger than 'normal' assemblages (CG19, 24, 25, 91 and 92). Furthermore these assemblages were distinctive, for instance incorporating many sherds representing single vessels and having almost no sherds with burnt internal residues (<2%). In one case, (CG19), a deposit of charred cereal crop waste was associated with a single vessel. A favoured interpretation is therefore that these features were specifically excavated for the structured placement of artefacts/ecofacts as 'offerings' and possibly that these were also marked by posts.

PIT/POST: CONTEXT GROUP 19 (FIG. 34)

Grid   1087/0971
Fill/cut   1601
Plan   Sub-rectangular
Profile   U-shaped
Dimensions   1.30 × 0.80 × 0.24m

An irregular, sub-rectangular cut having a depression in its base. The latter measured approximately 0.70m across and may have held a post. This feature was unusual as despite its small size, it contained abundant pottery (66 sherds) and charred cereal remains (Table 30) as well as a single flint, 13 fragments of daub and a small fragment of animal bone.

Most, if not all, of the pottery sherds derived from a single Late Bronze Age vessel and it seems likely that the charred cereal was deposited within a pot as part of a ritual deposit rather than having been casually discarded. The feature has no obvious other function and may therefore have been excavated specifically receive this 'offering'.

Two single grains of charred wheat provided radiocarbon dates from this feature (OxA-10791–2; Table 2).

PIT/POST: CONTEXT GROUP 23 (FIG. 34)

Grid   1083/0963
Fill/cut   1604
Plan   Sub-circular
Profile   U-shaped
Dimensions   0.47 × 0.29m

Shallow but distinct posthole with single very dark grey brown, sandy clay loam fill. Notable for including a considerable volume of pottery (27 sherds) in view of its small size. Several vessels were represented. Animal bone (47 fragments), charcoal and burnt stone were abundant within the feature which also produced flint (6).

PIT/POST: CONTEXT GROUP 24 (FIG. 34)

Grid   1079/1069
Fill/cut   1510

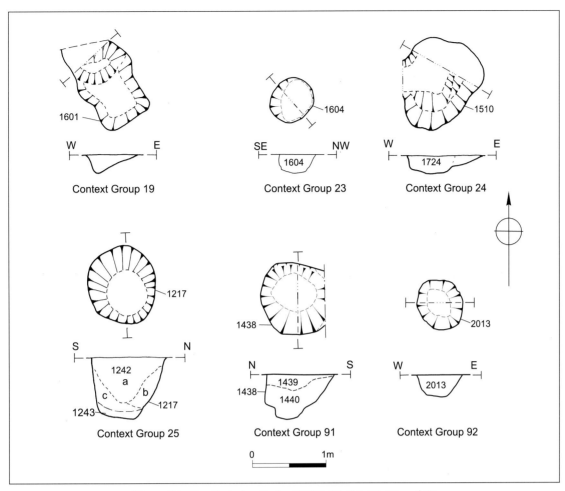

Figure 34. Small pits/postholes CG19, 23, 24, 25, 91 and 92.

Plan	Sub-oval
Profile	Basin-shaped
Dimensions	1.00 × 0.65 × 0.45m

Sub-oval pit with steeply sloping sides except at the northern end which had a shallow sloping side breaking nearly vertically to a flat base. Although somewhat shallow in depth, the profile suggests that this feature may have contained a substantial post. A single fill of dark grey brown, charcoal flecked, silty loam was identified. Burnt stone, animal bone (4), flint (2) and pottery (15) were all recovered, all bar one sherd of the pottery deriving from a single small fine vessel.

Pit/Post: Context Group 25 (Fig. 34)

Grid	1070/970
Cut	1217
Fill	1216, 1242, 1243
Plan	Sub-circular
Profile	U-shaped
Dimensions	1.00 × 0.82 × 0.95m

A near vertical-sided, flat-based cut with a distinctive sequence of fills. The eastern side was excavated as a single fill (1216) and this produced pottery (40), fired clay/daub (18), flint (5) and animal bone (65, including some calcined material noted as concentrated to the base of the feature). A substantial quantity of fossiliferous limestone some of which was burnt was also recovered (2.78kg).

Subsequent excavation of the western half divided the fills into two, an upper fill (1242) and a base fill (1243). Section evidence suggests further division of the upper fill into three parts. The uppermost element (1242a) was a dark grey brown sandy loam. This overlaid a yellow brown sandy

clay (1242b) occupying the northern side of the cut. A darker more heavily charcoal-flecked fill (1242c) pre-dated both of the others and occupied the southern side of the feature. This latter element contained abundant limestone (some burnt), animal bone (16 fragments, some burnt), flint (2), pottery (8) and heat-cracked pebbles. The base fill was a very dark grey brown, charcoal-rich, coarse sandy loam (1243). Occasional limestone, pottery (4) and heat cracked pebbles were all present in this base fill.

This feature is interpreted as a robbed posthole, possibly occupying an earlier pit. The uppermost fill appears to reflect the remains of an infilled post-pipe (1242a), with a packing of limestone to one side (1242b) and a disturbed earlier fill or slump (1242c) to the other. The base fill appears to have included a distinct charcoal-rich element intermixed with calcined bone. The latter was highly fragmentary and has not been identified to species, one possibility being that this represents a 'token' deposit of human cremated remains. A moderately large assemblage of pottery (52 sherds) was recovered representing several vessels. Although disturbed by the subsequent activity this may represent a ritual deposit (?an offering) placed below a post. Alternatively, since the putative 'post pipe' did not reach the base of the feature the post may have been a later insertion into an earlier small pit. Use or possibly re-use may be associated with the construction of a fence line (CG47).

Pit/Post: Context Group 91 (Figs 34 and 35)

Grid	1085/1032
Cut	1438
Fills	1439, 1440
Plan	Sub-circular
Profile	U-shaped
Dimensions	0.80 × 0.70m

Distinct, steep-sided, small pit or posthole with two fills. The lower fill (context 1440) was a dark grey brown, loamy deposit, moderately flecked with charcoal. This included burnt stone, pottery (201), fired clay/daub (7), flint (7, all burnt) and animal bone (15). The majority of the pottery assemblage derived from a single fine vessel which may have been deposited intact. Several other vessels (*c.* 6) were also represented, large proportions of several of which were also noted.

The upper fill (1439) was slightly paler in colour and less heavily charcoal-flecked but this also contained burnt stone, pottery and animal bone (2). The pottery assemblage was limited in this deposit (10 sherds)

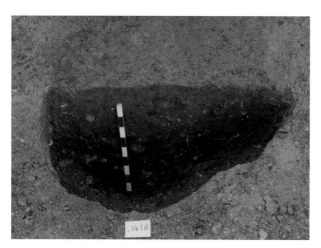

Figure 35. West facing section of CG91.

with no large chunks present, suggesting that this represents a backfill.

During excavation further material was mistakenly assigned to the context number allocated to the cut and thus cannot be ascribed to either upper or lower fill. This included pottery (41, including sherds which conjoined with those from 1440), flint (4) and animal bone (3).

PIT/POST: CONTEXT GROUP 92 (FIG. 34)

Grid	0868/1024
Fill/cut	2013
Plan	Sub-circular
Profile	U-shaped
Dimensions	0.66 × 0.62 × 0.26m

Well defined small pit or posthole not forming part of any obvious structure. This had a very dark grey brown, silty loam fill with charcoal flecking. The feature contained a significant quantity of pottery (50 sherds, representing at least 3 vessels), burnt limestone and animal bone (4) were also present.

Hearths/ovens

Nine features have been interpreted as hearths or ovens, most of which comprised shallow pits or depressions containing large quantities of burnt material (Fig. 16).

Of particular note, was a group of six of these features located towards the northwestern extents of the excavated area (CG41, CG43, CG44, CG45, CG46 and CG77; Fig. 36). These were shallow depressions associated with large quantities of charcoal, burnt gravel and burnt limestone.

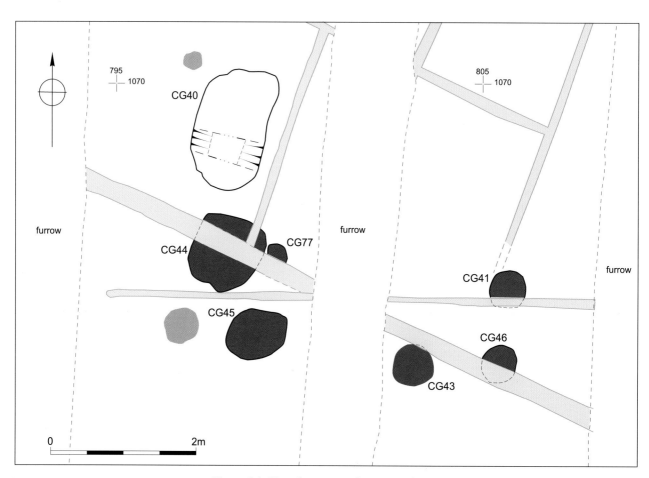

Figure 36. Hearth group and associated pit.

These probably form a contemporary grouping. Although direct dating evidence was not recovered, several Late Bronze Age features were present in the vicinity and it seems most likely that they correspond with this, the main period of activity. However, the possibility that they were of Beaker or earlier date should not be excluded. These features can be broadly interpreted as hearths, although the absence of burning of the surrounding natural suggests that the stone and gravel had been heated elsewhere and then been placed in a prepared hole whilst hot and the radiant heat used for some process. Close to this group of 'hearths', a shallow pit (CG40) has been tentatively interpreted as having been designed to contain water, while to the north an extensive depression in the natural clay (CG52) may represent a shallow pond, both features suggesting the possibility that activities associated with these 'hearths' required a water source.

The location of this 'hearth' group in relation to the later linear features which cut them (FS1, contexts 2054 and 2075) may be fortuitous, however, it may be that the location of the hearths was known and used in the layout of the later field system since several boundaries intersected at this point.

The remaining features interpreted as hearths or ovens differed somewhat. In one (CG28), to the southwest of the group, fired clay and daub fragments were present perhaps suggesting that this represented an oven. Further to the west, a shallow depression associated with charcoal and burnt stone may represent a further hearth but in the light of the nearby cremation deposit (CG96) may also potentially represent the remnants of a pyre.

Lastly, on the eastern side of the site a further hearth was identified (CG30), its use probably being associated with that of a nearby waterhole and soaking pit (CG8 and CG9). A craft or agricultural processing function may be indicated, although other uses should not be excluded.

Hearth pit/oven: Context Group 28 (Located on Fig. 16)

Grid	0774/1049
Fill/cut	2135/2134
Plan	Sub rectangular
Dimensions	2.16 × 1.52 × 0.56m

Shallow, sub-rectangular feature with an irregular based depression running along each side of its base. Partially obscured by a furrow. The yellowish mid grey-brown fill contained a considerable quantity of burnt daub fragments as well as flecks of daub and charcoal in its upper part. A number of unassigned postholes were present in the immediate area. The daub and charcoal along with a burnt patch of soil suggest that this may reflect the site of a demolished hearth of oven structure. No finds were recovered.

Hearth pit: Context Group 30 (Located on Fig. 16)

Grid	1128/1001
Fill/cut	1109
Plan	Sub-rectangular
Dimensions	2.50 × 1.50 × 0.18m

Shallow hollow filled with charcoal and burnt limestone in a dark brown grey, silty sand matrix. The feature was not well-defined and was more akin to a spread of burnt debris occupying a shallow depression than a cut feature. The material did not appear to have been burnt *in situ* but may

have been heated elsewhere and then placed into this depression and the radiant heat from it utilised. Possibly associated with nearby waterhole CG8 and lined pit CG9 both of which also contained considerable quantities of burnt material. No finds were recovered.

Hearth pit: Context Group 41 (Fig. 36)

Grid	0805/1065
Fill/cut	2028
Plan	Sub-circular
Dimensions	1.05 × 0.20m

Shallow, flat-based pit containing a single distinctive fill comprising a very dark grey/black sandy clay loam with 20%+ of volume filled by small fragments of burnt limestone and burnt gravel (*c.* 0.02–0.03m fragments). Charcoal was abundant and included a small quantity of cereal grain; however, the feature was otherwise sterile and the grain may have been accidentally incorporated with chaff and other crop waste used tinder. This feature appears to be some form of hearth, although the surrounding gravel showed no signs of reddening, the quantity and nature of the burnt stone material suggest that it had been placed in a prepared hole whilst hot and the radiant heat used for some process. No artefacts were recovered.

Hearth pit: Context Group 43 (Fig. 36)

Grid	0803/1063
Fill/cut	2051
Plan	Sub-circular
Dimensions	1.10 × 0.60m

Shallow, flat-based pit containing a single distinctive fill which very closely resembled the fill of CG41, being characterised by significant quantities of charcoal, burnt limestone and burnt gravel. No finds were recovered.

Hearth pit: Context Group 44 (Fig. 36)

Grid	0798/1065
Fill/cut	2052
Plan	Sub-oval
Dimensions	2.00 × 1.50 × 0.30m

Shallow, flat based pit. The lower fill was a charcoal rich dark grey clay, the upper fill (restricted to an area approximately 1m diameter and 0.2m deep) very closely resembled the fills of CG41 and CG43, being characterised by significant quantities of charcoal, burnt limestone and burnt gravel. This feature was truncated by several linear features (2053 and 2054). A single undiagnostic flint was recovered.

Hearth pit: Context Group 45 (Fig. 36)

Grid	0795/1063
Fill/cut	2081
Plan	Sub-oval
Dimensions	1.55 × 1.35m

Sub-circular feature, recorded only in plan. The fill was characterised by significant quantities of charcoal, burnt limestone and burnt gravel. No finds were recovered.

Hearth pit: Context Group 46 (Fig. 36)

Grid	0805/1063
Fill/cut	2079
Plan	Sub-circular
Dimensions	0.90m (diameter)

Sub-circular feature, recorded only in plan. The fill was characterised by significant quantities of charcoal, burnt limestone and burnt gravel. No artefacts were recovered.

Hearth pit: Context Group 77 (Fig. 36)

Grid	0799/1066
Fill/cut	2080
Plan	Sub-circular?
Dimensions	0.60m (diameter)

Sub-circular feature, recorded only in plan. The fill was characterised by significant quantities of charcoal, burnt limestone and burnt gravel. No finds were recovered.

HEARTH PIT: CONTEXT GROUP 97 (LOCATED ON FIG. 16)

Grid	0752/1047
Fill/cut	2137/2138
Plan	Sub-oval
Dimensions	1.90 × 1.40 × 0.20m

Shallow pit with burnt stone and heavy charcoal content in the fill. No finds were recorded. Liable to represent fire pit or hearth. Excavator suggested some possible link with cremation 2136 (CG96) – ?possible pyre location.

Undated cremation

A single undated and unaccompanied deposit of cremated bone was recorded in a small, shallow bowl-shaped pit towards the western limit of the excavated area (CG96; Fig. 16). The heavily calcined bone present was not firmly identifiable to species due to the very small quantity present and absence of definable elements (Pinter-Bellows, this volume).

The feature and its contents are, however, considered liable to represent a human burial deposit given the discrete nature of the feature, its location on the margins of occupied areas of the site and the highly calcined and fragmented nature of the bone.

The small size of the cremated bone deposit was noted on examination and the possibility that this represents a token representation with ritual significance rather than a full burial has been considered (Pinter-Bellows, this volume); however, caution should be exercised since the shallow depression was full of bone and in the light of the severe plough truncation of much of the site, it seems equally likely that the small volume of bone present reflects the level survival rather than of original deposition.

CREMATED BONE DEPOSIT: CONTEXT GROUP 96 (LOCATED ON FIG. 16)

Grid	0741/1050
Context	2136
Plan	Sub-circular
Profile	Bowl
Dimensions	0.45 × 0.05m

Shallow pit with a single compact, dark grey-brown sandy clay fill with abundant inclusions of highly burnt (?human) bone and charcoal.

Posthole structures

Eight roundhouses, five rectilinear structures, five four-post structures, two semi-circular structures, two T-shaped structures, two curvilinear gully-based structures and three small rectilinear post and gully structures have been identified along with three fencelines and three large post-defined enclosures. Several substantial but isolated postholes have also been recorded (Fig. 16).

These structures have been identified within substantial clusters of post- and stakehole-sized features, the majority of which were not excavated. As a result, identification has

been based upon plan analysis allied to information on fill characteristics where recorded. Many of the structures produced very limited or no dating evidence; however, in the light of the predominance of Late Bronze Age activity and the apparent relationship and proximity of many of these post-built structures to dated features, they are considered most probably to date from this period.

Apart from two of the roundhouses which overlapped (CG54 and 55), no sequence of construction was represented and even in the case cited the chronological relationship of the two roundhouses could not clearly be established. Truncation had clearly affected survival, the post/stakeholes for the most part remaining as only shallow depressions while no occupation deposits (*e.g.* floors or internal hearths) were present. Ridge and furrow cultivation had also substantially affected survival and clearly accounted for many of the gaps in the post/stakeholes defining these structures.

As a result of the truncation, many of the structure plans appear irregular; although the latter also seems in part to reflect the original pattern. Certainly a degree of irregular spacing was present originally, while the post/stakeholes themselves also appear not to have been of uniform depth or size. This may reflect variable histories of construction and dismantling; posts being replaced, structures remodelled and posts removed when structures were abandoned, some possibly for reuse. Furthermore, it is recognised that there is no requirement for posts to be of uniform diameter or length, thus a deeper posthole may simply reflect adjustment made for a longer post (Moore and Jennings 1992, 35) to ensure a level roof support or wall height.

Roundhouses

Eight roundhouses have been identified. Two potential groupings were present, both lying towards the northern side of the site (CG58, 59 and 60 and CG54, 55 and 56; Fig. 16). In the latter grouping, CG54 either replaced or was replaced by CG55, while the latter was also rebuilt on one occasion. The other two examples appear isolated, one being located towards the west side of the site (CG57), the other on its southern margins (CG78).

The diameters of seven of the roundhouses were defined by post circuits which varied between 7.00m and 13.5m, most falling towards the upper end of this range. It can be suggested that these post-rings represent roof supports for larger diameter structures which had wattle and daub walls lying beyond them. No traces of these walls survived although daub was regularly noted within posthole fills around the structures. This method of construction was first postulated for Bronze Age roundhouses identified at Shearplace Hill, Dorset (Avery and Close-Brooks 1969) and has been suggested at other Late Bronze Age sites comparable with Kemerton such as those at Reading Business Park (Moore and Jennings 1992; Brossler, Early and Allen 2004) and Shorncote (Hearne and Heaton 1992;

Hearne and Adam 1999). At both Reading Business Park and Shorncote diameters of the roof support post circuits ranged from 6.65–10.00m, with external wall dimensions being in the region of 13.00m as indicated by the position of porch posts which are assumed to have been situated on the line of the external wall. Four of the roundhouses at Kemerton (CG56, 58, 59 and 60) had comparable porches represented by paired postholes lying outside of the main post-circuit. These were located on the south/south-south-east sides of the roundhouses. Assuming the model of construction is correct this would suggest that the Kemerton roundhouses were slightly larger than those at Reading Business Park or Shorncote having external diameters of up to 16.00m.

In only one instance was there evidence for replacement of the structure, CG54 either having replaced or been replaced by CG55 which itself had been rebuilt or remodelled; the replacement being slightly off centre from the original structure. None of the roundhouses had identifiable central roof supports, although again this compares favourably with many examples from other sites.

The eighth roundhouse (CG78) is more tentatively identified and appeared to have been of different construction. This was represented by a curvilinear gully enclosing an area at least 9.00m in diameter. In the absence of postholes, details of construction are hard to establish though daub was present. One possibility is that the gully represented the construction trench for a mass wall or setting for a wall constructed from sections of wattle and daub, although it is also possible that this represents an eavesdrip for a smaller free standing structure. An entrance to the structure can be inferred on the north side from a break in the gully. It is possible that a second south-facing entrance was present as only the northern half of the structure lay within the site limits.

In the absence of internal features or surfaces and the paucity of material assemblages from the limited number of postholes which were excavated, it has not proved possible to determine functions for these buildings. However, evidence from comparably dated sites suggests that range of domestic and workshop functions are likely and this is supported by the presence of domestic waste and residues from metalworking, processing and craft activities within features such as pits and waterholes in the vicinity of many of the roundhouses.

ROUNDHOUSE: CONTEXT GROUP 54 (FIG. 37)
Grid   1039/1111

Roundhouse measuring approximately 11m in diameter. Only half of the structure lay within the recorded area. Nine fairly regularly spaced postholes were identified of which only one (1724) was excavated. The fill of this and the other postholes (as observed in plan) was grey to very dark grey in colour. Several of the postholes contained large volumes of charcoal indicating that perhaps the posts had been burnt or scorched.

The diameters of the postholes indicated that the posts may have been variable in size but that the majority probably measured between 0.40–0.50m in diameter. A number of postholes within the area of the structure have been assigned to Roundhouse CG55 which appears to have had

two phases of construction. Several other features present may represent internal features or other, undetermined structures that pre- or post-dated the roundhouse. No evidence for a porch was discerned, although this could have been situated to the west beyond the excavated area.

ROUNDHOUSE: CONTEXT GROUP 55 (FIG. 38)
Grid   1036/1104

Roundhouse with two phases of construction (CG55a and CG55b), one slightly offset from the other. None of the postholes was excavated and over half of both structures lay beyond the investigated area. CG55a comprised 11 postholes while CG55b comprised 10 postholes. Both were within the region of 12.5 to 13m in diameter. No internal features were identified and no porch structure was present although, if present, this may have lain to the west beyond the recorded area.

The roundhouse/s overlapped with another similar structure to the north, Roundhouse CG54; however, the fills of the postholes comprising CG55a and CG55b were less well-defined than those of CG54 perhaps suggesting that CG54 replaced CG55.

ROUNDHOUSE: CONTEXT GROUP 56 (FIG. 39)
Grid   1082/1120

Roundhouse comprising 15 rather irregularly spaced postholes with a further two representing a porch on its southern side. The main post circuit measured approximately 12m in diameter, while if the porch posts are taken to demarcate the position of the outer wall, the overall diameter of the roundhouse was *c*. 17m.

None of the postholes were excavated but in plan they were recorded to have grey to dark greyish fills, several of which were heavily flecked with charcoal. Posthole diameters varied between 0–25 to 0.70m but were mostly in the 0.45 to 0.50m range. A number of features within the structure are considered to represent either internal features or features which pre- or post-dated the structure.

ROUNDHOUSE: CONTEXT GROUP 57 (FIG. 40)
Grid   0810/1028

Group of six, unexcavated postholes recorded in plan as having distinct, charcoal-rich, dark fills. These were located in an area of the site containing few postholes and demarcated a circle *c*. 7m diameter. They are considered to represent the remains of a heavily truncated roundhouse. A number of postholes in the immediate vicinity may be associated although no porch could be identified. Two bowl-shaped pits (CG10 and CG11) were located close to the structure and both contained large quantities of domestic waste.

ROUNDHOUSE: CONTEXT GROUP 58 (FIG. 41)
Grid   0934/1115

Sub-circular structure, comprising a *c* 12m diameter circuit of 12 postholes. Two further postholes formed a possible porch to the southeast which if taken to demarcate the position of the outer wall provides an overall diameter of *c*. 15m.

None of the postholes was excavated but they were observed to be typically dark brown to very dark grey brown in colour and averaged 0.56m diameter. Charcoal flecking was observed in several and one exhibited signs of burning. No internal features were present.

ROUNDHOUSE: CONTEXT GROUP 59 (FIG. 42)
Grid   0898/1102

Sub-circular structure comprising a circuit of 9 postholes, with a further posthole possibly representing a porch to the southeast. The central post circuit measured c 12m diameter circuit, while if the porch post is taken to demarcate the position of the outer wall, the overall diameter of the roundhouse was *c*. 19m.

The postholes averaged 0.65m in diameter. Daub and charcoal were present within the only one of these to be excavated (context 1821) but no other finds were recorded. Four postholes were present within the area of the roundhouse and potentially represent an internal division separating the northeast side of the building from the rest.

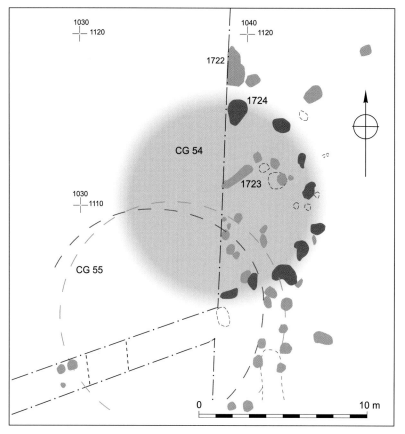

Figure 37. Roundhouse CG54.

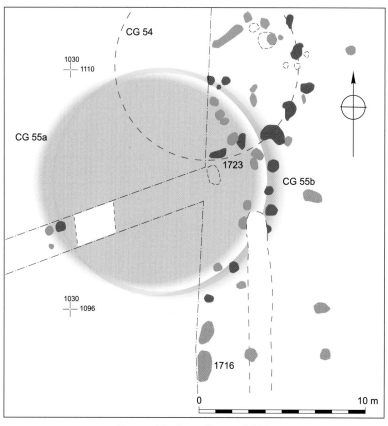

Figure 38. Roundhouse CG55.

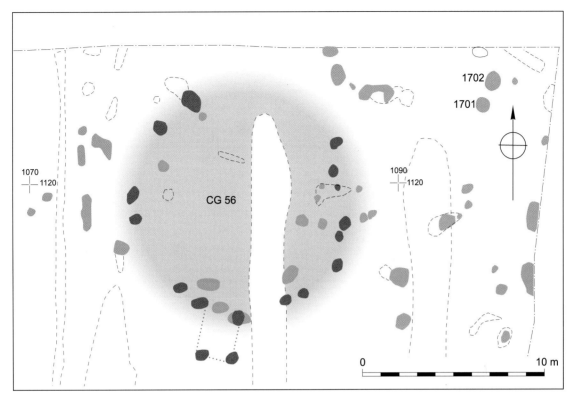

Figure 39. Roundhouse CG56.

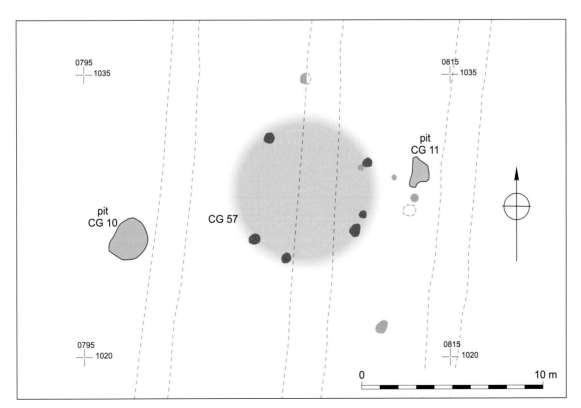

Figure 40. Roundhouse CG57.

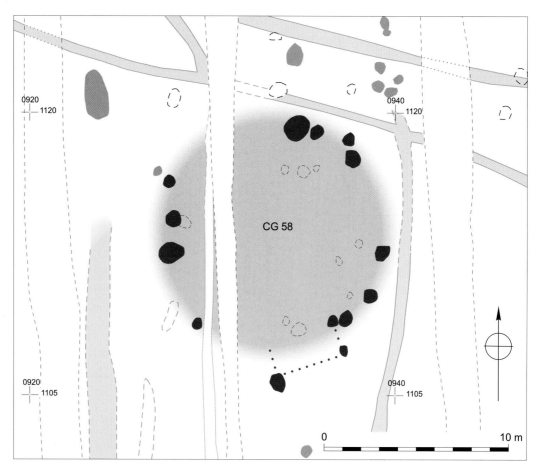

Figure 41. Roundhouse CG58.

ROUNDHOUSE: CONTEXT GROUP 60 (FIG. 42)

Grid   0915/1105

Rather irregular sub-circular structure, comprising a c 10m diameter circuit of 8 postholes. Two further postholes formed a possible porch to the southeast which if taken to demarcate the position of the outer wall provides an overall diameter of *c.* 14m.

The postholes averaged 0.46m in diameter and were observed in plan to be brown to dark brown in colour with charcoal flecking. One potential internal feature was present, its size suggesting that it might have been a pit.

Only one of the postholes (context 1820) was excavated. This proved to survive as little more than a shallow depression containing articulated animal bone (192 fragments) possibly representing a placed (?foundation) deposit in the base of an otherwise largely truncated feature.

ROUNDHOUSE: CONTEXT GROUP 78 (FIG. 43)

Grid   0937/0920

Probable roundhouse of which only the northern part lay within the excavated area. This comprised a curvilinear gully (context 1809) indicative of a diameter of at least 9.00m. It had a 2.00m wide entrance and enclosed an area of disturbed natural.

Two small pits or relatively large postholes lay within the area defined by the gully and, although only one was excavated (context 1805), both were observed to contain daub and charcoal. Several small stakeholes were also present and may be associated. The gully fill included burnt limestone and charcoal. It was unclear whether the gully represented the wall footing for the structure or an eavesdrip. No finds were recovered.

Rectilinear structures

Five rectilinear structures were defined (CG61, 62, 63, 64 and 65; Figs 44–6, 54 and 55). Two of these (CG61 and CG63) were relatively small structures measuring only 4.00 × 3.50m and 3.85 × 2.75m, but the remainder were of a reasonably large size, measuring between 6.25 × 3.00m and 8.00 × 6.25m. Parallels for these structures are less readily identified than for the roundhouses although rectilinear buildings have been identified as at Shorncote (Hearne and Heaton 1994; Hearne and Adam 1999).

One of the structures (CG62) at Kemerton was of very regular construction thus enabling the form of the structure to be determined with some degree of confidence. The arrangement of the twelve posts in two distinct sets of six indicates that the building probably comprised two enclosed bays set on either side of an open-sided central area. The two smaller internal posts suggest that the structure had a north to south aligned roof ridge along its central axis. Also of potential significance was that this central axis was aligned precisely onto a large limestone block set in a shallow depression located about 9.00m to the south of the building. This, along with the unusual form of the structure raises the possibility that it may have had a ceremonial function rather than a utilitarian one.

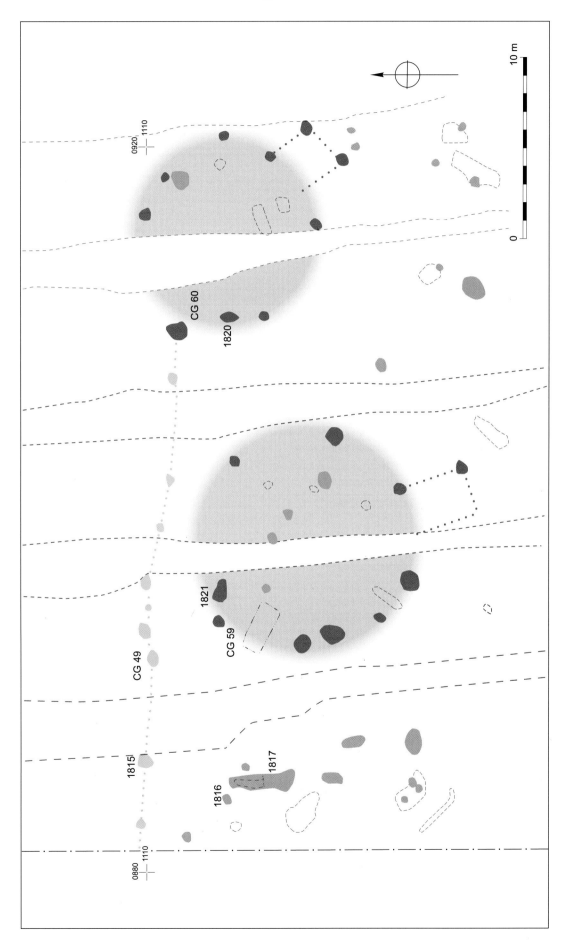

Figure 42. Roundhouses CG59 and CG60 and Fence CG49.

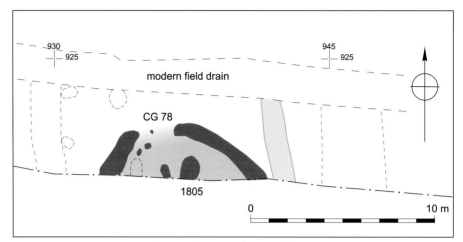

Figure 43. Roundhouse CG78.

The other rectilinear structures were of less regular construction and functions are liable to have been associated with providing shelter (stables/byres) or pens for animals, workshops or as storage facilities. In particular, the location of one of these (CG64) within a large post-defined enclosure (CG68) and close to two waterholes (CG6 and 7; see Fig. 55) allied to its size (8.00 × 6.25m) would strongly suggest use as an animal pen for separating out stock within the larger enclosure. Structure CG65 was of similar size (7.50 × 6.50m) and form and may also have been a pen located adjacent to another large post-defined enclosure (CG67; see Fig. 54) and close to several roundhouses. The two smaller structures (CG61 and CG63) appear more likely to have been roofed, CG61 also having a possible porch on its north side.

RECTILINEAR STRUCTURE: CONTEXT GROUP 61 (FIGS 44 AND 45)
Grid   0878/0950

Well defined, rectilinear post-built structure comprising at least 12 postholes. Ten posts (contexts 2004, 2061, 2062, 2063, 2064, 2065, 2066, 2067, 2068, 2069 and 2070) defined a sub-rectangular area measuring 4.00 × 3.50m with two further (unexcavated) posts defining an apparent porch structure on the northwest corner. Further (unexcavated) posts in the immediate vicinity may have been associated and the structure had been truncated at the east end by a temporary haul road.

No direct dating evidence was recovered; however, apart from a couple of residual Beaker finds in the Late Bronze Age waterholes 45m to the east (CG6 and 7), all activity in this area of the site was of Late Bronze Age date and therefore the structure is considered most likely to be of that date.

RECTILINEAR STRUCTURE: CONTEXT GROUP 62 (FIGS 44 AND 46)
Grid   0820/1047

A clearly defined, rectangular three bay structure measuring 6.25 × 3.00m represented by 12 shallow postholes averaging 0.24m deep (contexts 2015, 2016, 2017, 2018, 2019, 2020, 2021, 2022, 2023, 2024, 2025 and 2026). Truncation had clearly affected the area and no occupation horizons were identified. The smaller size of the two internal posts suggests that they may have supported the roof, while the arrangement of the external posts suggests that the structure may have comprised enclosed bays to the north and south of an open sided central area.

A single burnt flint and a single fired clay fragment were recovered

(from 2018) but no artefactual or stratigraphic dating evidence was recovered; however, a range of datable features lay within the close vicinity. Twenty metres to the south, two Late Bronze Age pits and an associated roundhouse (CG10, 11 and 57) were recorded, while 15m to the north, two Late Bronze Age post/pits (CG32 and 34) were located along with (slightly further north) a Late Bronze Age waterhole and associated soaking pit (CG3 and 5). Slightly further distant (35m), and to the east, three Beaker period pits were present. On the balance of probability the structure is considered most likely to be of Late Bronze Age date, given the rarity of Beaker structures and greater proximity of Late Bronze Age activity in the vicinity.

One further observation was that the structure was aligned on a northeast to southwest axis, directly on the line of which was a large limestone block some 9.00m to the southwest. The position of the block may be fortuitous; however, an alternative is that this represents a building with some ritual function.

RECTILINEAR STRUCTURE: CONTEXT GROUP 63 (FIG. 44)
Grid   1080/0958

Rectilinear structure measuring 3.85 × 2.75m and comprising at least 12 well defined shallow dark filled postholes (contexts 1301/1302, 1305/1306, 1307/1308, 1309/1310, 1354, 1355, 1356 and 1357). Two internal posts may have partitioned off the south end of the structure or formed roof supports.

Most of the postholes included charcoal flecks and two of them contained daub fragments. A single sherd of medieval pottery (from 1355) is considered intrusive and, in the light of the levels of Late Bronze Age activity in the vicinity, this structure is considered liable to be of such a date.

RECTILINEAR STRUCTURE: CONTEXT GROUP 64 (FIG. 55)
Grid   0935/0955

Rectilinear structure measuring 7.50 × 6.50m in plan, with 6 posts forming a well defined southwest side and three the northeast side. Most of the postholes could have held relatively large posts of a 0.60m+ diameter, although the two central posts on the southwest side were smaller (0.35m diameter) and may mark the location of an entrance into the structure. Although none of the postholes were excavated, the fills were all recorded in plan as being dark brown to dark grey brown in colour with daub and charcoal flecking also noted in some them.

No artefacts or dating evidence were recovered but the structure lay within a large fenced enclosure (CG68) which also included two substantial Late Bronze Age waterholes (CG6 and 7).

RECTILINEAR STRUCTURE: CONTEXT GROUP 65 (FIG. 44)
Grid   0917/1085

Virtually square structure comprising 8 postholes of an average 0.60m

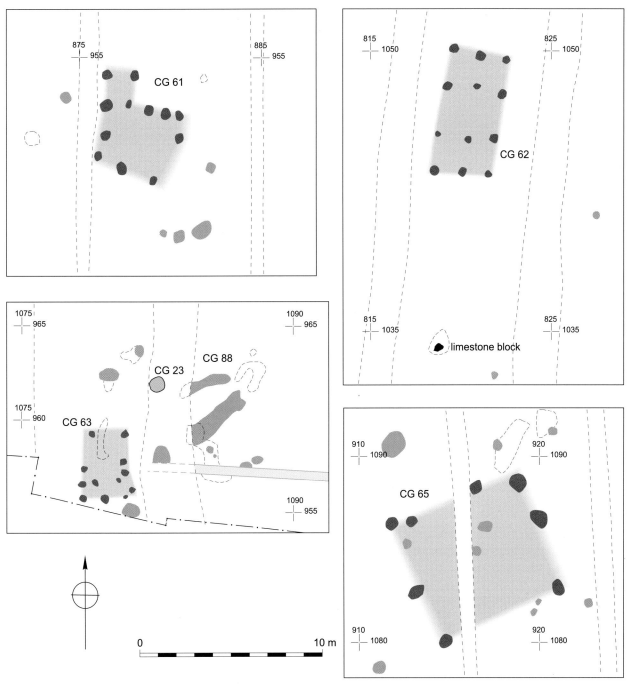

Figure 44. Rectilinear structures CG61, 62, 63 and 65.

diameter. The structure measured 8.00 × 6.25m. Further postholes may have been removed by a furrow which crosses the structure.

None of the features were excavated and no finds were recovered; however, fills were mostly noted in plan to be dark brown grey to grey brown in colour and in the light of Late Bronze Age activity in this area (Pits CG 1 and 2; Enclosure CG67; Roundhouses CG58, 59 and 60) this is considered to be of comparable date.

Four-post structures

Five four-post structures have been identified (CG70, 71, 72, 73 and 74; Fig. 47). All of these were located in the northeast part of the site (Fig. 16). Although no

dating evidence was recovered, Late Bronze Age activity predominates across the site and was present in this area and consequently these are liable to be of this date.

The structures were mostly rectilinear, although one (CG70) was square in plan. They varied in size measuring between 2.50 × 1.25m and 4.00 × 4.00m (3.125m² to 16.00m²). None of the structures was symmetrical. Comparable structures have been widely identified on Late Bronze Age sites including at Reading Business Park and Shorncote (Moore and Jennings 1992; Hearne and Heaton 1994; Hearne and Adam 1999; Brossler, Early and Allen

Figure 45. Rectilinear structure CG61 (from southwest).

Figure 46. Rectilinear structure CG62 (from north).

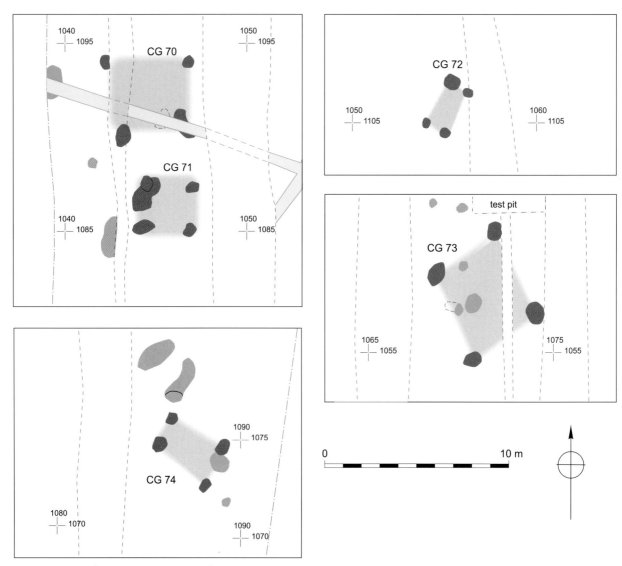

Figure 47. Four post structures CG70, 71, 72, 73 and 74.

2004), although at both of these locations the structures were generally somewhat smaller than the examples here.

Such structures are usually interpreted on both Bronze Age and Iron Age sites as representing small buildings with raised floors used as storehouses or granaries (Gent 1983). A similar interpretation is offered here.

FOUR-POST STRUCTURE: CONTEXT GROUP 70 (FIG. 47)
Grid   1045/1093

Four-post structure, measuring 4.00 × 4.00m. Disturbed by furrow on west side. Comprised well-defined posts with dark fills. These were only observed in plan but could have supported posts up to 0.40m in diameter.

FOUR-POST STRUCTURE: CONTEXT GROUP 71 (FIG. 47)
Grid   1046/1086

Four-post structure, measuring 3.00 × 2.50m. The two posts to the west side appeared considerably larger in plan than those on the east and both were half-sectioned (contexts 1521 and 1522), that to the south showing a distinct smaller post impression in its base. These two may have been replaced or possibly robbed at the end of the life of the structure thus accounting for the variable plan. Charcoal flecking was present in both excavated postholes and daub in one. Posts could have been up to about 0.35m in diameter.

FOUR-POST STRUCTURE: CONTEXT GROUP 72 (FIG. 47)
Grid   1055/1106

Four-post structure, measuring 2.50 × 1.25m. None of the four postholes were excavated, but all had dark coloured fills. Post diameters could have been up to 0.30m.

FOUR-POST STRUCTURE: CONTEXT GROUP 73 (FIG. 47)
Grid   1070/1057

Four-post structure, measuring 4.00 × 3.50m. None of the four postholes was excavated but all could have supported a post up to 0.45m in diameter. The two fills described in plan were both dark in colour.

FOUR-POST STRUCTURE: CONTEXT GROUP 74 (FIG. 47)
Grid   1087/1075

Four-post structure, measuring 2.50 × 1.50m. All four postholes were noted to have dark fills and one was excavated but produced no finds. These could have supported posts up to 0.35m in diameter.

Semi-circular structures

Two semi-circular structures were identified, one describing just under half a circuit measuring 6.00m across, the other a similar half circuit of some 5.00m across (Fig. 48). Similar structures have been recorded elsewhere, for instance at Reading Business Park (Moore and Jennings 1992).

These may represent partial post circuits of roundhouses which had no earthfast posts in the other portions. Alternatively they could represent distinct structures in their own right, perhaps functioning as windbreaks or open-fronted animal shelters.

SEMI-CIRCULAR POST STRUCTURE: CONTEXT GROUP 69 (FIG. 48)
Grid   0833/0999

Semi-circular structure comprising 6 regularly spaced and well defined postholes, each about 0.45m in diameter. These described just under half of a circle of about 6.00m in diameter. The enclosed area faced north and there was no evidence for either a northern side to the structure or of any internal features. It is suggested that either this was a semi-circular structure constructed to provide shelter from the wind or that it was a roundhouse where the northern side was either a free standing structure or has been fully truncated.

SEMI-CIRCULAR POST STRUCTURE: CONTEXT GROUP 89 (FIG. 48)
Grid   1040/0970

Semi-circular arrangement of six postholes with charcoal-rich fills. These formed a structure which appears to have been open to the west. The two postholes on the open western side were more substantial than the arc of four smaller postholes forming the remainder of the structure suggesting that these formed the main supports for the structure which only measured 5.00m across at it widest. This most probably represents a semi-circular structure constructed to provide shelter from the wind.

T-shaped structures

Two T-shaped structures were found in close proximity (Fig. 49). These are interpreted as representing structures having upright frames with supporting posts placed at right-angles to the frame. The structures therefore appear to face in opposite directions. Possible functions include as drying racks or supports for looms.

T-SHAPED STRUCTURE: CONTEXT GROUP 75 (FIG. 49)
Grid   0862/0943

T-shaped structure comprising distinct alignment of four posts with a fifth post set off at right-angles from this alignment. Four of the postholes were excavated (2001, 2002, 2003 and un-numbered). All produced charcoal but no artefacts were recovered. All of the postholes could have supported posts up to 0.45m across, although one (2003) could have held a considerably larger post (1.00m or more); however, the latter is believed more likely to reflect robbing or dismantling of the structure.

T-SHAPED STRUCTURE: CONTEXT GROUP 76 (FIG. 49)
Grid   0852/0947

T-shaped structure comprising 4 certain posts and 2 further possible posts. None of these were excavated but all had well-defined, dark coloured fills. This was located only 7.00m from the only other T-shaped structure which has been identified on the site (CG75), although CG76 appears to have been more heavily truncated or of slightly less substantial construction.

Curvilinear gully structures

Two structures with curvilinear 'construction' gullies lay close together on the southern margins of the site (CG50 and CG51; Fig. 50). Neither was fully excavated or revealed within the investigated area. The more extensively observed (CG50) also included postholes arranged in an arc around one end of the structure.

In both structures, the 'construction' gullies on one side were notable for the presence of narrow slots aligned parallel to a central ridge of fired or burnt clay. The latter possibly represents the stub of a partially fired clay or daub 'wall'. This may have been faced on both sides by hurdles set into the slots although no wattle impressions were visible within the burnt sandy clay. Another possibility is that the slots were used to support boards or hurdles used in construction of a cobb wall. The apparent use of a post-built wall at one end of CG50 indicates that the sides of this structure were not all of the same construction perhaps reflecting differing requirements or some degree of structural complexity. Regrettably both structures lay very close to the quarry face and there was insufficient time to make a detailed investigation.

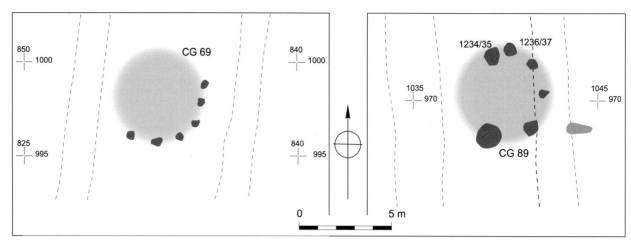

Figure 48. Semi-circular structures CG69 and 89.

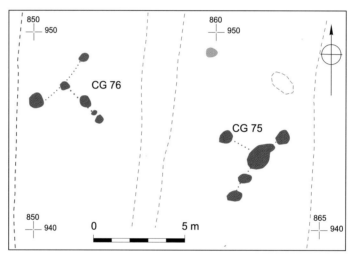

Figure 49. T-shaped structures CG75 and 76.

CURVILINEAR GULLY STRUCTURE: CONTEXT GROUP 50 (FIG. 50)
Grid   1040/0963

Irregular, rather poorly-defined, post and gully structure of unusual form and uncertain function. Although truncated to the east end by a furrow, this appeared to have comprised an irregular horseshoe-shaped gully, open to the west, along with 5 postholes. These formed a structure of broadly sub-oval plan measuring 6.00 × 5.00m.

Three small and one large posthole described an arc around the east end while a fifth posthole occupied the open end of the horseshoe-shaped gully. The gully was shallow and in two excavated sections (contexts 1223 and 1226) had a pair of narrow parallel slots running along its base with a ridge of soil between them. In the southern gully section (context 1223) this ridge comprised *in situ* burnt sandy clay material running along the centre of the feature. In contrast, the northern gully (context 1224) did not contain such slots or a ridge of burnt material. Along with the arc of posts at the east end, this suggests that the structure had differently constructed sides, possibly reflecting differing requirements such as an ability to withstand heat along one side. A similar structure lay a few metres to the east (CG51).

CURVILINEAR GULLY STRUCTURE: CONTEXT GROUP 51 (FIG. 50)
Grid   1050/0960

Structure, similar to CG50, comprising the northern part of a curvilinear gully (context 1222) with a pair of shallow parallel slots running along its length and sandwiching the remains of a daub/partially fired clay 'wall' *in situ*. This was only present in one section, suggesting that, as with CG50, the fired clay/daub 'wall' did not extend all the way round.

The structure measured at least 4.80m across and had been truncated to the east by a furrow. The majority of the interior lay in the former quarry area and there was no evidence for any associated posthole arrangements.

Rectilinear post and gully structures

Three small rectilinear post and gully structures (CG86, 87 and 88; Figs 50 and 51) were recorded in the southeast corner of the investigated area. These were of similar dimensions (approximately 3.35 × 3.00m, 4.00 × 2.50m and 4.00 × 3.00m respectively) and of comparable construction having irregular based gullies running down either side with posts aligned on the central axes of the structures.

One suggested reconstruction is that the central posts supported a roof ridge while the gullies held hurdles angled at 45° up to the supporting roof ridge, thus forming a small A-framed structure which could have been used as an animal shelter similar to those used today for pigs.

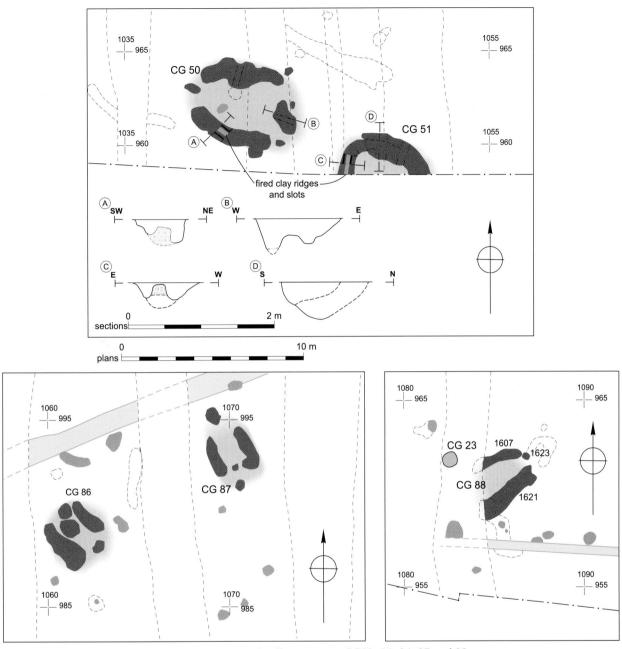

Figure 50. Post and gully structures CG50, 51, 86, 87 and 88.

POST AND GULLY STRUCTURE: CONTEXT GROUP 86 (FIGS 50 AND 51)

Grid   1061/0989

Two short parallel gullies, each containing a number of shallow postholes. A further three postholes and a stakehole lay between the gullies, which were 1.50m apart. The area between the gullies was slightly disturbed, possibly by trample. The fills of the features were all generally similar, however the soil colours varied locally within each feature.

The features define a small rectangular structure (context 1252) aligned approximately north to south and measuring c 3.35 × 3.00m. This is similar in size, plan and alignment to CG87 and CG88.

POST AND GULLY STRUCTURE: CONTEXT GROUP 87 (FIG. 50)

Grid   1070/0993

Structure comprising two short parallel gullies, having a disturbed area between them. Both gullies contained shallow postholes while three further postholes ran through the central axis of the structure. Less clear, but generally similar in size, plan and alignment to CG86. Interpreted as a small rectangular structure (context 1253) measuring c 4.00 × 2.50m.

POST AND GULLY STRUCTURE: CONTEXT GROUP 88 (FIG. 50)

Grid   1085/0961

Structure, truncated to the west by a furrow, comprising two roughly parallel gullies (contexts 1607 and 1621) and a posthole (1623). Both gullies contained shallow postholes and one produced a single flint (1607). The posthole lay slightly to the east of the gullies but on the central axis of this broadly rectilinear structure which measured c 4.00 × 3.00m. Similar in form and size to both CG86 and CG87.

Figure 51. Post and gully structure CG86 (from southwest).

Figure 52. Fence CG48 – Posthole with pyramidal ceramic weight used as packing.

Boundaries/fences

Four posthole alignments (CG47, 48, 49 and 53; Fig. 16) have been identified and are considered to represent fences providing boundaries, windbreaks or stock control features within the site. Of these CG47 in the southeast corner of the excavated area may represent a fence or barrier (?wind break) designed to separate off or shield a group of pits located to its immediate east while GC49 towards the north side of the site appears closely related to a group of roundhouses (CG58, 59 and 60), possibly separating these from an area of activity located to the north. The third fence or barrier identified, CG48, was located in the northwest part of the site and appears to have extended further north beyond the investigated area. This has a break in it, probably reflecting the location of a gate; however it is uncertain what this was associated with.

Fences have been identified on other Bronze Age settlement sites, as at Hornchurch, Essex (Guttmann and Last 2000) and Shorncote (Hearne and Adam 1999), although they were absent at Reading Business Park (Brossler, Early and Allen 2004). This may reflect that different strategies were being employed or were required to demarcate areas and control access to them at otherwise apparently similar sites.

The fourth example, CG53, located centrally within the investigated area may have a slightly different function since it comprises two short alignments providing a 'funnel-like' arrangement close to a conjunction of field boundaries. This may have operated as a stock drafting gate as have been identified elsewhere such as in the Fens of eastern England (Pryor 1998).

BOUNDARY/FENCE: CONTEXT GROUP 47 (FIG. 16)
Grid   1070/0967

North to south alignment of moderately large postholes or small pits running for some 20m in the southeast corner of the excavated area (contexts 1205, 1212, 1206, 1208, 1213 and 1216/1217/1242/1243 (also CG25),). These measured between 0.50 and 1.00m in diameter.

The identification of the alignment is only tentative as there was a marked disparity in depth of the excavated features and the possibility remains that the alignment may be an illusion created by the medieval ridge and furrow which was similarly aligned. However, all were characterised by dark fills and where excavated produced daub and charcoal. A single flint was recovered from fill/cut 1212, but otherwise the postholes were sterile with the exception of post/pit 1217. This was a distinct feature having a well-defined robbed post-pipe and indications of post packing, as well as having been reused as small pit (see CG25 for discussion of finds and re-use as a pit).

FENCE: CONTEXT GROUP 48 (FIGS 16 AND 52)
Grid   0846/1047

An alignment of 7 postholes located towards the northwest of the investigated area, averaging 0.24m diameter running northwest to southeast with a slight change of direction in the middle where a gap in the alignment may identify the location of a gate.

Two of the postholes (2057/2058 and 2059) were excavated and were well defined and U-shaped in profile. Both contained burnt limestone and charcoal flecking, and one of them (2058) had additionally been packed with ceramic loom weights, one pyramidal and one annular (Fig. 52). The loom weights, probably incomplete at the time of deposition had been crushed *in situ*, possibly by rocking of the post at the time of its removal. The other five postholes were not excavated, however, all had clearly defined, charcoal-rich, dark grey fills.

FENCE: CONTEXT GROUP 49 (FIG. 42)
Grid   0886/1110

Alignment of 10 postholes, extending for at least 25m across the site in a broadly east to west direction close to the northern boundary of the investigated area. The largest of the postholes (1815) was the only one of these features which was excavated. Animal bone (2), flint (1) and small sherds (3) of LBA pottery were recovered from the dark charcoal and daub flecked fill.

This fence is probably closely related to the three roundhouses (CG58, 59 and 60) in this area of the site, perhaps defining an occupation area and possibly protecting it (from stock?).

FENCE OR DRAFTING GATE: CONTEXT GROUP 53 (FIG. 16)
Grid   0973/1000

Arrangement of 9 postholes in two groups defining a 'funnel-shaped' area close to, and apparently associated with, a field boundary (part of FS1, Fig. 17). None of the postholes was excavated; however, all were observed in plan to contain well-defined, charcoal-rich, dark grey fills.

Post-defined enclosures

Three substantial post-defined enclosures have been identified (CG66, 67 and 68; Figs 53, 54 and 55).

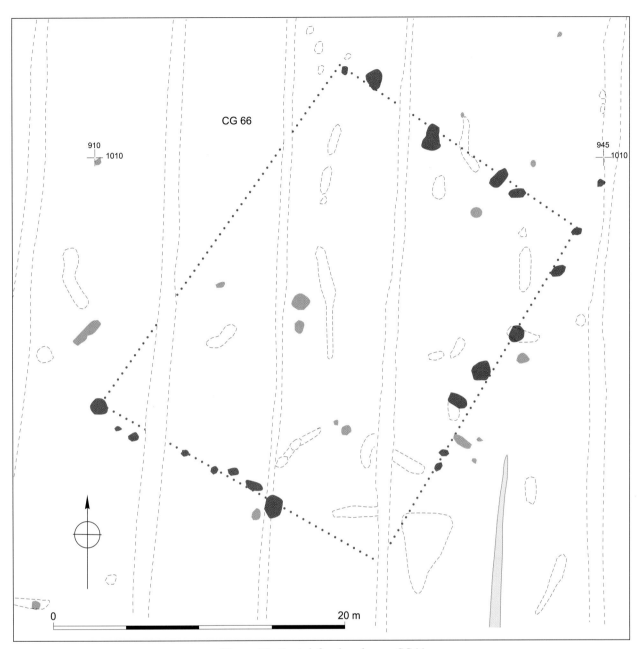

Figure 53. Post-defined enclosure CG66.

Two of these enclosed large sub-oval areas. One (CG67) measured some 36.00 × 32.00m and enclosed an area of approximately 825m². This had a funnel-shaped entrance on its southern side and appeared to have been cut by a substantial Late Bronze Age pit (CG2). Several postholes and possible pits were present within the enclosure, one set of postholes on the east side possibly separating off a small area within the enclosure. The second (CG68), measured some 45.00 × 35.00m and encompassed an area of approximately 1275m². This had a somewhat flattened southwest side with an entrance in it. The eastern side was poorly defined and no posts could be assigned here with any confidence. This may reflect truncation of the postholes in this area or indicate that it was attached to

the field boundary located on this side; a suggestion which may be supported by the presence of an entrance through the field boundary at this point which would have provided access into the enclosure. The enclosure contained a sub-rectangular post-built building (CG64) and two large waterholes (CG6 and 7).

Comparable sized enclosures have been identified at Hornchurch, Essex where two sub-circular examples were recorded (Enclosures C and D; Guttmann and Last 2000, 332–5). These were more fully excavated and better preserved than the examples at Kemerton and produced evidence for the deposition of placed deposits. It was also observed that the circuits (even allowing for truncation) appeared incomplete and it was suggested that they might

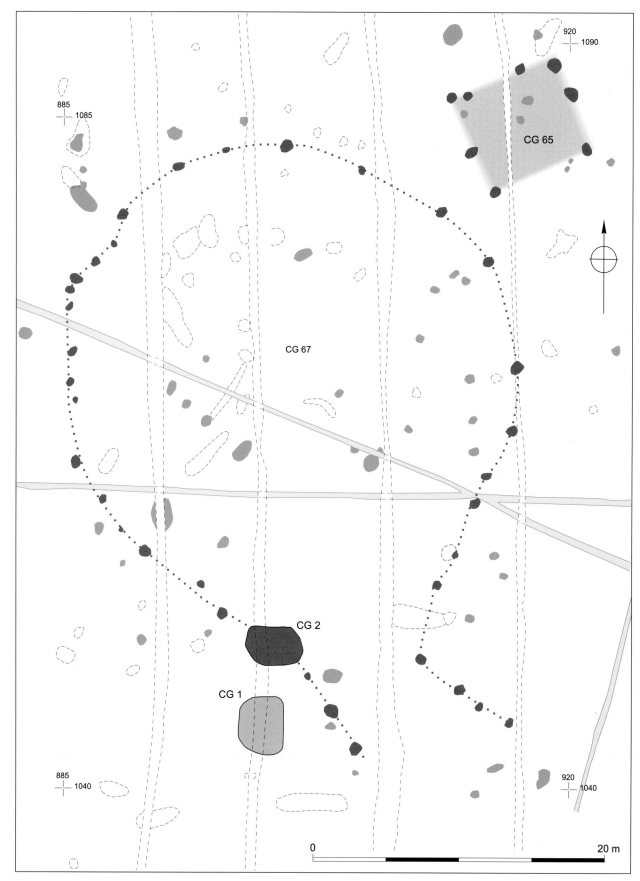

Figure 54. Post-defined enclosure CG67.

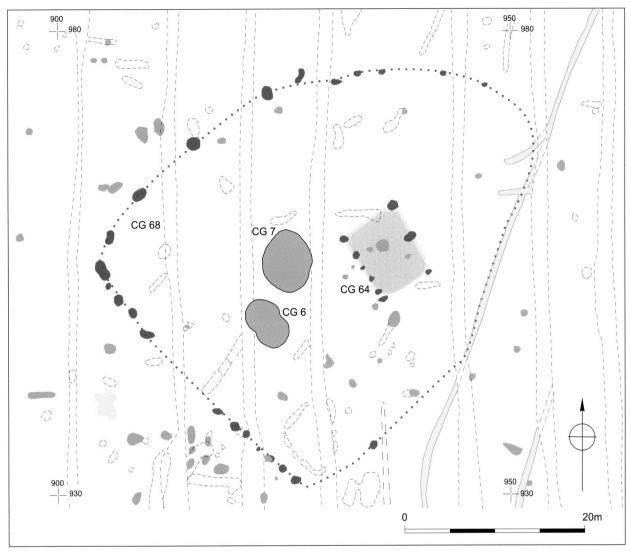

Figure 55. Post-defined enclosure CG68 and Rectilinear structure CG64.

not have formed substantial physical barriers. At Kemerton, there is no evidence for placed deposits in the postholes and it is felt more likely that the enclosures had a more utilitarian function as stock enclosures or stockyards; perhaps having supported hurdles and possibly being accompanied by, or reflecting the laying out of, hedges which would have provided more substantial barriers. The presence of two waterholes and a small posthole structure in CG68 provide some support for this suggestion since water would be required by the enclosed stock and some animals may have required shelter or separation from the rest of the herd or flock. However, there is a possibility that material in the large pits and waterholes closely associated with these enclosures does represent placed deposits. In particular it may be significant that one of the pits (CG1), associated with Enclosure CG67, and both of the waterholes, associated with CG68, were located close to the enclosure entrances and included the largest

concentrations of metalworking debris recovered from the site. Elsewhere, such an association of metalworking debris (and metalwork) with entrance areas of enclosures and even houses has been noted in the Late Prehistoric and Iron Age periods as at Springfield Lyons, Essex (Buckley and Hedges 1987) and Gussage All Saints, Dorset (Wainwright 1971).

The third large enclosure at Kemerton (CG66) was less well-defined, comprising only three sides of an apparently rectilinear enclosure measuring some 27.00 × 22.00m (*c.* 600m²). No internal structures were defined and no ready parallels have been identified, although the field enclosures at Chigborough Farm in the Blackwater Estuary, Essex (Wallis and Waughman 1998 cited in Guttmann and Last 2000) may be comparable.

In the light of the different form of each of the three enclosures, different functions might be represented but either enclosure or exclusion of stock seems liable to have been an important factor.

Enclosure: Context Group 66 (Fig 53)

Grid   0930/1000

Enclosure consisting of postholes with an average diameter of 0.59m defining three sides of an area measuring some 27.00m × 22.00m. None of the postholes was excavated. In plan, those forming the northeast and southeast sides of the enclosure were well-defined and consistently exhibited dark, to very dark grey brown fills flecked with charcoal. The southwestern side was less well-defined and in plan the fills were only recorded as being dark brown to brown mottled deposits. The northwestern side appeared open but the area was heavily truncated and this may account for this absence as well as the poor definition of the enclosure's southwest side. Alternatively the northwest side of the enclosure may have been formed by a hedge. Similar factors may account for the apparent gap in the south corner, although the possibility should not be excluded that this formed a wide entrance into the enclosure. The enclosure fell on a northeast to southwest axis and thus was aligned with elements of the ditches comprising the Bronze Age field system (especially those of FS2, see Figs 16 and 17).

Enclosure: Context Group 67 (Fig. 54)

Grid   0900/1065

A large, sub-oval enclosure, measuring approximately 36 × 32m in size and having an entrance to the south. The postholes defining the enclosure were generally dark brown or dark grey brown and averaged 0.42m in diameter. The enclosure was well-defined on its west side and around its north edge where many of the posts lay within 2.00–3.00m of each other. It was less clearly defined to the east possibly reflecting heavier truncation; however, surviving posts still were typically only about 4.00–5.00m apart. The posts forming the entrance provided a slightly funnel-shaped approach into the enclosure. None of the posts were excavated.

A number of postholes encompassed by the enclosure may represent internal structures or divisions. Two large pits were present in the vicinity; one was a largely sterile basin-shaped pit (CG2) sited on the line of the enclosure, the other, located just outside of the enclosure adjacent to its entrance was a bowl-shaped pit (CG1) with a wealth of material culture in its upper fills. These may both be contemporary with use of the enclosure; CG2 possibly having held water in the wetter months of the year and CG1 potentially having placed deposits including metalworking debris within its abandonment fills.

Enclosure: Context Group 68 (Fig. 55)

Grid   0925/0955

Substantial enclosure measuring some 45.00 × 35.00m. None of the postholes was excavated but in plan these varied considerably in size and fill; from 0.40m to 1.00m diameter and from reddish grey-brown through to very dark grey-brown. Many fills were heavily charcoal-flecked but no finds were noted.

The southwest side was the best-defined section of the enclosure circuit comprising 12 postholes, spaced at approximately 2.00m intervals. These formed a fairly straight alignment some 32.00m in length with a 10.00m wide entrance located opposite two substantial waterholes (CG6 and 7) and a rectilinear structure (CG64), situated within the enclosure. The northwest and north facing sections of the enclosure were also fairly well-defined comprising 10 rather unevenly spaced postholes describing a gentle arc. The remainder of the enclosure circuit (the east side) was less certain with only a solitary posthole located on its projected alignment, suggesting that this side was probably formed by the field boundary ditch sited in the area (part of FS2, Fig.17) and possibly an accompanying hedge. Certainly there appears to be a ditch defined entrance through this field boundary which could have provided access into the enclosure.

Isolated postholes (Fig. 16)

A number of well-defined, but apparently isolated, postholes were identified which were characterised by the presence of datable material and/or packing stones. In some respects these are similar to the isolated small pits/posts discussed previously; however, do not have the distinct finds rich fills of the latter.

These can most probably be interpreted as the sole surviving postholes of otherwise fully truncated structures, although the possibility that they represent a form of feature based on a single post, such as a marker post, should not be excluded.

Context Group 29 (Fig. 16)

Grid	0783/1021
Cut	2114
Fills	2112, 2113
Plan	Sub-circular
Profile	U-shaped
Dimensions	0.90 × 0.80 × 1.00m

Small vertical-sided cut located towards the west end of the investigated area. This had possibly been lined or had been rapidly filled after excavation since there was no evidence of weathering. A lower fill was a dark grey-brown loamy clay (2113) and this contained charcoal flecking, fired clay fragments, gravel and burnt stone. This was overlain by an upper fill (2112) which was paler, sandier and more compact. Pottery (4 sherds), bone (16 fragments) and part of a possibly pyramidal ceramic weight were recovered from these fills. The proportions and character of this feature support interpretation as a substantial but isolated posthole.

Posthole: Context Group 32 (Fig. 16)

Grid	0831/1059
Fill/cut	2029
Plan	Sub-circular
Profile	U-shaped
Dimensions	0.50 × 0.20m

Well-defined but isolated cut located towards the west end of the investigated area, with a single dark grey, compact, sandy clay loam fill flecked with charcoal. This contained some pottery (4 sherds, 2 from a fine bowl), a stone weight, bone (4 fragments) and burnt limestone.

Posthole: Context Group 33 (Fig. 16)

Grid	1043/1005
Fill/cut	1408
Plan	Sub-oval
Profile	Bowl-shaped
Dimensions	1.10 × 0.80 × 0.20m

Sub-oval feature located in southeast corner of the investigated area. This had a bowl-shaped depression at its south end within which a post appears to have been set. The fill contained burnt limestone, daub and charcoal but no artefacts. The feature may represent a small pit; however, more probably provided a setting for a large post set at the south end and packed with limestone.

Posthole: Context Group 34 (Fig. 16)

Grid	0819/1059
Fill/cut	2030
Plan	Sub-oval
Profile	U-shaped
Dimensions	0.60 × 0.42 × 0.20m

Well-defined but isolated cut with a single, compact, mid grey, clay loam fill flecked with charcoal. Contained pottery (3 sherds), bone (3 fragments) and burnt limestone.

Posthole: Context Group 35 (Fig. 16)

Grid	1081/1082
Fill/cut	1501
Plan	Lobed linear
Profile	Stepped/U-shaped
Dimensions	2.34 × 1.10 × 0.80m

Irregular, broadly linear, lobed feature disturbed on its eastern edge by a land-drain. Excavation revealed this to be a shallow irregular cut with a well-defined posthole on its east side. The latter measured 0.80 × 0.60 and was U-shaped in profile. The posthole was packed with burnt limestone and contained charcoal, pottery and flint. This feature is adjacent to CG36 and lies within a cluster of unassigned, unexcavated and rather indeterminate features at the east end of the investigated area; however, it does not form part of any readily identifiable structure.

POSTHOLE: CONTEXT GROUP 90 (FIG. 16)

Grid	0860/1066
Fill/cut	2042/2041
Plan	Sub-circular
Profile	U-shaped
Dimensions	0.58 × 0.45m

Well-defined posthole located near the north boundary of the investigated area but not forming part of any obvious structure. This had a dark grey brown upper fill with abundant charcoal and a less charcoal-rich paler lower fill containing burnt limestone fragments. The latter may represent packing for a post. Pottery (5 sherds), flint (2 flakes), bone (12 fragments) and a quantity of charred cereal were present.

Iron Age, Roman, medieval and later activity (by Mike Napthan)

The investigated area was notable for the highly limited range of activity represented post-dating the Late Bronze Age occupation. Both Iron Age and Romano-British settlement sites have been recorded to the north and south, however, with the exception of a couple of boundary features which potentially date to this period, certain evidence was limited to a handful of sherds of Roman pottery present as residual material in the modern ploughsoil. The boundary features were aligned on a north-south axis and could also relate to medieval activity, being similarly aligned to medieval ridge and furrow cultivation features, which had heavily affected the site. Although no longer visible as earthworks due to truncation by recent cultivation, these had clearly been a visible component of the local landscape until recently, 19th and 20th century ceramic land-drains having been laid along the base of many of the furrows.

Part 3.
Artefactual evidence

Prehistoric pottery (by Ann Woodward and Robin Jackson)

Introduction

A total of 4392 sherds weighing 33,043g (av. sherd weight 7.52g) were recovered through hand collection (numerous crumbs and small fragments from environmental residues were not included in the analysis). Of these, 29 sherds were of Roman, medieval or post-medieval date. A total of 354 belonged to Late Neolithic or Early Bronze Age traditions. The remainder, and most substantial portion, of the assemblage, 4009 sherds, dated to the Late Bronze Age period. Overall there were 333 rim sherds, 251 base angles and 18 diagnostic wall profiles.

The Late Neolithic, Beaker and Early Bronze Age assemblage provides an important contribution to the local and regional corpora. The association of much of this material in sealed pit groups along with other contemporary finds categories such as flintwork is especially noteworthy. Several vessels were associated with a small quantity of highly calcined bone recovered from a recut section of a ring-ditch and which may represent a disturbed cremation deposit (5 vessels from CG 79, context 1814).

The Late Bronze Age assemblage comes from a series of rich deposits in sealed context groups. It is one of the largest such assemblages excavated in the country and is of very great significance being comparable with the assemblages from Tinney's Lane (Tyler and Woodward 2009; 13,839 sherds), Reading Business Park (Moore and Jennings 1992: 7100 sherds), Green Park (Brossler, Early and Allen 2004: 3901 sherds), Aldermaston (Bradley *et al.* 1980: 6849 sherds) and Brean Down (Bell 1990: 4425 sherds). The nearest sizeable group derives from Shorncote in Gloucestershire, and dates from slightly later within the Late Bronze Age. Here, three phases of investigation of

areas of Late Bronze Age activity have recovered 745, 794 and 290 sherds respectively (Hearne and Heaton 1994; Hearne and Adam 1999; Brossler *et al.* 2002).

Methodology

The pottery was recorded by pro forma and data entered on an Excel spreadsheet by Robin Jackson, according to the Prehistoric Ceramics Research Group guidelines (PCRG 1992). The fabric and form series was established by both authors in consultation with Derek Hurst, and sherds representative of the main fabric groupings were analysed petrologically by Dr David Williams (this volume).

All tabulations and graphs were prepared using Excel software by Robin Jackson (Tables 4–11; Figures 58, 77–80; and Appendix 1). The text was prepared by Ann Woodward with descriptions of the illustrated sherds (Figures 56–57, 59–76) and other contributions by Robin Jackson. Identification of some of the later Neolithic/ Early Bronze Age pottery was facilitated by discussion with Dr Alex Gibson.

A very high proportion (86%) of the Late Bronze Age pottery derived from a series of pits and waterholes, which contained 100 or more sherds each (Table 4). Almost all of the prehistoric pottery was stratified; mainly in the pits and waterholes, but also in ditches, structural postholes, small pits and a ring-ditch. The distribution of Late Neolithic and Early Bronze Age material will be described below.

The types of context which produced Late Bronze Age pottery groups of less than 100 sherds are shown in Table 5.

Fabric

A series of 29 fabric types was defined macroscopically during the period of analysis. These were subsequently grouped into 14 categories, A to N, and 21 samples were

Table 4. Pottery: Count and weight data (major groups).

CG	Data	1828	1830	1831	1834	1836	1837	1838	1839	1840	1841	1842	1843	1848	1853	1854	1855	2032	2036	2037	2060	Total
1	Qty	14	607	1												5						627
	Wt (g)	38	2255	30												30						2353
4	Qty																		565		33	598
	Wt (g)																		6778		130	6908
5	Qty																			108	13	121
	Wt (g)																			374	354	728
6	Qty					369	52			39		12										472
	Wt (g)					4013	378			652		110										5153
7	Qty			157				4	4		84		122	49	95		13					528
	Wt (g)			1268				58	154		1412		912	527	627		387					5345

CG	Data	1102	1103	1104	1111	1216	1242	1243	1438	1439	1440	1517	1601	1801	1810	1814	2010	2011	2013	2043	2101	Total
8	Qty	11	74	7																		92
	Wt (g)	50	237	30																		317
9	Qty				404																	404
	Wt (g)				3809																	3809
10	Qty																130					130
	Wt (g)																1024					1024
11	Qty																	58				58
	Wt (g)																	337				337
12	Qty																			108		108
	Wt (g)																			632		632
14	Qty																				132	132
	Wt (g)																				512	512
17	Qty											198										198
	Wt (g)											1258										1258
19	Qty												66									66
	Wt (g)												294									294
25	Qty					40	8	4														52
	Wt (g)					242	57	14														313
39	Qty													94								94
	Wt (g)													429								429
79	Qty														1	96						97
	Wt (g)														4	243						247
91	Qty								32	10	201											243
	Wt (g)								160	58	1311											1529
92	Qty																		50			50
	Wt (g)																		180			180
Overall total: major groups																						**4070**
Overall weight: major groups																						**31368**

Table 5. Pottery: Count and weight data (lesser groups; by group type).

Feature type	No. of features	Sherd count	Av. sherd wt (g)
Waterholes	3	136	3.46
Basin-shaped pits	3	105	4.42
Bowl-shaped pits	2	73	5.16
Small pits/posts	5	210	4.71
Hearths/ovens	1	2	1
Postbuilt structures	2	4	3
Fences	1	3	2.67
Isolated posts	5	20	4 @ 3.5 1 @ 20
Ditches/gullies	3	3	1.67

submitted for petrological analysis (see below). Three of the groups (A to C) related to Late Neolithic and Early Bronze Age material while the remaining 11 groups (D to N) were Late Bronze Age in character.

The fabrics are described in outline, arranged by group, and with their proportional occurrence expressed as percentages of the total assemblage by sherd count (Figures derived from Appendix 1: Tables 1 and 2). The system of codes mainly derives from the Worcestershire County Council pottery fabric series, with site-specific sub-divisions and new codes added as necessary. Full descriptions for new fabrics have been produced by Derek Hurst and along with those few fabrics already recorded a full list is presented in Appendix 2.

GROUP A. LATE NEOLITHIC AND LATE BRONZE AGE (1%)
Fabric 5.8. Quartzite (1%)

GROUP B. BEAKER (7%)
Fabric 5.3. Quartz sand and grog (3%)
Fabric 5.7. Quartz and limestone (2%)

Fabric 5.9. Quartz sand   (1%)
Fabric 139. Grog   (1%)

GROUP C. EARLY BRONZE AGE (1%)

Fabric 4.12. Shell   (1%)
Fabric 5.13. Quartz sand   (< 1%)

Palaeozoic limestone: small fragments, unidentifiable to sub-group: fabric 4.8 (1%)

GROUP D. LATE BRONZE AGE: FINE PALAEOZOIC LIMESTONE (5%)

Fabric 4.8.3.   (3%)
Fabric 4.8.6.   (2%)

GROUP E. LATE BRONZE AGE: MEDIUM TO COARSE PALAEOZOIC LIMESTONE (8%)

Fabric 4.8.1.   (5%)
Fabric 4.8.2.   (3%)

GROUP F. LATE BRONZE AGE: VESICULAR PALAEOZOIC LIMESTONE (7%)

Fabric 4.8.4.   (7%)
Fabric 4.8.5.   (< 1%)

Shell: small fragments, unidentifiable to sub-group: fabric 4.9 (7%)

GROUP G. LATE BRONZE AGE: FINE SHELL (9%)

Fabric 4.9.1.   (9%)

GROUP H. LATE BRONZE AGE: MEDIUM TO COARSE SHELL (19%)

Fabric 4.9.2.   (16%)
Fabric 4.9.3   (3%)

GROUP I. LATE BRONZE AGE: VESICULAR SHELL (11%)

Fabric 4.9.4.   (11%)

GROUP J. LATE BRONZE AGE: SHELL AND GROG (6%)

Fabric 4.7.   (6%)

GROUP K. LATE BRONZE AGE: FINE QUARTZ (SAND) (< 1%)

Fabric 5.10.   (< 1%)

GROUP L. LATE BRONZE AGE: SAND AND LIMESTONE (11%)

Fabric 4.10.1.   (3%)
Fabric 4.10.2.   (2%)
Fabric 5.11.   (3%)
Fabric 5.12.   (3%)

GROUP M. LATE BRONZE AGE: SHELL AND QUARTZITE (1%)

Fabric 4.11.   (1%)

GROUP N. LATE BRONZE AGE: IGNEOUS/METAMORPHIC (< 1%)

Fabric 97 (indeterminate)   (< 1%)

The petrological analysis provided confirmation of the main fabric groupings defined during the programme of ceramic recording, and has produced information concerning the probable source of many of the types of inclusion encountered.

The inclusions in the Late Neolithic ware with quartzite filler possibly derived from Triassic sandstones, located west of the site. The Beaker fabrics contain varying mixtures of grog, local Triassic sandstone and local Jurassic shelly limestone. The Early Bronze Age fabrics include one with shelly limestone and grog and another with sand, mica and iron oxide inclusions which cannot be sourced with certainty.

The fabrics of the Late Bronze Age assemblage fall into two main groups, containing respectively Jurassic fossil shell (46% of the total assemblage) and Palaeozoic shelly limestone (21% of the total assemblage). There are also smaller quantities which contain grog as well as shell, or Triassic sandstone. In addition there is a small, but significant, proportion containing fine sand with mica flecks and iron oxide. Finally there is a small quantity (less than 1%) of material containing dark igneous or metamorphic rock inclusions, which matched neither of the typically encountered Malvernian or Doleritic wares (Derek Hurst pers. comm), but for which a Malvernian source remains likely (Williams this volume).

Form

Very few upper vessel profiles and no complete sections could be reconstructed, so most aspects of form have been considered on the basis of rim and base morphology.

A series of four profile types, three base angle forms and 13 rim types were devised. These apply to the Late Neolithic and Early Bronze Age material as well as to the major Late Bronze Age assemblage. In the absence of a local form series for such assemblages the coding system has been developed specifically for the Kemerton site and will hopefully form the basis for future work in Worcestershire.

The percentage occurrences of the rim and base angle forms listed below represent the percentage of total rims in the assemblage, by number of sherds (see Appendix 1: Table 3). The main form types are illustrated in Figures 56 and 57.

PROFILE FORMS
P1   ovoid; *e.g.* Fig. 56.1 and 56.5
P2   necked; *e.g.* Fig. 56.3
P3   weak shoulder; *e.g.* Fig. 56.9
P4   angular shoulder; *e.g.* Fig. 59.3

BASE ANGLE FORMS
B1   simple; *e.g.* Fig. 57.11; 32%

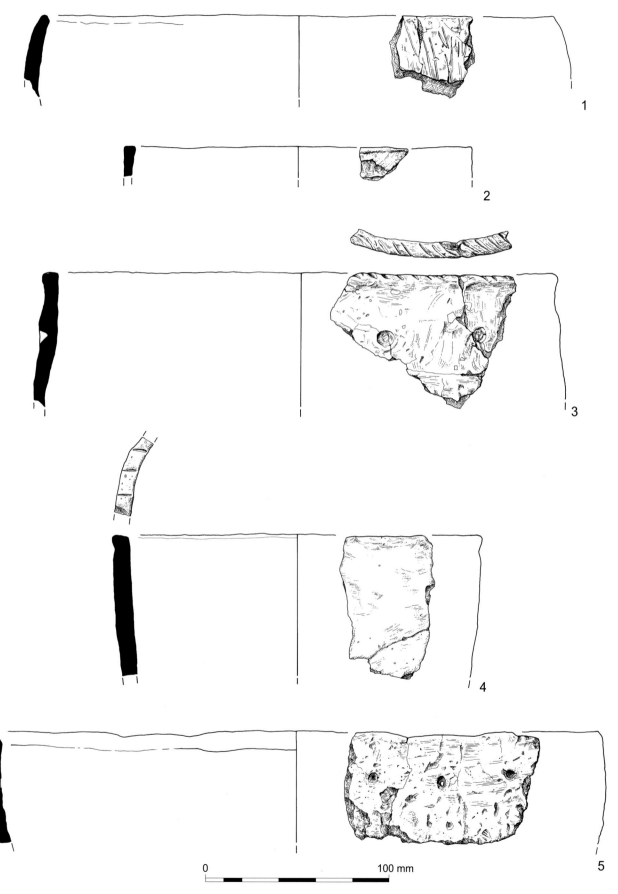

Figure 56. Form series (nos 1–5).

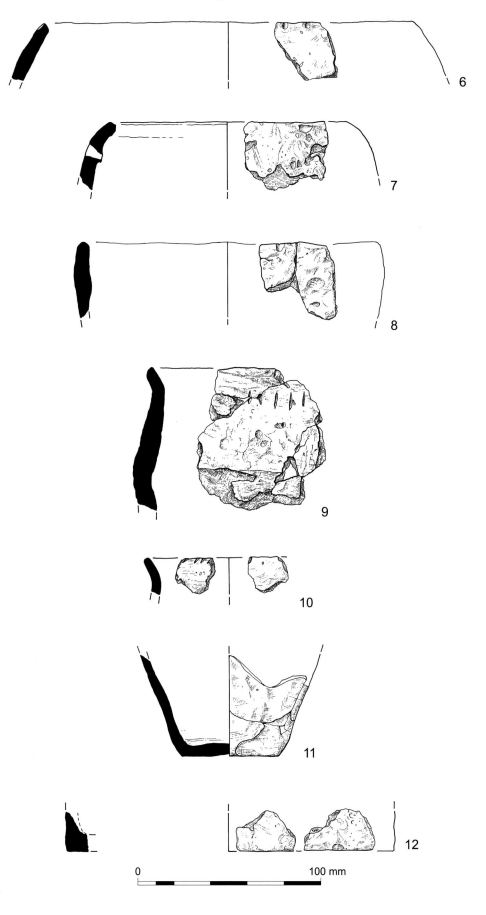

Figure 57. Form series (nos 6–12).

B2   expanded externally; *e.g.* Fig. 69.53; 51%
B3   expanded externally with row of thumb-prints; *e.g.* Fig. 57.12; 69.55; 17%

RIM FORMS

R1   simple, vertical; *e.g.* Fig. 56.1; 32%
R2   simple, flared; *e.g.* Fig. 60.5; 7%
R3   flat top, grooved; *e.g.* Fig. 70.57; <1%
R4   flat top, straight; *e.g.* Fig. 56.2; 11%
R5   flat top, externally expanded, slight neck; *e.g.* Fig. 56.3; 2%
R6   internal rim bevel; *e.g.* Fig. 56.4 and 5; 14%
R7   hook rim; *e.g.* Fig. 57.6–57.8; 20%
R8   everted, simple; *e.g.* Fig. 57.9–57.10; 7%
R9   everted, piecrust; *e.g.* Figs. 67.49 and 74.77; 2%
R10   externally expanded, straight; not illustrated; <1%
R11   T-shaped, flat; *e.g.* Fig. 74.78; 2%
R12   T-shaped, simple; *e.g.* Fig. 68.51; 1%
R13   flat top, internally expanded; *e.g.* Fig. 68.50; 2%

Where overall profiles could be determined they tend to be of simple ovoid outline. Necked vessels are very rare, except in the Beaker assemblage. The most common rim form is the simple straight variety R1. The next most common rims forms are the hook rim and internal rim bevel, R6 and R7; these are particularly characteristic of Late Bronze Age assemblages throughout the country. The only other rim form that occurs to a significant degree is the flat-topped straight category, R4. The base angle forms are dominated by the externally expanded varieties B2 and B3. Again these are found particularly within assemblages of Late Bronze Age date.

Form series (Figures 56 and 57)

1. Simple vertical rim, R1, fabric 4.9.1 (group G), context 2029, CG32
2. Straight rim with flat top, R4, fabric 4.9.1 (group G), context 511, CG18
3. Flat topped, externally expanded rim, slight neck, R5, decorated with diagonal incised lines on outer edge of rim, D12, and row of part perforations, D16, fabric 4.9.1 (group G), context 2029, CG32
4. Internal rim bevel, R6, with diagonal incised lines on top of rim, D11, fabric 4.8.2 (group E), context 1841, CG7
5. Rim with internal bevel, R6, decorated with a row of perforations, D15, fabric 4.9.4 (group I), context 1604, CG23
6. Hook rim, R7, decorated with fingertip or fingernail impressions on outer edge of rim, D2, fabric 4.10.2 (group L), context 1853, CG7
7. Hook rim, R7, with row of perforations, D15, fabric 4.8.4 (group F), context 1801, CG39
8. Hook rim, R7, fabric 4.8.3 (group D), context 511, CG18
9. Everted, simple rim, R8, with fingertip or fingernail impressions in neck, D3, weak shoulder, P3, fabric 4.9.4 (group I), context 1604, CG23
10. Everted, simple rim, R8, decorated with diagonal incised lines on top of rim, D11, fabric 4.7 (group J), context 1510, CG37
11. Simple base, B1, fabric 5.10 (group K), context 1801, CG39
12. Base angle expanded externally with row of thumb-prints, B3, fabric 4.8.1 (group E), context 1801, CG39

Decoration

A series of 19 decoration codes were used during the detailed recording of the assemblage. These have been divided into seven groups as listed below. The percentage occurrences are percentages of the total number of decorated sherds (Appendix 1: Table 4). The sum of the percentages exceeds 100% as some sherds carry more than one type of decoration.

GROUP A: FINGER IMPRESSIONS ON RIM

D1   Fingertip or fingernail impressions on top of rim. 3%
D2   Fingertip or fingernail impressions on outer edge of rim. 1%

GROUP B: FINGER IMPRESSIONS AT NECK AND SHOULDER

D3   Fingertip or fingernail impressions in neck. 4%
D4   Fingertip or fingernail impressions on shoulder. 3%

GROUP C: IMPRESSED AND INCISED MOTIFS, MAINLY BEAKER

D5   All over fingertip or fingernail impressions. 4%
D6   Whipped cord impressed 'maggots'. 1%
D7   Long rectangular tooth-comb impressions. 3%
D8   Short rectangular tooth-comb impressions. 9%
D9   Point tooth-comb impressions. 2%
D13   Incised linear motifs. 11%
D14   Stab and drag. <1%
D21   Stabbed dots <1%

GROUP D: INCISED DECORATION ON RIM

D11   Diagonal incised lines on top of rim. 2%
D12   Diagonal incised lines on outer edge of rim. 1%

GROUP E: PERFORATIONS EXECUTED PRIOR TO FIRING

D15   Row of perforations. 18%
D16   Row of part perforations. 7%

GROUP F: FINGER FINISHES

D10   Shallow finger grooving. 8%
D17   Finger smearing. 5%
D18   Smoothed surface. 7%
D19   Fine line smearing. 15%

GROUP G: APPLIED DECORATION

D20   Applied cordon. 1%

The main concentration of decoration occurred on the Beaker sherds. Amongst these the most common technique of decoration utilised is short rectangular tooth-comb impressions. Within the Late Bronze Age assemblage the most common decorative types involved rows of perforations and various finger applied surface finishes. Finger impressed decoration located on rims, necks or shoulders is relatively rare.

Form and fabric

Detailed tabulations displaying the correlations by number of sherds and weight between form and fabric, form and decoration, and between form, decoration and sherd

Table 6. Pottery: Occurrence of decoration (by form).

Dec	Data	B1	B2	B3	P3	P4	R1	R2	R3	R4	R5	R6	R7	R8	R9	R10	R11	R12	R13	Total
D1	Qty											7	5							12
	Wt (g)											126	36							162
D2	Qty						2					1	2							5
	Wt (g)						18					2	26							46
D3	Qty													12						12
	Wt (g)													94						94
D3/P3	Qty													5						5
	Wt (g)													40						40
D4	Qty				9															9
	Wt (g)				106															106
D5	Qty				5		4													9
	Wt (g)				24		50													74
D5/D12	Qty												1							1
	Wt (g)												28							28
D8	Qty							5												5
	Wt (g)							33												33
D9	Qty							1												1
	Wt (g)							2												2
D15	Qty						12	12		6		14	16		1			2		63
	Wt (g)						106	16		64		200	164		6			94		650
D16	Qty						4						3		4					11
	Wt (g)						82						24		142					248
D16/13	Qty						4													4
	Wt (g)						42													42
D17	Qty												2							2
	Wt (g)												132							132
D18	Qty		7							4										11
	Wt (g)		44							54										98
D19	Qty	11					2			2										15
	Wt (g)	110					14			20										144
none	Qty	69	118	41	1	3	78	1		28	3	20	35	2		1	6		7	413
	Wt (g)	1086	2128	853	2	44	704	8		130	26	126	238	26		12	48		54	5485
Total Qty		81	129	41	15	3	108	22	1	36	6	49	65	23	7	1	6	2	7	602
Total Wt (g)		1242	2346	853	132	44	1048	79	4	214	32	618	664	232	172	12	48	94	54	7888

Total number of decorated rims = 145

Total number of decorated bases = 23

Total number of decorated body shreds = 293

thickness were prepared (Tables 6–8; Appendix 1: Tables 5–8). Considering the whole assemblage as a single group, there are no clear correlations between any particular fabric groups and form types (Appendix 1: Table 5), or between fabric groups and styles of decoration (Appendix 1: Table 6), apart from the concentration of comb-decorated techniques within the Beaker fabric group, B.

Table 7. Pottery: Occurrence of abrasion (whole site).

	Abrasion						
	0	1	1/2	2	2/3	3	Total
Qty	166	186	2	3136	167	735	4392
Wt (g)	399	1500	2	27740	365	3037	33043

1 = Fresh
2 = Slightly abraded
3 = Very abraded

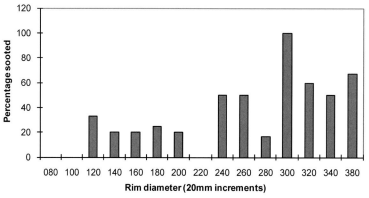

Figure 58. Occurrence of internal residues on rims.

Table 8. Occurrence of internal residues (whole site; by fabric).

Fabric	Fabric group	Data	Internal residue no	yes	Total
4	N/A	Qty	171	0	171
		Wt (g)	91	0	91
4.7	J	Qty	241	0	241
		Wt (g)	1208	0	1208
4.8	N/A	Qty	47	0	47
		Wt (g)	36	0	36
4.8.1	E	Qty	114	120	234
		Wt (g)	811	1431	2242
4.8.2	E	Qty	98	35	133
		Wt (g)	798	255	1053
4.8.3	D	Qty	113	21	134
		Wt (g)	1194	206	1400
4.8.4	F	Qty	102	186	288
		Wt (g)	443	862	1305
4.8.5	F	Qty	12	0	12
		Wt (g)	79	0	79
4.8.6	D	Qty	86	2	88
		Wt (g)	380	8	388
4.9	N/A	Qty	295	2	297
		Wt (g)	432	12	444
4.9.1	G	Qty	254	150	404
		Wt (g)	1897	1515	3412
4.9.2	H	Qty	561	155	716
		Wt (g)	6883	2254	9137
4.9.3	H	Qty	116	20	136
		Wt (g)	1696	290	1986
4.9.4	I	Qty	241	246	487
		Wt (g)	1707	1658	3365
4.10.1	L	Qty	105	10	115
		Wt (g)	500	58	558
4.10.2	L	Qty	59	39	98
		Wt (g)	642	666	1308
4.11	M	Qty	39	20	59
		Wt (g)	254	270	524
4.12	C	Qty	27	0	27
		Wt (g)	249	0	249
5.3	B	Qty	99	17	116
		Wt (g)	448	38	486
5.7	B	Qty	93	2	95
		Wt (g)	302	4	306
5.8	A	Qty	47	0	47
		Wt (g)	237	0	237
5.9	B	Qty	56	0	56
		Wt (g)	301	0	301
5.10	K	Qty	12	0	12
		Wt (g)	50	0	50
5.11	L	Qty	117	26	143
		Wt (g)	977	303	1280
5.12	L	Qty	102	25	127
		Wt (g)	383	304	687
5.13	C	Qty	13	0	13
		Wt (g)	92	0	92
97	N	Qty	20	3	23
		Wt (g)	62	40	102
139	B	Qty	40	0	40
		Wt (g)	267	0	267
Total Qty			**3285**	**1079**	**4364**
Total Wt (g)			**22443**	**10174**	**32617**

Most types of decoration occurred on vessels with a wide range of rim, base and profile forms, but a few types did show strong patterning (Table 6). Fine line smearing (D19) occurred particularly on simple bases (B1), while fingertip impressed styles of decoration (D1–4) were strongly correlated with shouldered profiles (P3) and with internally bevelled and hooked rims (R6 and R7). There was no clear variation in sherd thickness amongst the specific rim, profile and base forms (Appendix 1: Table 7) or types of decoration (Appendix 1: Table 8).

Deposition and use

The degree of abrasion of the pottery was recorded using three categories: fresh, slightly abraded and very abraded. Overall, most of the pottery was only slightly abraded (71%), with 21% highly abraded and only 4% in fresh condition (Table 7). This may indicate that the pottery was broken and deposited, perhaps in a midden, for a short period of time, prior to the deposition of the fragments in the pits and waterholes.

The average sherd weight of fragments from the major context groups (predominantly waterholes and larger pits) varied from 3g to 12g, with an average value of nearly 8g (7.71g) and *c.* 10g in the waterholes (Table 4). These results are higher than those obtained for Late Bronze Age pottery from small pits, postholes, ditches and tree throws in which the average sherd weight was typically *c.* 5g or less (Table 5). This may suggest that the pottery in the waterholes and large pits possessed a different life history than the general settlement debris.

Where pit fills were separately excavated or where section drawings were produced following rapid half sectioning, it was evident that the upper (secondary) fills contained the bulk of the pottery and other finds, often along with large quantities of burnt stone. In contrast, the silty lower (primary) fills and slumping deposits contained few finds with the notable exception of the presence in at least two of the large waterholes (CG6, context 1840; and CG7, contexts 1841 and 1855) of substantial chunks of vessel bases which may have served to scoop up water.

Blackened deposits representing either sooting or more probably burnt food residues were commonly recorded on the internal surfaces of vessels. They occurred on 26% of the pottery by sherd count (Table 8). This was fairly common amongst the two main fabric types, shell and Palaeozoic limestone, and there was no significant difference between the finer and coarser versions of these fabrics. However, there was a tendency for the finer fabrics, belonging to groups D, K and L, not to display evidence of such residues (Table 8). The presence or absence of these residues was not significantly correlated with any particular form types (Appendix 1: Table 9), but a plot of the percentage occurrence of residues against rim diameter, which is a good indication of vessel capacity, show that these occurred mainly on vessels of larger size (Fig. 58). Although detailed recording of the location of these deposits on the interior of the vessels was not undertaken, a notably high proportion of base sherds (40% by count) exhibited internal residues. In conjunction with the observation that finer fabrics generally did not have residues, this suggests that the use of the larger vessels in the coarser, main fabric types was for food preparation.

Interestingly, although not formally recorded, external sooting was not apparent on many vessels and this may indicate use of 'pot boilers' to heat food rather than placement directly over a fire, a suggestion supported by the large quantities of burnt stone present in the pit fills (especially the bowl-shaped examples) associated with the majority of the pottery. A similar conclusion has been drawn for the Late Bronze Age assemblage from Green Park (Reading Business Park), although at that site internal residues were also uncommon (Morris in Brossler, Early and Allen 2004, 69).

The Neolithic assemblage (Fig. 59)

A single pit (context 1520) produced a number of sherds from different vessels of probable Neolithic date, while later Neolithic sherds from a single vessel were recovered as residual material in a Late Bronze Age pit (context 1801, CG39).

1. A single unabraded rim sherd from a plain vessel was found in Late Bronze Age context 1801, CG39. Grooved Ware. The tapered rim is from a globular vessel with a rim diameter of 180mm. The shape of the rim conforms best to Longworth's form 23 (Wainwright and Longworth 1971, 57, fig. 20) and the soapy fabric with grog and some calcareous material (fabric 5.7), in this case limestone, is typical for this style of late Neolithic pottery. 18 wall sherds in a similar fabric were also present and probably represent further elements of this vessel.

Context 1520 (CG38)

2. Wall sherd from rounded shoulder vessel with all over randomly executed fingernail decoration, D5. Fabric 5.8 (group A), context 1520, CG38. Tradition indeterminate, but probably Neolithic. A close parallel is present in the assemblage from Runnymede Bridge (Longworth and Varndell 1996, 100 and fig. 58.NP68); this was tentatively ascribed to the Peterborough Ware tradition of the Middle Neolithic
3. Two angular shoulder sherds, P4, fabric 5.9 (group A), context 1520, CG38
4. Three wall sherds, fabric 5.8 (group A), context 1520, CG38. Tradition indeterminate, but possibly Early or Middle Neolithic on the grounds of form and fabric.

The Beaker assemblage (Figs 60 and 61)

Groups of Beaker sherds were found in the main features dated to this period, three closely spaced pits (CG12, CG13, and CG42; Table 9). Smaller groups of abraded fragments were also found in a series of postholes and small pits, and, in addition, there were residual sherds from some of the Late Bronze Age pits and waterholes.

Decorated Beaker sherds were found in two Late Bronze Age waterhole fills (context 2032, CG4; context 1848, CG7): these are illustrated below along with the main vessels represented in the major groups. A plain rim sherd was found in a posthole of probable Beaker date (context 1816, CG84). Here there were two flat-topped rim sherds and two wall sherds with three different fabrics represented. Plain wall sherds apparently in Beaker fabrics were recovered from several small pit/posthole features, which are also considered liable to be Beaker in date (contexts 1210, CG82; 1705, CG85; 1823, CG83; 2055, CG94; and 2110, CG95). Further probable plain wall sherds were recorded in several Late Bronze Age contexts, both from larger pits (1103, CG8; 1438, CG91; and 1517, CG17), and smaller pits or postholes (context 1604, CG23; 1708, CG16; and 2042, CG90). Several sherds were also recovered from a cleaning layer (context 1828) and as unstratified material (1856).

Context 2043, CG12 (Fig. 60)

5. 4 rim sherds and 13 decorated wall fragments from a vessel with simple flared rim, R2, decorated with short rectangular tooth-comb impressions, D8, forming zones of parallel horizontal lines and lattice. Fabric 5.3 (group B)
6. 2 rim sherds and 17 decorated wall fragments from a vessel with a simple flared rim, R2, decorated with incised linear motifs, D13, forming rough horizontal lines apparently arranged in several irregular zones. Fabric 139 (group B)
7. Single, simple, flared rim sherd decorated with incised linear motifs, D13. Fabric 139 (group B)
8. 2 decorated wall sherds with two incised horizontal linear motifs, D13, with stabbed dots, D21, above and below,. Fabric 5.3 (group B)
9. 2 decorated wall sherds from a vessel with short rectangular tooth-comb impressed overlapping multiple chevrons, D8, and incised linear motifs, D13, forming two horizontal lines with lattice below. Fabric 5.3 (group B)
10. 3 decorated wall sherds from a vessel with short rectangular tooth-comb impressions, D8. Fabric 5.3 (group B)
11. 2 decorated wall sherds from a vessel with long rectangular tooth-comb impressions, D7, forming two distinct zones of horizontal lines. Fabric 5.3 (group B)
12. 1 decorated wall sherd from a vessel with whipped cord impressed 'maggots', D6, arranged in horizontal lines. Fabric 139 (group B)
13. Entire base, in 6 pieces, possibly from the same vessel as 2 above, simple base angle form, B1, centre of base raised. Fabric 139 (group B)
14. 2 simple base angle sherds, B1, possibly from the same vessel as 1 above. Fabric 5.3 (group B)
15. 4 simple base angle sherds, B1, probably from the same vessel as 6 above. Fabric 5.3 (group B)
16. 2 simple base angle sherds, B1. Fabric 5.7 (group B).

Context 2043 contained fragments from a minimum of eight different fineware vessels.

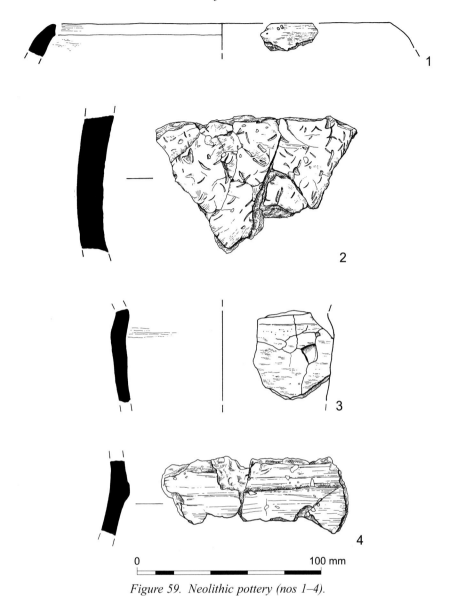

Figure 59. Neolithic pottery (nos 1–4).

Table 9. Composition of main Beaker pottery groups.

Context Group	context	number of sherds	rim	decorated wall	plain wall	base angle
12	2043	98	7	50	27	14
13	2046	17	1	9	7	-
42	2047	19	1	16	2	-

CONTEXT 2046, CG13 (FIG. 61)

17. 1 rim sherd from a vessel with a simple flared rim, R2, with short rectangular tooth-comb impressions, D8, forming a zone of horizontal lines and a single chevron below the rim. Fabric 5.3 (group B)

18. 1 decorated wall sherd from a vessel with point tooth-comb impressions, D9. Fabric 5.3 (group B)

19. 1 decorated wall sherd from a vessel with incised linear motifs, D13, forming three horizontal lines and a rough chevron motif below. Fabric 5.9 (group B).

CONTEXT 2047, CG42 (FIG. 61)

20. 8 decorated wall sherds from a vessel with short rectangular tooth-comb impressions, D8; motifs include horizontal lines and single chevron. Fabric 5.3 (group B)

21. 3 decorated wall sherds from a vessel with incised linear motifs, D13, forming multiple discontinuous chevrons. Fabric 5.3 (group B)

Not illustrated: 1 plain rim sherd and a wall sherd, decorated

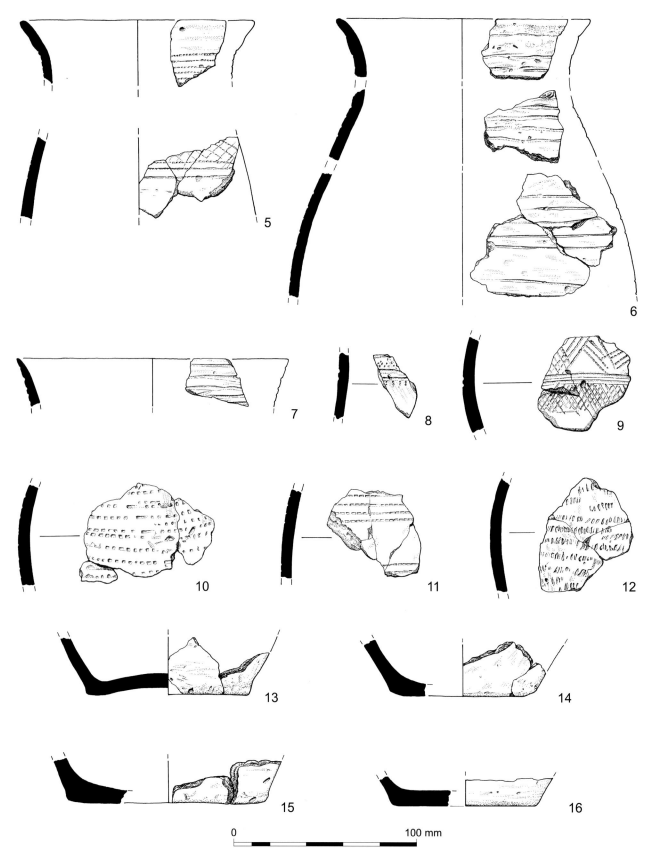

Figure 60. Beaker pottery (nos 5–16).

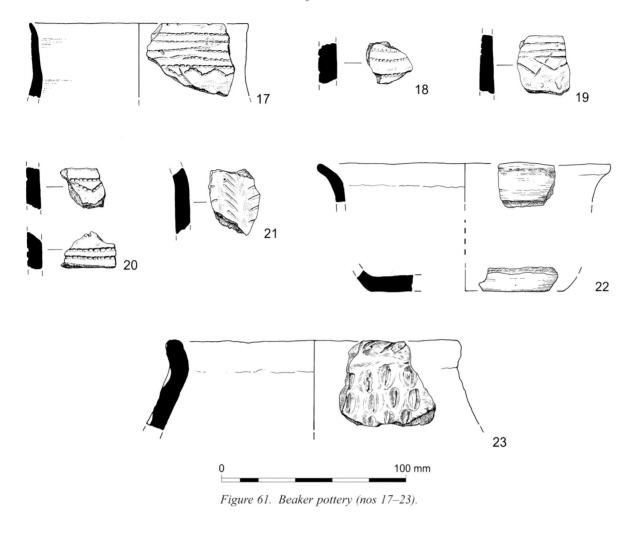

Figure 61. Beaker pottery (nos 17–23).

Figure 62. Early Bronze Age pottery (nos 24–26).

with a horizontal line and chevron in point tooth comb technique. Fabric 5.9 (group B)

OTHER CONTEXTS (FIG. 61)

22. 1 rim sherd and 1 base angle from a very fine vessel with an everted, simple rim, R8, and a simple base angle form, B1. Fabric 5.7 (group B), context 2032, CG4

23. Decorated rim sherd from a thick-walled domestic vessel with an everted, simple rim, R8, all-over fingertip or fingernail impressions, D5, and diagonal incised lines on outer edge of rim, D12. Fabric 4.9.2 (group H), context 1848, CG7.

The Early Bronze Age assemblage

Pottery of Early Bronze Age date was found in two features only. One context (1814) was a recut in the ring-ditch CG79; this contained the upper part of a small accessory vessel and was associated with cremated bone. The other material, fragments from a larger urn, was found in two different contexts (1836 and 1837) within a Late Bronze Age waterhole (CG6).

24. Upper portion, in 12 joining pieces, from an accessory vessel with a flat rim and a slightly ovoid profile. The deeply incised decoration comprises diagonal lines, possibly forming an irregular chevron design, below

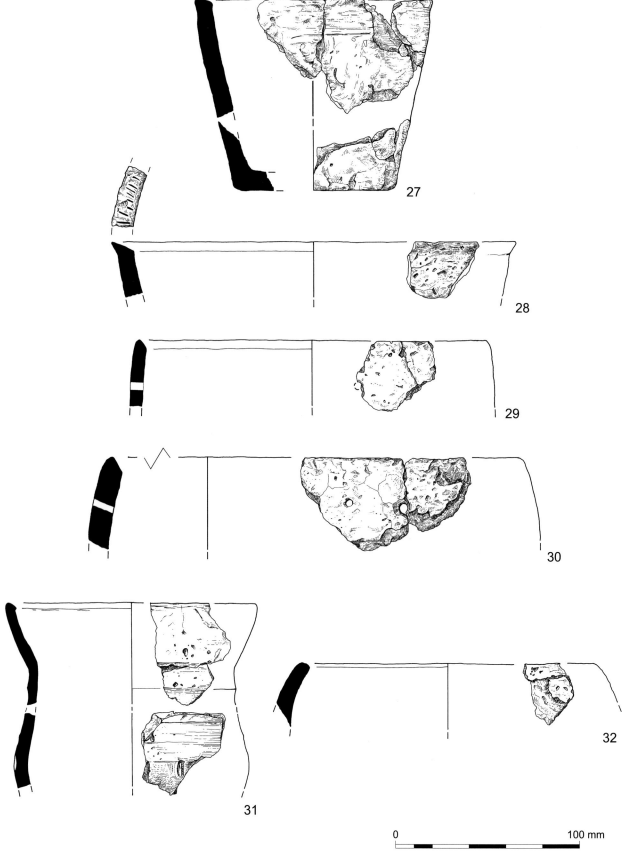

Figure 63. Late Bronze Age pottery from Pit CG1 (nos 27–32).

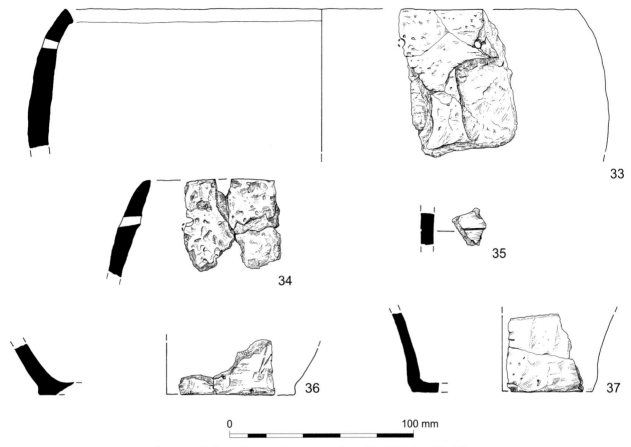

Figure 64. Late Bronze Age pottery from Pit CG1 (nos 33–37).

a single horizontal line. Fabric 5.9 (group B). Context 1814, CG79

25. Thick-walled plain rim sherd with an internal bevel, R6, diameter indeterminate. Fabric 4.12 (group C). Context 1837, CG6

26. Sharply angled plain shoulder sherd from a thick-walled vessel, probably the same as 25. Fabric 4.12 (group C). Context 1836, CG6.

The Late Bronze Age assemblage

Catalogue of illustrated vessels by major Context Group

The major rim and base forms have been illustrated and described above (Figs 56 and 57). In order to give an impression of the nature and variety of the individual groups of pottery from the large pit or waterhole assemblages further sets of vessels are illustrated below by context group.

CONTEXT GROUP 1: BOWL-SHAPED PIT (FIGS 63 AND 64)

27. 16 sherds from a vessel with internal rim bevel, R6, and externally expanded base, B2, fabric 4.9.1 (group G), context 1830

28. Vessel rim with internal bevel, R6, with fingernail impressions on top of rim, D1, fabric 4.9.4 (group I), context 1830

29. 2 sherds from a vessel with a rim with internal bevel, R6, and row of perforations, D15, fabric 4.8.4 (group F), context 1830

30. 2 sherds from a vessel with a rim with internal bevel, R6, and row of perforations, D15, fabric 4.9.4 (group I), context 1830

31. 3 rim sherds and 2 decorated wall sherds from a vessel with an internal rim bevel, R6, and a weak shoulder, P3. The shoulder has a row of fingernail impressions on it, D4, with shallow finger grooving just above, D10. Fabric 4.8.4 (group F), context 1830

32. 3 rim sherds from a hook rimmed vessel, R7, fabric 4.8.4 (group F), context 1830

33. 5 sherds from a hook rimmed vessel, R7, with a row of perforations, D15, fabric 4.9.4 (group I), context 1830

34. 3 sherds from a hook rimmed vessel, R7, with a row of perforations, D15, fabric 4.9.4 (group I), context 1830

35. Single body sherd, decorated with an incised linear motif, D13, fabric 4.8.6 (group D), context 1830

36. 5 sherds from a vessel with an externally expanded base, B2, fabric 4.8.6 (group D), context 1830

37. 2 sherds from a vessel with an externally expanded base, B2, fabric 4.8.4 (group F), context 1830.

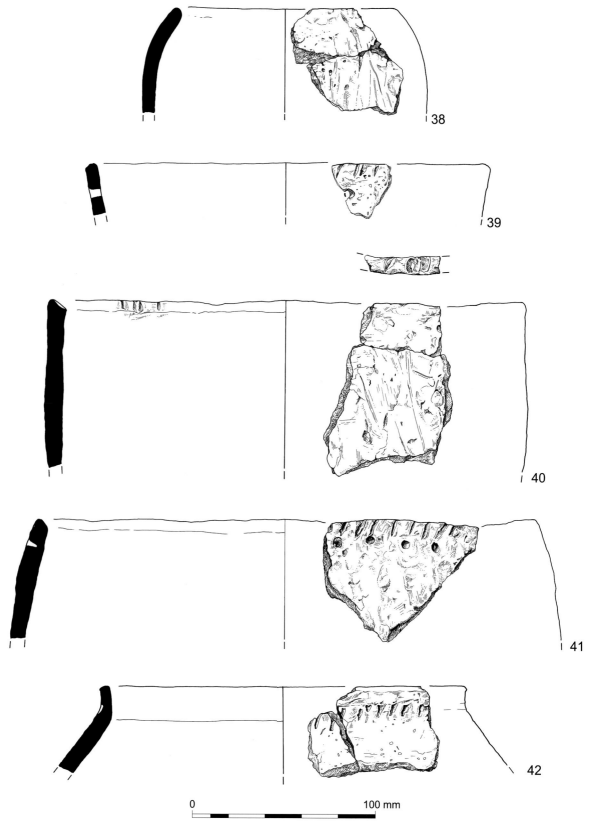

Figure 65. Late Bronze Age pottery from Waterhole CG4 (nos 38–42).

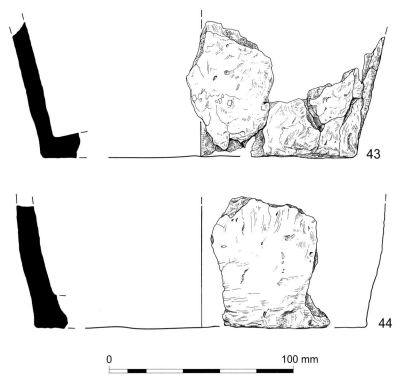

Figure 66. Late Bronze Age pottery from Waterhole CG4 (nos 43–44).

CONTEXT GROUP 4: WATERHOLE (FIGS 65 AND 66)

38. 2 sherds from a vessel with a simple, hook rim, R7, fabric 4.9.4 (group I), context 2032

39. Single sherd from a vessel with simple, vertical rim, R1, decorated with diagonal incised lines on outer edge of rim, D12, and row of perforations, D15, fabric 4.9.2 (group H), context 2032

40. 3 sherds from a vessel with a rim with an internal bevel, R6, and fingertip impressions on top of rim, D1, fabric 4.9.1 (group G), context 2032

41. Single sherd from a vessel with a rim with an internal bevel, R6, decorated with vertical shallow finger grooving, D10, a row of part perforations, D16, and diagonal incised lines on outer edge of rim, D12, fabric 4.9.2 (group H), context 2032

42. 2 sherds from a vessel with an everted, simple rim, R8, with stab and drag decoration immediately below rim, D14, fabric 4.9.2 (group H), context 2032

43. 8 sherds from a vessel with an externally expanded base, B2, fabric 4.9.4 (group I), context 2032

44. Single sherd from a vessel with an externally expanded base with row of thumb prints, B3, fabric 4.9.2 (group H), context 2032.

CONTEXT GROUP 6: WATERHOLE (FIGS 67, 68 AND 69)

45. 6 sherds from a vessel with a simple, vertical rim, R1, fabric 4.9.1 (group G), context 1836

46. Single rim sherd with internal bevel, R6, with fingertip or fingernail impressions on top of rim, D1, fabric 4.9.2 (group H), context 1836

47. Sherd from hook rimmed vessel, R7, with row of part perforations, D16, fabric 4.10.2 (group L), context 1836

48. Single sherd from vessel with a hook rim, R7, decorated with fingertip or fingernail impressions on its outer edge, D2, fabric 5.11 (group L), context 1836

49. 2 sherds from a vessel with an everted piecrust rim, R9, with a row of part perforations, D16, fabric 4.9.2 (group H), context 1836

50. 2 sherds from a vessel with a flat topped, internally expanded rim, R13, fabric 4.9.1 (group G), context 1836

51. 2 sherds from a vessel with a simple, T shaped rim, R12, decorated with row of perforations, D15, fabric 5.11 (group L), context 1836

52. Single sherd from a vessel with a flat topped, internally expanded rim, R13, fabric 5.11 (group L), context 1836

53. 19 sherds from a vessel with an externally expanded base, B2, fabric 4.8.1 (group E), context 1840

54. 5 sherds from a vessel with an externally expanded base, B2, fabric 4.9.2 (group H), context 1840

55. 5 sherds from a vessel with an externally expanded base with row of thumbprints, B3, fabric 4.9.1 (group G), context 1837.

CONTEXT GROUP 7: WATERHOLE (FIG. 70)

56. Single sherd from a vessel with a simple vertical rim, R1, fabric 4.9.2 (group H), context 1834

57. Single sherd from a vessel with a flat topped, grooved

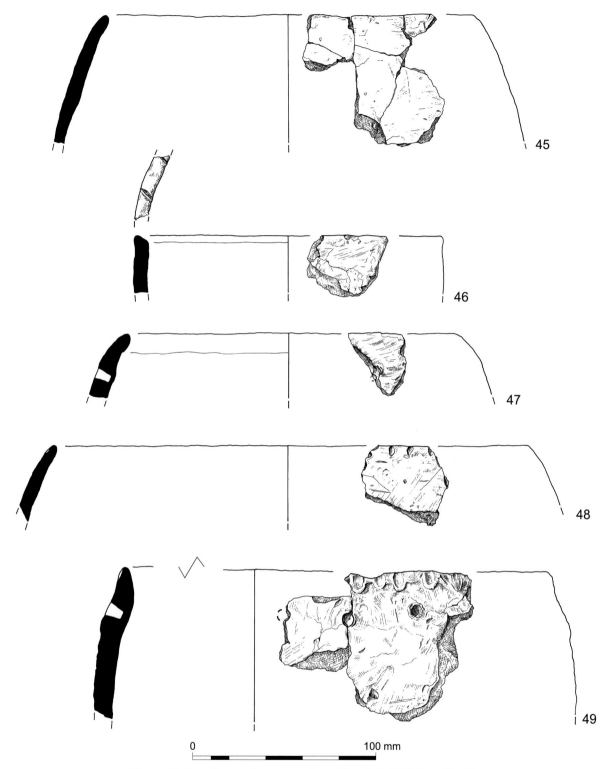

Figure 67. Late Bronze Age pottery from Waterhole CG6 (nos 45–49).

rim, R3, decorated with incised linear motifs, D13, below the rim, fabric 4.8.3 (group D), context 1834

58. Single wall sherd from a vessel with incised linear motif decoration, D13, forming filled triangles, fabric 5.10 (group K), context 1853

59. 11 sherds from a vessel with a (?) simple base form, B1, and vertical fine line smearing, D19, fabric 4.8.3 (group D), context 1834

60. 4 sherds from a vessel with an externally expanded base, B2, fabric 4.9.2 (group H), context 1834

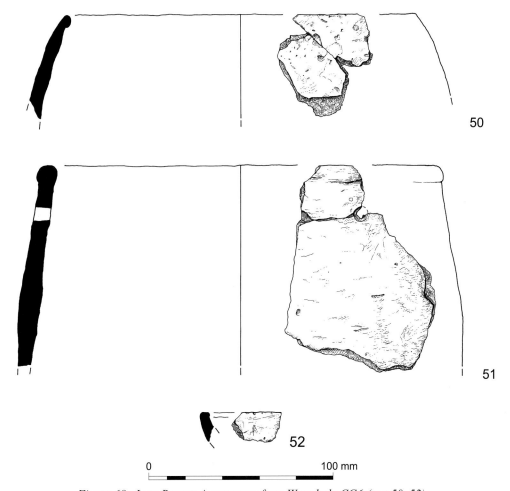

Figure 68. Late Bronze Age pottery from Waterhole CG6 (nos 50–52).

61. Sherd from a vessel with an externally expanded base, B2, fabric 4.8.2 (group E), context 1834.

CONTEXT GROUP 8: WATERHOLE (FIG. 71)

62. Sherd from a vessel with a simple vertical rim, R1, fabric 4.8.4 (group F), context 1103
63. Sherd from a vessel with a simple vertical rim, R1, fabric 4.9.2 (group H), context 1103
64. Sherd from a vessel with a flat topped, straight rim, R4, decorated with a row of perforations, D15, fabric 4.9.2 (group H), context 1103
65. 2 sherds from a vessel with a hook rim, R7, fabric 4.8.4 (group F), context 1102
66. Sherd from a vessel with an externally expanded base, B2, fabric 4.9.2 (group H), context 1103.

CONTEXT GROUP 9: BASIN-SHAPED PIT (FIGS 72 AND 73)

67. 5 sherds from a vessel with a simple vertical rim, R1, fabric 4.8.1 (group E), context 1111
68. 4 sherds from a vessel with simple vertical rim, R1, fabric 4.8.2 (group E), context 1111
69. 5 sherds from a vessel with a simple vertical rim, R1, decorated with row of part perforations, D16, and

incised linear motifs, D13, fabric 4.8.1 (group E), context 1111
70. 2 sherds from a hook rimmed vessel, R7, decorated with diagonal incised lines on top of rim, D11, fabric 4.9.2 (group H), context 1111
71. 2 sherds from a hook rimmed vessel, R7, decorated with vertical finger smearing, D17, fabric 4.9.2 (group H), context 1111
72. 4 sherds from a hook rimmed vessel, R7, decorated with fingertip or fingernail impressions on top of rim, D1, fabric 4.9.1 (group G), context 1111
73. Wall sherd from a vessel decorated with fine line smearing, D19, fabric 4.8.6 (group D), context 1111.

CONTEXT GROUP 10: BOWL-SHAPED PIT (FIG. 74)

74. 2 sherds from a vessel with a flat topped, straight rim, R4, fabric 4.8.4 (group F), context 2010
75. 2 sherds from a vessel with a rim with an internal bevel, R6, fabric 4.11 (group M), context, 2010
76. Single sherd from a vessel with a rim with internal bevel, R6, decorated with a row of perforations, D15, fabric 4.10.2 (group L), context 2010
77. 2 sherds from a vessel with an everted piecrust rim,

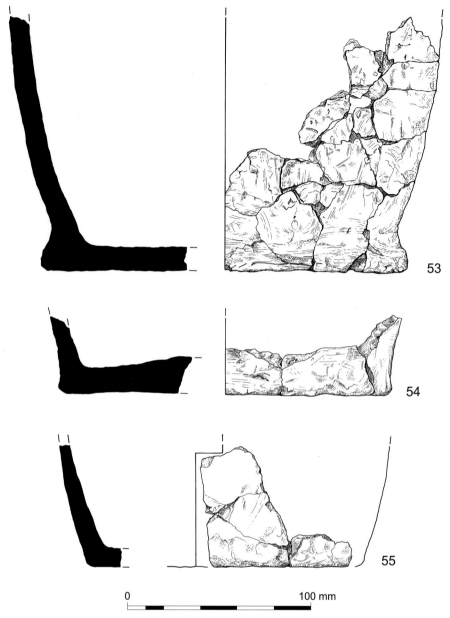

0   100 mm

Figure 69. Late Bronze Age pottery from Waterhole CG6 (nos 53–55).

R9, with row of perforations, D15, and vertical shallow finger grooving, D10, fabric 4.10.2 (group L), context 2010

78. 5 sherds from a weak shouldered vessel, P3, with a T-shaped flat rim, R11, fabric 5.12 (group L), context 2010

79. Single sherd from a vessel with an externally expanded base, B2, probably from the same vessel as 78 above, fabric 5.12 (group L), context 2010.

CONTEXT GROUP 25: PIT/POST (FIG. 75)

80. Single sherd from a vessel with a simple, vertical rim, R1, decorated with a row of part perforations, D16, fabric 4.10.2 (group L), context 1216

81. Single sherd from a vessel with a flat topped, straight rim, R4, fabric 4.9.2 (group H), context 1216

82. 5 sherds from a vessel with a rim with internal bevel, R6, decorated with a row of perforations, D15, fabric 4.9.4 (group I), context 1216.

CONTEXT GROUP 91: PIT/POST (FIG. 76)

83–6. 4 sherds all probably from the same vessel, a jar with a simple, everted rim, R8, weak shoulder, P3, and externally expanded base with a row of thumb-prints, B3. Decorated with a row of fingertip impressions on both the neck, D3, and shoulder, D4, and external finger smearing, D17. Fabric 4.7 (group J), context 1440

87. Single sherd from a shouldered vessel with a simple, everted rim, R8, decorated with a row of fingertip impressions on the neck, D3, fabric 4.7 (group J), context 1440

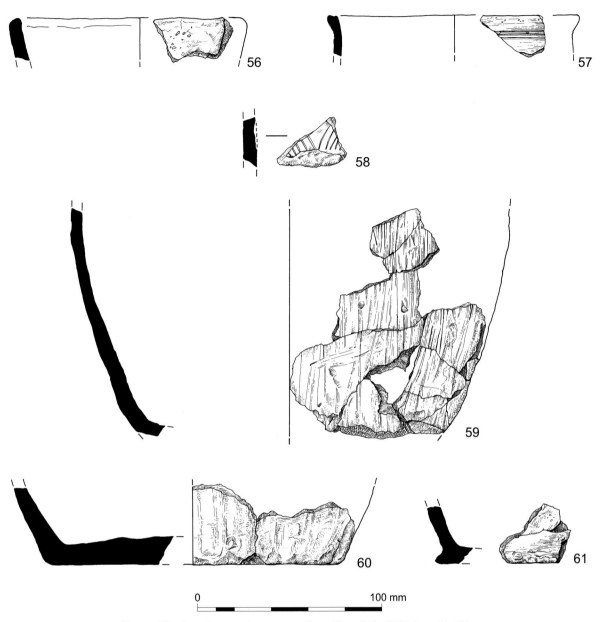

Figure 70. Late Bronze Age pottery from Waterhole CG7 (nos 56–61).

INDETERMINATE VESSEL FROM CONTEXT GROUP 4: WATERHOLE (FIG. 76)

88. 7 sherds from a small cup with a simple, vertical rim, R1, decorated on the exterior with random fingernail impressions, D5, fabric 5.13 (group C), context 2032

The pieces of this small vessel in a distinctive sandy fabric are much abraded. It was initially thought to be an Early Bronze Age accessory cup, occurring as residual material within its Late Bronze Age context. Although it might belong to Longworth's group 7 Trunco-Conic Cups (Longworth 1984, 52), no convincing parallels for the tall profile indicated for the Kemerton item appear to exist. An alternative possibility might be that the vessel is a fine cup of Late Bronze Age date, similar to two examples

from Aldermaston, one of which also carries fingernail impressions, but on the interior surface (Bradley *et al.* 1980, figs. 11, 11 and 14, 56F). However, if this were the case, it was more abraded than the rest of the Late Bronze Age pottery from Context Group 4, and therefore may still have been a residual item, or perhaps an heirloom.

The major Late Bronze Age context groups

In order to study the series of larger context group assemblages in more detail, data from such groups was tabulated separately (Appendix 1: Tables 10–14). For those groups which contained more than 100 sherds, the main results, by sherd count only, are presented in summary form in Table 10.

Table 10. Major Late Bronze Age Context Groups. Occurrence of fabric, form and decoration.

	CG1	CG4	CG5	CG6	CG7	CG9	CG10	CG14	CG17	CG91
No. sherds	627	598	121	472	528	404	130	132	198	243
Av. sherd weight	4g	12g	6g	11g	10g	9g	8g	4g	6g	6g
Fabric group:										
Limestone										
E	-	67	12	48	64	68	-	18	76	6
F	188	37	8	-	1	-	7	-	4	3
Shell										
G	19	43	14	161	36	47	2	26	24	1
H	12	240	2	40	324	70	-	8	50	56
I	193	49	5	2	13	-	73	7	35	7
J	-	2	-	-	-	-	-	-	-	161
Quartz/Limestone										
L	47	47	55	135	13	16	43	3	-	-
Quartz/Igneous										
M	5	2	-	25	5	1	4	-	-	-
No. rims	39	50	11	49	27	32	26	1	19	20
No. bases	29	45	4	50	42	13	6	3	7	8
Form										
R1	5	25	2	16	14	19	5	1	-	3
R2	-	-	-	-	-	-	-	-	12	1
R3/R4	5	-	3	3	5	4	3	-	6	2
R6/R7	29	20	3	17	7	9	8	-	1	-
R8/R9	-	4	-	4	1	-	3	-	-	12
R5/10/R13	-	1	3	7	-	-	1	-	-	2
R11/12	-	-	-	2	-	-	6	-	-	-
B1	3	15	-	4	15	5	3	-	3	1
B2	26	26	4	30	20	6	3	3	3	2
B3	-	4	-	16	7	2	-	-	1	5
P3	-	-	-	-	-	-	-	-	-	14
P4	-	-	-	1	-	-	-	-	-	-
Decoration										
D1/D2	2	12	-	2	2	4	1	-	-	6
D3/D4	1	1	-	-	-	-	-	-	-	22
D11/D12	-	13	3	-	12	2	13	-	-	-
D13	1	2	-	-	6	-	-=	-	-	-
D15/D16	21	14	1	16	1	6	2	1	17	1
D17/D19	11	19	-	-	18	60	-	-	-	3

Considering fabric first, it can be seen that various concentrations of the different fabric groups occur amongst the large assemblages. There is much vesicular pottery (Groups F and I) in CG1 and CG10 only (both bowl-shaped pits). This may be a reflection of localised chemical soil conditions which have leached out the calcareous inclusions, a suggestion supported by the failure due to leaching of bone sampled for radiocarbon dating from CG10. Waterhole CG4 shows a large concentration of medium to coarse shelly ware (Group H), while Waterhole CG6 has more fine shelly pottery (Group G) as well as quartz/limestone and shell/quartzite mixtures. By contrast, almost all of the pottery with shell and grog inclusions comes from Pit/post CG91 which, on the form data discussed below, is a feature of rather later date.

Nearly all the large context group assemblages contained more fragments from rims than bases, with only Waterhole CG7 having a predominance of base angles. Rims of simple (R1) and flat (R3, R4) form appear to have occurred fairly evenly across the groups. However three groups, Bowl-shaped pit CG1, and Waterholes CG4 and CG6 have high incidences of internally bevelled and hooked rims (R6, R7) and also of rows of perforations or part-perforations (D15, D16). As seen previously, these two characteristics of rim form and decoration are positively correlated. But in CG17, a basin-shaped pit, a high occurrence of perforations is associated with a relatively high level of flared rims (R2), which may be a later trait. Incised rim treatments (D11, D12) occur particularly in CG7 and CG10. The most divergent assemblage is that from Pit/post CG91 which is characterised by a different array of fabric types (see above) and by a set of different form attributes (Fig. 76). These include almost all examples of well-defined shoulders (P3), nearly all of the necks and shoulders bearing fingertip impressions, as well as several everted rims and those with piecrust treatment (R8, R9). All these features are found in decorated assemblages dated to the later stages of the Late Bronze Age period (Barrett

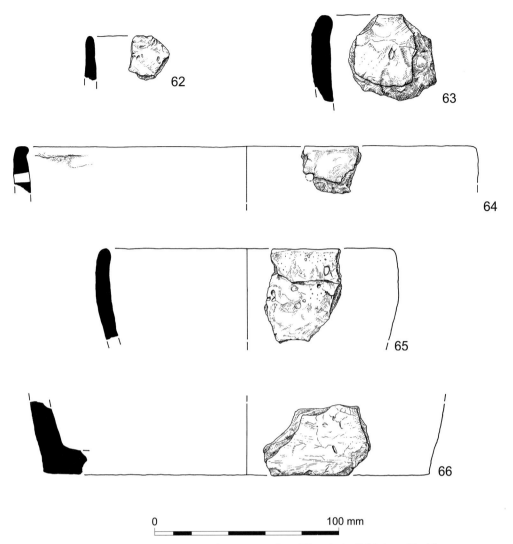

Figure 71. Late Bronze Age pottery from Waterhole CG8 (nos 62–66).

1980). These late features also occur sporadically in some of the other context groups. For instance, CG4 includes everted or piecrust rims and finger-tipped neck or shoulder sherds, and occasional late types also occur in CG1, CG6, CG10 and CG17. However, all the groups except CG91 are dominated by plainware assemblages, with a particular emphasis on the hook or bevelled rim jars carrying a row of perforations or part perforations below the rim.

VESSEL SIZE

No complete vessel profiles were recovered, but a fair impression of the variety of vessel sizes represented can be obtained by considering the ranges of rim diameter and base diameter measurements (Figs 77–80). The overall range of rim diameter variation is shown, for individual sherds in Figure 77 (see also Appendix 1: Figure 1 for minimum numbers of vessels). The distribution displays a strong double peak at the 160mm and 200mm levels. In Figure 78 the same data is broken down according to the major rim form categories. Simple rims and the hooked

and internally bevelled types occur in all rim diameter size ranges, but the flat, expanded and T-shaped forms are confined to vessels with medium to large rim diameters, with none falling below 140mm. There is little correlation between vessel size, as indicated by rim diameter, and styles of decoration (Appendix 1: Figure 2). The clearest pattern to emerge is for incised decoration (Group C), which occurs on pots of small to medium size. However, these rims mainly derive from Beakers in the later Neolithic/ Early Bronze Age assemblage. Fingertip embellished rims (Group A) are fairly evenly distributed amongst pots of small, medium and large size, and finger finishes are also found on vessels of varying size. The rows of perforations (Group E), however, display a tendency towards occurrence on larger vessels, with a marked preference for vessels of rim diameters between 220 and 240mm. The three forms of base angle all occur widely within the overall range of base diameters (Fig. 79), but the peaks may suggest that the externally expanded forms, with or without thumb printing (B2 and B3), occur more often on larger vessels;

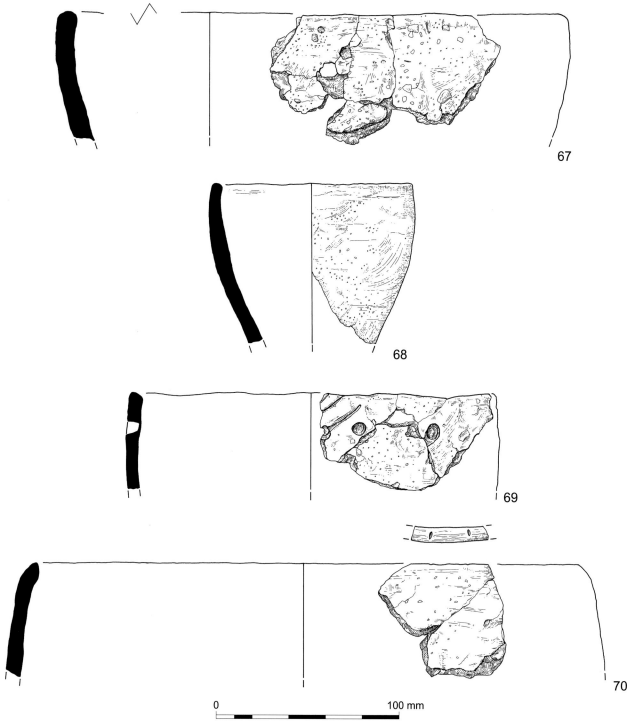

Figure 72. Late Bronze Age pottery from Pit CG9 (nos 67–70).

certainly the smallest groups, with rim diameters between 30 and 80 mm, mainly possess bases of simple form (B1).

In many cases there are not enough rim sherds from each major context group to allow meaningful comparisons of rim size ranges between the groups to be attempted (Appendix 1: Figure 3). However, the histograms for CG1, CG4, CG6, CG7, CG9 and CG91 can usefully be considered (Fig. 80). Bowl-shaped pit CG1 and Waterhole CG4 show

fairly even ranges of rim diameter measurements, but the histogram for Waterhole CG7 shows a tendency towards more small vessels, Waterhole CG6 to medium vessels and Basin-shaped pit CG9 to large ones. The pattern of rim diameter recorded for Pit/post CG91, which is the group containing the later decorated assemblage, shows a much tighter grouping of vessels mainly with middle-sized rim diameters.

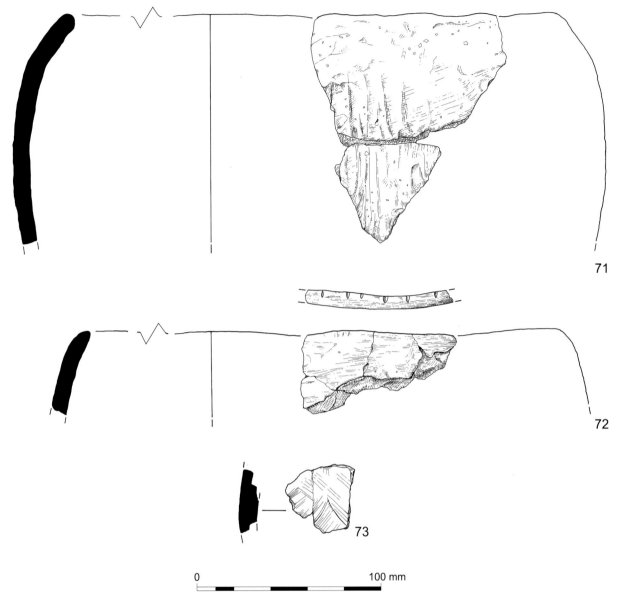

Figure 73. Late Bronze Age pottery from Pit CG9 (nos 71–73).

Discussion

The assemblage of prehistoric pottery from Kemerton is important in several ways. The substantial and well-preserved group of Late Bronze Age vessels provides a significant contribution to the national corpus of such assemblages and the occurrence of such a considerable number of large sealed groups is particularly unusual. In addition, the smaller groups of Neolithic and Early Bronze Age pottery have the potential to cast further light on ceramic periods which are not well known or understood within the county.

NEOLITHIC

The single rim sherd of Grooved Ware (Fig. 59.1) is an important find in regional terms. Very little Grooved Ware

is yet known in the area, although a substantial assemblage has recently been recovered from Clifton Quarry, Severn Stoke in either grogged or untempered fabrics (Edwards forthcoming). The only other pieces of pottery belonging to this Late Neolithic tradition within the county of Worcestershire are a single grooved wall sherd and two undecorated sherds, in a shelly fabric, from the nearby site of Aston Mill, Kemerton (Dinn and Evans 1990, fig. 16.1) and three highly decorated sherds from Broadway (Warren *et al.* 1936, fig 7.6–7.8). The various sherds from context 1520 may belong to an earlier period of the Neolithic; the most diagnostic piece (Fig. 59.2) may be from a Middle Neolithic Peterborough Ware bowl. Pottery of this tradition is also probably represented at Aston Mill (Dinn and Evans 1990, fig. 16.2).

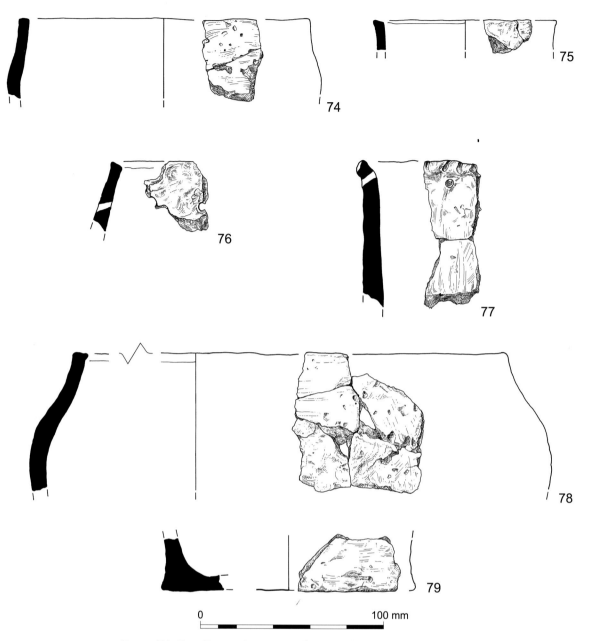

Figure 74. Late Bronze Age pottery from Pit CG10 (nos 74–79).

BEAKER

The Beaker fine wares display rim and body profiles, and schemes of decoration, which are matched amongst vessels of the Wessex/Middle Rhine type as defined by Clarke (1970). This can clearly be demonstrated by consideration of the two vessels, both from CG12 (Fig. 60.5 and 6), which are best represented in the fragmentary sherd assemblages.

The first has an outward flaring rim with a plain zone just below. The decorative scheme, which is executed by a comb with short rectangular teeth, includes zones of parallel horizontal lines and herringbone pattern. These designs are typical of Clarke's Basic European Motif Group 1 (Clarke 1970, 424–425) and commonly occur

on the tall vessels with flaring rims typical of his Wessex/ Middle Rhine group. The tall profile of the second (Fig. 60.6), with its pronounced neck and flaring rim is also typical of the Wessex/Middle Rhine type. The incised decoration is more unusual, but does occur on Beakers of this type, for instance on a large vessel from Fengate (Clarke 1970 no. 641, fig. 229). Wessex/Middle Rhine Beakers are traditionally dated to a fairly early stage within the currency of Beakers and were included in Case's Middle Style (Case 1977). However, recent reassessment of the available radiocarbon dates and detailed contextual studies have indicated that a simple unilinear pattern of stylistic development is unlikely to have taken place,

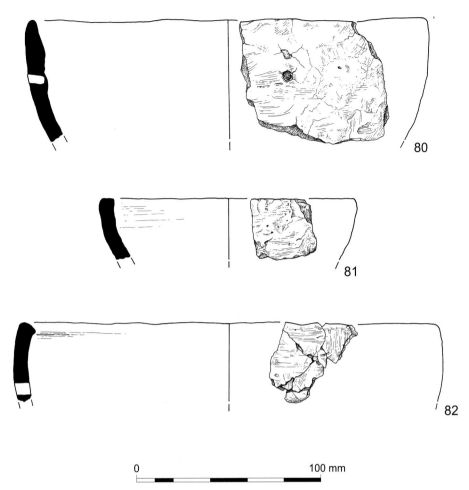

Figure 75. Late Bronze Age pottery from Pit/post CG25/47 (nos 80–82).

and that a much more complex situation, with significant chronological variation by region, probably existed (Case 1993). Case redefined his former Early, Middle and Late Styles as Styles 1, 2 and 3, each of which may occur at different times in the various regions. The Wessex/Middle Rhine tradition belongs to Case's Group D, which is Style 2 in the Midlands, Wessex and Wales and spans the third, and possibly fourth, quarter of the third millennium (Case 1993, 260–263).

Most of the Beakers from the counties of Worcestershire and Gloucestershire, as listed by Clarke, belong to his developed Northern and Southern Series, previously dated to the later stages of the Beaker tradition. However, a pair of Wessex/Middle Rhine Beakers which bear a remarkable similarity to the two best preserved vessels from Kemerton was found very close by, on Bredon Hill (Thomas 1965). The two Beakers came from the successive burials of a man and a woman under a barrow near to the Bredon Hill hillfort; interestingly this barrow would have been intervisible with the site at Huntsman Quarry. Both vessels included fragments of grog. The larger vessel was decorated with zones of horizontal lines in square tooth comb impressions below a collared rim, whilst the

slightly smaller vessel was decorated with a design of widely spread lines reminiscent of the pattern of Vessel 2 from Kemerton, but executed in a comb rather than an incised technique (Thomas 1965, pl. 2 and fig. 3). The Bredon Hill Beakers were dated to an early stage of the Wessex/Middle Rhine phenomenon by Clarke (in Thomas 1965, 68–70). The rich grave assemblage more recently excavated at Wellington Quarry, Marden in Herefordshire, with its fine intact Wessex/Middle Rhine Beaker of Group D, also belongs to this same early chronological horizon (Harrison *et al.* 1999).

It is very unlikely that the Kemerton Beakers derived from burials: they occur in very fragmentary condition and are associated with the remains of larger and thicker-walled vessels, some decorated with rusticated techniques, which are typical of contemporary assemblages of domestic pottery. For instance, the rim with all-over fingertip impressions (Fig. 61.23) is from a vessel similar in size and shape to that from Witton in Norfolk (Bamford 1982, fig. 44a) although the fingertip impressions on the Witton pot are paired. In Worcestershire, occasional sherds found on sites of later date may represent further domestic Beaker sites, as at Aston Mill, Kemerton where one sherd from an

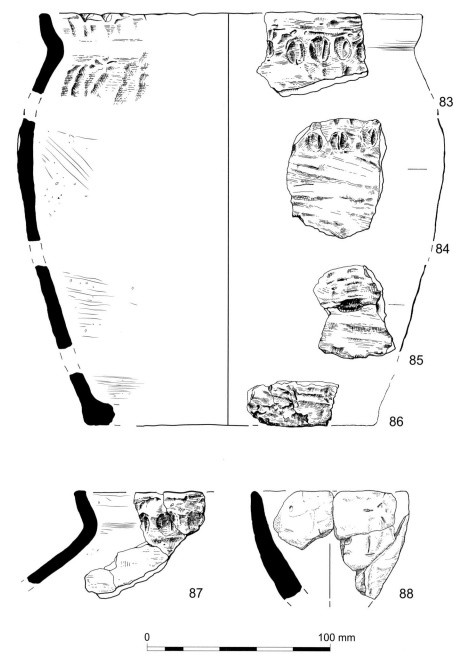

83

84

85

86

87

88

0   100 mm

Figure 76. Late Bronze Age pottery from Pit/post CG91 and indeterminate vessel from Waterhole CG4 (nos 83–88).

Early Style vessel decorated with all-over cord impressions was identified (Dinn and Evans 1990, fig. 16.5), or Beckford where five abraded sherds, all from different contexts, were mostly comb-decorated and of Style 2 or 3 type (Woodward undated). At Holt, on ring-ditch Site B, a pit group was recovered, but its stratigraphic relationship to the ring-ditch could not be determined. This sherd group contained fineware rims and rusticated domestic wares (Hunt *et al.* 1986, 14–16 and fig. 13). Amongst a total of 91 sherds, three fine ware and four coarse vessels were represented. Formal features suggested an early date within

the Beaker sequence, and again it is possible to suggest that this group may have belonged to Group D.

A similar group of domestic Beaker pottery from an isolated oval pit at Longmore Hill Farm, Astley comprised 125 sherds, representing a minimum of six fine Beakers and 11 coarse ware vessels. Once more the group was stylistically early, probably dating from the second quarter of the third millennium BC (Dinn and Hemingway 1992). Further small assemblages of domestic Beaker pottery are also known from Shropshire. These include material from a possible hearth at Rock Green, Ludlow (Carver and Hummler 1991, 92 and fig. 35), fragments of between three and five domestic vessels within a shallow pit (F263) beneath barrow B15 at Bromfield (Hughes, Leach and Stanford 1995, fig. 7) and redeposited sherds from pits north of the Bromfield Bronze Age urn cemetery (Stanford 1982, 288–289 and fig. 5). In the latter case, the general character of the assemblage yet again indicates an early date, in line with the vessel parallels cited by Stanford from Thickthorn, Dorset (Clarke's European type) and from Bulford, Wiltshire (Wessex/Middle Rhine).

Domestic Beaker assemblages containing vessels of definite Wessex/Middle Rhine style are very rare, and the Kemerton group provides important new information in this respect. The only other significant published assemblage of similar type is that from Dean Bottom on the Marlborough Downs in Wiltshire (Cleal in Gingell 1992, 62–67). This comprised a large group of 280 sherds representing a minimum of 20 vessels; most of the material came from a single pit. The sherds were in fresh condition and may have derived from a midden deposit. As at Kemerton, vessels with comb decoration were mixed with plain Beakers and vessels with rusticated fingertip treatments, but the vessels at Dean Bottom were not so varied in size. The weighted mean of two radiocarbon dates from Dean Bottom gives a range of 2484–2130 cal BC. A further range of pit deposits containing large fragments from Case's Group D vessels, including both fine and coarse wares, have also been excavated at Bestwall Quarry, Wareham in Dorset. The main pit deposit here was dated to 2340–2200 cal BC at 95% confidence (Ladle and Woodward 2009, 204–213).

A radically new approach to the classification of British Beakers has led to the definition of a new series of typological groupings which provide a better fit with the increasing numbers of radiocarbon determinations available (Needham 2005). Amongst vessels previously identified as belonging to the Wessex/Middle Rhine group those with strong shoulders fall within Needham's Tall Mid-Carinated Beaker group (TMC: Needham 2005, fig. 6), whilst those with more even profiles would belong to his group of 'S' profile Beakers (ibid, fig. 10). The two vessels from Bredon Hill are carinated and belong to the TMC category, but the surviving profiles from Kemerton, and those from Bestwall, are not carinated and are more S-shaped. However, both the TMC and 'S' profile groups fall within a similar time range, mainly between *c.* 2250 and 2000 cal BC, around and after the 'fission horizon' defined by Needham (2005, fig. 13).

EARLY BRONZE AGE

The accessory cup from a secondary context in the ring-ditch (CG79; Fig. 62.24) is of a common Early Bronze Age type. It belongs to the bowl-shaped Type 9d defined by Longworth (1984, 52–53), which is characterised by simple convex or ogee sides and a flat base. The flat rim and body profile of the Kemerton vessel is best matched on the cup from Acklam Wold, Yorkshire (Longworth 1984, pl 176d), although that is decorated with fingernail

and cord impressions. The incised geometric decoration is well matched by that occurring on the cup from Site E at Holt (Hunt *et al.* 1986, fig. 14 and pl. 4). This cup, with its internal rim bevel and double perforation, is a typical example of the class as a whole.

The fragments of plain rim and shoulder from an Early Bronze Age urn (Fig. 62.25 and 26), found as residual items in Waterhole CG6, probably come from a vessel of Collared type. Collared Urns occur only rarely in Worcestershire or in Gloucestershire. The fine group from Holt mainly comprises decorated vessels belonging to Longworth's Primary Series, but one is plain (Hunt *et al.* 1986, fig. 14.8), and plain examples in shapes typical of both the Primary and Secondary Series are known from the Cotswolds in Gloucestershire (Lower Slaughter: Longworth 1985, pl. 75d and Farmington: Longworth 1984, pl. 160f).

LATER BRONZE AGE

The considerable importance of the Late Bronze Age assemblage lies mainly in its large size and the internal variety of its formal and depositional characteristics. These aspects have been dealt with fully in the descriptive sections of this report. It now remains to discuss this material in relation to other groups of similar date from the region, and to some related pottery from sites further afield.

Within the Severn and Cotswolds areas there are fairly substantial assemblages of Late Bronze Age pottery from Brean Down, Somerset (Woodward in Bell 1990, chapter 11) and Shorncote in Gloucestershire (Morris in Hearne and Heaton 1994, 34–43; Mepham 1999, 58–63; Brown 2002, 64–66). Both these assemblages contain material which could be assigned to the successive plainware and decorated stages of Late Bronze Age ceramics and at Shorncote, as at Kemerton, there is evidence to suggest that most of the decorated material may have derived from specific and later features on the site (for Shorncote, see Hearne and

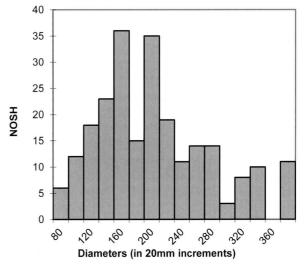

Figure 77. Rim diameters (whole assemblage).

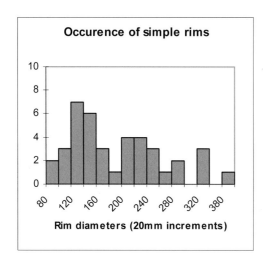

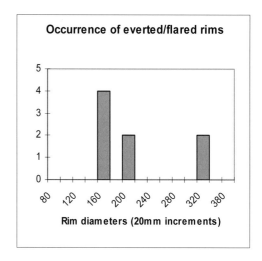

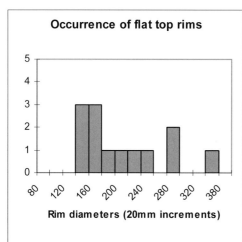

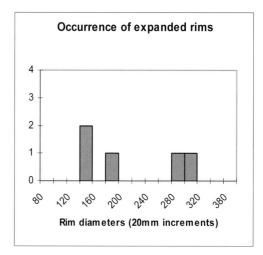

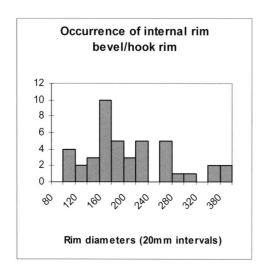

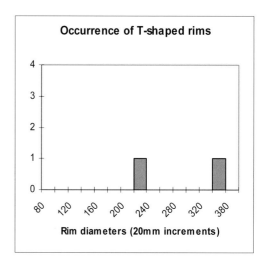

Figure 78. Occurrence of major form groups (by rim diameters).

Heaton 1994, 42). A general date of the ninth century BC was preferred by Morris for the Shorncote assemblage. At Brean Down there were three radiocarbon dates obtained for the Late Bronze Age deposits, but two may have related to residual charcoal, and only one gave a date within the expected range of the eleventh to ninth centuries. The series of radiocarbon dates obtained for the Kemerton assemblages (Bayliss, Jackson and Bronk Ramsey, this volume) suggests that the ceramics were used and deposited between *1130–1010 cal BC and 1050–960 cal BC (95%*

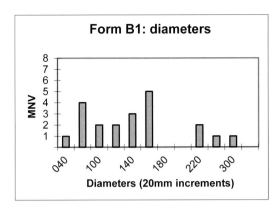

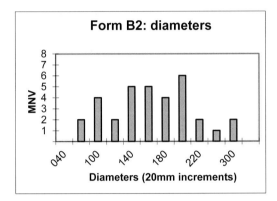

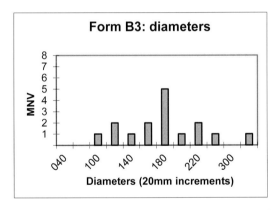

Figure 79. Occurrence of base forms (by diameter).

probability) or *1090–1020 cal BC and 1040–990 cal BC* (*68% probability*). They were in use for between *1 and 160 years* (*95% probability*) or *1 and 80 years* (*68% probability*). Thus the Kemerton pottery falls very firmly within the earlier plainware period of the Late Bronze Age, which is now thought to have been current between *c.* 1000BC and *c.* 800BC (Needham 2007). Furthermore it can be seen that the Kemerton material appears to have been used and deposited at the very beginning of this stage, around if not before 1000BC.

The absolute dating of plain ware assemblages belonging to the earlier phase of the Late Bronze Age in southern England has recently been discussed in relation to the radiocarbon dating programme undertaken for the site of

Bestwall, Dorset (Ladle and Woodward 2009, 270–271). Modelling of 16 dates for Late Bronze Age pottery from Bestwall was compared with 12 newly calibrated dates from five other sites that had produced plain wares. These sites comprised Cadbury Castle, Brean Down Unit 4 and Combe Hay, Eldon's Seat and Balksbury Camp. Taken together, the dates suggested that the plain ware stage of the Late Bronze Age was chronologically well defined within the south central region of England, with a period of use within the 10th and 9th centuries cal BC. These dates are in partial accord with radiocarbon dates from two sites in the Middle Thames valley: Rams Hill and Aldermaston Wharf. A second programme of dating at Rams Hill demonstrated that the second phase enclosure dated from the 11th century cal BC and the third phase enclosure belonged to the 10th century cal BC (Needham and Ambers 1994, fig. 6). Two determinations from Aldermaston (Bradley *et al.* 1980, 248) provided dates also within the 11th and 10th centuries' cal BC. Thus it would appear that the production of plain wares might have commenced earlier in the Thames valley than in the heartland of Wessex or Somerset. In confirmation of this observation, a particularly early group of shoulderless plain wares from Eynsham Abbey, Oxfordshire was dated by a series of six radiocarbon dates and would have been current *c.* 1270–1040 cal BC (Barclay *et al.* 2001, 158). Thus it seemed that in the Thames and Severn valleys plain wares were in use before 1000 cal BC while in central southern England they do not appear to have been current until the 10th century cal BC. However the phase of pottery production excavated more recently at at Tinney's Lane, Sherborne, Dorset has been dated to the very early period recognised for pottery associated with the second phase enclosure at Rams Hill, and at Huntsman's Quarry, Kemerton, or even a little earlier, as at Eynsham Abbey, in the 12th or 11th century cal BC. Modelling of the dates for the ceramic production phase at Tinney's Lane indicated that this ceramic production phase started *1150–1070* cal BC and ended in *1050–980* cal BC (*68% probability*). It may be that a newly defined stage of early plain wares can be defined in relation to this group of sites. This stage involved the demise of the decoration and strong globular profiles of the Deverel-Rimbury tradition and the development of a new wider range of vessel sizes and simple profiles.

The fabrics of Late Bronze Age pottery in Somerset, Wessex and the Thames valley are all characterised by prominent angular inclusions of pale-coloured materials: calcite in the west and flint further to the east. At Shorncote and Kemerton, the preferred inclusions are derived from Jurassic shelly limestone, again pale and conspicuous in colour, but much softer. At Shorncote, as in the other areas mentioned above all the fabrics contain inclusions that could have been obtained near to the sites, so the significant occurrence of Palaeozoic limestone fabrics and occasional presence of metamorphic/igneous types at Kemerton, is highly unusual and of extreme significance. Although there are a few other instances of non-local fabrics amongst

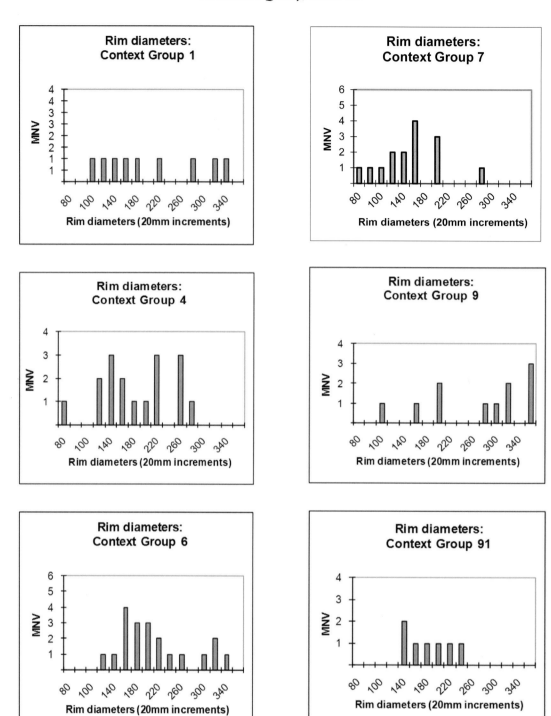

Figure 80. Occurrence of rim diameters in selected Context Groups.

certain other Late Bronze Age, and earlier, assemblages elsewhere in the country (Morris 1994, 374), this is the first time that the local Severn valley tradition of using rocks from specific sources that become common from the Middle Iron Age period onwards has been documented at such an early period. This tradition was first defined by Peacock (1968) who provides mapping of the probable source areas for the main rock type concerned, Palaeozoic limestone (his Group B1; *ibid.*, fig. 2). These lie between 22

and 35km west of the site at Kemerton. The metamorphic/ igneous inclusions identified at Kemerton are not readily matched within Peacock's Group A pottery group, which contains Pre-Cambrian rock from the Malvern Hills. However, use of an alternative source within the Malverns to that used in the Iron Age is possible, while consideration is also made in the light that many inclusions seem closer in appearance to those found in the Bromfield pottery of south Shropshire and identified as doleritic (Stanford

1982; Derek Hurst pers. comm). Whatever the case, such inclusions would certainly have come from a distant source. Interestingly, at Shorncote the fairly low but significant occurrence of grog fabrics (8%) correlated with the later decorated vessel forms (Morris in Hearne and Heaton 1994, 42). A similar correlation has been established at Kemerton where the shell and grog fabrics are confined almost entirely to the later group from CG91.

Many of the Kemerton rim forms correlate with those defined for the Shorncote and Brean Down assemblages. Thus Kemerton forms R1, R2, R6, R7 and R8 can be matched by Shorncote forms R1, R2/R6, R5/R7, R3 and R4 respectively. When percentage occurrences of rim forms are compared with the larger assemblage from Brean Down (Woodward in Bell 1990, 138), it can be seen that simple, flared and internally bevelled rim forms occur in roughly similar proportions. However, flattened rims are more common at Brean Down. A similar range of rim types also occur at Combe Hay, Somerset (Price and Watts 1980, fig. 24), and within the large plainware assemblages from the Thames valley, such as Aldermaston Wharf (Bradley *et al.* 1980) and Reading Business Park (Moore and Jennings 1992; Brossler *et al.* 2004), both in Berkshire, and Eynsham Abbey and Whitecross Farm, Wallingford (Barclay *et al.* 2001; Cromarty *et al.* 2006), both in Oxfordshire. The nearest Thames valley site which has produced a Late Bronze Age plainware assemblage of this type is Roughground Farm, Lechlade, Gloucestershire (Hingley in Allen *et al.* 1993, fig. 23). A particularly close parallel to the Kemerton ceramic groups is provided by the substantial and early dated assemblage from Tinney's Lane, Sherborne, Dorset (Tyler and Woodward 2009). Dominated by simple ovoid or straight-sided profiles and with very few shouldered vessels, or bowls or cups, this assemblage displays a very similar range of surface treatments to those represented at Kemerton. There is also a similarly low incidence of very simple decorative motifs.

There are, in addition, two formal characteristics that occur significantly at Kemerton which cannot be matched easily on any of the plainware sites that date from the 10th century cal BC onwards. These are the T-shaped and flat, internally expanded rims (R11–13), and the rows of perforations and part perforations (D15–16). However, a parallel for one of these features is the instance of two sherds with perforations from Brean Down (Woodward in Bell 1990, figs. 91.49 and 92.61). Interestingly, perforations and part perforations are evident within the very early plainware assemblage from Eynsham Abbey (Barclay *et al.* 2001, figs. 14, 9; 15, 18 and 27), and rows of perforations below the rim form one of the commonest forms of embellishment amongst the vessels from the early plainware pottery production site at Tinney's Lane, Sherborne (Tyler and Woodward 2009). Rows of perforations are more characteristic of domestic and burial assemblages of Middle Bronze Age date. They occur in Berkshire, Surrey, Sussex, Hampshire and Wiltshire, as well as in East Anglia where they form a particular characteristic of the ceramic groups

from Grimes Graves (Ellison in Longworth *et al.* 1988, 114, appendix II). But the incidence of perforations at Kemerton is much higher than that recorded even at Grimes Graves. The heavy T-shaped and internally expanded rims are also reminiscent of some Middle Bronze Age urn forms, and it may be that the presence of these two groups of traits at Kemerton may denote a date early within the plainware sequence, and such an early date has been confirmed by the results of the radiocarbon determinations. The plainware assemblage from Reading Business Park 2 (Green Park), like that from Kemerton, is dominated by simple ovoid or straight-sided forms with a significant presence of decoration located on rim tops but not on the vessel body or shoulders. A similarly early date for the Green Park material has been suggested by Morris, who argues that characteristics of the Late Bronze Age assemblage there were a direct development from the Middle Bronze Age pottery which was present on the same site. However no radiocarbon dates are available for the Late Bronze Age assemblage from Green Park (Morris in Brossler *et al.* 2004, 78–80).

The strengthened rims and rows of perforations, taken together with the evidence that the perforated vessels tend to be large in size, may also be indicative of functional factors. At Grimes Graves it was tentatively suggested that the large bucket forms common on that site may have been used in tasks connected with dairying, this being the main economic activity as evidenced by the faunal remains (Ellison in Longworth *et al.* 1988, 49). The rows of perforations and ledged rims at Kemerton might have facilitated the attachment of organic covers to the vessels, although the rows of part perforations could hardly have functioned in this manner. Environmental evidence from the site strongly suggests that the economy was based on pastoral activities within an open landscape. As at Grimes Graves it can therefore be suggested that the large bucket shaped vessels may indeed have functioned as pails for the collection and storage of milk (from cattle, sheep or goats). The substantial occurrence of burnt residues on these larger vessels, and often inside their bases (see above) further indicates that these pots were also being used to process or cook commodities. The process represented may have been the scalding of milk, facilitated by the use of pot boilers, prior to the preparation of dairy products such as cheese. Certainly, both cattle and sheep/goat were present at the site, in relatively equal numbers, and the fact that the majority of the cattle were kept into maturity as well as some of the sheep (Pinter-Bellows, this volume) supports the suggestion that dairy products may have been important.

The pattern of occurrence of rim diameters, as indicative of vessel size, is not as clear as those obtained for the Unit 4 assemblage at Brean Down or that from Aldermaston Wharf. At these two sites three size peaks, plus a few very large vessels, were apparent (Woodward in Bell 1990, 141, fig. 101). At Kemerton distribution of rim diameter measurements is more even, and peaks at 160mm and 220mm are more similar to the pattern given by the rim

Table 11. Percentage occurrence of selected ceramic attributes amongst settlement zones.

Attribute	South/central zone	South-east zone	North central zone	West zone
	CG 6, 7	CG 8, 9	CG 1, 2, 4, 39, 92	CG 3, 5, 10, 11 & 14
Fabric group				
Limestone (E, F)	13	31	33	13
Shell (G, H, I, J)	66	62	55	50
Quartz and limestone (L)	17	7	10	35
Quartz and igneous (M)	4	<1	2	1
Form				
R1	39	57	35	33
R3/R4	11	13	5	20
R6/R7	32	30	55	27
R8/R9	7	-	4	-
R5/R10/R13	9	-	1	20
R11/R12	2	-	-	-
Decoration				
D1/D2	7	5	14	-
D3/D4	-	-	2	-
D11/D12	21	3	13	50
D13	10	-	3	-
D15/16	30	9	37	33
D17/D19	32	83	31	17
Total sherds	867	233	1041	244

diameters of the published vessels from Reading Business Park (data in archive, measured from Hall in Moore and Jennings 1992, figs. 44–51). At that site the main peaks for both the plainware and decorated Late Bronze Age assemblages were around 160mm and 220mm, with an additional minor peak at 300mm. At Tinney's Lane, Sherborne analysis of rim diameters displayed a slightly more complex pattern with four-fold peaks, at 120mm, 180mm, 240mm and 320/340mm. At Grimes Graves, where rows of perforations similar to those recorded at Kemerton are common, the Middle Bronze Age pots are in general rather larger in size (Longworth *et al.* 1988, 50, fig. 21).

The general absence of fineware jars and particularly bowls at Kemerton occurs also at Shorncote, but not at Brean Down. Looking ahead in time to the local published assemblages of Iron Age date it is interesting to note that the range of rim diameter sizes at Kemerton in the Late Bronze Age is similar to that displayed by the Intermediate Iron Age phase defined at the hillfort on Bredon Hill (Cruso Hencken 1938, figs. 17–18) rather than to the generally smaller bag-shaped pots of the Early Iron Age phase of that site (*ibid.* figs. 14–16).

Within the large area excavated at Huntsman's Quarry

it has been possible to define five main zones of activity, each considered to represent an area of settlement (see Part 5). Each of these zones included a series of posthole structures and one or more groups of waterholes of which four contained substantial quantities of pottery (in the fifth, the northeast zone, the only waterhole present was subject to only very limited investigation and few other pits were present thus limiting the quantity of material culture from this zone). The excavator has further suggested that each settlement zone may have been occupied by a single generation of a farming family, and that the zones may indeed have been successive. A comparison of the main ceramic characteristics of the pottery assemblages from the four occupation areas with substantial quantities of pottery is provided in Table 11. From this it can be deduced that pottery from the south central zone included unusually high quantities of pottery containing shell and igneous inclusions, and also the highest concentration of everted rim types (R5/R10/R13). The southeast zone was characterised by high instances of simple rims (R1) and finger surface finishes (D17/D19) but a low occurrence of rows of perforations (D15/D16). In the north central zone there were higher numbers of internally bevelled and hook rims (R6/R7) and finger-impressed rims (D1/D2), whilst the large zone to the west produced the highest occurrence of the quartz plus limestone fabric group (L) and high incidences of flat rims (R3/R4), expanded rims (R5/R10/R13) and also of incised decoration on rims (D11/D12). This subtle variation in ceramics between occupation zones may reinforce the idea that the different zones were populated by different kin groups, and that they may have been occupied successively. It is generally accepted that as the Late Bronze Age progresses, decoration becomes more common, so it might also be feasible to suggest that the two zones characterised by higher occurrences of rim decoration, those located in the north central and western sectors of the site respectively, may have been occupied slightly later than the southern and eastern groups.

It may be concluded that the Late Bronze Age pottery from Kemerton was used in a domestic and agricultural context and that the vessels may have been designed and used for specific purposes such as the collection and processing of dairy products. Obvious fine tablewares are virtually absent and the pots are mainly medium to large in size. Although most of the pottery derives from large waterhole and pit assemblages, the context groups are not at all similar to the small groups of Late Bronze Age vessels deposited as chunks in isolated pit deposits at sites in the West Midlands and elsewhere. These appear to contain sets of one very large thin-walled vessel together with a few medium-sized jars and small cups in fine fabrics and adorned with unusual decorative techniques (Woodward 2000). These 'drinking set' deposits are characterised by the presence of very large joining portions from a small number of vessels of varying size and have been interpreted in relation to episodes of ritualised feasting.

The Kemerton context groups seem to have resulted from a rather different process. The context assemblages are larger and contain fragments from a much larger range of vessels, with each vessel being represented by only a few sherds. On the grounds of evidence concerning fragmentation and abrasion it has been suggested that the Kemerton potsherds had been lying in middens before they were introduced to the secondary fillings of the various waterholes. The deposits do appear, however, to have been placed into the waterholes deliberately and it may be that they represent closing deposits: the symbolic placing of pieces of everyday equipment within significant structures when an area of settlement was abandoned or moved to another location. The depositing of pieces from the vessels which were used to store and process a commodity (milk), which was essential to the livelihood of the inhabitants, were thus employed to mark the final filling of the holes which had provided water for the animals who produced that milk. Closing deposits containing large amounts of pottery associated with Bronze Age roundhouses in Cornwall have been identified and discussed by Nowakowski (2001). These deposits were found to overlie the remains of the houses themselves, but at Bestwall Quarry in Dorset similar closing deposits

associated with a Middle Bronze Age house had been placed in pits. In this case however several of the vessels were represented by very large fragments, or sets of joining fragments, and it was possible to suggest that the pots represented in the closing deposits had also functioned as one or more feasting sets (Ladle and Woodward 2003; 2009, 255–265). As the pottery from the Kemerton waterholes appears to have derived from intermediate contexts, such as middens, the possibility of a final usage of the vessels in feasting episodes cannot be investigated. However it is tempting to postulate that the closing deposits contained the remnants of vessels used in feasts or rituals enacted to mark the last stages of occupation and activity within each of the settlement zones identified on the site.

Petrology (by David F. Williams)

Introduction

A thin section examination was undertaken on twenty-one selected sherds of early prehistoric pottery recovered from the investigations at Huntsman's Quarry, Kemerton. Prior to analysis, all of the sherds were examined in the hand-specimen with the aid of a binocular microscope (×20) and their surface colours described with reference to Munsell Charts.

Kemerton is situated some 5 miles northeast of Tewkesbury and lies on the Jurassic Lower Lias formations, with Triassic sandstones and mudstones about 5 miles to the west (Geological Survey 1" Map of England sheet 216).

Petrology and fabric

Grog/Shell/limestone

Sample 1. Context 1440: Fabric 4.7
Soft, slightly rough, sandy fabric with a soapy feel, light brown (7.5YR 7/4) outer surface, darker brown (7.5YR 5/2–4/2) inner surface and core. Small scattered plates of white shell and irregular-shaped pieces of limestone can be seen together with pieces of argillaceous material.

Sample 2. Context 1111: Fabric 4.9.2
Soft, roughish fabric, patchy reddish-brown (2.5YR 6/6–5YR 5/3) throughout. Frequent plates of shell are scattered throughout the fabric, together with pieces of argillaceous material.

Sample 3. Context 1836: Fabric 4.12
Soft, somewhat rough fabric with a slightly soapy feel, light red (2.5YR 6/8) surfaces with a dark grey core. There is more evidence of the presence of shell and the sherd is harder fired than Sample 1, otherwise a similar fabric.

Sample 4. Context 2032: Fabric 5.7
Soft, smoothish, thin-walled fabric with a soapy feel, a weak red (2.5YR 4/2) colour throughout. A similar fabric

to Samples 1 and 3, although there is more argillaceous material present with shell less obvious.

SAMPLE 5. CONTEXT 1601: FABRIC 5.11

Soft, rough, friable sandy fabric, light reddish-brown (2.5 YR 6/8–5YR 5/3) outer surface and core, dark grey inner surface. Pieces of a light-coloured argillaceous material can quite clearly be seen scattered throughout the fabric.

Thin sectioning shows that all five sherds contain pieces of grog (*i.e.* previously fired crushed-up pottery introduced to the clay of the vessel by the potter). These are more common in Sample 3 and especially Sample 4.

All of the sherds have a fairly fine-textured clay matrix, containing moderately sparse ill-sorted grains of quartz ranging to over 1mm in size, flecks of mica and some opaque iron oxide. Pieces of fossiliferous shell and cryptocrystalline limestone are present in Samples 1–4, especially in Sample 2, where some of the grog has small pieces of shell in it, and in Sample 3. Sample 5 seems to lack the shell but does contain sparse cryptocrystalline limestone. Unfortunately, the shell and limestone inclusions, which presumably occur naturally in the clay, are lacking in any diagnostic fossils which might suggest a particular geological source. In view of this, and as the site is situated in a shelly/limestone area, there is nothing here to point to anything other than a fairly local source or sources for the making of the pottery.

Shell

SAMPLE 6. CONTEXT 2032: FABRIC 4.9.1

Soft, smoothish fabric, light reddish-brown (5YR 6/4) outer surface and part core, dark grey inner surface and part core. Moderately frequent plates of shell can be seen in fresh fracture.

SAMPLE 7. CONTEXT 2032: FABRIC 4.9.3

Soft, rough fabric, reddish-brown (5YR 5/3) throughout. Abundant large plates of shell are scattered throughout the fabric.

SAMPLE 8. CONTEXT 1836: FABRIC 4.11

Soft, rough fabric, reddish-brown (5YR 5/3) throughout. Large plates of shell are scattered throughout the fabric.

Thin sectioning shows that the shell is fossiliferous and pieces of bryozoa can be seen scattered throughout the fabric. It is difficult to be certain, but in the absence of other evidence, the closeness of Jurassic formations to the site suggests that these sherds may well be from a fairly local source.

Limestone (?)

SAMPLE 9. CONTEXT 2043: FABRIC 139

Soft, smooth, thin-walled fabric, reddish-yellow (5YR 7/8)

surfaces and part core, dark grey part core. Thin sectioning shows a fine-textured fabric with little in the way of non-plastic inclusions except some silt-sized quartz grains and sparse small pieces of cryptocrystalline limestone. Difficult to source on this evidence but again could be local.

Grog/Sandstone

SAMPLE 10. CONTEXT 1836: FABRIC 4.10.2

Hardish, rough, sandy fabric, red (2.5YR 5/6) throughout.

SAMPLE 11. CONTEXT 2043: FABRIC 5.3

Soft, rough, sandy fabric, light red (2.5YR 6/6) throughout.

SAMPLE 12. CONTEXT 2046: FABRIC 5.9

Soft, rough, sandy fabric, light red (2.5YR 6/6) outer surface and dark grey inner surface and core.

Samples 10 and 11 are similar in the hand-specimen and thin section. Under the petrological microscope small pieces of grog can be seen scattered throughout the clay matrix, together with small fragments of a quartz-sandstone. Also present are ill-sorted grains of quartz, which can reach up to 7mm in size, and in Sample 11 some sparse shell. Sample 12 also contains grog and small fragments of a quartz-sandstone, but the accompanying quartz grains are well-sorted, average size below 0.40mm across. The quartz-sandstone in all of these sherds may well have derived from the local Triass to the west of the site.

Large Quartz

SAMPLE 13. CONTEXT 1520: FABRIC 5.8

Soft, rough, sandy fabric containing conspicuous large angular white and glassy quartz grains, light red (2.5YR 6/8). Thin sectioning shows a fairly fine-textured clay matrix containing a scatter of large (up to 6mm across) grains of quartz, some of them polycrystalline, and occasional pieces of quartzite.

The large size and apparent angularity of the quartz grains suggests that they represent crushed tempering material which was deliberately added to the clay by the potter. Kemerton is not that far from Triassic sandstones and it is possible that the large quartz grains may have derived from these.

Malvernian Igneous/Metamorphic

SAMPLE 14. CONTEXT 2032: FABRIC 97

Soft, rough fabric, buff (7.5YR 7/4) outer surface and part core, dark grey inner surface and part core.

SAMPLE 15. CONTEXT 1814: FABRIC 97

Soft, rough fabric, greyish-brown (10YR 5/2) surfaces, dark grey core.

In the hand-specimen both these sherds can be seen to contain frequent angular rock and mineral inclusions. Thin sectioning shows that these include a variety of crushed igneous and metamorphic rocks similar in composition to those described by Peacock (1968) for certain prehistoric pottery (Peacock Group A) thought to have been made in the Malvern Hills region, on the borders of Herefordshire and Worcestershire. An alternative suggestion is that these inclusions may be of dolerite, another igneous/metamorphic rock known to have been used in ceramics during the prehistoric period, a likely source of which exists in southern Shropshire (Derek Hurst pers. comm).

Malvernian Shelly Limestone

SAMPLE 16. CONTEXT 1111: FABRIC 4.8.1
Soft, rough, friable fabric, light buff (7.5YR 7/4) outer surface and part core, dark grey inner surface and part core. Frequent large angular inclusions of white or off-white limestone are scattered throughout the fabric.

SAMPLE 17. CONTEXT 1111: FABRIC 4.8.3
Soft, roughish, more dense fabric than Sample 16, reddish-brown (5YR 5/1) throughout. The visible white limestone inclusions are smaller and more evenly distributed than in Sample 16.

SAMPLE 18. CONTEXT 1801: FABRIC 4.8.5
Soft, rough, thin-walled fabric, reddish-yellow (5YR 7/6–6/6) outer surface, dark grey inner surface and core. This is a vesicular fabric with sparse inclusions of off-white limestone.

In thin section all three sherds can be seen to contain fragments of shelly limestone. These are less common in Sample 18, but the size and angularity of the vesicles in this sherd suggest that more of these inclusions were once present. The shelly limestone contains fossil brachiopod test and crinoid ossicles set in a matrix of recrystalline calcite. Discrete pieces of bryozoa and calcite are scattered throughout the clay matrix, together with some grains of quartz. This fabric description is very close to that noted by Peacock (1968, Group B1) for certain Iron Age pottery of the Herefordshire-Cotswold region for which he suggested an origin in the area of, or west of, the Malvern Hills. A similar source for these three sherds seems likely.

SAMPLE 19. CONTEXT 2010: FABRIC 5.12
Soft, rough, vesicular sandy fabric, pale brown (10YR 7/4) throughout. In thin section this sherd contains a fairly clean clay matrix with a moderately frequent scatter of well-sorted quartz grains average size up to 0.40mm across. Irregular-shaped vesicles of various sizes occur throughout the fabric. It is difficult to be certain, but these may once have contained limestone or shelly limestone and thus the sherd may be connected to this group.

Quartz

SAMPLE 20. CONTEXT 1801: FABRIC 5.10
Soft, rough, sandy fabric, dark grey (10YR 4/1) surfaces, lighter grey core. Thin sectioning shows a groundmass of silt-sized quartz grains with some slightly larger grains, flecks of mica and some opaque iron oxide.

SAMPLE 21. CONTEXT 2032: FABRIC 5.13
Soft, rough, quite sandy fabric, reddish-yellow (5YR 7/6) outer surface and part core, grey inner surface and part core. Thin sectioning shows little but well-sorted quartz grains ranging up to an average size of 0.40mm across, some flecks of mica and a little opaque iron oxide.

Both of these sherds contain a range of common inclusions that make it difficult to suggest any particular source area for them.

Ceramic weights (by Derek Hurst)

Description

A total of 284 fragments of fired clay weighing 6.624kg have been identified as representing at least 39 separate clay weights (Table 12). The function of these objects is usually attributed to textile manufacture and hence they are often labelled loom weights. However, a less specific term, weights, is used here in recognition of some uncertainty about the use of these objects, and the possibility that several uses might have been applicable.

Two types were identified, pyramidal (*e.g.* Fig. 81.1–81.3) and cylindrical (*e.g.* Fig. 81.4–81.6). The majority were recovered from well-dated Late Bronze Age contexts; however, two examples were recovered from an Early Bronze Age recut within a ring-ditch (CG79), one of indeterminate form, the other of possible pyramidal form.

By weight there was little difference in the frequency of these types, but the cylindrical form was much commoner by count, suggesting that it was subject to a greater degree of fragmentation, possibly as result of being less well fired than the other type, or possibly the former was made locally giving rise to the survival of firing failures in the archaeological record. In terms of quantification by minimum number the pyramidal type was more common than the cylindrical type (63% and 37% respectively; 17 instances to 10) based only on examples where a positive identification of type could be given.

The pyramidal form was of a more consistently executed shape than the other type, the only observable variation being a greater tendency to rounding of corners on one example (Fig. 81.3). The size range for the pyramidal type was also less variable than that for the cylindrical type, at between 0.296kg and up to about 0.50kg.

The cylindrical type was more variable. Some examples were considerably more extended in form (Fig. 81.4), while the weight of the individual items also varied, with one example only weighing 0.256kg (context 2032, Fig. 81.6) but another probably having weighed in the order of 1.kg (context 2010, Fig. 81.5). The increased weight was not accounted for by the extended cylinder type, suggesting that this variation in form was to do with function rather than simply increasing size. It has been suggested that smaller weights could have been used for the weaving of flax (Neal 1987, 335), the cultivation of which was evidenced in the Kemerton site pollen record (Greig, this volume).

There were two basic fabrics:
a)   coarse quartz with occasional oolitic lumps (fabric A)
b)   fine quartz with mica and occasional plate shell (fabric B).

Fabric A was the more common. As the weights are likely to have been made locally, this suggests that there were two sources of clay being exploited by the inhabitants. Fabric A may be particularly local to the site as it includes oolitic material which is also a feature of soils in the vicinity of the site (British Geological Survey 1:10,000 sheet SO93NW).

Illustrated ceramic weights (Fig. 81)

Pyramidal type
   1   1834, Waterhole CG7
   2   1848, Waterhole CG7
   3   1853, Waterhole CG7
Cylindrical type
   4   1830, Bowl-shaped pit CG1
   5   2010, Bowl-shaped pit CG10
   6   2032, Waterhole CG4

Dating and comparison with other sites

The only site in the locality that has produced a quantity of prehistoric weights is Beckford (Hurst 1984), where the use of ceramic weights was dated to the Iron Age/Roman period, and both pyramid and triangular types were present. Elsewhere it has been noted that the pyramidal type post-dates the cylindrical type, and that both pre-date Iron Age types of weight (Bradley *et al.* 1980, 244).

Cylindrical weights have been regarded as typical of the Middle Bronze Age (Bradley and Hall 1992, 87), but also occur on some Late Bronze Age sites as at Green Park (Barclay 2004, 92–94) and Shorncote (Morris 43–44). At Reading Business Park (immediately adjacent to Green Park) and at Aldermarston Wharf both cylindrical and pyramidal types were present in Late Bronze Age contexts (Bradley 1980, 244; Bradley and Hall 1992, 87). At Kemerton, as at Aldermarston, pyramidal weights were the more common type. Given the relatively early date within the Late Bronze Age period of the activity at Kemerton, it seems likely that some chronological overlap is represented or that the period of occupation spans the transition between these types.

Comparison of the Kemerton weights with examples from other Late Bronze Age sites suggests that the cylindrical types have more typologically in common with weights of this type from Aldermarston and Knight's Farm in Berkshire (Bradley *et al.* 1980, fig. 19.5 and fig. 37.3) rather than those from the slightly earlier site at Black Patch in East Sussex (Drewett 1982, fig. 34.3). This comment is based upon general form, as defined particularly by the ratio of length:width.

Spatial distribution

The majority of the weights (78% by weight) were recovered from large pits or waterholes, which accounted for the bulk of the excavated material from the site; although a cylindrical weight and at least one other weight of indeterminate form had been used as packing in a posthole (context 2057/2058, CG63). In one case both cylindrical and pyramidal types were certainly present in the same feature (Waterhole CG4) but elsewhere either type occurred in isolation (*e.g.* the cylindrical type in CG1 and the pyramidal in CG6 and CG7). Given the dating usually attributed to these types this may indicate that settlement may have undergone some migration or expansion southwards.

Conclusion

The quantity of ceramic weights from Kemerton is exceptional. The most likely use of these objects is as loom weights, suggesting that textile manufacture was an important activity on this site. The absence of any associated spindle whorls is notable, though a similar absence at a number of comparable sites in the Thames Valley has been interpreted to indicate that such objects were made of wood (Moore and Jennings 1992, 122).

Stone weight (by Derek Hurst)

A limestone weight weighing 1.276kg was recovered from an isolated small pit or posthole (context 2029; Fig. 81.7). This was heavier than the ceramic weights but may have had a similar function associated with textile production. Alternatively this could have functioned as a thatch weight.

Fired clay (by Derek Hurst)

There was a total of 352 fragments of fired clay weighing 3.441kg. There was a similar range of fabric types as for the ceramic weights (see above). Some fragments of the fired clay showed smoothed surfaces, but without any further diagnostic features the material could not be attributed to its original use. The general similarity, however, of many fragments to the weights suggested that some of this material is likely to have come from this type of object. Other structures likely to have been associated with fired clay would typically be domestic hearths and ovens, though the presence of metalworking on the site

Table 12. Occurrence of weights (by context/Context Group).

Context	Data	1102	1103	1517	1814	1830	1831	1834	1836	1841	1843	1848	1853	1856	2010	2032	2036	2040	2058	2101	2113	Total
Context Group		8	8	17	79	1	1	7	6	7	7	7	7	N/A	10	4	5	77	63	14	29	
Type																						
Cylindrical	MNW	1				1										1			1			4
	Frags	2				1										1			70			74
	Wt (g)	302				488										256			198			1244
Cylinder - extended	MNW														1							1
	Frags														1							1
	Wt (g)														282							282
Cylindrical?	MNW		1				1									2				1		5
	Frags		2				2									7				4		15
	Wt (g)		252				176									418				282		1128
Indeterminate	MNW		2	1	1							1	1	1		2	1	1	1			12
	Frags		11	1	1							1	2	1		7	45	2	75			146
	Wt (g)		142	26	24							54	30	12		262	296	60	90			996
Pyramidal	MNW							6	1	1		1	1			1						11
	Frags							24	7	2		1	1			6						41
	Wt (g)							1266	300	44		382	296			218						2506
Pyramidal?	MNW		1		1						2				1						1	6
	Frags		1		1						3				1						1	7
	Wt (g)		200		48						100				92						28	468
Total weights represented		1	4	1	2	1	1	6	1	1	2	2	2	1	2	6	1	1	2	1	1	**39**
Total fragments		2	14	1	2	1	2	24	7	2	3	2	3	1	2	21	45	2	145	4	1	**284**
Total Weight		302	594	26	72	488	176	1266	300	44	100	436	326	12	374	1154	296	60	288	282	28	**6624**

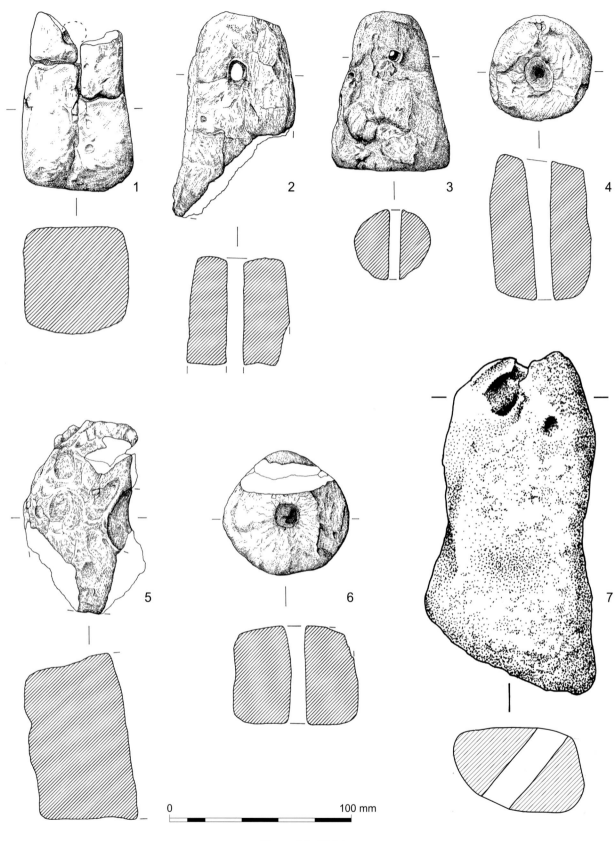

Figure 81. Weights.

Table 13. Ceramic wrap and mould pieces and hearth material.

Context Group	Context	Mould pieces	Mould weight (g)	Wrap pieces	Wrap weight (g)	Hearth material	Hearth weight (g)
N/A	515	0	0	0	0	2	15
1:Pit	1830	64	546	26	61	1	21
	1854	3	34	2	9	0	0
4:Waterhole	2032	12	86	15	49	6	67
6:Waterhole	1836	25	136	14	39	1	9
7:Waterhole	1843	2	22	0	0	0	0
	1834	4	16	0	0	0	0
Totals		110	840	57	158	10	112

in this period also gives rise to the possibility that some of the fired clay was derived from structures or moulds associated with this process.

In terms of distribution, the material was thinly scattered in features across the whole site, mainly in the larger pits and waterholes (CG1, 6 and 7). The significance of this is unclear; however, the bias in distribution towards these larger features was noted for other categories of finds.

The mould fragments and slag (by Roger C. P. Doonan)

Introduction

A collection of in excess of 150 mould fragments (mould and wrap pieces) was recovered along with some hearth

material and unstratified slag debris (Table 13). These were assessed and in some cases analysed by X-ray flourescence spectrometry. With the exception of a small quantity of hearth material from a later deposit (context 515), all the material derived from six Late Bronze Age contexts within four features; a bowl-shaped pit (CG1, contexts 1830 and 1854) which produced the largest quantity of material, and three waterholes (CG4, context 2032; CG6, context 1836; and CG7, contexts 1834 and 1843).

Mould fragments

Description

The fragments submitted for analysis comprised the total assemblage from the site, and derived from two parts of the casting process. Some fragments were of true mould

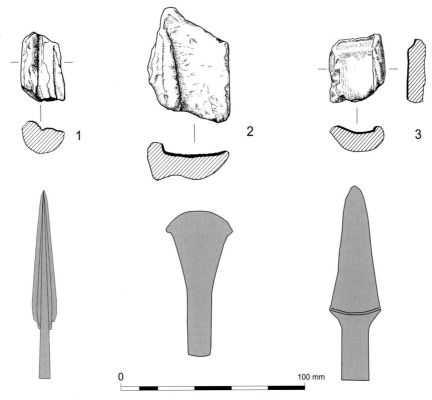

Figure 82. Ceramic mould fragments.

surfaces (*e.g.* Fig. 82) and would have been in contact with molten metal, whilst other fragments were of clay that had been wrapped around the true mould to ensure that they stayed in place whilst the molten metal was being poured into them. Over half of the assemblage (by both count and weight) derived from a large bowl-shaped pit (CG1) located adjacent to the entrance of a large post-defined enclosure (CG67), the remainder coming from three waterholes distributed through the central part of the investigated area (CG4, 6 and 7).

The main criteria for differentiating between wraps and mould pieces are that mould pieces are often grey as a consequence of being heated in a reducing atmosphere and exhibit morphological details relating to the cast artefact (Table 13). Mould wraps in contrast tend to be red orange in colour and of indeterminate form.

Clay mould fragments are not encountered prior to the end of the Middle Bronze Age (Tylecote 1986, 82) and their presence is thus consistent with the Later Bronze Age dating of the site and can be considered quite usual for this period.

It is possible for copper alloys to be cast by three different techniques, all of which use clay to form the mould. These are open moulds, piece moulds, and lost wax or investment moulds. Of these techniques, open moulding is the least complex and is only useful for simple two-dimensional objects. Piece moulding and lost wax moulding are considerably more complex and are capable of forming intricate three-dimensional objects. In Britain, it is generally thought that the lost wax technique was not used until the Early Iron Age (Tylecote 1986, 80). The mould fragments from Kemerton are all consistent with this model for development, all deriving from piece moulds and, where discernable, from two piece or bi-valve moulds. Such moulds can only be used once.

Shape analysis

Some of the mould fragments survived to the extent that the type of artefacts that were cast in them can be suggested (Table 14; Fig 82), and this indicates that the main artefacts being cast at the site were weapons; including a palstave, a spearhead socket and two weapons with mid-ribs, all of which derived from CG1.

XRF analysis of mould fragments

Among the true mould fragments (*i.e.* the mould pieces), it was possible to detect traces of metal left on the modelled surface of the mould in some instances (~20%). Analysis of these mould fragments was performed using XRF spectometry. The instrument used was a LINK XR200 with a tube voltage of 40kV, a current of 20mA and a 3mm collimator.

In all the analysed samples there were traces of copper, lead and tin. There was no evidence for any arsenic or antimony on any of the mould surfaces. It is not possible to extrapolate, from a qualitative analysis of these residues, a precise alloy composition. However, the presence of these three elements suggests that the alloys used in the castings were either leaded tin bronzes or tin bronze with a little lead. Such alloy types would be typical for the Late Bronze Age period (Northover 1980; Tylecote 1986, 30).

Lead was frequently added to tin bronze in the Late Bronze Age as it offered enhanced castability, meaning that fine detail could be depicted and fewer castings failed. This benefit is evident in alloys containing over 2wt% of lead (Tylecote 1986, 80). Such low levels of lead have little effect on the mechanical properties of the alloy, although if excessive amounts of lead are added, for instance greater than 15%, then the mechanical properties of the allow begin to deteriorate.

Hearth material

Amongst the mould material were found a small number of fragments of hearth material (Table 13). This is vitrified refractory material derived from the walls of metallurgical hearths.

The slag debris

None of the slag debris examined exhibited any evidence of being associated with non-ferrous metallurgy. The presence of copper was not detected by either XRF spectrometry or microstructural analysis. In the light of this, and the unstratified nature of the material (which was recovered during soil stripping), this cannot be considered to offer any insight into the nature of the metallurgy associated with the moulds and casting. Microstructural analysis of one piece (KEM1) found numerous inclusions of iron sulphide

Table 14. Mould fragments for which the objects cast in them were identifiable.

Context	Context Group	Identification	Figure
1830	1: Pit	Weapon with mid rib (×2)	81.1
1830	1: Pit	Flat blade	-
1830	1: Pit	Palstave	81.2
1830	1:Pit	Weapon with mid rib	-
1830	1:Pit	Flat blade	-
1830	1:Pit	Spearhead socket (part of)	81.3
2032	4:Waterhole	Flat blade	-

in a pyroxene matrix (calcium iron silicate) saturated in magnetite. It is likely that such a slag was formed during iron smithing whilst using coal as a fuel.

Conclusion

Morphological and chemical analysis has provided some insight into the nature of the casting operations that were carried out at Kemerton in the Late Bronze Age. It is apparent that the alloy selected was bronze, which was most probably leaded. The artefacts made appear to have been predominantly weapons.

Worked flint (by Peter Bellamy)

Introduction

The analysis of the worked flint was approached with several themes in mind. The first theme is raw material procurement. Is flint from more than one source being used? Are these sources local? How is the material brought to the site (as nodules or as prepared cores)? The second theme is an investigation of the character of the flintworking on the site. Does the flint represent a single industry or are there several technological traditions present? Are these chronologically diagnostic? What are the products of the industry or industries? Does the nature and the scale of the flintworking change over time? The third theme is one of use and deposition on the site. Are there specific areas where flint is being used and/or discarded? Are different parts of the site used for different processes? What are the deposition processes?

The total worked flint assemblage from the site comprises a total of 397 pieces (1749g), of which, 314 (1392g) was recovered from stratified contexts, 39 pieces (164g) were unstratified excavation finds and 44 items (193g) came from the fieldwalking (Table 15). In addition, a small quantity of burnt unworked flint (204g) was recovered from both the excavations and the fieldwalking. The assemblage is not homogeneous and though the bulk of the material appears to derive from a flake industry, there is evidence for the presence of narrow blade industries as well. The diagnostic artefacts suggest that the flint spans a chronological range from the Late Palaeolithic to the Bronze Age.

Raw material

The raw material used was exclusively flint. As the majority of the assemblage had a fairly heavy white or bluish-white patination, it was difficult to determine the colour of the flint. The small number of unpatinated or very slightly patinated pieces indicated that the flint was mid brown to grey-brown in colour with very few inclusions. Occasional flakes of slightly coarse cherty flint were also noted. On the whole, the flint appeared to be relatively free from thermal fractures and faults. Where there is surviving cortex, this indicates that the vast majority of the pieces were derived from flint gravel nodules. The cortex was generally white, buff or brown in colour, often fairly pitted and worn, with a number of glossy worn patches. Some pieces had no surviving cortex but had well-rolled glossy thermal surfaces, many of which were iron-stained. The gravel flint was probably derived from the flint gravels available on site and from the immediate vicinity.

A small number of pieces (approximately 11) had a thin smooth brown cortex with no signs of rolling evident, and three others had a thick chalky cortex. These pieces may not be derived from the gravels and could have been imported to the site. The slight evidence available suggests that this material was prepared on site rather than being brought in as prepared cores.

The size of the nodules used is difficult to determine from the assemblage itself. Nearly all the cores have been extensively worked and estimation of the original size of the nodules is almost impossible. The cores are all very small (between 24–49mm max dimension) and in general the flakes are also small (mainly between 20–30mm in length with a small number up to 50mm long). This suggests that the size of the nodules may also have been fairly small. In general, the flint appears to be of fairly good knapping quality, with few faults and fractures evident.

The character of the flintworking on the site

It is clear that there is more than one industry represented in the assemblage. The vast majority of pieces are products of flake production with a small number of items derived from a narrow blade industry.

The blade industry is represented by a small number of cores, narrow blades and bladelets and some retouched forms also. There are three blade cores in the assemblage (Table 16). The number of blade cores may be underrepresented as almost all the cores have been worked out and the final removals may not be representative of the removals earlier in the life of the core. A number of flake cores have some indication of previous blade or blade-like flake removals. One core tablet from a blade core and three crested blades indicate the rejuvenation of blade cores on site. The blades included both small narrow blades and some larger broad blades. The small number of blade tools present indicates at least two separate industries, one Upper Palaeolithic and one Late Mesolithic. The Upper Palaeolithic artefacts are a shouldered point (Fig. 83.1) and a backed blade fragment (Fig. 83.2). Both of these pieces were white patinated and the shouldered point was lightly burnt also. The Late Mesolithic artefacts comprise two broken geometric rod-like microliths; one with oblique trimming at one end (Fig. 83.3–83.4) and two butt microburins, notched on the right hand side (Fig. 83.5–83.6). In addition, there are three miscellaneous retouched blades, two with oblique retouch at the distal end.

The flake industry, unlike the blade industry, is widespread, with pieces found in many contexts across the site;

Table 15. Flint assemblage composition.

Site area	Context/description	Flakes	broken flakes	burnt flakes	blades	broken blades	burnt blades	cores	broken cores	tools	broken tools	burnt tools	chips	burnt chips	misc debitage	total
N/A	Fieldwalking	13/41	9/32	5/20	1/2	1/4		1/12	1/7	2/15	3/28	1/6	1/0		6/26	44/193
2	All features	1/1				2/2	2/1	1/30		2/7	1/0			2/1		11/42
3	All features			1/4					1/14				1/0			3/18
4	All features	1/4														1/4
5	All features	1/1		3/9					1/17		1/0		2/0	1/0		9/27
7	All features	1/1														1/1
11	All features	3/10	3/7					1/9		1/9	1/8		2/1	2/2	1/7	14/53
12	All features	3/20	2/5					1/20		2/21						8/66
13	All features	1/5														1/5
14	All features	2/11								2/18			1/1		1/3	6/33
15	All features	3/6		1/9	1/0	2/0			1/14				7/1	3/0		18/30
16	All features	2/7	2/5		1/0	1/0		1/23	1/8	2/26						10/69
17	All features	8/70	3/19	2/1	3/5	4/2		1/27		2/8	3/5		9/0	6/0		41/137
18	Ring-ditch CG 79	2/10		2/1												4/11
18	Pit CG 1	18/86	2/4	2/9		3/7		5/97	3/16	2/20	1/2		9/3	1/0	3/6	49/250
18	Waterhole CG 7	4/20	2/2					1/9					1/0	1/0		9/31
18	Waterhole CG 6	6/12						1/22		1/1	1/4					9/39
18	Other features	1/1											2/0	2/0	2/4	7/5
20	Beaker pits CG 12, 13 & 42	4/9	4/27	3/7				3/45	2/21	7/41	2/7	1/3			3/10	29/170
20	Pit CG 10							1/28			1/7					2/35
20	Waterhole CG 4	19/82	7/33	2/26	2/3	2/4			1/11	4/35	2/12	2/12	6/4	1/0	1/4	49/226
20	Waterhole CG 3	1/4	1/1							1/9						3/14
20	Other features	3/4	1/4	2/9						1/10	1/9				1/8	9/44
21	Waterhole CG 14	6/9	2/6			1/1		4/47		2/2					2/5	17/70
21	Other features	1/1						1/7		1/4			1/0			4/12
All	Unstratified	7/31	9/24	5/55		1/4		3/26			1/5		10/2	2/0	1/17	39/164
Total		111/446	47/169	28/150	8/10	17/24	2/1	25/402	11/108	32/226	18/87	4/21	52/12	21/3	21/90	397/1749

Table 16. Flint core typology.

Site area	Context/ description	single-platform blade cores	multi-platform blade cores	single-platform flake cores	multi-platform flake cores	discoidal flake cores	tested nodules, etc	core fragments	mean wt of complete cores (g)
2	All features			1					29
3	All features							1	
5	All features							1	
11	All features						1		11
12	All features	1							15
15	All features							1	
16	All features					1		1	26
17	All features		1						27
18	Pit CG 1			2	2	1		3	18
18	Waterhole CG 7							1	
18	Waterhole CG 6				1				22
20	Beaker pits CG 12, 13 & 42			1	2			2	15
20	Pit CG 10				1				28
20	Waterhole CG 4							1	
21	Waterhole CG 3			1	3				11
21	Other features				1				9
All	Unstratified	1		1		1			8
Total		**2**	**1**	**6**	**10**	**3**	**1**	**11**	**17**

although the largest quantity was recovered from features containing Beaker pottery. A number of these features also contain Late Bronze Age pottery and the question is whether there are two flake industries present, one Late Neolithic/ Early Bronze Age and one Late Bronze Age in date, or whether there is a single industry which is residual in the later period features. Visual inspection suggested there was little difference in the character of the flintworking in the various features. However, in order to test this, it was decided to undertake metrical and attribute analysis on the flint from the three Beaker pits (CG12, 13 & 42) and from a Late Bronze Age pit (CG1) and waterhole (CG4), despite the small sample sizes involved. These metrical and attribute data have been retained in archive rather than presented in this report because of the potential unreliability of the small sample sizes. Nevertheless, the results from the Beaker and the Late Bronze Age pits were almost identical, thus confirming the initial visual impression, so consequently, it has been assumed that the flint from the Late Bronze Age pits is primarily a residual Beaker assemblage. Despite this, the possibility that the Late Bronze Age features also include some Late Bronze Age flintworking cannot be ruled out completely as there are a small number of pieces from the site which would fit comfortably within a Later Bronze Age flint assemblage.

The assemblage is dominated by debitage (Table 15) with elements present from all stages of the reduction process, from initial core preparation to finished tools and utilised pieces, indicating that there was both production and use of flint tools on the site. No evidence for core tool production was recognised, which is perhaps not surprising given the size and quality of the locally available raw material.

The flake cores included both single platform and multi-directional cores (*e.g.* Fig. 84.17 and 18). These latter were worked out in one direction then the core rotated and the previous flake scars used to create a new platform. Up to three different platforms were utilised. There is virtually no evidence for the use of abrasion to strengthen the platform edge. Three discoidal cores were recovered (Table 16; *e.g.* Fig. 84.19), at least two of which were on large flakes. The flake cores are between 5–38g with a mean weight of 17g (Table 16). A single broken flake from a Levallois core recovered from Waterhole CG7 indicates the use of this technique also within the industry.

The flakes are generally intermediate in shape between 15mm and 53mm in length and 9–52mm in width with either plain or cortical butts averaging *c.* 5 mm wide. They appear to have been largely removed by a hard hammer, though for the vast majority of flakes the hammer type is indeterminate. The flakes include preparation flakes (*c.* 8%), core trimming flakes (*c.* 56%) and other miscellaneous 'waste' flakes. Three rejuvenation flakes removing a previous flaking face and two crested flakes were recovered from Waterhole CG4 confirm the evidence of the cores for the creation of new platforms utilising the previous flake scars.

The tools and other pieces showing signs of utilisation comprise about 13% of the assemblage. The majority of retouched forms are of Late Neolithic/Beaker type and include chisel and oblique transverse arrowheads, thumbnail and other scrapers, piercers and knives (Table 17). Apart from the miscellaneous retouched pieces, scrapers are the most numerous tool type present in the assemblage. The scrapers tend to be small and neatly worked with abrupt retouch round the end and down the sides and include

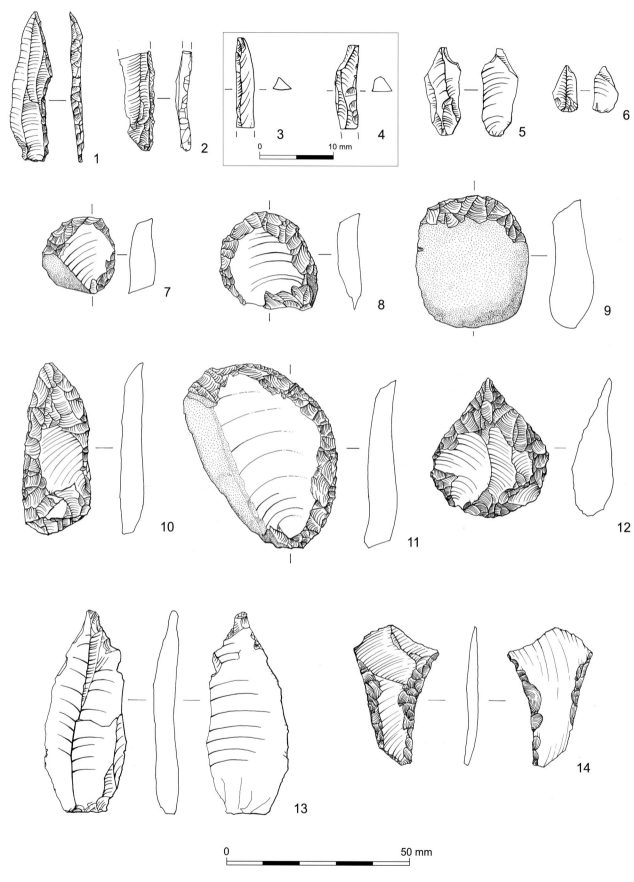

Figure 83. Flint.

Table 17. Retouched forms.

Site area	context /description	knife	scraper	piercer	scraper/ piercer	backed blade	shouldered point	transverse arrowhead	oblique arrowhead	projectile point	microlith	microburin	misc retouched blade	misc retouched flake	utilised
N/A	Fieldwalking	1	4												1
2	All features		1					1					1		
5	All features												1		
11	All features				1									1	
12	All features													2	
14	All features		1											1	
16	All features													1	1
17	All features		1							1	2	2			
18	Pit CG 1		1	2											
18	Waterhole CG 6	1	1												
20	Beaker pits CG 12, 13 & 42	2	1						1					6	
20	Pit CG 10	1													
20	Waterhole CG 4		2										1	4	1
20	Waterhole CG 3														1
20	Other features	1		1											
21	Waterhole CG 14					1	1								
21	Other features	1													
All	Unstratified		1												
Total		7	13	3	1	1	1	1	1	1	2	2	3	15	4

four thumbnail scrapers (Fig. 83.7–83.8). One scraper has a straight scraping edge and two examples have fairly shallow retouch. A variety of different blanks were used for scrapers including core preparation flakes (Fig. 83.9) and a core fragment. Several of the scrapers are heavily worn. Knives are the next most numerous tool type and two types are represented – plano-convex knives and naturally-backed flake knives. Two plano-convex knives are present in the assemblage, both made on long flakes with regular fine invasive retouch (Fig. 83.10). One other possible example has some bifacial retouch but it is too fragmentary to be certain whether it is a knife or not. The rest of the knives have shallow invasive retouch along one side and with natural backing (usually cortical) on the other side (Fig. 83.11). The piercing and boring tools comprise a piercer with a finely worked point on a broad thick flake (Fig. 83.12); a borer on the end of a broad blade (Fig. 83.13); and a piercer on a broad flake with a point formed by minimal retouch. Two arrowheads, a chisel transverse (Fig. 83.14) and an oblique (Fig. 84.15) were recovered together with another heavier possible projectile point (Fig. 84.16). The miscellaneous retouched pieces are the most common retouched form and include a wide variety of flakes with mainly small areas of regular fine retouch along one side or end of a flake.

There is a small number of possible Middle–Late Bronze Age retouched forms present in the assemblage, including a composite scraper/piercer (Fig. 84.20) and two flakes with coarse denticulate retouch (*e.g.* Fig. 84.21) and one with a thinned butt. A single possible end-blow Janus flake was also found in the assemblage.

The analysis of the flint assemblage has confirmed the presence of three or four different chronological periods. Both the Upper Palaeolithic and the Late Mesolithic periods are represented by only a very small number of residual items, making it difficult to assess their character. There is no evidence for flint knapping on site during the Upper Palaeolithic and the artefacts may represent no more than chance losses. The presence of blade cores and rejuvenation flakes of possible Mesolithic date, together with microburins indicate that some knapping and tool production was taking place on site. In contrast, the Late Neolithic/Beaker period is the only period which has evidence for anything other than very small-scale flintworking on site. The range of debitage indicates that flint gravels were being procured and worked on site. It does not appear to have been a specialised industry and a range of tools were produced consistent with a domestic settlement context. The possible Later Bronze Age use of flint is much more difficult to define. The very small quantity of material which may belong to this period indicates that flint working and use was not a significant part of the settlement activity at this time.

Use and deposition of flint on the site

An examination of the distribution pattern of the flint, the types of features which contain flint and the composition of the assemblage in these features was undertaken to support understanding of patterns of use and deposition across the site.

Firstly the distribution of the flint from the different chronological periods was examined to see if it was possible to isolate chronologically distinct areas of the site. The two possible Upper Palaeolithic artefacts were

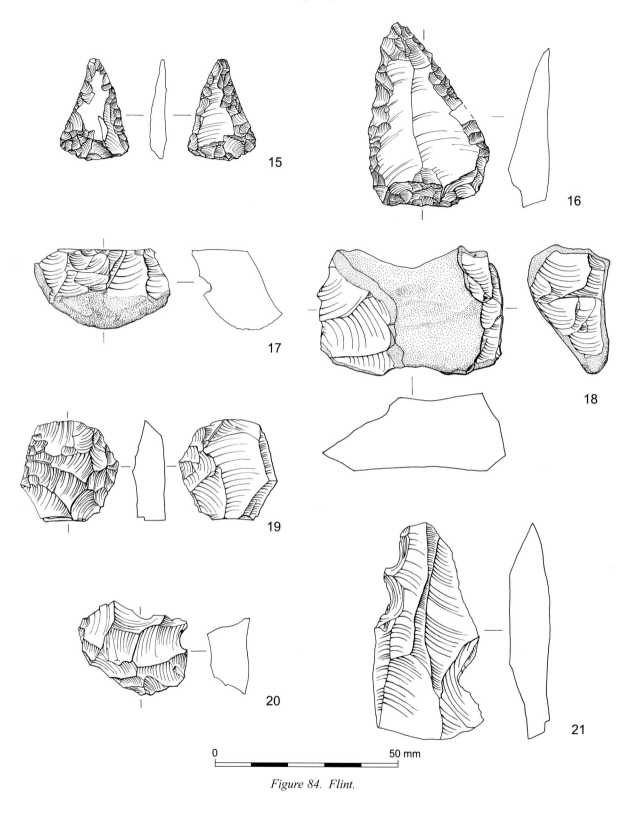

Figure 84. Flint.

residual, both being recovered from a Late Bronze Age pit (context 2102, CG14) towards the western end of the site. No other flintwork which could be confidently assigned to this period was found in the vicinity and it is likely that the finds represent casual losses rather than evidence for an Upper Palaeolithic settlement site. In contrast, all the diagnostic Mesolithic artefacts were found in the northeastern part of the site centred on Area 17 (Fig. 11; contexts 212 and 1722). These were associated with a number of pieces of blade debitage, blade cores and two retouched blades (contexts 1714, 1716, 1717 and 1722), which are assumed to be Mesolithic on the basis of their proximity to the diagnostic Mesolithic material. There was only a very sparse scatter of blade debitage elsewhere. This restricted distribution suggests the presence of a Mesolithic settlement in this area, though the quantity of material recovered is not large enough to be able to confidently characterise the nature of this site.

Although the Late Neolithic/Beaker flint is widely scattered across the site, unlike the earlier material, this distribution is not even across the whole of the site and there is a clear pattern of flint being concentrated in pits rather than being associated with other features. The largest quantity of flint came from the centre of the site, focussed on the Beaker pits (Fig. 11; CG12, 13 and 42), and two Late Bronze Age features, a waterhole (CG4) and a bowl-shaped pit (CG1; Fig. 11). Smaller quantities were recovered from the Late Bronze Age waterholes to the south (CG6 and 7) and west (CG14; Fig. 11). It is unclear how much of this patterning reflects the 'true' distribution of the flint and how much is a result of the excavation strategy which focussed on excavation of these substantial and evidently artefact rich features. Nevertheless the lack of flint from excavated house structures, the ring-ditch, and the boundary ditches indicates that there are areas where there is only a sparse scatter of flint and, therefore, the perceived concentrations may accurately reflect real archaeological differences.

A closer examination of the main concentration may provide some insights into the nature of the Beaker activity. The composition of the flint assemblage from the Beaker pits and two of the Late Bronze Age features (CG1 and CG4) suggests that the activity represented is non-specialised and is likely to indicate settlement. There is evidence both for knapping and for the use of flint tools with no specialised areas of production or use. There is a fairly wide range of different tool types present including scrapers, piercers, knives and miscellaneous retouched pieces, together with an oblique arrowhead and another possible projectile point. None of the material refitted and the majority of the pieces were not in mint condition and some of them were burnt,

suggesting that the material was not immediately deposited in the pits. The residual material in CG1 and CG4 may have been accidentally incorporated from the immediately surrounding ground surface but it is less clear whether the material in the Beaker pits was deliberately deposited or not. There is little difference in the assemblage composition and condition between the Beaker and Late Bronze Age pits, though it must be noted that the Beaker pits contained the highest proportion of retouched pieces of any feature on site. It is interesting to note that only one of the three Beaker pits (CG12) contained a respectable quantity of flint, yet the adjacent pit (CG13) contained only a single flint flake and no flint was recovered from the third of these pits (CG42). Given the close proximity of the pits to each other, this difference is interesting and suggests that the flint was incorporated through deliberate deposition of selected material, as refuse. If it was the result of accidental incorporation from the surrounding surface then a more even distribution might be anticipated.

The ring-ditch, possibly of Beaker or Early Bronze Age date, only produced four flint flakes. It is likely that these represent accidental losses and there is no evidence for any flint associated with the construction and use of this funerary monument.

In contrast with the Beaker settlement, the Later Bronze Age settlement appears to have no associated flintwork. There is little or no flint in many of the features and it seems unlikely that the small quantities present are any more than part of a residual background scatter. The one exception to this is perhaps in the southeastern part of the site (Areas 11, 12 and 16) where there is a slightly greater concentration of flint found in postholes and other features. It is pertinent to note that all of the possible Middle–Late Bronze Age flint artefacts came from this area (*e.g.* CG9; Fig. 16). It is likely that most of the flint in this area was accidentally incorporated into the features.

Illustrated flint

Fig.	*description*	*period*	*CG/context*	*CG type*
83.1	tanged point	Upper Palaeolithic	CG14: 2101	Waterhole
83.2	backed blade	Upper Palaeolithic	CG14: 2101	Waterhole
83.3	rod microlith	Late Mesolithic	N/A: 212	Gully
83.4	microlith	Late Mesolithic	N/A: 1722	Tree-throw
83.5	microburin	Mesolithic	N/A: 1722	Tree-throw
83.6	microburin	Mesolithic	N/A: 1722	Tree-throw
83.7	thumbnail scraper	Late Neolithic/Beaker	CG12: 2043	Pit
83.8	thumbnail scraper	Late Neolithic/Beaker	CG4: 2032	Waterhole
83.9	scraper	Late Neolithic/Beaker	CG4: 2032	Waterhole
83.10	plano-convex knife	Late Neolithic/Beaker	N/A: 2106/7	Pit/posthole
83.11	flake knife	Late Neolithic/Beaker	CG12: 2043	Pit
83.12	piercer	Late Neolithic/Beaker	CG1: 1830	Bowl-shaped pit
83.13	borer	Late Neolithic/Beaker	CG1: 1830	Bowl-shaped pit
83.14	chisel arrowhead	Late Neolithic/Beaker	N/A: 204/5	Gully
84.15	oblique arrowhead	Late Neolithic/Beaker	CG12: 2043	Pit
84.16	projectile point?	Late Neolithic/Beaker	CG4: 2032	Waterhole
84.17	single platform core	Late Neolithic/Beaker	CG1: 1830	Bowl-shaped pit
84.18	two platform core	Late Neolithic/Beaker	CG1: 1830	Bowl-shaped pit
84.19	discoidal core	Late Neolithic/Beaker	CG1: 1830	Bowl-shaped pit
84.20	scraper/piercer	Middle-Late Bronze Age?	CG9: 1111	Basin-shaped pit
84.21	retouched flake	Middle-Late Bronze Age?	Area 16: 1614	Posthole

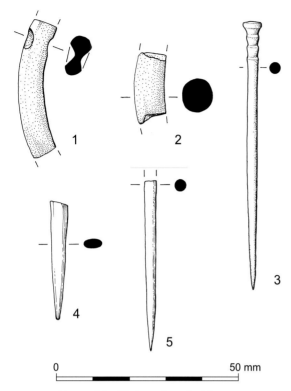

Figure 85. Shale and worked bone.

Other finds

Shale objects (by Robin Jackson)

Catalogue

CG4: Context 2032 (Fig. 85.1)
Armlet fragment from one of the upper fills of a large waterhole. Oval section. Well made and finely finished. Original internal diameter 80mm. Original external diameter 93mm. Two opposing depressions were present on one end of this segment. These had been drilled or gouged out and appear likely to represent a setting for some form of mount or fastening, or alternatively had been drilled to enable the object to be repaired.

CG3: Context 2039 (Fig. 85.2)
Small fragment of worked shale possibly from an armlet, recovered from the upper fill of a large waterhole. Circular sectioned. Well-made and finely finished fragment of which too little survived to determine diameter.

Discussion

The two shale objects recovered both derived from Late Bronze Age contexts (CG3, context 2039; CG4, context 2032). Both appear to be fragments of armlets, this term being used (after Calkin 1953, 46) to avoid any implication as to where they might have been worn on the arm.

Shale has been widely found in Bronze Age contexts, being used for a variety of items of dress and personal adornment including beads, buttons and armlets, as at Swine Sty, Derbyshire (Mackin 1971), Brean Down, Somerset (Foster 1990, 159–160; fig. 112: 37–39), Potterne (Wyles 2000, 208–213), Runnymede Bridge (Needham and

Longley 1980) and Green Park (Boyle 2004, 98–99). Such shale objects reflect the wide range of external contacts evidenced at some of these sites, the ability to acquire such objects possibly reflecting a relatively high status.

At Brean Down, Potterne, Runnymede Bridge and Green Park shale armlets or bracelets were recorded in Late Bronze Age contexts while at Swine Sty evidence of Early Bronze Age shale working, including production of armlets was recorded. Internal diameters vary widely from as small as 15mm (at Eagleston Flat, Curbar, Derbyshire; Beswick 1994) to as much as 90mm at Green Park. Evidence suggests that roughouts were produced at sites like Swine Sty using a combination of flaking, gouging, pecking and cutting. The roughouts were finished by abrasion and polishing. Completion sometimes occurred at the site of production but there is also evidence that trading of the blanks was commonplace, the latter having been found for example at Brean Down and Potterne, both sites located away from the nearest shale source.

The best preserved of the two examples from Kemerton (from 2032; Fig. 85.1) clearly represents part of a finished item with its diameter (250mm circumference) falling towards the upper end of the range recorded. This may suggest that it was designed for a man or to be worn high on the arm. The evidence for some form of mount or fitting is unusual, although similar objects at Potterne (Wyles 2000, 210 and fig. 81.15 and 16) were suggested to be bracelet fragments reused as pendants. Alternatively it might provide evidence of a form of staple used to repair a valued item.

Distance from the likely source of the shale is also of some considerable interest. Even though some trade is evident from distribution of shale objects, it is most commonly the case that the distances involved are not great. However, Kemerton is a long way from known and utilised sources either on the Dorset coast (Kimmeridge; Calkin 1953) or in Derbyshire (Swine Sty; Mackin 1971), 175km or 140km distant respectively, thus suggesting that the site was integrated into a long-distance exchange network.

Other worked stone (by Derek Hurst)

Apart from the objects discussed above, two other worked stone objects were recovered.

One of the fills within a large waterhole (CG4, context 2034) produced a small fragment of quern or rubber with a worked surface. This has been identified as being made from May Hill sandstone (Fiona Roe pers. comm). May Hill sandstone has been used as a quern material since the Neolithic, when it was imported into sites in Gloucestershire (Roe 1999, 415–418) and remained the most common quern material used in the region throughout the prehistoric period .

The other item was a piece of architectural stonework made from oolitic limestone derived from a pit which was otherwise sterile but is clearly not of Late Bronze Age date.

Unworked stone (by Derek Hurst)

Unworked but utilised stone was recovered, in the form of 'pot-boilers' and limestone pieces, which were all burnt. The burnt limestone far outweighed the amount of 'pot-boilers', and was concentrated in the upper fills of some of the large pits and waterholes (particularly in CG1 and CG7). However, this material was only selectively retrieved on site, and so little could be stated other than in general terms about its incidence and distribution across the site.

'Pot-boilers' are conventionally understood to have been used for heating water, and the burnt limestone may also have had a culinary use. Occasionally the latter comprised plates of limestone, flat on one side, and scorched (especially on one side), and this could imply a use as a hot surface for cooking. More often, however, the limestone fragments were irregularly shaped, and only partially burnt. Such pieces may have functioned as the local counterparts of the more familiar pebble 'pot-boilers', which were otherwise relatively poorly represented.

Worked bone (by Robin Jackson)

Catalogue

Context 1103 (Fill within waterhole CG8; Fig. 85.3)
Very well-made and polished bone pin with a finely decorated, ?turned, head. Circular sectioned with a fine tapered point. Length 72mm. Section 3mm (main shaft); 5mm (head).

Context 1111 (Fill within basin-shaped pit CG9; not illustrated)
Burnt fragment of worked bone point. Possibly from an awl or chisel. Tip broken off. Irregular oval shape in section with two flattened faces as if 'pared'. Length 19mm.

Context 1841 (Fill within waterhole CG7; Fig. 85.4)
End of a well-made and polished bone pin. Slightly flattened oval in section with a fine tapered point. Length 31mm. Section 4mm/2mm

Context 2032 (Fill within waterhole CG4; Fig. 85.5)
End of a well-made and polished bone pin. Circular sectioned with a fine tapered point. Length 45mm. Section 3mm.

Discussion

The four bone objects described were all recovered from Late Bronze Age contexts. The identification of three bone pins and a possible awl or chisel fragment from contexts of this period is not unusual for a site of this date. Similar finds were recorded at Brean Down, Somerset within a larger group of worked bone objects for which it was observed that items were mainly practical (Foster 1990, 160–162).

In this respect the Kemerton material appears typical, however, the pin in context 1103 stands out as an unusually well made example having a finely worked decorative head. In the light of this, it is felt to have most probably been a highly valued dress or hair pin, rather than a simply utilitarian article.

The other two pin ends are also well worked and highly polished, however, since only the points survive it is impossible to determine whether they were also decorated. These may have fulfilled a similar function, however,

the possibility that they were associated with weaving or sewing should not be excluded.

Worked timbers (by Ian Tyers)

Introduction

Ten fragments of timber derived from the lower silting fills two waterholes of Late Bronze Age date (CG4 and CG8) were submitted for species identification and technological analysis.

The material was primarily lengths of roundwood, some with cut ends and others with broken or rotted ends and was of diverse size. The largest being pieces *c.* 70cm by *c.* 10cm diameter, whilst the smallest were *c.* 10cm by *c.* 2cm diameter.

Identification

The identification of timbers from archaeological sites can be either a microscopic or a macroscopic procedure, depending upon which species the sample is and upon its preservation characteristics. For many of the native hardwood species, and in particular for oak (*Quercus* spp), beech (*Fagus* sp), ash (*Fraxinus* sp) and elm (*Ulmus* sp), the characteristics visible using hand-lenses or low-power binocular microscopes (both typically ×10 magnification) are sufficient to determine safely the species of timber. For most of the other native hardwood species and all softwoods it is necessary to prepare slides of thin sections to examine using high-power microscopes (magnifications up to ×400) in order to separate the species involved. The identifications reported here are a result of both these procedures combined with the use of biological keys and reference volumes (*e.g.* Schweingruber 1978, 1990 and Wilson and White 1986).

Technological analysis

Different tools used in the past to convert or shape wooden objects leave a variety of 'signature marks' upon well-preserved timbers such that reconstruction of the methods and tools used is frequently possible. Distinctions can be made between the marks left by hewing with axes, or adzes etc., and also the types of marks made by tools used for more complex operations such as sawing and auguring can be distinguished. Although no comprehensive handbook serves as a complete reference to this subject, papers such as those in the Somerset Levels Papers series (*e.g.* Coles and Orme 1984, 1985), the Flag Fen report (Pryor 1991) or covering Roman and medieval material from London (*e.g.* Goodburn 1992) provide a series of examples. In exceptional material (both of large assemblage size and exceptional waterlogging) it is possible to follow individual tools being used on different timbers which assists more standard stratigraphic analyses with linking the process of construction or modification of wooden structures.

Table 18. The analysed timbers.

Context	Context Group	Latin name	English name	Technology	Comment
1115	8	*Alnus* spp	Alder	Double facet cut end plus ?notch	
1115	8	*Alnus* spp	Alder	Single facet cut end	
1115	8	*Alnus* spp	Alder	Single facet cut end	
1115	8	*Alnus* spp	Alder	Modern flat top	
1115	8	*Alnus* spp	Alder	Modern flat top	
1115	8	*Alnus* spp	Alder		
2034	4	*Quercus* spp	Oak	Possible notch	Rotted heart
2034	4	*Quercus* spp	Oak	?Single facet cut end plus possible notches	Rotted heart
2034	4	*Quercus* spp	Oak		Badly preserved
2050	4	*Quercus* spp	Oak		Badly preserved

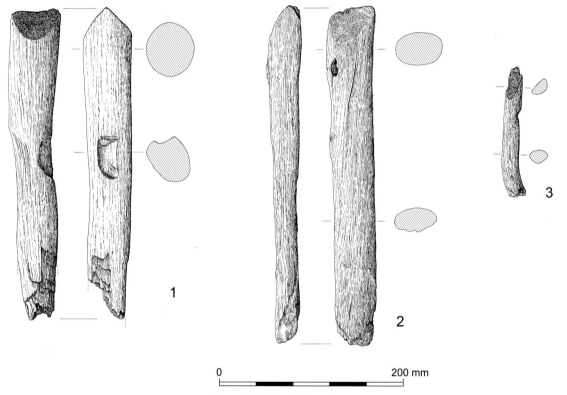

0   200 mm

Figure 86. Worked wood.

Results

Ten separate fragments of material were examined (Table 18; Figs 86 and 87). Although some were relatively large pieces, the majority were smaller twig-like fragments.

CONTEXT 1115 (CG8)

All six pieces of timber submitted for analysis from this context, the basal fill of a large waterhole, were of alder (*Alnus* spp). Alder is a relatively soft timber, frequently encountered at sites of all periods. This group includes three timbers with clear cut marks, apparently aimed at putting pointed ends on to stakes (Fig. 86). The preservation was too poor to identify the exact tool involved but the concave surfaces and stop lines across the facets suggested use of an axe. Alder is particularly prone to breaking

across the grain and several of the timbers were markedly broken in this way, at least two flat ends appear to be non-archaeological in origin, perhaps being derived from the excavation process, but cannot be identified with absolute certainty. The material is somewhat knotty and a small broken piece may have a coppice heel surviving, although the fragmentary survival makes identification difficult. All this material shows some evidence of woodworm (*Anobium punctatum*) damage suggesting the timbers had been exposed for some time.

CONTEXTS 2034 AND 2050 (CG4)

All four pieces of timber examined from these contexts were of oak (*Quercus* spp). Oak is a hard strong timber predominant in structures from all periods and it is often

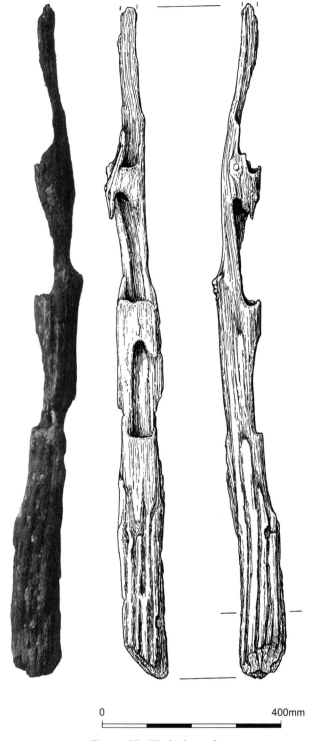

0   400mm

Figure 87. Worked wood.

preserved even under imperfect conditions. The material was sufficiently poorly preserved that little further analysis was possible. The possibility of timbers of other species being entirely lost due to the poor preservation conditions cannot be discounted. Two smaller fragments (one from 2034 and one from 2050) were barely recognisable and were impossible to examine in any greater detail.

The two larger fragments (both from 2034) conjoined and included one possibly cut end (see below), but the preservation was far too poor to identify with any certainty the tools used. These timbers were unusual in having hollow centres presumably rotted out, this weakness may indicate they derived from a single parent log.

Note (by Robin Jackson): The illustration made of the two timber fragments from 2034 (Fig. 87) was produced when these were first excavated some 3 years prior to analysis. At the time they clearly conjoined and were in somewhat better condition than when seen by the specialist who did not have the benefit of the illustration. Both the illustration and the on-site description record three notches in the face of this timber which as noted above appeared to have had a cut end. This timber was broken during recovery being embedded in 2050 but extending into 2034 and lying at an angle against the sloping side of the pit. This closely resembles notched timbers interpreted as ladders found in similar situations on Late Bronze Age and Iron Age sites as at Sutton Common, South Yorkshire (Parker Pearson and Syde 1997, 233), Loft's Farm, Essex (Brown 1988) and at Eight Acre Field, Radley, Oxfordshire (Taylor in Mudd *et al.* 1995) and is felt to represent the poorly preserved remains of such a ladder.

Discussion

The material in Waterhole CG4 is not especially notable either in terms of its implications for structural techniques or the local environment. The poor quality of preservation meant that this material was not worth conserving and it has been discarded.

The material in Waterhole CG8 is slightly better in preservation. However, it would be hard to name a prehistoric site in England or Wales that has not included pointed alder stakes of some sort. The material is thus hardly of national significance. The drawings prepared record the pertinent features in reasonable detail (Figs 86 and 87) and in the light of their state of preservation (somewhat deteriorated by shrinkage and some physical damage since original excavation), these were also not deemed worthy of conservation and were discarded.

The updated project design for the site (Napthan *et al.* 1997) identified a number of themes for the analytical work. Unfortunately the small size of the assemblage makes it difficult to identify aspects of the timber component that can contribute usefully to these themes. The material may all be derived from backfill rather than structures in the pits; it is therefore unclear whether the material contributes to an understanding of the structural practises in the settlement area or its waste disposal processes. The species concerned are extremely common to archaeological excavations of all periods in this country, and reveal nothing unexpected about the local environment. The tools indicated by the few identifiable facets reveal nothing unexpected in terms of available crafts and technologies. The small size of the assemblage and fragmentary nature of the material do not allow significant discussion of woodland management practises, if any, and nothing of timber selectivity beyond a preference for roundwood of appropriate size.

Summary

One pit exclusively contained alder timbers, the other exclusively oak timbers the reason for this distinction is not clear. The obviously worked timbers in both oak and alder were identified. Axes seem to have been used to work points onto the timbers.

Part 4.
Environmental evidence

Animal bone (by Stephanie Pinter-Bellows)

Material and Methods

The excavation produced a total of 3189 animal bones and bone fragments from Neolithic, Beaker and Late Bronze Age features. The majority of the faunal material c. 95% (3,009 fragments) came from the Late Bronze Age contexts, the remainder, c. 5% (180 fragments), deriving from Late Neolithic/Beaker contexts.

The following mammal and bird species were identified: cattle (*Bos taurus*), pig (*Sus scrofa*), sheep (*Ovis aries*), red deer (*Cervus elaphus*), roe deer (*Capreolus capreolus*) and dog (*Canis familiaris*). Sheep and goat can be difficult to identify to species; deciduous cheek teeth (dP3 and dP4), distal scapula, distal humerus, distal radius, astragalus, calcaneous, and distal metapodia were used in the differentiation of sheep and goat (see Boessneck 1969, Payne 1985, and Prummel and Frisch 1986). Bones which could not be identified to species were assigned to higher order categories: sheep/goat, small artiodactyl (sheep-, roe deer- or pig-size), large artiodactyl (cow- or red deer-size), large mammal (cow-, red deer-, or horse-size), and dog/fox.

Due to the age of the bones and the state of preservation, all bones which could be identified were recorded. Tooth eruption and wear data, fusion data, and measurements were recorded systematically; and pathology and butchery data were noted. Recording of the material followed Jones *et al.* (1981). Dental eruption and attrition data were recorded using the wear stages defined by Grant (1982) for cattle and pig, and the stages defined by Payne (1973, 1987) for sheep/goat. Measurements follow von den Driesch (1976) with additions as described in Davis (1992). Withers heights were calculated following von den Driesch and Boessneck (1974).

Two methods of quantification were used to estimate the relative importance of the major animal species: simple fragment counts (often termed number of identified specimens per taxon) and minimum numbers of individuals (following Gilbert and Steinfeld 1977: 333).

Results

Neolithic/Beaker

The assemblage from this phase is very limited (180 fragments; 0.695kg; av. wt. 3.86g). The condition of the

Table 19. Animal bone from Neolithic, Beaker and Early Bronze Age contexts.

Context Group	Date	Type	Count	Weight (g)
38	Neolithic	Pit	30	36
12	Beaker	Pit	132	554
13	Beaker	Pit	4	49
42	Beaker	Pit	5	9
79	Early Bronze Age	Ring-ditch	9	47
Total			**180**	**695**

Table 20. List of animal species from Neolithic/Beaker and Late Bronze Age contexts.

Animal Species	Neolithic/Beaker NISP	Late Bronze Age NISP	MNI*
Cow (*Bos taurus*)	10	260	11
Pig (*Sus scrofa*)	-	138	8
Sheep (*Ovis aries*)	-	10	*
Sheep/Goat	3	145	9
Dog (*Canis familiaris*)	-	10	1
Red deer (*Cervus elaphus*)	-	35	1*
Roe deer (*Capreolus capreolus*)	-	8	2
Sheep/Goat/Deer	-	33	
Dog/Fox	-	1	
Small Artiodactyl	3	89	
Large Artiodactyl	-	63	
Large Mammal	7	215	
Unidentified Mammal	114	1818	
Total	137	2825	

Notes

The most frequent element used for calculated MNI for the cattle and sheep/goat is the first or second lower permanent molar, for the pig it is the first molar, and for the roe deer it was the mandible.

With no fragments identified as goat, fragments of sheep and sheep/goat bones have been grouped together for the remainder of the analysis.

While the fragments of antler are included in the fragment count they have not been included in the calculation of MNI as antlers can be collected without the killing of the animal and the three antler coronets present all show that the antlers had been dropped.

bones was universally poor, very eroded and abraded, some almost past recognition. The majority of this material derived from a Beaker pit group (comprising CG12, 13 and 42; Table 19), but quantities were also present in a Neolithic pit (CG38) and the recut section of an Early Bronze Age ring-ditch (CG79, context 1814). Fragments which could be identified to species are presented in Table 20 and the single measurable element on Table 21.

Late Bronze Age

PRESERVATION AND TAPHONOMY

A total of 3,009 fragments, weighing 23.878kg (av. wt. 7.9g) of animal bone was recovered from Late Bronze Age contexts; the majority deriving from the large basin- and bowl-shaped pits and waterholes (Table 22).

Condition of the bone was subjectively noted on three characteristics. Charred bone was noted for colour – black through blue through white – and the amount of the bone affected. Eroded and abraded bone was considered together as the characteristics were found together in almost every case. Eroded bone was defined as bone which was pitted, battered, having a 'woody' appearance or occasional bones where the outer surface had gone. Abraded bone was defined as bone which had rounded edges, instead of retaining sharply angular margins to old breaks and cut surfaces. The colour of the bone was also noted; from chalky white to a dark brown tannin-like colour. Gnawed

bone was noted for the element and portion of the bone affected and the species believed to have gnawed it.

Fragmentation was examined by the amount of unidentified bone (mostly fragments of long bone shafts and admittedly a most subjective characteristic based on the time spent and the experience of the observer).

In considering the condition of the bone, it was questioned whether there were any differences between the larger assemblages (>200 fragments) deriving from three of the waterholes (notably CG4, CG6 and CG7) and one of the major pits (CG1), and that coming from other pits and postholes (Table 23). Preservation of bone from most contexts was recorded as fair to poor. Charring and gnawing were recorded to have affected only a small percentage of bones from across the site; the little gnawing noted was all carried out by dogs. Unidentified fragments were also found in similar percentages in the larger assemblages to those of the smaller ones and thus the levels of fragmentation (as suggested by the unidentified bone) do not reveal any meaningful patterns; although average weights were somewhat higher in the major features across the site in comparison to the smaller ones (Table 22). There were, however, a higher percentage of bones showing a variety of colours and fewer bones showing signs of erosion and abrasion within the assemblages recovered from the large pits and waterholes. Erosion and abrasion of bone was not only more numerous in the material from the smaller features but was also more severe. The appearance of the eroded bone suggested that much of it was affected

Table 21. Measurements from Neolithic/Beaker and Late Bronze Age contexts.

Neolithic/Beaker

Cattle

First phalanx
GLpe 53.2	Bp 28.7	SD 23.7	Bd 26.0

Late Bronze Age

Cattle

Scapula
	GLP 58.2	LG 50.9	BG 43.9		

Humerus
	Bd 64.5	BT 57.4	HTC 29.9		
	Bd 67.2	BT 61.1	HTC 28.0		
	Bd 76.6	BT 72.2	HTC 32.8		

Acetabulum
| | LA 59.1 | MW 12.8 | | | |
| | LA 65.5 | MW 13.9 | | | |

Astragalus
		GLm 54.1		Dm 33.1	Bd 38.6
	GLl 56.9	GLm 53.2	Dl 31.8	Dm 27.8	Bd 37.3
	GLl 60.1	GLm 54.5	Dl 32.1	Dm 28.8	Bd 38.0
	GLl 60.5	GLm 55.2	Dl 33.9	Dm 29.1	Bd 37.3
	GLl 61.9	GLm 56.8		Dm 32.1	Bd 40.8
	GLl 64.1	GLm 57.0			Bd 41.9

First Phalange
	GLpe 58.9	Bp 28.6	SD 23.7	Bd 28.3	

Pig

First Mandibular Molar
	L 15.2	W 10.5		

Third Mandibular Molar
	L 30.2	Log ratio -0.108	Wa 14.9	Log ratio -0.163
	L 30.8	Log ratio -0.100	Wa 15.2	Log ratio -0.155
	L 34.9	Log ratio -0.046	Wa 16.2	Log ratio -0.127
	L 35.3	Log ratio -0.041	Wa 16.2	Log ratio -0.127
	L 35.5	Log ratio -0.039	Wa 16.3	Log ratio -0.124

Scapula
	GLP 38.8	LG 30.1	BG 26.1	

Tibia
	Bp 37.1

Red deer		*Roe deer*			
Antler		Antler			
	41 203.2		41 77.1		
Tibia		Humerus			
	Bd 54.2		Bd 27.2	BT 26.1	HTC 12.2

Sheep/goat

Metatarsus
	SD 11.8	DD 10.3	B at F 22.8	

First Phalange
	GLpe 32.2	Bp 11.1	SD 8.4	Bd 9.4

by water – pitting across the entire surface; being either woody in texture or having the outer layer of bone wholly missing. One interpretation of this patterning is that all the bone was treated similarly before disposal, but that it may have been affected differently by the size and content of the pit into which the bone came to rest.

Table 22. Animal bone from Late Bronze Age features.

CG	Type	Count	Weight (g)	Average wt (g)
4	Waterhole	692	4977	
6	Waterhole	355	2904	
7	Waterhole	464	5301	
8	Waterhole	131	1359	
14	Waterhole	113	636	
18	Waterhole	54	314	
	Sub-total	*1809*	*15491*	*8.81*
2	Basin-shaped pit	62	349	
5	Basin-shaped pit	124	468	
9	Basin-shaped pit	164	1795	
15	Basin-shaped pit	9	116	
17	Basin-shaped pit	108	1595	
26	Basin-shaped pit	30	22	
39	Basin-shaped pit	2	22	
	Sub-total	*499*	*4367*	*8.75*
1	Bowl-shaped pit	294	967	
10	Bowl-shaped pit	95	1726	
11	Bowl-shaped pit	19	82	
16	Bowl-shaped pit	13	68	
21	Bowl-shaped pit	6	17	
27	Bowl-shaped pit	2	4	
37	Bowl-shaped pit	4	2	
	Sub-total	*433*	*2866*	*6.61*
19	Pit/post	1	2	
23	Pit/post	49	185	
25	Pit/post	81	309	
91	Pit/post	20	81	
92	Pit/post	4	28	
	Sub-total	*155*	*605*	*3.90*
29	Posthole	10	106	
32	Posthole	4	26	
34	Posthole	3	4	
35	Posthole	22	48	
90	Posthole	12	20	
	Sub-total	*51*	*204*	*4.00*
49	Fence	2	1	0.50
77	Hearth pit	60	344	5.73
	Totals	**3009**	**23878**	**7.93**

Table 23. Preservation and taphonomy of bone from Late Bronze Age contexts.

Condition	Major pits %	Other pits %
Charred	1.8	2.3
Eroded, Abraded	33.0	51.8
Gnawed	0.5	0.4
Coloured	54.7	35.6
Unidentified fragments	61.1	68.5
Total number of fragments	1588	1237

SPECIES ABUNDANCE

The species identified are listed in Table 20 as numbers of fragments (NISP) and the minimum number of individuals (MNI). The table shows the assemblage as a whole, since when the large pits and waterholes were sub-divided from the lesser features and examined by statistical analysis using chi square the differences in NISP were not significant ($X2 = 5.36$, $P>.05$).

The bulk of the identifiable bones belong to the domestic mammal species: cattle, sheep/goat, and pig.

Table 24. Relative frequency of skeletal elements from Late Bronze Age contexts.

	Cattle		Pig		Sheep/goat	
	Total	O/E	Total	O/E	Total	O/E
Mandible	10	2.3	12	4.3	6	2.3
Scapula, glenoid	5	1.1	4	1.4	2	0.8
Humerus, distal	6	1.4	0	0.0	2	0.8
Radius, distal	3	0.7	0	0.0	0	0.0
Acetabulum	3	0.7	1	0.4	0	0.0
Femur, distal	0	0.0	1	0.4	0	0.0
Tibia, distal	5	1.1	2	0.7	4	1.5
2+3 Carpal	2	0.5	0	0.0	0	0.0
Astragalus	9	2.0	1	0.4	0	0.0
Calcaneum	2	0.5	0	0.0	0	0.0
Metapodia, distal	7	0.8	2	0.2	2	0.4
Phalanx, first	4	0.2	0	0.0	3	0.3
Molars, lower first and second*	33	3.8	22	3.9	33	6.3
Molar, lower third*	7	1.6	6	2.1	4	1.5

Notes

The counts of the teeth include those in the jaws.

The species total will not equal the total from the list of animals table because only selected element fragments were used.

An example of the calculations. For cattle the total counts for the elements are added up, after dividing the number of first phalanges by 4 and the metapodia and combined total of first and second molars by 2, giving a total of 62. This is divided by the number of elements being used (14) giving an expected total, if the elements were all equally abundant, of 4.4. The observed values (O) are then divided by this calculated expected value (E) to show whether the elements are under- or over-represented relative to one another. The elements for sheep/goat are treated the same way as cattle. For pig however, the metapodia are divided by 4 as pig have a greater number and all were used in the calculation.

The fragment count gives the impression that cattle were the more numerous species; however, the MNI suggests almost equal numbers. Since the MNI calculations were made using teeth, an explanation for the larger number of cattle bone fragments may be that the larger cattle bones were being broken into more fragments. As cattle have several times the amount of meat of pigs and sheep, when the importance of these animals as a food source is considered, cattle again become more important. The only other domestic mammal found on the site was dog. Only a small number of bones were found, the majority from one partial skeleton (context 2036, CG5).

Wild mammals in the form of red deer and roe deer are present, but in small numbers – thus indicating a supplement to the diet rather than a major component. Most of the elements identified from the red deer are antler fragments. They do not necessarily mean that the deer were being killed for their antlers, as antlers drop off in the autumn; and the two coronets (antler bases) recorded are from antlers which have dropped off. The fragments of roe deer, on the other hand, include only one antler fragment (a 'dropped' coronet).

RELATIVE FREQUENCY OF SKELETAL ELEMENTS

Examination of the range of skeletal elements recovered shows them to be relatively equally distributed across the site, however, deposition was clearly not entirely random. A left and right cattle astragalus of similar size from one of the basin-shaped pits (CG5, context 2036) appear to represent a pairing, while articulating cattle thoracic vertebrae were recovered from one of the bowl-shaped pits (CG10, context 2010).

The distribution of selected skeletal elements for the most common mammalian species represented in the assemblage is summarised in Table 24. This shows the assemblage as a whole, since when the rankings of the elements were examined between the larger assemblages (from substantial pits and waterholes) and the smaller assemblages (from the lesser features) by statistical analysis using Kendall's tau the rank order was the same (cattle, $z = 1.98$, $P<.05$; pig, $z = 2.55$, $P = .01$; sheep, $z = 2.56$, $P = 0.01$). The calculations used to examine the relative frequency of selected skeletal elements in the table follow O'Connor (1991); selected elements used in the calculations come from different parts of the body and include some smaller parts of the skeleton. The expected total for elements has been calculated by taking the total count of the elements (compensating for elements of which there are more than two in the skeleton: metapodia, first phalanx, and first and second mandibular molars taken together) and dividing by the number of elements involved to obtain an expected total, if the elements were all equally abundant. The observed value (O) is then divided by this calculated expected value (E) to show whether the number of specimens of a given element in the sample was under-represented ($O/E < 1.00$) or over-represented ($O/E > 1.00$) relative to one another. A sample calculation is shown at the bottom of the table.

The pattern which emerges from this analysis shows various elements are over-represented, such as mandibles, mandibular teeth and astragali; while other elements such as the first phalanx, calcaneum, carpals and distal femora are under-represented. These differences can mostly be

Table 25. Mandible and mandibular tooth ageing data for cattle from LBA contexts.

Mandibles

dP4	M1	M2	M3
-	B	1	-
k	D	-	-
j	F	1	-
k	G	b	-
-	K	k	g
-	L	k	k

Individual teeth (including both loose teeth and those in mandibles)

dP4	wear stage	a	b-e	f-k	>k			
		-	-	7	-			
M1/2	wear stage	a	b-e	f	g/h	j	k-m	>m
		3	9	5	7	1	6	-
M3	wear stage	a	b-f	g/h	j	k-m		
		-	-	5	-	2		

Table 26. Mandible and mandibular tooth ageing data for sheep/goat from LBA contexts.

Mandibles

dP4	M1	M2	M3
14	6	-	-
17	7	v	-
16	9	4	u
23	9	-	-
-	15	11	11

Individual teeth (including both loose teeth and those in mandibles)

dP4	wear stage	0-12	13	14	16	>16
		-	-	2	1	3
M1/2	wear stage	0	1-4	5-8	9	>9
		1	2	11	13	5
	cumulative % age	3%	9%	44%	84%	100%
M3	wear stage	0	1-4	5-10	11	>11
		1	1	1	1	1

explained by taphonomic and recovery factors. There is differential preservation of weaker parts of the skeleton, *i.e.* those with more cancellous bone and those not yet fused (Brain 1967). There are also lower recovery rates for smaller bones. This differentiation in number of small bones not only holds true for elements of a smaller size but can be seen in the higher incidence of over-representation among the cattle bones (where the fragment size may be bigger than in relatively small species such as pig and sheep/goat).

The assemblage appears to be consistent with disposal on a multi-use site. There do not appear to be noticeable concentrations of elements associated with disposal during butchery separate from culinary or industry purposes.

AGEING

Tables 25–27 summarise the age distribution of cattle, pig and sheep/goat in terms of teeth eruption and wear. Due to the small size of the assemblage, interpretation of the age of animals is confined to the individual context of this particular site and attempts are not made to explore questions of animal husbandry or human diet at this period on a larger scale.

The dental eruption and wear evidence indicate that the

Table 27. Mandible and mandibular tooth ageing data for pig from LBA contexts.

Mandibles

dP4	M1	M2	M3
J	c	l	-
-	d	a	-
-	-	b	3
-	f	c	-
-	f	d	-
-	j	c	-
-	j	g	c
-	j	g	c
-	k	j	d

Individual teeth (including both loose teeth and those in mandibles)

dP4	*wear stage*	a	b-d	e-h	j-m		
		-	1	-	1		
M1	*wear stage*	a	b	c/d	e/f	g/h	j/n
		1	-	2	2	1	6
M2	*wear stage*	a	b	c/d	e/f	g/h	j/n
		2	1	3	-	2	1
M3	*wear stage*	a	b	c/d	e/f	g/h	j/n
		1	1	5	-	-	-

majority of the cattle were kept into maturity, with most having been killed between four and eight years and some at eight years and over. There is a smaller peak killed before a year and a half, indicating that only a few animals were killed specifically for meat; adolescent animals (second molar in wear, third molar not yet in wear) are often of a size to provide a good ratio of meat yield to fodder consumed. However, the majority were killed over this age (of prime beef) and this implies that the importance of the animal lay as much, if not more, in their value for traction or providing dairy products.

The majority of the pigs were killed by the time they reached the end of adolescence (in their third year, before their third molar erupts). Pigs are usually slaughtered by late adolescence as they have gained much of their body weight by this age. The dental eruption and wear indicate that the pigs died at a variety of ages before late adolescence; more being killed as they came closer to full body weight ('more' in the small sample available being single digit numbers).

The dental eruption and wear data for sheep show animals killed at all ages, though few were very young (first molar under stage 4) or over approximately 6 years (second molar over stage 9). This suggests an unspecialised sheep husbandry, with sheep killed for meat and kept for milk and/or wool.

MEASUREMENTS

All measurements taken are presented in Table 21 and none fall outside expected ranges. Measurements of pig third

molars were converted into log ratio values, the standard (value 0) being the Kizilcahaman wild boars studied by Payne and Bull (1988). These values are all smaller than the Kizilcahaman boar, indicating that the pigs are all probably domestic; though it must be noted that the Kizilcahaman wild boar is by no means a universal standard.

Conclusions

Preservation of bone from most contexts is fair to poor. The range of skeletal elements appears consistent with disposal on a multi-use site. There do not appear to be noticeable concentrations of elements associated with disposal during butchery separate from culinary or industrial purposes.

The majority of the bones come from cattle, pig and sheep/goat. The cattle appear to be the most important meat source, though the three species may be represented in relatively equal numbers in this assemblage. While the size of cattle makes them an important source for meat, in life they were probably more valued as a source of dairy products and for traction. The sheep were also multi-purpose animals valued for milk and/or wool as well as meat. The pigs, seemingly all domestic, had a more one-dimensional role being valued for their meat.

The red deer from the site is mainly represented by antler fragments, the evidence available pointing to most of the antlers having been already dropped from the deer. The bones present from the red and roe deer point to them playing only a minor role in the diet. Dogs were present

Table 28. Cremation fragment size and anatomical distribution.

Cremation 1814 (CG79)

Fragment size distribution			*Anatomical fragment distribution*		
≥10mm	5.0g	38%	Unid	13.0g	100% of total
≥ 5mm	3.0g	24%			
≥ 2mm	5.0g	38%	Skull	0g	0% of identified frags
			Axial	0g	0% of identified frags
			Long bone	0g	0% of identified frags

Cremation 2136 (CG96)

Fragment size distribution			*Anatomical fragment distribution*		
≥10mm	60.0g	63%	Unid	54.0g	57% of total
≥ 5mm	15.0g	16%			
≥ 2mm	20.0g	21%	Skull	1g	2% of identified frags
			Axial	0g	Axial
			Long bone	0g	Long bone

on the site in small numbers and may have been used for hunting or working with stock.

Human bone (by Stephanie Pinter-Bellows)

One human bone was identified within one of the uppermost, 'abandonment' fills of a waterhole (context 2032; CG4); the spinous process of an adult thoracic vertebra, the shape of which suggests it was an upper thoracic vertebra.

Cremated bone (by Stephanie Pinter-Bellows)

The cremated bone from two deposits was examined. The fragment size and anatomical distribution of both are shown in Table 28.

The bone from 1814 (CG79), a recut section of ring-ditch, totalled 13.0g in weight. The maximum length of a fragment was 16mm. It was not possible to identify the anatomical elements from which any of the fragments derived; or to determine certainly whether the species was human or non-human.

The bone from 2136 (CG96), a small pit comprised a total of 95.0g in weight. The maximum length of a fragment was 38mm. From this assemblage, it was possible to discern skull and long bone fragments (these long bone fragments could not be identified to specific elements) but not from which species the bones came from; however, the pit was small and heavily truncated, and apart from the calcined bone only contained charcoal.

The weight of both groupings is very small. The quantity of bone recoverable from a modern adult cremation is between 1600–3600g; and archaeological adult cremations usually range from 200g to almost 2000g with an average of *c.* 800g (McKinley 1989). The colour of bones was an almost universal greyish-white with hints of blue on a few of the fragments. There are some twisting and fissuring of the fragments. The colour is suggestive of a

burning temperature of between 645–<940°C (Shipman *et al.* 1984). The colours indicate a thorough burning of the bones; however, it is much more common to find the colours indicating a range of temperatures depending on the placement of the individual bones to the heat and the amount of fat and muscle surrounding them (McKinley 1994).

These two small assemblages of burned bone fragments possibly represent cremation burials. The small, uniform and relatively unidentifiable nature of the fragments suggests, however, that this is less a burial meant to represent an individual than a token representation with ritual significance. Although other reasons for small collections of burned bones being buried in such locations should be considered, the otherwise sterile and isolated character of CG96 is certainly consistent with interpretation as an unaccompanied cremation burial, while the funerary association of the other deposit is highly probable given its location within a recut of a ring-ditch (CG79).

The plant macrofossils (by Elizabeth Pearson)

Methods

Fieldwork and sampling policy

The environmental sampling policy was as defined in the County Archaeological Service Recording System (1995 as amended). Samples of 10 to 70 litres were taken from 71 contexts dating to the Beaker/Early Bronze Age and Late Bronze Age periods. On account of the rarity of environmental remains from deposits of this date, all samples were fully sorted.

Processing and analysis

Non-waterlogged samples were processed by flotation followed by wet-sieving using a Siraf tank. The flots were

Table 29. Plant remains from Beaker pit and EBA ring-ditch.

Botanical name	Family	Common name	Habitat	CG79 1814	CG12 2043
Charred plant remains					
Hordeum vulgare grain	Gramineae	barley	F		6
cf *Hordeum vulgare* rachis	Gramineae	barley	F		1
Cereal sp indet grain	Gramineae	cereal	A		7
Bromus sp grain	Gramineae	brome grass	A		2
Gramineae spp indet grain	Gramineae	grasses	AF		1
cf *Rumex conglomeratus*	Polygonaceae	sharp dock	CD		4
Uncharred plant remains					
Chenopodium/Atriplex sp	Chenopodiaceae	goosefoot/orache	AB		+
Lycopus europaeus	Labiatae	gipsywort	BE	+	

Key:

A= cultivated ground
B = disturbed ground
C = woodlands, hedgerows, scrub etc
D = grasslands, meadows, and heathland
E = aquatic/wet habitats
F = cultivar

+ = 1-10
++ = 11-50
+++ = 51-100
++++ = 100+

collected on a 300μm sieve and the residue retained on a 1mm mesh. This allows for the recovery of items such as small animal bones, molluscs and seeds. The residues were fully sorted by eye and the abundance of each category of environmental remains estimated. The flots were fully sorted using a low power EMT stereo light microscope and remains identified using modern reference collections housed at the County Archaeological Service.

Two samples (contexts 1115 and 2050) from the bases of two large Late Bronze Age waterholes (CG4 and CG8) were rich in waterlogged organic remains. A sub-sample of 500mls to 1 litre from this material was processed by the wash-over technique as follows. A sub-sample was broken up in a bowl of water to separate the light organic remains from the mineral fraction and heavier residue. The water, with the light organic fraction was decanted onto a 300μm sieve and the residue washed through a 1mm sieve. The wet flots were sorted and subsequently stored in alcohol, while the residue was dried. The habitat information for the plant remains has been taken from Clapham *et al.* 1987.

Charred plant remains

Charred plant remains were poorly preserved over the whole site, with the exception of a relatively rich assemblage of cereal grain from a Late Bronze Age pit/posthole (CG19, context 1601).

These remains are likely to have been accidentally charred as a result of piecemeal processing of cereal crops (for example, parching grain prior to storage or milling), or spillage of cereal grains into domestic fires during cooking.

Beaker/Early Bronze Age activity

A small quantity of charred plant remains was recovered from a Beaker pit (CG12, context 2043). This included barley (*Hordeum vulgare*) grains in association with grass grains (Table 29). The only chaff identified was a possible barley rachis. The seeds of sharp dock (cf *Rumex conglomeratus*) may be a crop contaminant which has come from plants growing at the edges of the field, perhaps in a hedgerow.

Late Bronze Age activity

Charred plant remains were only sparsely present from features of this date (Tables 30 and 32), although one rich assemblage was recovered from a small pit of this date (CG19, context 1601) and is discussed separately from the remainder which are discussed as a group.

CG19: PIT/POST 1601

The remains from this feature, a small pit or posthole, are the only example of concentrated charred cereal crop waste recovered from the site. They were recovered in association with 64 sherds of pottery all apparently from a single vessel; perhaps suggesting deliberate and selective deposition of this material. Two sub-samples taken from the assemblage have produced radiocarbon dates of 2885±40 BP (OxA-10791, 1260–920 cal BC) and 2891±36 BP (OxA-10792, 1260–930 cal BC).

One third of the flot from a 20 litre sample was quantified. The assemblage was dominated by cereal grain, a large number of which were identifiable as emmer (*Triticum dicoccum*) or emmer/spelt wheat (*Triticum dicoccum/ spelta*). Hulled six-row barley (*Hordeum vulgare*) was identified on the basis that both straight and twisted

Table 30. Charred plant remains from major Late Bronze Age pits/waterholes.

Botanical name	Family	Common name	Habitat	CG1 1830	CG2 709	CG2 1845	CG2 1846	CG4 2032	CG4 2049	CG4 2050	CG6 1836	CG8 1102	CG8 1103	CG8 1104	CG8 1110	CG8 1112	CG8 1114	CG8 1115	CG9 1111
Triticum dicoccum grain	Gramineae	emmer wheat	F	3					2	3	1	2	3	1					
Triticum cf *dicoccum* grain	Gramineae	emmer wheat	F							3	1	2	3	1					3
cf *Triticum dicoccum* tail grain	Gramineae	emmer wheat	F	3															
Triticum dicoccum glume base	Gramineae	emmer wheat	F						1			1							
Triticum dicoccum/spelta grain	Gramineae	emmer/spelt wheat	F							1		1							
Triticum dicoccum/spelta glume base	Gramineae	emmer/spelt wheat	F												1				
Triticum sp (free-threshing) grain	Gramineae	free threshing bread wheat	F								1			2					
Triticum sp grain	Gramineae	Wheat	F	3		1		1	1				1						1
cf *Triticum* sp	Gramineae	Wheat	F														1		
Hordeum vulgare sp grain	Gramineae	Barley	F									1	1	1					
straight, hulled grain	Gramineae	Barley	F						3										
twisted, hulled grain	Gramineae	Barley	F			1													
cf *Hordeum vulgare* grain	Gramineae	Barley	F			1						1							
Triticum/Hordeum sp grain	Gramineae	wheat/barley	F					5				1		1			1		
Triticum/Secale sp grain	Gramineae	wheat/rye	F										1						
Cereal sp indet grain	Gramineae	Cereal	A	11	1	5		12	3	2	1		1	2					8
Bromus sp	Gramineae	brome grass	AF					1	1		1								1
cf *Bromus* sp	Gramineae	brome grass	AF										1						
Avena sp	Gramineae	Oat	AF	1					1										
Gramineae spp indet grain	Gramineae	Grasses	AF	20	1	3		8	6+frag	2			4	1	4	1	1		2
Gramineae sp indet culm node	Gramineae	Grasses	AF		1														
Vicia/Lathyrus sp	Leguminosae	vetch/vetchling/pea	A								1								
cf *Vicia/Lathyrus* sp	Leguminosae	vetch/vetchling/pea	A																
Leguminosae sp indet	Leguminosae	legume	A										1						
Rumex acetosella sgg	Polygonaceae	sheep's sorrel	A									1							
Corylus avellana shell frag	Corylaceae	Hazelnut	C	1															
Galium aparine	Rubiaceae	goosegrass, cleavers	BCD				1												
unidentified	unidentified			4				1											

Key:
A= cultivated ground   + = 1-10
B= disturbed ground   ++ = 11-50
C= woodlands, hedgerows, scrub, etc   +++ = 51-100
D= grasslands, meadows, and heathland   ++++ = 100+
E= aquatic/wet habitats   * = fragments
F= cultivar

grains, with glume impressions, were present. Three grains (*Triticum/Secale* sp) had some rye like characteristics, but could not confidently be distinguished from wheat. Only a small quantity of chaff (emmer and emmer/spelt wheat glume bases) was recorded.

This appears to represent a relatively clean grain assemblage (with the exception of large grass grain contaminants) which may have been accidentally charred as a result of parching grain prior to storage or milling, or from grain used in cooking being spilt into a domestic hearth. A few hazelnut shell fragments were also present.

The apparently careful disposal of this charred grain in a small pit or posthole along with sherds from a single vessel (which may have been complete at the time of deposition) is perhaps indicative of a structured deposit of some significance to those who placed it here.

Other features

In other features, charred plant remain assemblages were small; however, cereal grains were predominant (and in some cases large grass grains), while only a few chaff fragments and small weed seeds were recovered. A few hazelnut shell fragments were found in two pits (CG1, context 1830; and CG91, context 1440) as well as those noted in CG19 (above).

The scarcity of these remains, particularly the delicate chaff fragments and small weed seeds, may, to some extent, reflect deterioration resulting from constant wetting and drying on the well-drained soils overlying gravel. Indeed these conditions are likely to have resulted in a preservation bias towards the more robust cereal grains and large grass grains.

The identifiable cereal grains were dominated by wheat, many of which could be distinguished as emmer (*Triticum dicoccum*) or emmer/spelt wheat (*Triticum dicoccum/ spelta*). A small quantity of a free-threshing type of wheat grain was recovered from two of the waterholes; from contexts 1104 (CG8) and 1836 (CG6). Hulled barley (*Hordeum vulgare*) was recovered from several contexts, a basin-shaped pit (CG2, context 1845), two of the waterholes (CG4, context 2049; CG8, contexts 1102, 1103 and 1004) and two pit/posts (CG19, context 1601; CG25, context 1243) that from CG19 forming part of a notably cereal rich deposit.

The weed seeds are likely to derive from plants growing in arable fields, or growing around the site. As so few were recovered, it was difficult to make any interpretation of the soil conditions under which the crops were grown.

Waterlogged and uncharred plant remains

Uncharred plant remains were sparsely distributed over much of the site, with the exception of those from fills within two Late Bronze Age waterholes where they were relatively abundant (CG8, context 1115; CG4, contexts 2049 and 2050; Tables 31 and 32). In the case of both waterholes, preservation had resulted from waterlogging of deposits at their bases.

The seeds in the other deposits which do not appear to have been waterlogged are likely to be intrusive material from the ploughsoil, introduced into the features by reworking of the soil by earthworms. Although these remains are unlikely to be contemporary with the Bronze Age deposits, the data is presented in the tables as a record of the 'background contamination' which may be useful for comparison with other sites.

Beaker/Early Bronze Age

Only occasional uncharred seeds were recovered which are likely to be intrusive from the ploughsoil and not contemporary with the deposits.

Late Bronze Age waterholes (CG4, contexts 2049 and 2050; CG8, context 1115)

Plant remains were well-preserved at the base of these two waterholes. There was an abundance of fragmented herbaceous and woody plant material as well as seed remains, presumably from vegetation immediately surrounding the features.

Seed remains were most abundant in context 1115, the basal fill of this waterhole (CG8). Here, there was only slight evidence of plants which would have been growing either in water at the bottom of the pit, or at the wet muddy margins of the water's edge, for example, water crowfoot (*Ranunculus* sbgen *batrachium*), gipsywort (*Lycopus europaeus*) and sedges (*Carex* spp). In contrast, there was an abundance of twig, stem and leaf fragments, thorns and seeds of shrubby plants such as bramble (*Rubus fruticosus* agg), elderberry (*Sambucus nigra*) and dogwood (*Cornus sanguinea*) and these are indicative of either a hedgerow or woodland scrub in the immediate proximity. Other species indicate an element of grassland or herbaceous woodland undergrowth (*Prunella vulgaris*), while corn salad (*Valerianella dentata*) is considered to be a cornfield weed. The abundant blackberry and elderberry seeds and fragments of a sloe stone are all evidence of plants which may have been collected for food. One item appears to be a shrivelled berry, but remains unidentified.

In the lowermost fills of the other waterhole which produced waterlogged plant remains (CG4, contexts 2049 and 2050), the few seed remains recovered, suggest that similar environments were represented, although only seeds of goosefoot/orache (*Chenopodium/Atriplex* sp), which may have grown on disturbed ground around the pit, were abundant. Herbaceous vegetation and woody plant material (stem, twig, wood, root and unidentified leaf fragments), were more abundant in 2049 than in the other waterhole examined (CG8). Fool's parsley (*Aethusa cynapium*) may have been growing cornfields nearby, while collectable food (blackberry, elderberry, sloe and hazelnut) were also present.

Table 31. Uncharred plant remains from major Late Bronze Age pits/waterholes.

Botanical name	Family	Common name	Habitat	CG2 1845	CG2 1846	CG4 2032	CG4 2049	CG4 2050	CG6 1836	CG8 1102	CG8 1103	CG8 1115
Ranunculus acris/repens/bulbosus	Ranunculaceae	Buttercup	CD				+					++
Ranunculus sb gen Batrachius	Ranunculaceae	Crowfoot	E									++
Fumaria sp	Fumariaceae	Fumitory	ABC				+					
Silene sp	Caryophyllaceae	Campion	CDE	1					+			
Stellaria media	Caryophyllaceae	Chickweed	AB								+	
Chenopodium album	Chenopodiaceae	fat hen	AB				+	+++				+
Atriplex sp	Chenopodiaceae	Orache	AB				+					
Chenopodium/Atriplex sp	Chenopodiaceae	goosefoot/orache	AB			+						
Rubus fruticosus agg	Rosaceae	blackberry/bramble	CD				+	+		+	+	+++
Prunus spinosa	Rosaceae	Sloe	C				+					2*
Cornus sanguinea	Araliaceae	Dogwood	C									18
Aethusa cynapium	Umbelliferae	fool's parsley	A			+		+		+		
Polygonum aviculare	Polygonaceae	Knotgrass	AB									+
Corylus avellana shell fragment	Corylaceae	Hazelnut						+				
Solanum nigrum	Solanaceae	black nightshade	BC				+					++
Lycopus europaeus	Labiatae	Gipsywort	BE									4
Prunella vulgaris	Labiatae	Selfheal	CD					+		+		
Stachys sylvatica	Labiatae	hedge woundwort	C				+	+				2
Plantago major	Plantaginaceae	Plantain	B					+				
Sambucus nigra	Caprifoliaceae	Elder	BC			+	+			+	+	+++
Valerianella dentata	Valerianaceae	narrow-fruited cornsalad	B									2
Carduus sp	Compositae	Thistle	ABCD									1
Carduus/Cirsium sp	Compositae	Thistle	ABCD									4
Sonchus asper	Compositae	sow thistle	AB									1
Carex spp	Cyperaceae	Sedge	CDE		+		+					5
Unidentified seed												4
unidentified leaf frags								++			+	+
stem frags							+++					
twig fragments							++++	+++				+++
wood fragments							+++	++++				++++
root frags												
thorns												++

Key:

A= cultivated ground
B= disturbed ground
C= woodlands, hedgerows, scrub, etc
D= grasslands, meadows, and heathland
E= aquatic/wet habitats
F= cultivar

+ = 1-10
++ = 11-50
+++ = 51-100
++++ = 100+
* = fragments

Table 32. *Plant remains from lesser Late Bronze Age features.*

Botanical name	Common name	Family	Habitat	CG25 1242	CG25 1243	CG91 1440	CG17 1501	CG17 1517	CG19 1601	CG23 1604	CG39 1801	CG39 1802	CG10 2010	CG92 2013	CG90 2042
Charred plant remains															
Triticum dicoccum grain	emmer wheat	Gramineae	F						93						5
Triticum cf *dicoccum* grain	emmer wheat	Gramineae	F		3	2									
Triticum dicoccum glume base	emmer wheat	Gramineae	F						8						
Triticum dicoccum/spelta grain	emmer/spelt wheat	Gramineae	F		1				30	4					3
Triticum dicoccum/spelta glume base	emmer/spelt wheat	Gramineae	F		1				4						
Triticum sp grain	wheat	Gramineae	F			1			13	1					
Triticum sp ?tail grain	wheat	Gramineae	F			1			2						
Triticum/Secale grain	wheat/rye	Gramineae	F						3						2
Hordeum vulgare grain	barley	Gramineae	F		1				5						
H.vulgare hulled, straight grain	barley	Gramineae	F		3				6						
H.vulgare hulled, twisted grain	barley	Gramineae	F						4						
Triticum/Hordeum sp grain	wheat/barley	Gramineae	F												2
Cereal sp indet grain	cereal	Gramineae	A	1	1+frags	6		1	86	10		+ frag			11
cf *Lolium/Festuca* sp	fescue/rye-grass	Gramineae	A		1	1			7	1					
Bromus sp	brome grass	Gramineae	AF												
Gramineae spp indet grain (large)	grasses	Gramineae	AF	3	1				13	2			2		5
Gramineae spp indet grain (small)	grasses	Gramineae	AF								1		1		
Vicia sp (small)	vetch	Leguminosae	A						1						
cf Leguminosae sp indet		Leguminosae	A			1									
Corylus avellana shell frags	hazelnut	Corylaceae	C			6			4						
Cyperaceae sp indet		Cyperaceae	AE			2									
Uncharred plant remains															
Chenopodium album	fat hen	Chenopodiaceae	AB											+	
Chenopodium glaucum/rubrum	glaucus/red goosefoot	Chenopodiaceae	AB										+		
Chenopodium/Atriplex	goosefoot/orache	Chenopodiaceae	AB		+		+								
Rubus fruticosus agg	blackberry/bramble	Rosaceae	CD								+				
Aethusa cynapium	fool's parsley	Umbelliferae	A										+		
Polygonum aviculare	knotgrass	Polygonaceae	AB				+			+					
Mentha sp	mint	Labiatae	ABCDEF							+					
Lycopus europaeus	gipsywort	Labiatae	BE				+								
roots						+									

Key:

A= cultivated ground
B= disturbed ground
C= woodlands, hedgerows, scrub, etc
D= grasslands, meadows, and heathland
E= aquatic/wet habitats
F= cultivar

+ = 1-10
++ = 11-50
+++ = 51-100
++++ = 100+
* = fragments

Table 33. Pollen and other microfossils from context 2031 (Waterhole CG4).

Context	2032	2049	2050	
pollen	**nr/%**	**nr/%**	**nr/%**	
Ranunculus	20 (6)	40 (8)	1(1)	buttercups
Ulmus	2 (1)	3 (1)	-	elm
Betula	-	1 (+)	-	birch
Alnus	10 (3)	17 (3)	2 (2)	alder
Corylus	65 (19)	71 (12)	12 (10)	hazel
Chenopodiaceae	10 (3)	18 (3)	2 (2)	goosefoot
Caryophyllaceae	4 (1)	4 (1)	-	pink fam.
Persicaria maculosa-type	1 (+)	1 (+)	-	persicaria
Persicaria bistorta-type	1 (+)	18 (3)	4 (3)	bistort
Polygonum aviculare	+ (+)	1 (+)	-	knotgrass
Tilia	-	1 (+)	1 (1)	lime
Brassicaceae	3 (1)	1 (+)	-	crucifers
Ericales	-	1 (+)	-	heathers
Potentilla-t	1 (+)	-	-	cinquefoils
Crataegus-type	-	1 (+)	-	hawthorn
Trifolium repens-type	1 (+)	4 (1)	-	white clover
Trifolium pratense-type	2 (1)	6 (1)	-	red clover
Linum usitatissimum	-	1 (+)	-	flax
Hedera	-	1 (+)	-	ivy
Apiaceae	2 (1)	-	-	umbellifers
Mentha-type	-	1 (+)	-	mint etc.
Plantago lanceolata	26 (8)	60 (10)	7 (6)	plantain
Rhinanthus-type	-	1 (+)	-	
Galium-t	1 (+)	-	-	bedstraws
Cirsium-type	2 (1)	+ (+)	1 (1)	spear thistle
Centaurea nigra	+ (+)	-	-	knapweed
Lactucae	24 (7)	88 (15)	18 (15)	
Artemisia	5 (1)	4 (1)	33 (28)	mugwort
Anthemis-type	11 (3)	5 (1)	-	mayweeds etc.
Aster-type	13 (4)	4 (1)	1 (1)	daisies etc.
Cyperaceae	4 (1)	18 (3)	7 (6)	sedges
Poaceae	88 (26)	167 (29)	22 (18)	grasses
Cerealia-type	40 (12)	23 (4)	2 (2)	cereals
Secale-type	-	1 (+)	-	rye
tree and shrub total	82 (24)	136 (23)	21 (18)	
land herb total	253 (74)	408 (70)	87 (73)	
aquatic total	6 (2)	38 (7)	11 (9)	
total pollen	341 (100)	582 (100)	119(100)	
spores				
Filicales	-	1 (+)	-	ferns
Polypodium	-	3 (+)	+ (+)	clubmoss
Pteridium	3 (1)	1 (+)	2 (2)	bracken
parasite ova				
Trichuris	2	-	1	whipworm

The pollen (by James Greig)

Introduction

The 3 pollen samples examined derived from a large Late Bronze Age waterhole (CG4), which contained bone, charcoal and wood in a largely grey coloured silty matrix. Going from top to bottom, the following fill contexts were sampled, 2032, 2049 and 2050. The material was submitted for pollen analysis as part of the general biological analysis of the material, which mainly otherwise contained plant macrofossils.

Methods

A sub-sample of each sample was prepared for pollen counting by ultrafine sieving and swirling, followed by acetolysis, staining and mounting. The pollen was counted with a Leitz Dialux microscope, using a pollen reference collection for the confirmation of critical identifications. The pollen counts ranged from 119–582 grains. Each slide was also completely scanned under low power to record the presence of a few more taxa. The pollen was well-preserved and present in good quantity in two of the three samples (contexts 2032 and 2049), but was less well-preserved in the third (context 2050), as listed in Table 33.

Results

The pollen in context 2032 was quite well-preserved, although some grains were crumpled. In 2049 the pollen varied, being both well and poorly preserved. In 2050, it was rather poor, and it was only worth making a fairly small count. Pollen analysis usually shows up trees and woodland well, and also many grassland plants. Weeds may be detected, but usually in less detail than from the macrofossil records.

CG4: CONTEXT 2032

This was one of the uppermost fills of the waterhole comprising a sequence of artefact rich layers interspersed with charcoal and burnt stone rich horizons and representing disuse of the feature. As the pollen spectra are generally rather similar across the three samples taken from the waterhole, the results from context 2032 will be discussed in some detail, and those from the other two spectra will then be compared to it.

Tree and shrub pollen amounted to 24% of the total, mainly *Corylus* (hazel) and *Alnus* (alder), which can be regarded as part of the natural background of pollen deposited from the atmosphere. There were also some traces of *Ulmus* (elm) one of the main constituents of the original wildwood, and this may reflect survival of some more or less natural woodland somewhere in the area.

At least some of the pollen from herbs probably also arrived in the deposit by natural means. This forms the main part of the pollen spectra, with 74% in 2032, and therefore is considered to represent the site surroundings. Grassland taxa are represented by the pollen records of plants such as *Ranunculus-t* (buttercups), *Trifolium repens* and *T. pratense* (white and red clovers), *Plantago lanceolata* (ribwort plantain), *Centaurea nigra* (knapweed), Lactuceae (a large group of composites which includes cat's ears, hawkbits, sow-thistles, hawkweeds and dandelions) and Poaceae (wild grasses). Some of this generally grassland pollen could also have been deposited from derivatives of grassland plant materials such as animal dung. The presence of Cyperaceae (sedges) could represent damp grassland.

Weeds are probably indicated by records such as *Chenopodiaceae* (goosefoot, orache), Caryophyllaceae (such as chickweed), *Persicaria maculosa* (persicaria), *Artemisia* (mugwort), and *Anthemis*-type (mayweeds). These could easily have been growing very locally. The records of *Polygonum aviculare* (knotgrass) pollen are somewhat unusual as this pollen is rarely found in archaeological material, probably because knotgrass produces and disperses little pollen. These finds may show that there was a lot of knotgrass growing in a trampled or trodden area around the waterhole, although some could also have been deposited from whole plant material dumped into the feature.

Crop plants are represented by the 12% Cerealia-type pollen record in 2032. Although Cerealia-type does include some wild grasses such as *Glyceria*, the latter mainly grow in wet habitats and would not be expected to have made a large contribution to material from an essentially dry site, such as this. The cereal pollen may not represent the standing crops, but would seem more likely to have been deposited in secondary form from dung and straw, or from the dust arising from local crop processing. Of course, the cereal crops themselves would have probably grown in the general vicinity of the site, since it lies on what was good farming land, but the amount of pollen dispersed from cornfields is rather low.

The small pollen records from a limited range of wetland plants such as *Persicaria bistorta* (bistort type) shows that this feature was probably a water-filled pit or pond in an otherwise generally dry landscape.

Finally, this context (2032) as well as one of the other fills in this waterhole (2050) contained parasite ova of *Trichuris* (whipworm), suggesting a low level of sewage contamination most probably from humans, dogs or pigs.

CG4: CONTEXT 2049

This was part of the lower group of silting and slumped fills at the base of the waterhole and probably relates to the period of use of the feature. The tree and shrub pollen spectrum here includes several species not present in context 2032 (as discussed above). *Tilia* (lime), another principal constituent of the original wildwood, and *betula* (birch) are both represented, as is *Crataegus* (hawthorn); the latter possibly reflecting the presence of scrub or hedges, which are also indicated within the waterlogged plant remains record for the site and seem to have been a feature of many prehistoric landscapes where there was livestock.

Cereal pollen is lower at 4% in this context. One grain of *Secale*-type probably represents rye, which at this stage was probably a crop weed among crops of other cereals (*c.f.* Runnymede; Greig 1991, 254). The single grain of flax (*Linum usitatissimum*) is a rarity, for flax distributes extremely small amounts of pollen, and is probably very under-represented. The pit could even have been used for flax retting.

CG4: CONTEXT 2050

The pollen in this sample was not well-preserved. However there are very large amounts of *Artemisia* (mugwort) pollen, 28%, which might suggest deposition of plant material. *Artemisia* was present in all the other samples, but at a more usual level of 1%.

Discussion

Waste disposal patterns

The organic content of the pit suggests that it received plant material, probably in the form of rubbish and dung. The presence of the *Trichuris* intestinal parasite also suggests the presence of other waste material, such as faeces.

Local environment

The landscape was substantially cleared of woodland, certainly around the occupied site, where there may have been scrub and hedges. There was probably some woodland surviving further away. The character of the surrounding landscape seems to have been of grassland. The occupied site probably had a rich flora of weeds, while some wetland plants would have grown around the waterhole.

Food and other resources

There is plentiful evidence of cereals although these cannot readily be distinguished from the pollen evidence alone. Potential sources of wild food resources are also represented, including hazel charred nutshell fragments of which were also present in CG4.

Flax also seems to have been in use.

Comparison with other results; environmental history

These results can be compared with other environmental data from the area, both elsewhere along the Carrant Brook as well as the River Avon (of which the Carrant is a tributary). A pollen profile from 1km east of Beckford, about 4.5km east of the Kemerton site, on peaty material buried under alluvium, showed that much of the woodland had gone from the valley somewhat before the lowest dated horizon of 1800+ 110 cal BC (3750±110 BP, HAR 3954; Greig and Colledge 1988). This Early Bronze Age date is unsurprising, as widespread evidence of woodland clearance around 3800 BP is shown in many pollen diagrams from England (Greig 1986, 70). These Beckford results have pollen spectra generally similar to those from Kemerton, suggesting that the latter reflect the wider environment along the Carrant Valley as well as that immediately surrounding the site; namely an occupied landscape with plenty of pasture and some cereal crops. The Beckford sequence continues with little change until an inorganic sediment, probably alluvium from increased ploughing and cultivation of winter cereals, was deposited some time after an organic horizon dated 950+70 cal AD (1010±70 BP, HAR 3624) was laid down.

A similar picture to that from Kemerton was also obtained from an organic lens in the alluvium of the River Avon at Bidford about 22km northeast of Kemerton (Greig 1987). The pollen spectrum was very similar to the one from Kemerton, although the amount of cereal pollen was rather less, probably because the deposit was further from human settlement. It is dated 2270±90 uncal BP (HAR 3069), and seems to indicate an essentially open pasture landscape, perhaps with drinking pools by the river Avon, together with some cereal growing.

In contrast to the clearly occupied and cleared landscape located along the Avon and its tributary the Carrant Brook, evidence from Ripple Brook, *c.* 8km west of Kemerton, suggests that the floor of the Severn Valley remained covered by alder carr until about 2800 uncal BP; indicating a relatively unoccupied part of the landscape which was only more gradually cleared of its woodland, mainly during the Iron Age (Brown and Barber 1985).

This period of later prehistoric landscape change therefore seems to have occurred in the Avon Valley by the Early Bronze Age but not until the Late Bronze Age or Early Iron Age in the Severn Valley. Geomorphological changes to the valley floors also occurred through the prehistoric period with both the Severn and Avon gradually shifting from a pattern of multiple courses to a single main channel, incising through increasingly deep accumulations of alluvium deposited during overbank flooding. This process appears to have especially accelerated after around 2500 uncal BP, according to sedimentary, molluscan and beetle evidence (Shotton 1978) and may in part be attributed to increased sediment loads washing off the cleared and farmed terraces flanking the rivers.

Conclusions

The three pollen spectra examined show that this waterhole was more or less permanently waterfilled thus enabling for the preservation of organic material.

The pollen shows a predominantly cleared, open and occupied landscape. Some scrub survived, maybe in hedgerows, and although only limited woodland was evident in the vicinity, some areas probably still survived further away.

The open, grassy landscape probably supported grazing animals which would have used the waterhole. Cereal pollen shows that grain was probably grown, stored or processed nearby, and flax pollen shows that flax was being cultivated as well. The waterhole also contained some sewage, as indicated by parasite ova.

Molluscs (by Andrew Moss)

Introduction

A number of samples were presented for mollusc analysis. Molluscs are normally well-preserved in alkaline calcareous soils and it was expected that the mollusc fauna would give an insight into local environmental conditions at the time of occupation.

Methods

The snails were extracted during processing of bulk environmental samples as described above; being recovered from both flots and residues. Thirteen samples were selected for analysis (Table 34). One of these (CG17,

Table 34. Molluscs from Late Bronze Age contexts.

Context	2043	302	1103	1109	1110	1111
Context Group	12	16	8	50	9	
Type	Pit	Pit	Waterhole	Post/gully	Pit	
Carychium sp.						
Succinea putris (L.)					1	
Cochlicopa lubrica (Müll)						
Vertigo pygmaea (Drap)						1a
V. angustior (Jefferys)						
Acanthinula aculeata (Müll)						
Vallonia pulchella (Müll)		2a	1a			2a
V. excentrica (Støki)				1a:1j	1a	3a
V. spp		1j			2j	9j
Clausilia bidentata (Strom)						
Ceciloides acicula (Müll)	12a:7j	10a:24j	19a:95j	2a:38j	8a:46j	6a:27j
Discus rotundatus (Müll)						
Aegopinella nitidula (Drap)						
Zonitidae indet.					1j	
Cepaea sp.	1				1	1
Trichia hispida (L.) gp					1a:1j	2j
Candidula gigaxii (Pfeiffer)		1j		1j		
Lymnaea truncatula (Müll)					2j	
Segmentina nitida (Müll)					1j	

Context	1201	1440	1501	1601	1836	1844
Context Group	N/A	91	35	19	6	2
Type	Posthole	Pit/post	Posthole	Pit/post	Waterhole	Pit
Carychium sp.					1a	
Succinea putris (L.)					1j	
Cochlicopa lubrica (Müll)			1j		1a:1j	
Vertigo pygmaea (Drap)			1a:2j			
V. angustior (Jefferys)					1a	
Acanthinula aculeata (Müll)					1a	
Vallonia pulchella (Müll)		1a	3a			
V. excentrica (Støki)	3a			1a	6a	2a
V. spp	3j		14j		10j	
Clausilia bidentata (Strom)			1a			
Ceciloides acicula (Müll)	10a:11j	3a:4j	16a:43j	8a:21j	1a:6j	1a:1j
Discus rotundatus (Müll)					3a:18j	
Aegopinella nitidula (Drap)						1a
Zonitidae indet.			1j		3j	
Cepaea sp.	1	1	1			
Trichia hispida (L.) gp	1j	3j	2j		2j	
Candidula gigaxii (Pfeiffer)	1j					
Lymnaea truncatula (Müll)			3j		1j	

context 1517) contained only unidentifiable fragments, so analysis and discussion focuses on the remaining 12 samples. Each sample tube had a limited number of individuals making statistical analysis impossible. The full data set is given in Table 34.

Further samples derived from the flots and residues were subjectively scanned but contained nothing further to add to the discussion.

Identification was based on the keys of Cameron and Riley (1994) and Macan (1977), employing a Kyowa stereozoom microscope. Adults and juveniles were counted separately to see if the population was local and breeding or if the snails had in some way been sorted by taphonomic processes by size.

Ecological information comes principally from Macan (1977) Boycot (1934) and Kerney and Cameron (1979).

Results

Preservation

Preservation at the site was not very good: the larger species such as Helicellids being represented only by fragments. Only juveniles plus adults of the smaller species were found whole, but usually damaged. However, there is sufficient material to make reliable inferences about local environment.

Miscellaneous fossil fragments were noted such as oyster shell, coral and nummulite, derived from the underlying Jurassic bedrock.

The most abundant mollusc in all samples was *Ceciloides acicula*. This is a subterranean species. Evans (1972) considers it to be a recent introduction, and no reliable sub-fossil record exists. Given this and the fact that the number of adults and juveniles indicate a local breeding population, the species may probably be defined as intrusive – *i.e.* not contemporary with the rest of the fauna. It will therefore not be considered in the analysis.

Beaker

Only one sample from a pit is of this date (CG12, context 2043). Apart from *Ceciloides*, there are a number of fragments from at least one adult of *Cepaea* sp. This mollusc is ubiquitous and nothing can be gleaned from its presence.

Late Bronze Age

Ten samples from waterholes, pits and postholes were analysed. The faunas are too small to analyse individually so they are grouped together. Differences in species composition at the various locations may then be used to infer spatial variation and thus differences in the local environment. *Ceciloides* is again abundant and is discounted.

The family Helicellidae is represented by three species, *Cepaea* sp. a ubiquitous species, *Trichia hispida* (juveniles common) and *Candidula gigaxii* (occasional juveniles). The latter two species occur in open calcareous grassland, not too dry – although *Trichia* may also be found in wetter habitats.

A few unidentifiable juveniles of the Zontidae were recovered. The only recognisable species was a subadult of *Aegopinella nitidula*. The Zontidae prefer damper, shaded habitats such as woodland or hedgerows, but may also be found in the shadier, damper parts of open grassland.

The commonest occurrence is the family Valloniidae, *Vallonia excentrica* being the most frequently observed. This prefers open grassland, neither too dry or too wet. This species and *V. costata* are the two most abundant snail species in Bronze Age soils (Evans 1972). *V. costata* prefers drier grasslands than *V. excentrica* and its absence here is noteworthy. Occasional individuals of *V. pulchella* were recovered. These prefer damper habitats than *V. excentrica*. One tiny specimen of *Acanthinula aculeata* was recovered; this is a leaf-litter dweller of woodland and hedgerow.

Other species common in open damp grassland recovered here are *Discus rotundatus* (abundant in Waterhole CG6, context 1836), *Cochlicopa lubrica* and *Vertigo pygmaea* although the latter may also be found in wetlands.

Succinea putris belongs to a family of wetland species but this particular species is more tolerant of slightly drier habitats and may thus occur in the damper parts of grassland. Similarly *Lymnaea truncatula*, an amphibious species usually found at water margins, may also be found in the damper parts of grassland (Boycott, 1934).

Two other species are also noteworthy. One minute juvenile of the rare *Segmentina nitida* was recovered. This is an aquatic species living in ditches etc. *Vertigo angustior* is only found subfossil in Britain today, except in East Anglian wetlands, although in the past it may have

had a wider range of habitats including damp grasslands (Evans, 1972).

Discussion

Taken as a whole, the assemblage indicates open damp grassland perhaps with damper, darker microhabitats. The shade-loving Zonitidae and *Acanthinula* and to some extent *Discus rotundatus* may be found in longer grass. However, the occurrence of a number of *D. rotundatus* in a waterhole sample (CG6) may suggest that the feature was shaded, either naturally of artificially, attracting this species and possibly others too.

On the other hand, the presence of one aquatic snail, and other species whose habitat encompasses the wetland environment may suggest that reeds, wet grass, mud or water may have been present in and around some features, and this seems likely in the case of Waterholes CG6 and CG8 as well as Pit CG9, a substantial clay-lined feature. Alternatively such material could have been collected from a local source and the snails inadvertently brought back to the site. This seems the likeliest explanation for the occurrence of *Segmentina nitida*, although its minute size raises the possibility that it may be a contaminant.

Conclusions

The material from this site has been heavily contaminated by the intrusive snail *Ceciloides acicula*. The remaining fauna consists of a damp grassland assemblage with both lighter/shadier and drier/wetter microhabitats. Some wetland species do occur but these are not exclusively wetland, and may be found in damp grassland.

One exclusively aquatic snail was recovered and either indicates that the large clay-lined pit it derived from contained water or alternatively that it may have been brought to the site in mud etc. It is possible that other species may also have been inadvertently introduced in this way, however, in the case of the waterholes these would have provided appropriate wetter habitats.

Little insight can be gained about spatial distribution but the occurrence of *Discus rotundatus* in numbers in one waterhole may be explained by localised shading (natural or artificial) perhaps merely by longer grass surrounding the feature.

Environmental synthesis (by Elizabeth Pearson)

Beaker/Early Bronze Age activity

The plant remains from this phase provided only very limited of the local environment, as all material apart from charred cereal crop waste was considered to be intrusive from the ploughsoil. Unfortunately, the lack of waterlogged features and hence organic environmental remains makes it impossible to make comparisons with the apparently open grassland landscape of the Late Bronze Age indicated by pollen and molluscan evidence, and the hedgerow or scrub surrounding the large pits and waterholes indicated by macrofossil plant remains.

Barley is recorded as a crop in use during this phase, and is recorded from other archaeological sites of this date around the British Isles. Too few contexts of this date produced macrofossil plant remains to interpret waste disposal patterns and apart from the barley, very little evidence has been acquired on the food products consumed during this phase of the site. However, it is becoming increasingly accepted that collected plant food was an important component of the diet in combination with farmed cereals countrywide, providing a muesli-like plant diet (Moffett *et al.* 1989). Richmond (1999) takes this view further by suggesting that even in the Early Bronze Age 'it appears crop and perhaps certain species of livestock, still represented 'ranked foods' within society circulating under certain specific conditions'. That is, cultivated crops were viewed as prestigious foods, traded or grown for use on special occasions, particularly ritual feasts, and were a symbol of economic status. As a result, crop production was certainly in its infancy across much of British Isles at this time. It appears that the economic base of society saw pastoralism, associated with a broad-spectrum economy involving wild resources, as being more important than cereal cultivation. The idea is supported by presence of cattle and sheep in Neolithic/Beaker contexts at Kemerton, which although not abundant are certainly more prevalent than charred plant remains. Also the results from the nearby site at Beckford, where an Early Bronze Age date has been secured for the start of a pollen sequence, show a cleared landscape with grassland and some pasture as evidenced by dung beetles. Some cereal cultivation was also indicated (Greig and Colledge 1988).

Late Bronze Age activity

Local environment

Evidence for the local environment comes from waterlogged deposits at the base of large pits and waterholes. Woodland scrub or hedgerow appears to have been present in the immediate vicinity of these features as abundant remains from this type of vegetation (wood, twig, leaf or thorn fragments) are unlikely to have been dispersed over a long distance. Moreover, abundant seeds of blackberry and elderberry are also likely to represent nearby vegetation. Occasional seed remains from grassy or disturbed environments may not represent vegetation growing at the pit edges, but are, nevertheless, likely to be relatively local.

These results suggest a rather different environment in comparison with pollen and molluscan analyses which show a grassy and open environment. However, pollen and molluscan remains tend to reflect the environment over a larger area, whereas the plant macrofossil remains largely represent vegetation growing more or less *in situ*. Hedgerow or scrub may therefore have bordered the pits and waterholes, and hence dominated these particular plant macrofossil assemblages. This type of vegetation is also likely to have formed hedged boundaries along the edges of fields and trackways, and this is reflected to some degree by the pollen and molluscan evidence.

Waste disposal patterns

Crop waste appears in low levels over most of the site in waterholes, pits and postholes, but there is no evidence that special areas or feature types were selected for crop processing or disposal of crop waste. A concentrated deposit of charred crop debris found in one feature (1601; CG19) was the sole exception. In this case, the charred material was in a small pit or large posthole and associated with a single vessel. It may therefore represent a deliberate deposition perhaps an offering.

Otherwise these remains are likely to have been accidentally burnt as a result of crop processing or cooking. The scarcity of these remains generally suggests that these activities were probably carried out on a small-scale, and in a piecemeal manner. Although poor preservation may be partly responsible for their scarcity, it is nevertheless expected that any large-scale activity of this nature would still be evident in the archaeological record and thus these remains probably represent limited activities, perhaps undertaken at a household level.

Food, resources, cultivation and diet

Emmer wheat appears to have been the main wheat in cultivation reflecting the pattern most typically observed on sites of this period in southern Britain. However, some grains were indistinguishable from spelt wheat, which, although it does appear in Bronze Age contexts elsewhere in the country, does not appear to have become a major crop until the late Iron Age; and certainly its presence is rare locally until the Roman period. Similarly the occasional free-threshing type wheat grains found in Late Bronze Age contexts are known throughout the prehistoric period, but this did not generally become a major crop until the mid Saxon period. Six-row, hulled barley was cultivated and rye may have been growing as a weed of the crop charred in 1601 (CG19). Rye type pollen was also identified from a large waterhole (CG4).

It is difficult to determine whether these crops were grown on the site or imported from elsewhere as there is a lack of cereal straw and culm bases which are often considered as evidence of crop waste associated with producer sites (Hillman 1981). There is also a lack of chaff remains generally, and it is, therefore uncertain whether crop processing such as winnowing, threshing and sieving was carried out on the site. However, it should be borne in mind that if crops were processed in small quantities, and the preservation is biased towards the survival of cereal grains, the quantity of chaff surviving may not appear to be significant.

Overall, the evidence points to any cereal crop cultivation being on a small-scale, with the possibility that some, or all, of the crops were imported onto the site. Elsewhere in the country, charred cereal crop remains are similarly scarce at many comparably dated sites such as those in the Thames Valley area, for example, at Reading Business Park (Campbell 1992); Shorncote Quarry, Gloucestershire (Ede, 1992, 1999; Robinson 1995) and Runnymede Bridge (Greig 1991).

There is some information on sources of wild plant food which were available on the site from the large pits. These include fruits such as blackberry, elderberry and sloe, while hazelnuts are also likely to have been collected as a component of the diet, although there is no direct evidence of their use. Some limited evidence for the hunting of red and roe deer for meat was also present, although these are liable to have only formed a small element of the diet.

Domestic animals were also being farmed, although it is difficult to interpret the significance they had for the inhabitants of the site directly from the animal bone assemblage. There is no evidence from the animal bones of any ritual treatment of animals, so it is presumed that this represents waste from normal domestic activities. Although cattle would have produced the largest quantity of meat, cattle, pig and sheep/goat may have been kept in relatively similar numbers. The metrical data suggests that sheep husbandry was unspecialised. Dog was recorded in this assemblage, and it is likely that they would have been used for hunting and for herding animals, particularly sheep. Although it has been stated in the literature on ancient farming that primitive sheep cannot be worked with a dog, Pryor (1998) disputes this, and finds that dogs are the most efficient way of moving all sheep, even primitive varieties.

Although the bone assemblage itself does not allow detailed interpretation of the importance of livestock farming at the site, other strands of evidence would suggest that this was highly significant part of the settlement's economy. Evidence for an open grassland landscape emerges from the pollen and molluscan records, while the field boundaries, trackways or droveways and associated waterholes provide strong indications of a landscape organised for livestock control. Further support derives from the evidence for hedgerow species present in the plant macrofossil record. These suggest that these fields and tracks were possibly bounded by thorny hedges which are ideal for managing stock. Similar landscapes have been recorded widely along the Thames Valley and although environmental evidence is limited, indications are that livestock management was a major priority for these communities (Yates 2001). In terms of the overall balance of the agricultural economy for these sites, Richards (1999) has stated that:

> Whilst it appears that communities specialised largely in livestock farming, small-scale cultivation may also have taken place throughout the valley (Thames) and its tributaries. Evidence suggests however, that arable farming was generally limited. Arable activities have been recorded at a number of sites (eg Shorncote Quarry, Runnymede Bridge)…but whilst crop processing can sometimes be identified it is not always certain that actual cultivation took place.

This appears to reflect the pattern at Huntsman's Quarry, although this was not necessarily the case countrywide since in other areas, such as in Sussex and Kent, settlement expansion is linked to intensive arable agriculture (Richards 1999).

Craft and production

A single grain of flax pollen in one of the Late Bronze Age waterholes may have resulted from flax retting activities, particularly as this feature was also associated with fragments of loom weights. Although this is only a single pollen grain, as noted above, flax distributes extremely small amounts of pollen and is probably under-represented. A similar example is found at Reading Business Park (Campbell 1992) where flax seeds and capsules, and *Camelina* seed pods (a weed of flax) were found in five pit deposits. Here also loom weights were found, indicating that textile production was taking place.

Textile production of some kind evidently took place at Kemerton as reflected in the number of ceramic weights recovered and, apart from the potential flax production, the presence of adult sheep suggests that this probably largely reflects production of woollen textiles.

Part 5.
Discussion and synthesis

Upper Palaeolithic and Mesolithic

Although considered stray losses rather than representative of settlement, the two Upper Palaeolithic items represent important finds in Worcestershire and the wider region, an area within which any finds of this date are of note due to their scarcity (Myers 2007).

Mesolithic activity was better represented with a concentration of finds recovered within tree-throws located in the northeast part of the investigated area. Tree-throws and natural hollows have been widely recorded to have formed focal points for the accumulation and possibly deliberate deposition of material during the Mesolithic; examples in Worcestershire including at Aston Mill, Kemerton (Dinn and Evans 1990) and Lightmarsh Farm, near Kidderminster (Jackson *et al.* 1996). These reflect transitory occupation at these sites, perhaps by small hunting groups repeatedly returning to a favoured location. Unfortunately at Huntsman's Quarry, the assemblages recovered do not allow further refinement of dating or characterisation of the nature of the occupation. However, in the light of the presence of Mesolithic material at Aston Mill and Beckford, as well as at Huntsman's Quarry, it seems that the gravel terraces along the Carrant Valley may have provided a favoured location for the local population. One possibility is that the distinct rise of Bredon Hill was an important landscape feature, marking a major route around the north side of the Cotswolds towards the confluence of the Rivers Severn and Avon and perhaps also a feature associated with local beliefs and superstitions. Whatever the case, the site provides an important addition to the generally limited evidence for Mesolithic activity recorded within Worcestershire, and particularly in the south of the county.

Neolithic

A single pit (CG38) was identified and dated to the Middle Neolithic on the basis of material tentatively identified as from a Peterborough Ware bowl. Although only a small assemblage was present, at least two other vessels were also represented, possibly reflecting deliberate selection and structured deposition of material into the feature, a pattern commonly suggested for features of this date (Thomas 1999, 62–88; Edmonds 1999, 29–30 and 110–129). A small quantity of cattle bone was also recovered. A second potentially contemporary pit lay nearby (CG98). This also had a single fill and contained a small assemblage of flint but no other artefacts.

The single fills and the presence of potentially selected items incorporated within them typifies pits of this date (Thomas 1999). As is commonly the case no structural features were present; however, these pits can probably be interpreted as the remains of a short-lived domestic settlement. Their excavation and infilling may potentially have included some ritual significance for the local population perhaps marking their association with this particular area.

These pits and the small quantity of residual Grooved Ware pottery which was recovered, represent significant finds which add to a small but growing body of such material from the West Midlands. These include two further sites located within the Carrant Valley and to the south of Bredon Hill. A pair of pits associated with Grooved Ware and Early Bronze Age flint were recorded at the nearby site of Aston Mill, Kemerton and have been interpreted as domestic and/or ritual activity in the vicinity of, but pre-dating a ring-ditch (Dinn and Evans 1990). Secondly, slightly further to the east, at Beckford, although no Neolithic features were identified, small quantities of Neolithic residual material were recovered including

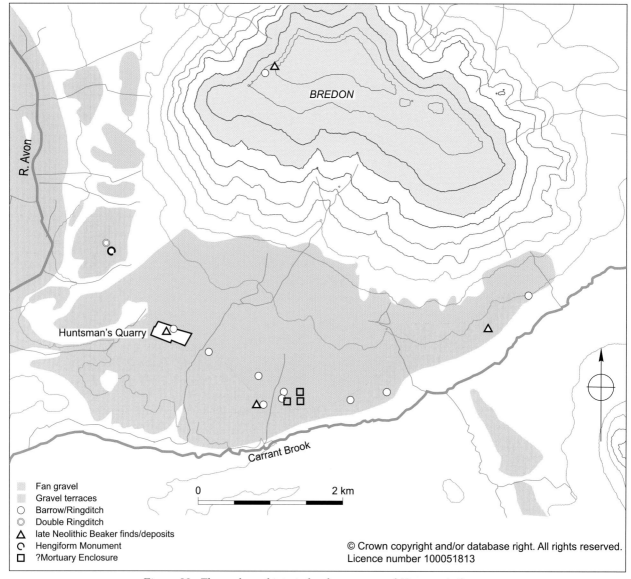

Figure 88. The early prehistoric landscape around Huntman's Quarry.

several sherds of Middle to Late Neolithic impressed ware (Woodward nd).

It can be tentatively suggested on the basis of this evidence, that this area at the southwest end of Bredon Hill may represent a focus for Neolithic activity. Apart from the handful of features and findspots described above, this area has revealed a number of cropmarks, most of which are as yet untested but, which feature several possible Neolithic sites. These include several potential mortuary enclosures which, if proven, are liable to be of Middle to Later Neolithic date (Fig. 88; Dinn and Evans 1990). In addition, an apparent hengiform monument identified through cropmark evidence at Bredons Norton has recently been subject to a small-scale investigation. Several phases of use of the monument were present including the cutting of a curvilinear ditch and the insertion of cremation deposits into the slighted remains of an external bank spreading over the uppermost fills of a substantial ditch (Jodie Lewis

pers comm). Several Later Neolithic to Early Bronze Age ring-ditches, some tested by excavation, are also present in the vicinity, as is evidence for Beaker period activity (see below) and Early to Middle Bronze Age secondary (funerary) use of earlier monuments; and it may be that this area was marked out as one with special meaning for local communities from an early date. In particular, it has been observed that the postulated mortuary enclosures and the ring-ditches appear to occupy the edge of local fan gravel deposits (from Bredon; Dinn and Evans 1990); although in the light of more recent cropmark evidence it seems more probable that their distribution coincides with the limits of the gravel terrace (Fig. 88). This distribution may reflect the marking of a boundary of some cultural, religious or even economic significance to the local population.

Within the wider region, it is notable that the very limited known activity of this date and type appears to be especially prevalent along the Warwickshire/Worcestershire

Avon and its tributaries. Similarly early material, including both Peterborough Ware and Grooved Ware assemblages, has been recovered from a range of features at sites along the River Avon in Warwickshire, as at Wasperton (Hughes and Crawford 1995), Barford (Oswald 1969), Broom (Palmer 2000) and along the Churchover to Newbold Pacey pipeline (Palmer 2007). It has been observed that these have typically been associated with small monument complexes (Palmer 2000), or as at Broom having been suggested as indicative of 'temporary encampment in a location of cultural significance' (*ibid* 2000, 36).

Evidence has been less forthcoming in the Severn Valley, which perhaps notably appears to lack monuments and small monumental complexes of the type seen in the Avon Valley. However, Middle to Late Neolithic Peterborough Ware assemblages have been identified in a pit and associated features in Tewkesbury which is located where the Avon joins the River Severn. To the south of this confluence, in the Severn Valley several sites in and around Gloucester have also produced Peterborough Ware assemblages, while Grooved Ware has been recovered from Saintbridge, Gloucester and Peterborough Ware from a pair of pits at Cam, near Dursley (Darvill 1987). Again the quantities of material and range of features are limited but it seems likely that small and short-lived settlements are represented (Darvill 1987).

The evidence for this period, is therefore of small monuments in the Worcestershire/Warwickshire Avon Valley but principally, as at Kemerton, this seems to relate to short-lived periods of residence indicated by the survival of pits containing carefully selected and deposited residues of domestic occupation.

Beaker

This period was characterised by widely dispersed but low intensity activity across much of the investigated area and by one apparent area of slightly more intense activity, focused on a group of three pits (CG12, 13 and 42) considered to be contemporaneous. The three pits were closely spaced in a line from north to south. They appeared to have been left open for some time allowing weathering of the sides prior to backfilling. In two cases backfilling appeared to be in a singe episode, but the third had a finds and charcoal-rich spread overlain by two further charcoal flecked deposits.

In the absence of any evidence for permanent structures and in the light of the restricted character of the deposits and associated assemblages, it seems probable that these were associated with one or more short-lived periods of activity. Stylistically the ceramics were early in the Beaker tradition (Wessex/Middle Rhine style) suggesting that this activity fell within the third, and possibly the fourth quarter of the third millennium BC.

Both the pottery and flint artefacts recovered strongly suggest domestic occupation with a range of activities represented including tool production, hunting, hide

working, food preparation and other activities. The small animal bone assemblage was poorly preserved but included both cattle and sheep or goat, while barley was represented within the limited charred plant remains recorded. As is commonly the case in features of this date, the material recovered may have been carefully selected and deposited within the pits and thus represent structured deposition reflecting ritual activity associated with one or more periods of use of the site. The material might for instance be considered as representing gifts to the gods in thanksgiving for a successful period of occupation or to ensure the replenishment of resources for future visits.

Locally very small quantities of Beaker period material have been recorded at both Aston Mill and Beckford and may be associated with further domestic sites. As noted previously, two Beakers discovered under a barrow on Bredon Hill are remarkably similar in style to those from Huntsman's Quarry, although they were located within a funerary context. Further afield within Worcestershire, a pit group at Holt and an isolated pit at Longmore Hill Farm, Astley have both produced Beaker domestic assemblages. At Longmore Hill Farm the pottery was also stylistically early and was accompanied by flint, burnt stone, charred plant remains (cereal and hazelnut shells) and small fragments of burnt animal bone (Dinn and Hemingway 1992). To the south, at Trinity Farm, Gloucestershire a row of three closely spaced pits has been recorded (Mudd, Williams and Lupton 1999) and bears close comparison with the pit group at Huntsman's Quarry. Only single fills were present containing both pottery and flint. As at Huntsman's Quarry, the ceramic assemblage was stylistically early. The fragmentary nature of the pottery assemblage was suggested as potentially reflecting broken material stored in a midden prior to deposition in the pits (Mudd, Williams and Lupton 1999), and a similar situation may be postulated for the material deposited at Huntsman's Quarry. As at many other early prehistoric sites, structured deposition of carefully selected material was suggested for the Trinity Farm material and this seems likely to have been the case at Huntsman's Quarry.

Charred plant remains including barley grains and a single chaff fragment were also present at Huntsman's Quarry. Evidence from the nearby site at Beckford shows that by the Early Bronze Age some cereal cultivation was undertaken in the area within a cleared landscape with grassland and some pasture as evidenced by dung beetles. (Greig and Colledge 1988). Therefore, cereals, although limited in number, may have been cultivated locally in small stands.

The Huntsman's Quarry material therefore provides a small but significant addition to the evidence of Beaker activity in the region. It also provides an important addition to the small number of domestic Beaker assemblages containing vessels of definite Wessex/Middle Rhine style known nationally. In conjunction with evidence from other sites in the region which have produced stylistically early material, this allows a number of observations to be made about local traditions and depositional practice. Pits are the main feature type and typically contain single fills or simple fill sequences. Material deposited usually includes fragmentary pottery from a more than one vessel and occasionally from a considerable number of vessels. Flint assemblages usually indicate both production and use of tools with tool assemblages dominated by scrapers. Charred food waste and animal bone have also been identified and it may be of note that barley has been recorded at two sites. Although seemingly representing domestic refuse from a wide range of activities, material deposited in these features appears to have been carefully selected, possibly from nearby middens, and probably held particular significance for the local population.

This reflects the national pattern for sites of this type and date (Thomas 1999, 64–74) and it is also evident that this reflects the pattern discussed previously for Neolithic activity in this region. Despite these strong themes of continuity and the apparent similarity of practices involved, caution must be exercised since the manner in which material was used and the symbolism with which it was imbued may potentially have varied widely from place to place and may also have changed though time as did the style and range of ceramics and other material culture (Thomas 1999, 64–74).

Early Bronze Age

The Early Bronze Age ring-ditch located on the north side of the investigated area almost certainly marks the position of a former burial mound, although no trace of any barrow mound or primary burial survived. Dating of the construction of the original monument is uncertain. A recut section of the ditch contained cremated bone and an accessory cup reflecting the insertion of a secondary burial into the monument during the Early Bronze Age. This indicates that the monument had remained a recognised feature in the landscape. Such re-use, or continuing use, of monuments for subsequent burial rites is a widely recognised practice during this period (Burgess 1980; Woodward 2000c).

The alignment of ditches flanking a later boundary/ trackway may also be some considerable significance since both features pass through the ring-ditch. These may reflect the recognition of the barrow as a territorial marker or as a feature within the landscape used to align boundaries. Although it is uncertain how much of the former monument would have been visible, it is also possible that a deliberate attempt has been made to integrate this in the newly laid out landscape either as a sign of respect to the ancestors; alternatively a deliberate slighting and appropriation of a formerly significant place could be represented.

The ring-ditch although badly truncated and lacking any evidence for a primary burial represents an important addition to the very limited number of recently excavated examples of such features in the region (Garwood 2007).

A further ring-ditch has been excavated in the immediate

vicinity, at Aston Mill, Kemerton. Again evidence for a primary burial was absent and this had also been re-used for secondary burial rites. Here, cremations and associated finds had been inserted into pits cut into the infilled ring-ditch during the Middle to Late Bronze Age (Dinn and Evans 1990), a pattern also potentially echoed at the recently investigated cropmark site at Bredons Norton (Jodie Lewis pers comm). Further ring-ditches, including a double-ditched example are known in the area from cropmark evidence and, as noted above, appear to be located along the edge of the gravel terrace; perhaps marking an important boundary for the local population (Fig. 88).

Lastly, the Collared Urn fragments, although residual, are important finds in a region which has produced very little material of this date.

Late Bronze Age

Late Bronze Age activity comprised a range of posthole structures, other structures and pits all of which were set within a system of fields and tracks or droves and associated with substantial waterholes. The posthole structures can be interpreted as representing a range of domestic buildings, workshops, storage facilities and animal shelters along with fences and three large posthole enclosures.

These structures and associated pits were widely dispersed across the entire excavated area. Unfortunately, due to a combination of truncation, limited stratigraphic relationships and absence of dating evidence from many features it has not been possible to phase the activity represented with any certainty. It does, however, appear from the radiocarbon dating of organic material within waterlogged basal fills of some of the waterholes that these, and presumably some elements of the associated field system, were the earliest features having been dug and laid out within the period *1210–1040 cal BC* (95% probability). Disuse of the waterholes was also well-dated, by radiocarbon dating of charred internal residues on pottery dumped as part of domestic debris deliberately dumped into the upper parts of these features. This disuse dated to the period between *1130–1010 cal BC* and *1050–960 cal BC* (95% probability), a period felt liable to reflect the main period of domestic occupation.

Settlement areas are therefore concluded to have been established within an already existing network of fields and waterholes. These occupation areas appear to have been otherwise unenclosed. Situations where the field system pre-dates the settlement have been recorded elsewhere at comparable Late Bronze Age settlement sites which have been extensively investigated as at Reading Business Park (Moore and Jennings 1992; Brossler, Early and Allen 2004), although in other instances the settlement and field system appear to have been established together as at Fengate, Cambridgeshire (Pryor 1978; 1998). At Huntsman's Quarry, it seems that although some waterholes and elements of the field system were established before

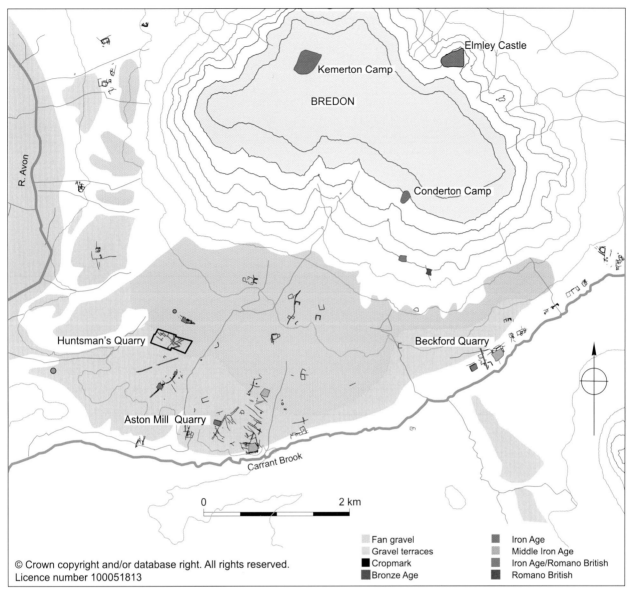

Figure 89. The later prehistoric and Romano-British landscape around Huntsman's Quarry.

the settlement, the system was not a static one. Fields were adapted, extended and altered through time and new waterholes were created while others were abandoned. Similarly it is unlikely that all elements of settlement were contemporary and it is believed that occupation shifted across the area, albeit within a relatively short timeframe of no more than about 160 years (and probably somewhat less) centering on the eleventh century cal BC. Indeed the whole period of Late Bronze Age activity was relatively short with no more than 250 years elapsing between the establishment of the first waterholes and elements of the field system and the abandonment of the settlement, waterholes and presumably the field system as well.

Ceramic evidence supports this impression of a short-lived period of occupation, the pottery falling firmly within the plainware tradition of the Late Bronze Age and only one specific and relatively isolated feature producing material

of the subsequent decorated stage. The total absence of Iron Age material and presence of only a handful of Roman dated material from the whole site provides further support for the majority of the evidence to relate to a short-lived sequence of activity.

Fields and farming

The earliest features of the Late Bronze Age landscape appear to have been some of the waterholes and elements of the field-systems and droves which were presumably laid out along with them. Certainly one of the waterholes (CG14) can be seen to be associated with one of the boundaries on which it lay. However, unfortunately there were generally very few stratigraphic relationships either between the boundary features or indeed with any other features, and only very limited dating evidence was present.

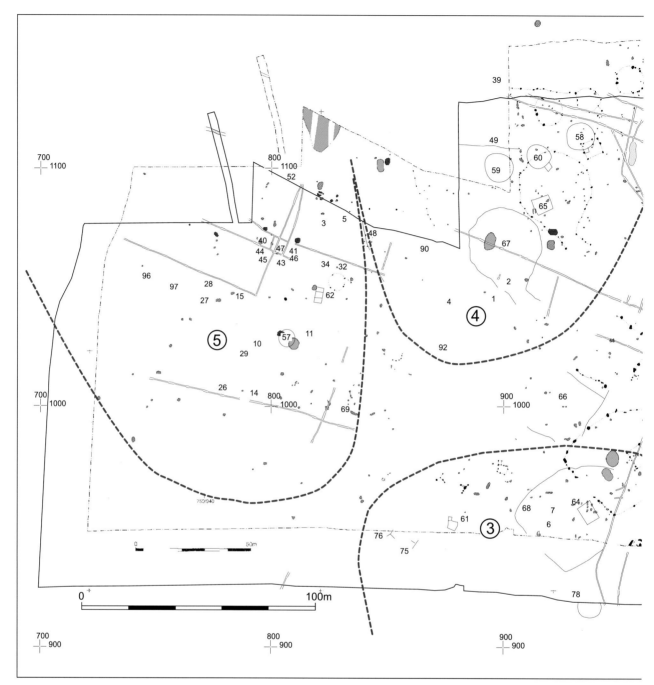

Figure 90. Suggested Late Bronze Age settlement zones.

As a result, the sequence in which the field system and waterholes were laid out has proved impossible to establish with any certainty; although using alignments and the limited relational data available it has proved possible to exclude some features and suggest two main phases of development (Fig. 17). This indicates that initially the landscape was divided into a number of rectilinear fields with associated waterholes and two potential droves. Several of the waterholes appear to have been positioned on field boundaries so that they could service two separate land parcels.

Dating of the basal fills of some of the waterholes suggests that this field system may have been established sometime between the end of the 13th century and the middle of the 11th century cal BC, although a slightly earlier date should not be excluded for some elements. A second system replaced the earlier one. Although also poorly dated, several elements were associated with Late Bronze Age pottery and it seems that this system may date from towards the end of the period of occupation represented, or possibly even slightly post-date it. This later system was more open in layout with a clearly defined

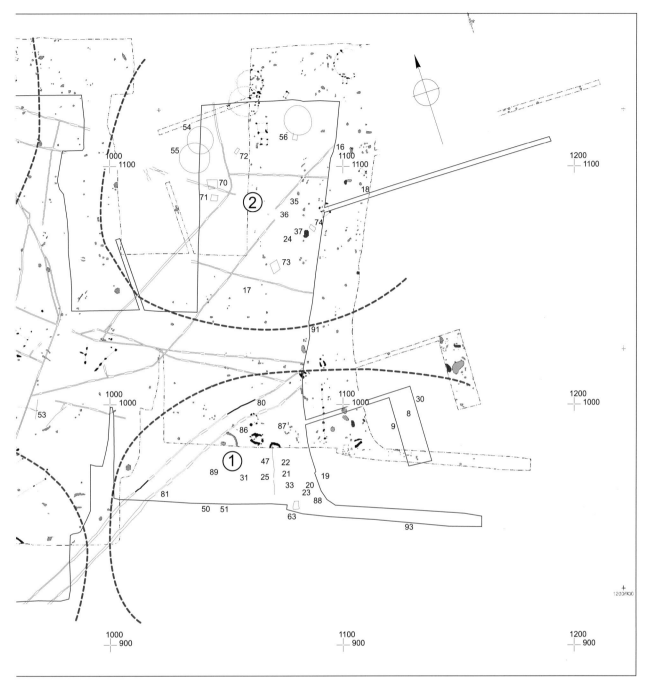

Figure 90. continued

drove; the system apparently having been designed to move stock from the north or northeast to the south and west or vica versa. The relationship of this later system to the waterholes is less evident than for the earlier system; however, within the apparently more open landscape provision of water may have been a less important issue with local streams perhaps having been more widely accessible.

The provision of waterholes for the earlier system is felt to be significant indicating that the system of droves and fields was probably created for controlling stock, since where stock are not allowed to roam freely, it is essential to provide an abundant supply of water. This also implies that pressure of stock on available grazing resources had reached levels where it was necessary to carefully control their movement. Further support for this model derives from analysis of the field systems at Huntsman's Quarry amongst which stockyards, a sheep run and a drafting gate can possibly be identified comparable to those noted and discussed elsewhere (Pryor 1998). These help control and manage stock, enabling herds to be divided, pregnant or sick animals to be removed and animals selected for culling or shearing; processes probably supported by the use of dogs to work both sheep and cattle. In such a pastoral economy, the droves facilitate stock movement, perhaps in this case between spring and summer grazing on the meadows of Carrant Brook floodplain to the south, and drier grazing on the adjacent terraces and upland landscape of Bredon Hill to the north.

Evidence from the waterlogged deposits in the base of some of the waterholes suggests that these fields and droves were probably bounded by hedgerows of hawthorn, bramble and other scrubby bushes. The ditches were also probably much more substantial than their much truncated surviving elements indicate and may have held water for much of the year. This may be supported by the presence of a single example of the rare mollusc *Segmentina nitida*, an aquatic species which favours wet ditches; although this may also reflect the presence of wet muddy habitats around the waterholes. Again the evidence indicates that stock management was an important element of the site economy, since arable fields do not need bounding by large ditches and hedges but both are important in controlling livestock.

Other environmental evidence from the site and the wider area provides further support for this model. A pollen diagram from the nearby site at Beckford (Greig and College 1998) suggests that the landscape in the Carrant Valley had been substantially cleared during the Early Bronze Age and given over to grassland pasture interspersed with some cultivation of cereals. At Huntsman's Quarry, the wide range of environmental evidence from the Late Bronze Age waterholes and pits indicates a landscape dominated by open grassland.

The predominantly pastoral agricultural regime indicated is reflected in the faunal assemblage that included considerable quantities of cattle and sheep. Although some cattle were killed young, most lived into maturity suggesting that their principal value may have been for milk and traction, their use for meat only coming at the end of their usefulness for these other purposes. This contrasts with the evidence from Reading Business Park where although dairy products were identified as being of some potential importance, cattle were mostly killed before they reached maturity (Levitan 1992; Wilson 2004). The reasons for this discrepancy are unclear but one possibility is that winter fodder was more readily available at Kemerton or that cattle were less valued for their meat than other products, thus leading to more animals being kept alive into maturity.

The age at which sheep were killed appears to vary, though as at Reading Business Park (Levitan 1992; Wilson 2004) most reached maturity. This suggests that unspecialised sheep husbandry was being practised with use for meat, milk and wool; the importance of the latter probably being reflected in the quantities of ceramic (loom) weights recovered from the site. The potential importance of milk products (from both cattle and sheep) may be reflected in the pottery assemblages from the site. These included many large bucket-shaped vessels with perforations and rim forms perhaps consistent with their use as milk pails with organic covers. Burnt residues in many vessels may suggest the scalding of milk as part of the preparation of dairy products such as cheese which may have been important parts of the diet and could also have been exchanged for other products.

The alignment of the field systems and droveways at Huntsman's Quarry is paralleled at many cropmark sites along the terraces on the north side of the Carrant Brook. These seem to indicate an extensive field-system laid out around Bredon Hill with tracks or droves possibly radiating from the hill. Two further parallel tracks or droves (including one of those investigated at the site) also extend to the west, possibly providing access to a tongue of higher ground situated towards the confluence of the Carrant Brook and the River Avon (Fig. 89). Although these cropmarks remain largely uninvestigated, at Beckford a major boundary feature was identified on a broadly north–south alignment. Although its dating was somewhat ambiguous and Iron Age pottery was present in upper fills, the feature also produced Bronze Age pottery and clearly pre-dated Middle Iron Age settlement while charred material produced a radiocarbon date of 1410+ 200 bc (Birm 431; Britnell 1975). This strongly indicates that a major phase of land division was undertaken on the south side of Bredon Hill, probably occurring sometime during the last quarter of the second millennium BC. The potential alignment of one element of this system at Huntsman's Quarry onto an earlier ring-ditch may also be significant, suggesting that this parcelling up of the landscape during the Late Bronze Age may have referenced earlier patterns of landscape division.

Clear evidence for the establishment of such an extensive system of landscape division as is represented at Kemerton is currently unique in the West Midlands but can be readily compared with the widespread examples known elsewhere in southern and eastern England as on Dartmoor and other upland areas (Fleming 1988) and the across Fens of eastern England (Pryor 1998; Malim 2001). Systems such as these have also been widely identified on the terraces of the Thames Valley (see Yates 2001) and, whilst the evidence from Kemerton stands out in the West Midlands, tentative evidence is beginning to emerge for more widespread Bronze Age land division in this region at this time (Yates 2007, 101–106). Such formal and widespread division of the landscape can be seen as reflecting greater intensification and regulation of farming and land division, and was perhaps associated with new forms of farming, increasingly sophisticated livestock management and changing ideas of land tenure (Pryor 1998).

Against this extensive evidence for a predominantly pastoral economy, it is difficult to assess the relative importance of arable cultivation in the area. Yates (1999; 2001) has suggested that for parts of the Thames Valley pastoralism was the 'paramount aim' and it is possible that this was the case at Kemerton and along this stretch of the Carrant Valley. However, some evidence for cereal production and consumption was present. Cereals were recovered indicating use of wheat and also six-row, hulled barley. These both appear to have been common crops throughout the Bronze Age, having been widely recorded elsewhere as at Reading Business Park (Campbell 1992). Rye was also present but may have been a weed rather than a deliberate crop. Some cereal pollen was also present, although this could have derived from material brought onto the site. Waterlogged plant remains included some weeds such as corn salad and fool's parsley which are typically associated with cornfields. Generally, however, this evidence was limited and in conjunction with the very small quantities of chaff suggests that much of the material may have derived from processed crop remains brought onto the site from adjacent arable farming areas. Despite this, some limited cultivation of cereals was probably undertaken, possibly in smaller, 'garden' type plots close to areas of settlement. Similar patterns have been observed at sites in the middle and upper Thames Valley where it has been suggested that the majority of cereals may have been imported in exchange for meat, wool or dairy surplus (Yates 1999).

Lastly, cultivation of flax may also have been undertaken as indicated by the presence of flax in the pollen record, as was also the case at Reading Business Park (Moore and Jennings 1992; Brossler, Early and Allen 2004). This is a crop requiring either rotation or intensive manuring (Moore and Jennings 1992) and thus may well have been cultivated in some of the smaller plots at Kemerton.

As noted previously, many of the scrubby species present in the environmental record probably reflect the widespread presence of hedgerows in the landscape; however, scrubby woodland is also liable to have been present. This would have provided suitable areas for keeping pigs which were also well represented in the faunal assemblage. These appear to have been culled in late adolescence indicating that they were used primarily for meat. This contrasts with the site at Reading Business Park where pig was not well represented.

In conclusion, it seems that the site at Huntsman's Quarry formed part of a carefully organised landscape spreading from Bredon Hill down to the Carrant Brook. This was laid out with hedged and ditched fields supplied with waterholes and interconnected with droves or tracks. The organisation of this landscape was designed to support an economy primarily based on pastoralism with cattle and sheep kept as much for milk, wool and traction as for meat. Pigs were also kept, probably in areas of scrubby woodland in the vicinity. Limited cereal cultivation and possibly the growing of flax were undertaken in small plots probably located close to areas of settlement.

Settlement structure

Evidence for the settlement associated with this landscape derives from a range of post-built structures, pits and other features of varying form and probably function. Structures included roundhouses, rectilinear buildings, four-post structures, fences and three large enclosures, the majority of which can be closely paralleled at comparable Late Bronze Age settlement sites.

Lack of stratigraphy and extensive truncation make it difficult to discern the function of many of these settlement components. These factors also affect understanding of settlement development and organisation of space. However, five separate zones of activity can be identified within the site (Fig. 90). Not all of the activity represented in any one zone was necessarily contemporary; however, it seems reasonably safe to assume that for most part broadly contemporaneous activities are represented within each zone. It is similarly difficult to determine whether the separate zones represent different but broadly contemporary activity areas or whether the various zones represent several phases of occupation. The radiocarbon dating programme has indicated that the period of occupation represented was short-lived (under 150 years of domestic occupation); however, it seems unlikely that the wide spread of activity and numerous post-built structures were all occupied or in use at any one time. It is therefore probable that more than one phase of occupation is represented and that some shift in the focus of the settlement has occurred during this period. The potential sequence represented by the five zones identified is discussed in more detail below.

Zone 1: southeast

This zone occupies the southeastern corner of the investigated area. A drove, part of the later of the field systems (FS2), runs across its northern side and appears to have either post-dated or been contemporary with, and largely bounding, other activity in this zone.

The zone incorporates a range of structures and features, the most notable of which are a large waterhole (CG8) and an associated clay-lined pit (CG9). No roundhouses were recorded but domestic structures could have lain beyond the excavated area, particularly to either the south or east. In the light of the large quantities of domestic refuse present within features in the area, domestic activity seems likely to have been undertaken in the immediate vicinity, especially close to the waterhole and associated pit noted above. This area is notable for the presence of several small structures. A rectilinear post-built structure (CG63), a small curvilinear post-built structure (CG89) and all three examples of the small gully and post structures (CG86, 87 and 88) are small structures probably representing storage facilities or animal shelters. The location of three of these (CG86, 87 and 89) alongside the track or drove may therefore be of note and linked to the use of the latter for moving stock around the landscape.

Two unusual curvilinear structures associated with remnants of partially fired, clay walls (CG50 and 51) suggest that craft or production activities requiring the use of heat were located in this zone, perhaps representing remnants of the bases of ovens or drying structures. A hearth was also present (CG30) located close to the waterhole and clay-lined pit, both of which included substantial dumps of burnt limestone. These three features may therefore have had closely related functions; the hearth perhaps being used to heat stones which were then used to heat or boil water drawn from the waterhole in the adjacent pit. Comparable deposits were widely recorded across the site and appear to reflect significant craft or agricultural processing activities which are discussed in more detail below.

Several pits were also present in the area including two basin-shaped (CG20 and 31) and three bowl-shaped (CG21, 22 and 93) examples. Little of note was recorded within these, although burnt stone, charcoal and daub were commonly present within their fills suggesting perhaps that these were also associated with processing activities. Of greater interest were two small pits or large postholes (CG19 and 23) and a substantial posthole (CG25) which formed part of a fence or alignment of small pits running north to south across the area (CG47). These three features were all unusual since despite their small size they contained significant quantities of pottery. In the case of CG19, nearly all the pottery derived from one vessel and this was accompanied by a charred deposit of processed cereal crop which may have been deposited within the vessel. CG23 also contained a considerable quantity of pottery, in this case accompanied by large volumes of charcoal and burnt bone as well as animal bone. CG25 was also distinctive including a base deposit of calcined bone accompanied by quantities of pottery representing several vessels. This was overlain by deposits providing evidence of a robbed-out substantial stone-packed posthole which formed part of the fence alignment (CG47). All three features therefore had an association with apparently carefully selected, distinctive and probably special deposits. These may have been placed as offerings or other structured, ritual depositions marking a particular event or a significant location within the settlement. The fence or pit alignment based around one of these features with 'special' deposits probably demarcated or separated certain areas of site activity and the material placed within it could have symbolically emphasised and marked this division.

Zone 2: northeast

The area defined as Zone 2 occupies the northeast corner of the site and is characterised by the presence of several roundhouses (CG54, 55 and 56) and also all of the four-post structures identified on the site (CG70–74). Several pits were also present, including two basin-shaped (CG17 and 36), two bowl-shaped pits (CG16 and 37) and a small pit/posthole (CG24). A well-defined but isolated posthole (CG35) was also present and contained burnt limestone packing. A waterhole (CG18) was recorded in an evaluation trench to the east and may be associated.

Domestic refuse was not as abundant as in Zones 1, 3 and 4, and this probably reflects the absence of any extensively excavated and substantial features in this area; such features having produced the vast majority of the material culture recovered. Nevertheless, several features produced quantities of domestic refuse in the form of pottery, animal bone and burnt stone.

The roundhouses lay towards the northwest side of this zone. One of these (CG56) was well-defined and had a south-facing porch. The other two (CG54 and 55) overlapped, indicating that at this location, the one replaced the other, while CG55 itself had been replaced or remodelled on one occasion since it comprised two closely overlapping post circuits. Since only half of these overlapping structures fell within the excavated area, it was not possible to determine whether any of these buildings also had porches. The evidence suggests that at no time were there more than two roundhouses in this zone, although others could exist beyond the site boundaries. It is possible that the roundhouses functioned as domestic structures, although in the absence of internal surfaces or occupation horizons this could not be determined with any certainty. However, it is equally possible that one served a residential function, with the other representing an associated workshop. This would be a typical arrangement for a Late Bronze Age settlement, examples elsewhere having been noted to comprise a major residential hut with one or two ancillary buildings (Ellison 1981). The replacement of a structure on possibly two occasions each time on basically the same site as its predecessor suggests that either the location was considered important or less probably that space was at a premium.

The only four-post structures identified on the site were located in this area with three lying near the roundhouses and the other two close to an entrance through one of the field boundaries. These structures are usually interpreted as representing raised structures used as granaries or for storage of straw, hay and other crops (Bradley *et al.* 1980; Gent 1983). At Reading Business Park (Green Park), the smaller four-post structures were felt to have only limited use for storage and it was suggested that, despite comparable layouts, these may have had different functions (Brossler, Early and Adam 2004). This may be the case at Kemerton, although all five examples either exceeded or fell within the range suggested for such storage facilities (3.00–12.00m²; Gent 1983, 245) and use as raised granaries or stores seems most likely.

Of the pits, CG17 was the most notable having been lined with clay and containing a large quantity of domestic refuse and burnt limestone. The small pit or large posthole (CG24) was also of some interest containing pottery mostly derived from one fine vessel which potentially represents a deliberate deposit. An isolated posthole (CG35) also contained pottery and appeared packed with burnt limestone but no clear associations could be determined. The pits in this zone also typically contained burnt limestone, charcoal and occasionally daub and these probably fulfilled a range of disposal and other functions.

This zone of activity appeared to be cut across by

elements of the later of the two field systems defined (FS2), indicating that it pre-dated this element of the field system; a suggestion strongly supported by the truncation of one of the pits in this zone (CG16) by one of the field boundaries.

Zone 3: south central

To the west of Zone 1, a third area of activity can be identified. This was focused upon one of the large post-defined enclosures (CG68). Within the enclosure were a waterhole (CG7), and adjacent to this a second possible waterhole or large water holding pit which had been recut on at least occasion (CG6). Adjacent to these waterholes was a rectilinear post-built structure (CG64), while beyond the enclosure were a further rectilinear structure (CG61) and two small T-shaped structures (CG75 and 76). Lastly within this zone, located on the southern margins of the investigated area, was the northern part of a curvilinear gully tentatively interpreted as representing a roundhouse (CG78).

As in Zone 1, there was only limited evidence for domestic buildings, the putative roundhouse representing the most likely candidate. However, again the substantial features in this area produced significant quantities of domestic waste including pottery, animal bone and burnt stone and it is suggested that the focus of domestic occupation was probably located to the south, beyond the recorded area.

Two possibilities are advanced for the use of the features identified in this part of the site. One possibility is that the large enclosure may have been designed to hold stock separated from the rest of the herd, for example pregnant animals or those recently having given birth along with their young. If this were the case then the waterholes would have provided a ready supply of drinking water for the animals, while the rectangular buildings both within and just outside of the enclosure could have been shelters or byres. Alternatively this area could be associated with production or craft related activities as suggested for the waterhole and clay-lined pit in Zone 1. A considerable number of clay weights, mostly of pyramidal form, were recovered from the waterhole and are liable to have functioned as loom weights, perhaps indicating an association of this area with processing and use of wool or possibly even flax. Certainly water for washing or even flax retting would have been in plentiful supply (from CG7) and could have been additionally stored or used in the adjacent pit (CG6). Large volumes of burnt limestone present suggest that the water may have been heated as part of any processing undertaken. If this were the case then the adjacent rectangular building may represent a related or storage facility. Beyond the enclosure, a second rectilinear building could have fulfilled a similar function while the two T-shaped structures could represent drying racks or even upright looms sited so that the weavers operated facing each other.

Another productive/craft related function represented in this area is bronzeworking; notable quantities of mould and wrap fragments having been recovered from the large pit (CG6) and some from the waterhole (CG7). Some of the burnt limestone is likely to have been associated with this metalworking activity, casting in particular having been suggested to have made use of stones to support crucibles and moulds in intense fires for considerable periods of time and to form superstructures to retain heat (Heaton and Hearne 1994).

Zone 4: north central

The area defined as Zone 4 includes evidence for settlement and other structures accompanied by pits and a substantial waterhole. One of the large post-defined enclosures was also present within this area and may be related to the occupation represented or slightly pre- or post-date it. A fenceline on the west side of this area of activity possibly defined the limits of the focus of occupation and associated activity.

A row of three roundhouses (CG58, 59 and 60), two with southeast facing porches, formed the focus of this area of activity. As in other parts of the site, truncation had removed any traces of internal surfaces, hearths or occupation deposits which may have been present and consequently the function of these cannot be determined with any certainty. As noted previously, Late Bronze Age settlement areas elsewhere have been observed to typically contain one major residential building and one or two associated workshops or other ancillary buildings. In this instance the central of the three buildings was the smallest and most irregular in plan (CG60) and thus may represent a workshop. Of the other two, the roundhouse to the east (CG58) appeared to have been the more substantially constructed and had a porch, thus may represent the main living quarters.

In front of the roundhouses was a rectilinear post-built structure. In the light of its form, this probably served a different function to any of the roundhouses, the most likely uses being as a workshop, store or animal shelter. Although no evidence survived for its presence, a path probably ran between this rectilinear building and the roundhouses. To the rear of one of the roundhouses (CG59) was a fence (CG49) which appeared to extend to connect with the rear wall of the central roundhouse (CG60). This clearly served to demarcate space, possibly keeping livestock away from one area of the settlement.

Large pits containing substantial assemblages of domestic refuse lay to both the rear (CG39) and front of these buildings (CG1 and 2). That to the rear may have held a substantial organic component and was notable in that the relatively large pottery assemblage recovered included residual Beaker and Grooved Ware pottery in sufficient quantities to indicate either deliberate inclusion or total truncation of an earlier focus of activity in the immediate vicinity.

To the south, one of the large pits (CG1) had a weathered or silting lower fill which was virtually sterile. The surviving depression over this lower fill was subsequently infilled with dumps of material, one of which contained significant quantities of charcoal, burnt limestone and domestic debris. The latter included pottery, bone, flint and fired clay as well as a considerable quantity of debris from bronze casting in the form of mould and wrap fragments. Identifiable mould fragments indicated that manufacture may have been predominantly of weapons. A notable quantity of residual Beaker pottery and flint were also recovered.

The other pit (CG2) contained a comparable fill sequence with weathering or silting deposits being overlain by dumped deposits incorporating large quantities of burnt limestone, charcoal and fired clay/daub; however, only very small quantities of pottery and bone were recovered. Since it penetrated through sand and gravel into underlying clay deposits, this feature may have been used to hold or store water, possibly filling naturally from groundwater at certain times of the year. The pit lay on the southern boundary of a large post-defined enclosure (CG67) which may have functioned as a stock enclosure or corral, its funnel-shaped entrance perhaps being designed to help drive animals into it. Although no physical relationship was established between the pit and the enclosure, they may have had a related use with the pit being sited in such a way that, if used to hold water, this would have been accessible to stock both within the enclosure and beyond. The enclosure either pre- or post-dated the earlier field system on the site, a major element of which ran across it.

To the west of these two pits, was a substantial waterhole (CG4). This had a deep sequence of weathering or silting deposits infilling its lower portion with some evidence for recutting or cleaning out at periodic intervals. The poorly preserved remains a log ladder lay against one side of the waterhole. Upon abandonment the waterhole seems to have been left open for a short while before being deliberately infilled with two dumps of material rich in charcoal, burnt limestone, pottery, flint, clay weights, animal bone and other finds. The deposition of these dumps was probably rapidly completed with little time elapsing between abandonment and infilling. Notable among the finds were further quantities of discarded clay mould fragments, wrap pieces and hearth debris reflecting metalworking in the area. In common with several other features in this zone, the waterhole also produced a notable quantity of Beaker period material. This waterhole lay on the projected alignment of one of the boundaries forming the earlier of the two field systems identified (FS1), suggesting contemporaneity with that field system and access to the waterhole from either side of the boundary.

To the south of the waterhole, a small pit or large posthole (CG92) provided a further example of a small feature containing a potential placed offering; in this case producing burnt limestone, animal bone and over 50 sherds of pottery representing at least three separate vessels. A small and apparently isolated posthole (CG90) can also potentially be associated with this zone of activity, its function remaining undetermined.

Lastly, to the far west of this zone and potentially demarcating its limits, was a fenceline on a northwest to southeast alignment.

Zone 5: west

Zone 5 encompasses the activity present in the western part of the investigated area and includes a group of hearths as well as several structures, pits, waterholes and a pond.

The most distinctive feature within this zone was a rectilinear structure (CG62) which was of more regular construction than any of the other buildings on site. The surviving plan suggested that it had comprised two enclosed bays to either side of what may have been an open-sided central area. The structure, although potentially having east and west facing entrances appeared to have been broadly north-south orientated with a central roof ridge. To the south, a large block of limestone in a shallow depression was aligned precisely with the postulated roof ridge. The unusual character and careful construction of the building may suggest that this had a different function to other structures on the site. A rectilinear building at Shorncote occupying an otherwise relatively bare area of site was suggested to be a non-domestic structure (Heane and Adam 1999); the inference being that the building may have fulfilled a religious function, perhaps representing a shrine. Small rectilinear structures at other Bronze Age settlement sites have been similarly interpreted, as at Broads Green and Newman's End, near Harlow both in Essex (Brown 1988; Guttmann 2000, cited in Guttmann and Last 2000). At these sites the presence of placed deposits and unurned cremations provides strong support for this interpretation. Unfortunately at Huntsman's Quarry, no associated finds were recovered from the severely truncated structure; however, the careful construction, unusual form and apparent relationship between the structure and the large limestone block suggest that this may have fulfilled such a function.

To the northwest and west of the postulated shrine, were a series of hearths, notably a closely-spaced group (CG41, 43, 44, 45, 46 and 47) which may have been associated with a nearby pit (CG40). The hearths were characterised by the presence of large quantities of charcoal, burnt limestone and also burnt gravel, although the absence of burning of the surrounding natural suggests that the stone and gravel had been heated elsewhere and then been placed in a prepared hole whilst hot and the radiant heat used for some process. The majority of the burnt stone recovered from other features on the site consisted of larger and more angular fragments than the predominantly small and rounded stones in these features. A deliberate selection of small stone evidently had a perceived advantage – perhaps radiating a more even heat. The nearby pit (CG40) has been tentatively interpreted as a shallow pit designed to contain water while to the north an extensive depression in the natural clay (CG52) may represent a shallow pond. In the light of this observation, the role of hearths seems most likely to have been to provide hot stones to heat water. In the absence of ceramics and animal bone there is no indication that they served as domestic hearths or ovens. Consequently some form of craft related or agricultural processing function seems most probable, although a wide range of other potential uses for hot stone technology have been postulated including, for many Bronze Age sites, use in saunas associated with ritual cleansing (Hodder and Barfield 1991).

Large quantities of burnt limestone and charcoal were also recovered from the fills of a waterhole and large pit in this part of the site (CG3 and CG5). The waterhole had limited quantities of such material in its base fill which predominantly comprised weathering or silting deposits. However, as was the case for all of the waterholes on the site, the upper fills comprised dumps of apparently rapidly deposited material, the final one of which contained large quantities of burnt material as well as domestic refuse. The adjacent pit was clay-lined and had a concentrated dump of burnt limestone in its base, many of the limestone fragments having charcoal adhering to them. A series of dumped deposits infilled the feature and all contained quantities of charcoal and burnt limestone; in two cases these deposits were particularly charcoal-rich. An associated function for these two features can be suggested, the waterhole providing water which was probably heated in the adjacent lined pit. Cooking or a craft related or agricultural processing function again seems most likely. However, as noted above, a wide range of functions can be postulated while the possibility that a burnt mound was present should not be excluded, since such a feature would not be out of place in these circumstances and could lie to the north beyond the investigated area or could potentially have been entirely truncated by later ploughing.

More or less central to this zone, was a roundhouse (CG57) with two associated pits (CG10 and 11). Although the roundhouse had been severely truncated and no internal surfaces survived, significant quantities of domestic debris were recovered from one of the pits (CG10) and moderate quantities from the other (CG11). These included a large pottery assemblage along with flint, burnt stone, animal bone (some articulated) and horncores. These appear to represent waste from a range of domestic functions (*e.g.* food preparation) and suggest that the roundhouse was a domestic residence; the pits representing either storage pits which had been later used as rubbish pits, rubbish pits or alternatively short-term storage facilities for midden-like material prior to its re-use.

A further post-built structure (CG69) was located in the southeast corner of this zone. This comprised a semi-circular arrangement of regularly spaced postholes. This may represent a shelter, providing a windbreak from the prevailing southwesterly wind, or the surviving portion of a roundhouse of which the north side has either been truncated or was of non-earthfast construction. This lay in the corner of a land parcel defined by two ditches.

The southernmost feature within this zone was a major

waterhole (CG14) which was sited on a field boundary within the earlier of the two field systems identified (FS1). This waterhole therefore had access from land parcels to both the north and south. The waterhole had some indications that it may have had revetted sides; however, otherwise this was typical, the base fills reflecting silting and weathering deposits as well as some slumping, the upper fills reflecting deliberate infilling with artefact rich material including pottery, bone and large quantities of charcoal and burnt stone.

Near to the waterhole, a pit (CG26) contained silting or weathering fills as well as dumped infilling deposits; however, few finds were present and the function of the pit remains undetermined. Other pits within this zone included two (CG15 and CG27) which may have been revetted. Burnt limestone, charcoal and finds were recovered but only small quantities and storage or other specialist functions seem likely.

A shallow depression containing large amounts of daub, possibly representing a demolished hearth or oven (CG28), and three isolated large postholes (CG29, 32 and 34) of indeterminate function were also present in this zone.

Finally, at the far western extent of the zone and somewhat removed from all other activity on the site, were two potentially associated features. One of these was a small pit or hearth (CG97) associated with lots of charcoal and some burnt stone, the other a heavily truncated depression containing a deposit of highly calcined bone (CG96). Although the small quantity of surviving bone and high level of fragmentation precluded firm identification of the bone as a human cremation, this seems the most likely interpretation; suggesting that this represents a funerary deposit, the nearby hearth or pit possibly representing the location of the pyre or disposal of pyre material. The small quantity of calcined bone may reflect truncation but alternatively these may be 'token' deposits as have been suggested for similarly small deposits of cremated bone recovered elsewhere as at Hornchurch, Essex (Guttmann and Last).

Other features

Two features of some potential significance could not readily be associated with any of the five zones discussed above.

The first of these was a small pit or very large posthole (CG91) situated on the eastern limits of the main excavated area and lying half way between Zones 1 and 3. This feature was notable for the presence in its primary fill of a large ceramic assemblage which included most of a single fine vessel as well as large chunks of several more vessels. Fabrics, forms and decorative features of these vessels differed from others on the site, being more consistent with decorated assemblages of the later stages of the Late Bronze Age period rather than plainware assemblages which otherwise dominate the site assemblages. In the light of this apparently later date for the feature, its relative isolation is perhaps not surprising whilst functional interpretation is also problematic. However, elsewhere on the site such features have been suggested to have had a ritual function, the associated material assemblages apparently having been carefully selected and placed possibly as offerings. A similar function therefore seems probable for this particular feature.

The other feature of note was a rectilinear enclosure (CG66) located between Zones 2 and 4. Only three sides were recorded and it is possible that this reflects the original form of the enclosure. However, since the most likely function was as a stock enclosure it seems more probable that truncation has removed the fourth side or perhaps that this side was hedged.

Craft, production and trade

Apart from the agricultural subsistence base for the settlement discussed above, a range of evidence for craft, production and trade was identified.

Textile manufacture

The large number of weights which were recovered from a range of features across the site indicates the undertaking of craft activities, especially within Zones 3, 4 and 5. Since sheep formed an important component of the pastoral economy and were kept to maturity, wool was probably an important product and the majority of the weights are therefore liable to relate to textile production and have been used as loom weights. It can also be suggested that one function of the clay-lined pits sited adjacent to waterholes and associated with large volumes of burnt stone may have been to provide hot water for fulling, washing and dying of fleeces (see Jeffrey 1991). Textile production appears to have been a typical component of Late Bronze Age settlement economies, having been identified at comparable sites, as at Reading Business Park (Moore and Jennings 1992; Brossler, Early and Allen 2004) and Shorncote (Hearne and Heaton 1992; Brossler *et al.* 2002). The hearths located in Zone 5 close to a waterhole and clay-lined pit may be similarly associated, especially since they seem to have been created to hold hot stones rather than to heat them thus potentially having been used for the creation of steam by the addition of water from the waterhole.

The recording of flax pollen has been suggested as evidence for the cultivation of this crop at the site and a further potential function for the loom weights could be in the production of linen rather than woollen textiles. The waterholes and lined pits might therefore have been utilised for retting, a process which requires large quantities of water and is more efficient if warm water is used to encourage the growth of the required bacteria to break down the fibres. Flint present in the waterholes is mostly understood to represent residual Beaker material but small quantities of potentially Middle to Late Bronze Age material were present and it is possible that flint scrapers

were used stages of flax processing following retting (*e.g.* for stripping bark from stems) as has been suggested at Reading Business Park (Brown 1992).

Although bone points were also recorded, the absence of spindle whorls for spinning of either wool or linen is somewhat surprising. Similar situations have been noted at some sites in the Thames Valley where it has been suggested that perhaps spindle whorls were made from wood and therefore have not survived (Moore and Jennings 1992). However, this seems unlikely in the light of the considerable evidence for the use of clay spindle whorls from Runnymede (Needham 1991) and Potterne (Hall and Seager Smith 2000) and this absence remains somewhat surprising unless there were strong regional traditions in the selection of raw materials used for the manufacture of such items.

Another point of note may be the variety of forms of clay weight present. These could reflect typological changes reflecting the observed transition from Middle Bronze Age (cylindrical) to Late Bronze Age (pyramidal) traditions. However, both types have been recorded on a range of Late Bronze Age sites and in light of the short period of occupation established by the radiocarbon dating programme at Huntsman's Quarry this seems unlikely. An alternative is that different forms were used for different purposes either for practical reasons or as a result of tradition; thus perhaps one type may have been associated with linen production, the other with wool. Different functions should also not be excluded, potential other uses including netmaking and ropemaking. Similarly other functions can be proposed for the bone points such as for sewing leather.

Metalworking

Nearly 170 piece mould and wrap fragments along with a small quantity of hearth material provided significant evidence for the on-site working of bronze. The distribution of this activity (present in both Zones 3 and 4) indicated that more than one phase of metalworking occurred within the lifetime of the settlement. Deposition of this material occurred in both pits and waterholes within what are argued below to represent closure deposits of some significance within the lifecycle(s) of the settlement. The location of this metalworking waste in Zone 4 may also be significant since the material was located within a pit (CG1) situated adjacent to the entrance of a large post-defined enclosure (CG67). Elsewhere the association of metalwork and metalworking debris with entrances to both enclosures and houses has been noted during the Late Bronze Age and into the 1st millenium BC, as at Springfield Lyons, Essex (Buckley and Hedges 1987), Cladh Hallan in the Outer Hebrides (http://www.shef.ac.uk/archaeology/research/cladh-hallan/cladh-hallan03.html; accessed 7 March 2011) and Gussage All Saints, Dorset (Wainwright 1971). Whether such material was brought from elsewhere to this location for disposal (as at Cladh Hallan) or the metalworking was undertaken in the vicinity, disposal at this location was probably deliberate, placing waste from a process which would have been important both socially and practically at an entrance.

Although highly fragmented as a result of the breaking out of the finished items at the end of the casting process, the survival of these rather soft and friable clay mould and wrap fragments suggests that the material has not moved far from the point of production, or at least that it has not been significantly subject to abrasion and further fragmentation.

Analysis of the form of the surviving pieces and of traces of metal surviving within the fabric indicated the production of leaded tin bronzes or tin bronze with a little lead. Identifiable objects included flat blades, a socketed spearhead, a palstave and a weapon with a mid rib; weapons thus appearing to be the principal products. In the light of the radiocarbon dating for the site, metalworking traditions represented should extend from the transition from the Penard to the Wilburton tradition and into the latter period (mid 12th century BC to late 11th/early 10th century BC; Needham *et al.* 1997; Barber 2003), dating which is consistent with the weapon types identified from the mould fragments.

This mould and wrap material is highly significant representing the first direct evidence for bronzeworking of this period to have been identified in Worcestershire or the wider region. In addition, although similar evidence has been recorded at several comparable Late Bronze settlements in the Thames Valley as at Reading Business Park (Moore and Jennings 1992) and Shorncote, (Hearne and Heaton 1994), finds of production debris are generally rare and more limited than the relatively extensive assemblage from Huntsman's Quarry.

Where present at Late Bronze Age settlement sites, evidence for bronzeworking is often considered as a high status or prestige activity; the production, control, use, trade/exchange and deposition of metal artefacts having had important roles in Bronze Age society, weapons in particular being seen as symbols of power (Champion 1999). Unfortunately, as is commonly the case on settlement sites, no bronze artefacts were recovered. Of probably slightly later date than Huntsman's Quarry, a single looped socketed axe has been recovered nearby on the lower slopes at the northwest end of Bredon Hill (Moray Williams 1954). Of perhaps a slightly earlier date, a double-looped, socketed spearhead has been found at Ashton-under-Hill, towards the east end of Bredon Hill (Moray Williams 1954). Overall, however, bronze artefacts are rare in the general area and therefore this production debris provides very important evidence for the consumption of bronze in this region and raises questions about the long term deposition and use of the finished products.

Trade

The presence of a considerable quantity of middle distance traded pottery tempered with palaeozoic limestone is highly significant. The use of a distinct temper from a particular regional geological source mirrors the recognised Mid to Late Iron Age practice, when the use and regional trading of palaeozoic limestone, Malvernian metamorphic and dolerite tempered wares was widespread in the West Midlands (Peacock 1968; Morris 1994). Recent work in Gloucestershire has suggested that potentially this tradition may have earlier origins, Malvernian rock tempered wares having been identified in association with a Late Bronze Age burnt mound at Sandy Lane, Charlton Kings just outside Cheltenham (Timby 2001). Malvernian wares were also potentially present in Late Bronze Age/Early Iron Age contexts at Hucclecote, near Gloucester, although their association with this phase of activity was not firmly established (Timby 2003). At Kemerton, the evidence of common usage of Palaeozoic limestone tempered material (as well as occasional use of igneous or metamorphic rock tempered material) recovered from securely dated contexts firmly establishes that this tradition extended back to at least the earlier part of the Late Bronze Age. This is a period when it is widely understood across southern Britain that local ceramic production dominates assemblages and few if any regional wares were produced (Morris 1994), and therefore this emerging evidence in south Worcestershire/ north Gloucestershire is of very considerable importance.

Trade and exchange patterns for other commodities might also be expected and given the geographical location of the settlement these are liable to extend south, down the Severn, and east, along the Avon. Apart from the pottery noted above, both the shale objects and bronze (or bronze raw materials) must have been brought to the site from a considerable distance. One possibility is that Severn River trade and possibly even western seaboard exchange mechanisms affected the settlement; shale and tin possibly being brought up the river from southern and southwestern England. Alternatively, such trade and exchange mechanisms might have drawn goods from the east from the Thames Valley and along the Avon.

Clearly further data is required before such trade and exchange patterns can be determined with any confidence and the importance of the evidence from Kemerton lies in raising these issues.

Disposal of material assemblages

The Late Bronze Age material assemblages from the site can basically be interpreted as the residues of domestic occupation, agricultural production and associated craft industries, comprising for the most part pottery, loom weights, animal bone, charred plant remains and large quantities of burnt stone and charcoal. This 'refuse' has largely been deposited as a component of the upper fills within waterholes, large pits closely associated with waterholes and other substantial pits across the site.

This 'refuse' derived for the most part from one or more dumps of material deposited into the uppermost part of these features upon their disuse as part of what appears to be a relatively rapid and deliberate backfilling process.

This material appears not to be discarded at its original location of use (*i.e.* it is not primary as defined by Schiffer 1988). However, the presence of large chunks of vessels, numerous conjoins and relatively low abrasion indicate that the pottery has not been extensively reworked or trampled. Other classes of artefacts as well as the animal bone assemblages are similarly relatively complete and unabraded, animal bone for instance showing only limited signs of gnawing.

These deposits are therefore considered to represent dumps of secondary refuse (*i.e.* it has been moved from its original point of use). However, the condition of the majority of the material incorporated indicates that has moved perhaps on only one occasion and then only a short distance from its original point of discard or breakage. Two possibilities are suggested. The first is that these have been taken from a nearby deposit of material which has been removed from its original sphere of use and stored for re-use, for instance in a short-term midden. Another possibility is that they derive from clearance of occupation debris from an abandoned area of the site. Whatever the case, their deposition into these pits appears to have occurred relatively soon after their original point of discard and appears to have been intended as a final act of disposal.

The reason for this apparently deliberate disposal into these pits is one which warrants further consideration. Numerous other lesser pits, structural features and gullies were also present and yet, in contrast to the waterholes and major pits, most seem to have attracted very little cultural material. Furthermore, the material itself has an intrinsic value as manuring material; the potential importance of manuring for instance for flax growing having already been noted. Consequently, this material appears to have been purposefully dumped into these particular features, all of which would have required a considerable investment of effort to establish and therefore for whatever reason must be considered to have been deliberately abandoned and infilled.

In conclusion, it is felt that the majority of the assemblages recovered from the site represent material deliberately deposited within these features when they were abandoned. Since this is a pattern seen repeatedly across the site, since domestic refuse had a potential use as manure and in the light of a widespread acceptance that refuse is not usually simply thrown away by prehistoric communities, it is concluded that these deposits reflect deliberate closure of these features with material specifically selected for the purpose. The potential symbolism of these deposits and reasons behind deliberate closure of these features are examined in more detail below. Other smaller features with notable concentrations of material may have symbolic meanings as well and these are also discussed.

Settlement lifecycles and the symbolic meaning of material deposition

The pattern and symbolism of disposal of cultural material on Late Bronze Age and Early Iron Age sites is an issue which has attracted much attention in recent years, much of it informed by the models proposed for structured deposition in both the Neolithic (Richards and Thomas 1984) and the Middle to Later Iron Age (Hill 1995). Discussion has focused upon special or placed deposits from a range of features including enclosure ditches, entrances, postholes and pits at both Middle and Late Bronze Age sites. These structured deposits have been suggested to have been placed at symbolically significant locations within the settlements or have been associated with ceremonies taking place at key moments within the 'lifecycle' of the settlements, such as upon foundation or abandonment (Brück 1999; Guttmann and Last 2000; Brück 2001). Considerable attention has also been paid to artefact rich material deposited over and around apparently dismantled buildings as part of a structured abandonment process at Middle Bronze Age sites at Trethellan Farm and several other locations in Cornwall (Nowakowski 2001), as well as at Bestwall, Dorset (Ladle and Woodward 2003). Another area of focus has been the remarkable large spreads or 'middens' of Late Bronze Age date such as those at Potterne (Lawson 2000), East Chisenbury (McOmish 1996), Runnymede Bridge (Needham and Spence 1996, 1997), and locally at Whitchurch, Warwickshire (Waddington and Sharples 2007), at all of which strong 'ritual' connotations have been argued for the material being deposited.

In contrast to these deposits, the major concentrations of material from waterholes and large pits associated with Late Bronze Age sites have attracted remarkably little attention in terms of potential symbolism and depositional practice. This is despite the fact that at sites such as Reading Business Park, Berkshire (Moore and Jennings 2001; Brossler, Early and Adams 2004) and Shorncote Quarry, Gloucestershire (Hearne and Heaton 1992; Hearne and Adam 1999; Brossler *et al.* 2002), the material assemblages from waterholes and other large pits dominate the overall site assemblages as they do at Kemerton. However, discussion of these assemblages has generally been restricted to their use as indicators of site function and economy, interpretation typically viewing them as domestic refuse.

As discussed above, at Kemerton the pattern of infilling of the waterholes and the closely associated substantial pits with can be argued as representing deliberate acts of closure. A rapid appraisal of the character of waterholes elsewhere (for instance at Aldermarston Wharf, Bradley *et al.* 1980; Shorncote, Hearne and Heaton 1994, Hearne and Adam 1999, Brossler *et al.* 2002; Reading Business Park, Moore and Jennings 1992, Brossler, Early and Allen 2004; Eight Acre Field, Radley, Mudd 1995) shows that these features have comparable sequences of use, abandonment and discard to those at Kemerton; material rich deposits typically occurring in the upper (discard) part of the fill sequences. It is therefore suggested that, rather than representing 'rubbish', these represent deliberate and symbolic closure deposits and that these are commonplace on Late Bronze Age settlement sites in both waterholes and large pits. This raises the question of whether they had similar symbolic values and meanings to those deposits which have already been widely discussed.

Elsewhere it has been argued that during the Middle and Late Bronze Age there may have been a close symbolic relationship between settlements and their occupants Brück (1999; 2001); the lifecycles of the settlements/ features being linked to those of the more important inhabitants. Major events in this lifecycle such as the birth or coming of age of an important heir within a kin group may therefore have been marked by the construction of a new house and establishment of a new settlement area. Such an event would have been accompanied by the completion of ceremonies during which significant artefacts and other symbolic deposits would have been made. It is suggested here that similar ceremonies were enacted in the Late Bronze Age; the excavation of a new waterhole perhaps forming part of this 'act of creation' and marking the start of the lifecycle of an important new member of the community as well as part of the settlement. Within a predominantly pastoral society such as that postulated for Kemerton, waterholes would have had a very important practical role providing water for stock ensuring their well-being and enabling them to be closely controlled within a bounded landscape. Thus the waterhole performs an important economic and social function and thus may have had a potentially powerful symbolic as well as practical role within the community.

At the other end of the settlement 'lifecycle', the death of the head of the household or head of the wider kin group would have represented the other key event in this suggested lifecycle. This has been proposed at a number of sites (see Nowakowski 2001; Brück 2001; Ladle and Woodward 2003) and it has been suggested that this event may have been accompanied by a practical as well as symbolically resonant 'death' of the associated settlement. As part of this process, houses appear to have been abandoned in a deliberately structured and orderly manner (Nowakowski 2001), and closing rituals were enacted (Bruck 1999, 2001); including possibly communal feasting and conspicuous consumption to mark the event (Ladle and Woodward 2003).

It is argued that at Kemerton, as with the foundation ceremonies at the start of the lifecycle, the end of this lifecycle may have been intimately tied to waterholes and large pits. Thus the abandonment and closure of these features, symbolically as well as practically, may have marked the end of the 'lifecycle' of an area of settlement as well as the death of a key member of the community. Such rituals at 'birth' and 'death' and the material deposited may have been closely related to beliefs about fertility, regeneration and rebirth. Perhaps the deposition of material symbolised a belief that through returning significant items to the ground and 'harnessing death' the success of a new settlement area and its community could be secured. At the same time, the relationship of the abandoned settlement and the dead member of the community with the rest of the

kin group could be formally closed and transformed, thus ensuring that they could not detrimentally affect the life of the new settlement and surviving community. During a period when the physical burial of individuals became much less visible than it had previously had been (Brück 1995), the potential importance of such ceremonies could have been considerable, possibly reflecting the increasing importance of the household and settlement yet maintaining 'traditional' links to individuals and ancestors.

Support for this suggestion derives from a number of observed characteristics of the material infilling the waterholes and large pits at Kemerton. Firstly, the presence of large chunks of individual vessels, some of which may have been carefully selected, may reflect a symbolic breaking up of the household as has been suggested for similar material derived from pits cut at the end of the 'life' of a roundhouse at Broom, Bedfordshire (Mortimer and McFadyen 1999). Another possibility at Kemerton, is that the vessels deposited had a symbolism derived from their use to store and process milk. Milk appears to have been an important commodity essential to the livelihood of the community, its production being dependant upon livestock the well-being of which was in turn dependent upon water from the waterholes.

An alternative relationship for the vessels might be to communal feasting and conspicuous consumption of food and drink undertaken as part of these closing rituals as has been suggested at Bestwall (Ladle and Woodward 2003). Although the characteristic feasting sets identified at Bestwall and elsewhere (Woodward 2000) were not present at Kemerton, it can be postulated that the pottery deposited in the closing deposits derived from carefully curated, short-term, midden deposits which included the remnants of vessels used in feasts or rituals enacted to mark the last stages of occupation and activity within each zone of the site. Similar processes have been suggested at Hornchurch (Guttmann and Last 2000). At Kemerton a link with feasting may be indicated by the presence of thick burnt residues on many of the vessels which possibly results from the final meals cooked within them; from the large quantities of animal bone present which included burnt, butchered and jointed pieces consistent with use as food; and from the large volumes of burnt stone and charcoal which may reflect use of hot stone technology in roasting meat and heating stews and similar meals held in the pots. A final possibility is that the material deposited simply represents a carefully selected range of the material culture in use at the settlement. This also could have derived from a midden and have been chosen to symbolically reflect the end of the everyday processes undertaken during its lifecycle; thus including domestic refuse as well as items such as the clay weights which are liable to have been associated with commonplace craft activities such as weaving. Lastly, the possibility is raised that the timber posts dumped into one of the waterholes (CG8) may actually represent part of a dismantled building, thus the closure deposits not only contained residues from the settlement but actually potentially incorporated elements of the buildings themselves.

Whatever the case, the symbolic importance of the selection and structured deposition of material culture in these features is emphasised by the generally sterile fills of other features across the site. This may indicate that incorporation of material culture and other residues of everyday life in middens prior to selective use in ceremonies or as manure on arable fields was the norm (Gingell 1992, cited in Brück 2001) and that selection of waterholes as receptacles for some 'rubbish' was, as noted above, a conscious choice imbued with symbolism.

Further areas of symbolism can be suggested for this use of material. Firstly, the 'pollution' of the all important water supply by 'rubbish' may have had considerable resonance to the local community. It has been widely suggested that 'refuse' may have had connotations of danger and an association with death at this time (Brück 1999; 2001) and therefore, in the light of the lifegiving properties of water (for both humans and animals), its deposition into the waterholes may have been particularly symbolic.

Secondly, the presence of a human vertebra in one of the waterholes (CG4) may also have held considerable significance. Brück (1995; 2001) has discussed the regular occurrence of human remains in various contexts at Late Bronze Age settlement sites and their potential symbolic connection with belief systems surrounding the cyclical process of life and death. Thus the inclusion of human remains within one of the 'closure' deposits at Kemerton is consistent with a widely observed phenomenon. Further, this reinforces the suggestion that these deposits formed an element of carefully observed rites undertaken to ensure the successful transformation between life and death and to secure the renewal of life for the community. Another resonance may have been to provide a link to ancestors and ancestral rights, matters which may have been important in establishing and maintaining ownership of the newly bounded landscape. Such a concern with reinforcing ancestral links as a way of demonstrating landownership rights might also be reflected in the incorporation of Beaker material in some of these 'closure' deposits. Although these finds may be residual and accidentally incorporated, the quantities present in some of the waterholes and larger pits (*e.g.* CG1 and CG4) were considerable and may reflect deliberate attempts to create an ancestral link to the surrounding land.

The case for the excavation and closure of waterholes marking the beginning and end of Late Bronze Age settlement lifecycles seems strong. However, a link needs to be established between this process and the widespread extent of the settlement evidence present at both Kemerton and other similar sites. Much of the evidence examined by Brück (1999) and others derives from well-preserved Middle Bronze Age enclosed settlement sites. These only witnessed short-lived periods of occupation within relatively small, fairly closely defined and enclosed

settlements. Brück (1999), using anthropological studies, has suggested that these settlements may reflect what is known as a neolocal residence pattern whereby children leave their parental home to set up their own households upon marriage. The resultant new settlement or household is then inhabited for the lifetime of the head of the household; or perhaps slightly longer if one or more members of the family do not marry, or if resources and space do not enable the setting up of a new household. In the light of variable estimates of the durability of a single phase construction roundhouse which fall between 15–25 years and up to 100 years, a typical lifecycle for a roundhouse of a few decades would fit well with the proposed residence model and a pattern of single generational (or slightly longer-lived) settlements or households might evolve.

However, Late Bronze Age sites differ significantly, with many such as that at Kemerton being unenclosed and having extensive areas of settlement activity. In the light of the limited stratigraphic relationships and the generally poor preservation of structures at these sites, the weight of evidence rests with the waterholes and major cut features and their relationship to the overall site plan. As at Kemerton, it has widely been argued that not all areas would have been occupied at any one time. Shifting patterns in the focus of occupation have therefore been suggested as at Knight's Farm (Bradley and Barrett 1980, 290), Shorncote (Hearne and Heaton 1992; Hearne and Adam 1999) and Reading Business Park (Moore and Jennings 1992; Brossler, Early and Adam 2004). At Shorncote, it was further suggested that each focus of domestic activity reflected a short-lived phase of occupation by a small group or community (Hearne and Adam 1999). It can therefore be suggested that at these Late Bronze Age settlements, similarly short-lived periods of occupation may be represented to those identified for Middle Bronze Age settlements as discussed by Brück (1999), each zone perhaps having been occupied for a single generation.

If applied to Kemerton, this hypothetical model works well. Five zones of activity each with one or more associated waterholes have been identified. If a period of between 20–30 years is allowed for each generational lifecycle, this might indicate a maximum period of occupation across the excavated area of between 100 and 150 years. This figure tallies with the estimated span of deposition for the ceramic assemblage as determined by the radiocarbon dating programme which indicated that the material was deposited over a period of between 1 and 160 years (95% probability). Although the dating programme suggested that some of the waterholes may have been established prior to this period, extending the Late Bronze Age activity to up to 250 years, there was no indication that this earlier use was associated with settlement; the waterholes almost certainly forming part of a field system laid out some time prior to domestic occupation. Unfortunately the dating of the ceramic assemblages was not sufficiently refined to allow such a shifting pattern from zone to zone to be firmly established. However, careful analysis of the ceramic assemblages from each zone has identified subtle variations in their composition and in increasing elements of decoration of the vessels appears to indicate a potential shift over time, from the south and east of the site towards the north and west. Thus it is suggested that the zones may have been sequentially established and abandoned in the order in which they have numbered, namely from 1 to 5 (Fig. 90).

Apart from the larger features with major finds concentrations discussed above, a number of small pits or large, isolated postholes also produced considerable concentrations of material. Of particular note was the large posthole in Zone 1 which appears to have been excavated for the placement of a vessel containing a charred cereals (CG19); a small pit or large posthole (CG92) in Zone 4 which included large chunks of at least three vessels; and the apparently late small pit or posthole (CG91) lying between Zones 1 and 2 containing a large ceramic assemblage, including most of a fine decorated vessel and substantial chunks of several others. Similar 'odd' deposits have been noted and discussed at other sites, and such features may have had associations with settlement lifecycles and the marking of significant events, locations and boundaries within the community (Brück 1999). Alternatively they may reflect the placement of offerings to give thanks or seek help from the gods at a more individual level for instance in relation to poor health or the successful conception or birth of a child.

In conclusion, the majority of artefacts deposited on the site seem to have been selectively deposited in a regular way in particular features. These repeated patterns of disposal and the character of the material incorporated are felt to reflect beliefs associated with death and regeneration, beliefs in which settlements as well as the inhabitants of the settlements were seen to have lifecycles. These ideas of lifecycles may have extended to many of the objects being deposited, while the rituals within which they were deposited may have been designed to ensure the proper treatment of the dead and ensure regeneration and continuing prosperity for the community. Elements of the material may also have specifically been chosen to reinforce ties between the living, the deceased and the ancestors, thereby establishing or re-iterating tenurial rights to the land being farmed by the local community.

The wider context

Yates (2001) has noted from the extensive evidence for Late Bronze Age activity identified along the Thames Valley that well organised field systems and associated settlements with specialised pastoral economies occur in discrete zones or enclaves spaced along the river valleys, with less well populated and managed areas between them. These zones or enclaves in the Thames Valley are associated with metalworking, metal deposition, specialist craft activity and distinctive regional pottery styles, and may represent wealthy socio-economic zones dotted along

river valley with relatively empty areas and less prosperous areas between.

These managed landscapes reflect a period of major social and economic change for local communities. These changes possibly occurred in response to increasing agricultural intensification; the creation of fields reflecting a point where grazing resources came under sufficient strain from the animal population to require careful control. This could reflect the demands of a growing human population; however, social change may have been a more important factor and it has been suggested that at this time the expression of power and wealth become intimately tied to the creation of agricultural surplus. Such surplus may have had an important function in supporting the provision of feasting to local populations by an emergent hierarchy, in underpinning exchange mechanisms involving prestige goods such as metalwork and in creating and meeting a wide range of social obligations (Champion 1999).

At Huntsman's Quarry, the predominantly pastoral economy might therefore have created an agricultural surplus which the local elite used to lay on feasts and through exchange to secure prestige goods like shale and bronze; the latter being cast at the site into weapons which themselves could be exchanged or displayed. Such prestige items were symbols of power at this period. A key factor in the exercise and generation of power and wealth by the local elite, may have been the location of the site beneath Bredon Hill. This situation has been noted earlier to have been ideally placed to overlook and control a potentially important strategic communication and trade route passing between Bredon and the northern end of the Cotswolds (Cruso Hencken 1934). This route runs towards to the confluence of the Severn and Avon and links the east–west route of the Avon Valley with the north–south route provided by the Severn Valley. Similar economic and social factors have been suggested to lie behind the development of key sites in southeastern England, several of which also lie on important communication routes (Yates 2001, 78).

The middle distance trade in palaeozoic limestone tempered and possible Malvernian tempered wares identified at Huntsman's Quarry as well as at several sites in north Gloucestershire may also indicate other socio-political developments in the region. During the Iron Age it has been widely suggested that this tradition relates to cultural, and possibly tribal (*Dobunnic*), affinities, potentially indicating beliefs in ancestral links to certain natural features or geologies (for instance the Malverns and Malvernian igneous rocks; or Clee Hill and dolerite). This raises the question of whether such tribal identities were already emerging during the Late Bronze Age or even earlier. If so, might these be reflected in common cultural traditions, and trade and exchange patterns to the south, west and east of the Malverns in common with the apparent distribution bias of the Iron Age material?

At the moment, Huntsman's Quarry remains an isolated example of this kind of very extensive and unenclosed Late Bronze Age settlement in this region. However, it seems likely that further examples will emerge along the Severn and Avon Valleys. The unique high status pyre site at Broom, Warwickshire with its associated bronze cauldrons and nearby pit containing a pottery feasting set (Palmer 2000) provides an indication of the potential for wealth generation in the region, while Middle to Late Bronze Age boundaries at Park Farm, Barford, Warwickshire (Cracknell and Hingley 1994), at Rudgeway Lane and the Gastons, near Tewkesbury, Gloucestershire (Walker, Thomas and Bateman 2004) and on the Malverns, Worcestershire (Field 2000) indicate other areas where formal division of the landscape had been undertaken. Lastly, other sites, like the extensive and material rich surface scatter at Whitchurch on the Stour, Warwickshire (Hingley 1988; Waddington and Sharples 2007) and the apparently comparable site at South Littleton, Worcestershire (WSMR 7338), provide intriguing potential parallels to the better studied and known sites at Potterne (Lawson 2000) and East Chisenbury.

In conclusion, analysis of the evidence from the Late Bronze Age settlement at Huntsman's Quarry and surrounding area strongly suggests that communities living to the immediate north and west of the Cotswolds were integrated into a similar pattern of Late Bronze Age social and economic change to that known from the more widely studied Upper Thames Valley region to the south and east of the Cotswolds scarp. Unfortunately, the specialised pastoral regime and community established at Huntsman's Quarry appears not to have lasted for any great length of time. The waterholes and presumably the accompanying field systems and occupation areas were abandoned sometime early in the first millennium BC, a pattern seen at many Late Bronze Age settlements. Indeed, it appears that after a period of agricultural intensification, specialisation, expansion and prosperity throughout much of the Late Bronze Age, that the end of this period witnessed a crisis for these communities possibly as a result of deteriorating climate, human over-exploitation and widespread social dislocation (Yates 2001). Around Kemerton, as in many areas of the country, there is no evidence for the pattern of settlement and landscape in the following period, the Early Iron Age remaining a prehistoric 'dark age', and it is not until almost 500 years later that the widespread appearance of enclosures associated with Middle Iron Age activity that the landscape was again visibly occupied and farmed.

Bibliography

Allen, T. G., Darvill, T. C., Green, L. S. and Jones, M. U. (1993) *Excavations at Roughground Farm, Lechlade, Gloucestershire: a prehistoric and Roman landscape.* Oxford Archaeological Unit, Thames Valley Landscapes: the Cotswold Water Park, Volume 1. Oxford.

Avery, M. and Close-Brooks, J. (1969) Shearplace Hill, Sydling St Nicholas, Dorset, House A: a suggested reinterpretation. *Proceedings of the Prehistoric Society* 35, 345–351.

Bamford, H. M. (1982) *Beaker Domestic Sites in the Fen Edge and East Anglia.* East Anglian Archaeology Report 16. Dereham.

Barber, M. (2003) *Bronze and the Bronze Age. Metalwork and society in Britain c. 2500–800 BC.* Stroud: Tempus.

Barclay, A. (2004) Fired clay. In Brossler, Early and Allen (2004), 92–94.

Barclay, A., Boyle, A. and Keevill, G. D. (2001) A prehistoric enclosure at Eynsham Abbey, Oxfordshire. *Oxoniensia* 66, 105–162.

Barfield, L. H. and Hodder, M. A. (1987) Burnt mounds as saunas, and the prehistory of bathing. *Antiquity* 61, 370–379.

Barfield, L. H. (1991) Hot stones: hot food or hot baths? In Hodder and Barfield (1991), 59–68.

Barker, P. (1994) Geophysical Survey carried out at Kemerton pit. Unpublished client report, Stratascan.

Barrett, J. C. (1980) The pottery of the later Bronze Age in lowland England. *Proceedings of the Prehistoric Society* 46, 297–319.

Bell, M. (1990) *Brean Down excavations 1983–87.* English Heritage Archaeological Report 15. HBMCE.

Beswick, P. (1994) Shale ring. In J. Barnatt (1994) Excavations of a Bronze Age unenclosed cemetery, cairns and field boundaries at Eagleston Flat, Curbar, Derbyshire 1984, 1989–90. *Proceedings of the Prehistoric Society* 60, 287–370.

Boessneck, J. (1969) Osteological differences between sheep (Ovis aries Linn) and goat (Capra hircus Linn). In D. Brothwell and E. Higgs (eds.) (1969) *Science in Archaeology*, 331–358. New York: Praeger.

Boycott, A. E. (1934) The habitats of the land mollusca in Britain. *Journal of Ecology* 22, 1–38.

Boyle, A. (2004) Shale bracelet. In Brossler, Early and Allen (2004), 98.

Bradley, R., Lobb, S., Richards, J. and Robinson, M. (1980) Two Late Bronze Age settlements on the Kennet Gravels: excavations at Aldermarston Wharf and Knight's Farm, Burghfield, Berkshire. *Proceedings of the Prehistoric Society* 46, 217–295.

Bradley, R. and Hall, M. (1992) Fired clay objects. In Moore and Jennings (1992), 87.

Brain, C. K. (1967) Hottentot food remains and their bearing on the interpretation of fossil bone assemblages. *Scientific Papers of the Namib Desert Research Station* 32.

Briggs, D. J., Coope, G. R. and Gilbertson, D. (1975) Late pleistocene terrace deposits at Beckford, Worcestershire. *Geological Journal* 10, 1–16.

Britnell, W. J. (1975) An interim report upon excavations at Beckford. *Vale of Evesham Historical Society Research Papers* 5, 1–12.

Bronk Ramsey, C. (1995) Radiocarbon calibration and analysis of stratigraphy. *Radiocarbon* 36, 425–430.

Bronk Ramsey, C. (1998) Probability and dating. *Radiocarbon* 40, 461–474.

Bronk Ramsey, C. (2001) Development of the radiocarbon calibration program OxCal. *Radiocarbon* 43, 355–363.

Bronk Ramsey, C. and Hedges, R. E. M. (1997) A gas ion source for radiocarbon dating. *Nuclear Instruments and Methods in Physics Research B* 29, 45–49.

Bronk Ramsey, C., Higham, T. F. G., Owen, D. C., Pike, A. W. G. and Hedges, R. E. M. (2002) Radiocarbon dates from the Oxford AMS system: Archaeometry datelist 31. *Archaeometry* 44, 1–149.

Brossler, A., Gocher, M., Laws, G. and Roberts, M. (2002) Shorncote Quarry: excavations of a Late Prehistoric landscape in the Upper Thames Valley, 1997 and 1998. *Transactions of the Bristol and Gloucestershire Archaeological Society* 120, 37–88.

Brossler, A., Early, R. and Allen, C. (2004) *Green Park (Reading Business Park): Phase 2 Excavations 1995 – Neolithic and Bronze Age sites.* Oxford Archaeology: Thames Valley Landscapes monograph 19. Oxford.

Brown, A. (1992) Worked flint – Late Bronze Age. In Moore and Jennings (1992), 90–93.

Brown, A. G. and Barber, K. E. (1985) Late Holocene

palaeoecology and sedimentary history of a small lowland catchment in central England. *Quaternary Research* **24**, 87–102.

Brown, N. (1988) A Late Bronze Age enclosure at Loft's Farm, Essex. *Proceedings of the Prehistoric Society* 54, 249–302.

Brück, J. (1995) A place for the dead: the role of human remains in Late Bronze Age Britain. *Proceedings of the Prehistoric Society* 61, 245–277.

Brück, J. (1999) Houses, lifecycles and deposition on Middle Bronze Age settlements in southern England. *Proceedings of the Prehistoric Society* 65, 145–166.

Brück, J. (2001) Body metaphors and technologies of transformation in the English Middle and Late Bronze Age. In Brück (ed.) (2001), 149–160.

Brück, J. (ed.) (2001) *Bronze Age landscapes. Tradition and transformation.* Oxbow, Oxford.

Buck, C. E., Cavanagh, W. G. and Litton, C. D. (1996) *Bayesian approach to interpreting archaeological data.* Chichester.

Buck, C. E., Christen, J. A., Kenworthy, J. B. and Litton, C. D. (1994) Estimating the duration of archaeological activity using ^{14}C determinations. *Oxford Journal of Archaeology* 13, 229–240.

Buck, C. E., Kenworthy, J. B., Litton, C. D. and Smith, A. F. M. (1991) Combining archaeological and radiocarbon information: a Bayesian approach to calibration. *Antiquity* 65, 808–821.

Buck, C. E., Litton, C. D. and Scott, E. M. (1994) Making the most of radiocarbon dating: some statistical considerations. *Antiquity* 68, 252–263.

Buck, C. E., Litton, C. D. and Smith, A. F. M. (1992) Calibration of radiocarbon results pertaining to related archaeological events. *Journal of Archaeological Science* 19, 497–512.

Buckley, D. and Hedges, J. (1987) *The Bronze Age and Saxon settlements at Springfield Lyons, Essex: an interim report.* Essex County Council Occasional Paper 5, Chelmsford.

Burgess, C. (1980) *The Age of Stonehenge.* London, Dent.

Campbell, G. (1992) Bronze Age plant remains. In Moore and Jennings (1992), 103–107.

Cameron, R. A. D. and Riley, G. (1994) *Keys for the identification of land snails in the British Isles.* AIDGAP, Field Studies.

Calkin, J. B. (1953) Kimmeridge coal money. *Proceedings of the Dorset Natural History and Archaeological Society* 75, 45–71.

Carver, M. O. H. and Hummler, M. R. (1991) Excavations at Rock Green, Ludlow, 1975. In M. O. H. Carver (ed.) (1991) Prehistory in Lowland Shropshire. *Transactions of the Shropshire Archaeological and Historical Society* 67, 84–97.

C. A. S. (1995) *Manual of Service practice: fieldwork recording manual.* County Archaeological Service, Hereford and Worcester County Council, internal report 399, as amended.

Case, H. J. (1993) Beakers: deconstruction and after. *Proceedings of the Prehistoric Society* 59, 241–268.

Case, H. J. (1977) The Beaker Culture in Britain and Ireland. In R. Mercer (ed.) (1977) *Beakers in Britain and Europe.* British Archaeological Reports (Supplementary Series) 6, 71–100. Oxford.

Champion, T. (1999) The Later Bronze Age. In J. Hunter and I. Ralston (eds) (1999) *The archaeology of Britain.* Routledge.

Clapham, A. R., Tutin, T. G. and Moore, D. M. (1987) *Flora of the British Isles* (3rd. edn.). Cambridge University Press.

Clarke, D. L. (1970) *Beaker Pottery of Great Britain and Ireland.* Cambridge.

Coles, J. M. and Orme, B. J. (1984) Ten excavations along the Sweet Track. *The Somerset Levels Papers* 10, 5–45.

Coles, J. M. and Orme, B. J. with drawings by Rouillard, S. (1985) Prehistoric Woodworking from the Somerset Levels: 3. Roundwood. *The Somerset Levels Papers* 11, 25–50.

Cook, M. and Hurst J. D. (1994) *Evaluation (fieldwalking) at Huntsman's Quarry, Kemerton.* County Archaeological Service, Hereford and Worcester County Council, internal report 274.

Cracknell, S. and Hingley, R. (1994) Park Farm, Barford: excavation of a prehistoric settlement site, 1988. *Transactions of the Birmingham and Warwickshire Archaeological Society* 98 (1993), 1–30.

Cromarty, A. M., Barclay, A., Lambrick, G. and Robinson, M. (2006) *Late Bronze Age Ritual and Habitation on a Thames Eyot at Whitecross Farm, Wallingford. The Archaeology of the Wallingford Bypass 1986–92, Oxford.* Oxford Archaeology, Thames Valley Landscapes Monographs 22.

Cruso Henken, T. (1938) The excavations of the Iron Age Camp on Bredon Hill, Gloucestershire (1935–7). *Archaeological Journal* XCV, 1–110.

Darvill, T. C. (1987) *Prehistoric Gloucestershire.* Alan Sutton.

Davis, S. (1992) *A rapid method for recording information about mammal bones from archaeological sites.* English Heritage Ancient Monuments Laboratory report 19/92.

Dinn, J. and Evans, J. (1990) Aston Mill Farm, Kemerton: excavation of a ring-ditch, middle Iron Age enclosures and a grubenhaus. *Transactions of the Worcestershire Archaeological Society* (3 ser.) 12, 5–66.

Dinn, J. L. and Hemingway, J. A. (1992) Archaeology on the Blackstone to Astley aqueduct. *Transactions of the Worcestershire Archaeological Society* (3 ser.) 13, 105–119.

Drewett, P. L. (1982) Excavations at Blackpatch, Sussex. *Proceedings of the Prehistoric Society* 48, 321–400.

Ede, J. (1992) Carbonised plant remains. In C. M. Hearne and M. J. Heaton (1992) Excavations at a Late Bronze Age settlement in the Upper Thames valley at Shorncote Quarry near Cirencester, 1992. *Transactions of the Bristol and Gloucestershire Archaeological Society* CXII, 17–57.

Ede, J. (1999) Carbonised plant remains. In C. M. Hearne and N. Adam (1999) Excavation of an extensive Late Bronze Age settlement at Shorncote Quarry, near Cirencester, 1995–6. *Transactions of the Bristol and Gloucestershire Archaeological Society* 117 (1999), 35–73.

Edmonds, M. (1999) *Ancestral geographies of the Neolithic.* Routledge.

Edwards, E. (2009) Neolithic and Bronze Age pottery. In A. Mann and R. Jackson (2009) *Watching brief and contingency excavation at Clifton Quarry, Severn Stoke, Worcestershire (PNUM 5379).* Historic Environment and Archaeology Service, Worcestershire County Council, internal report 1612, 24–30.

Ellison, A. (1981) Towards a socioeconomic model for the Middle Bronze Age in southern England. In I. Hodder, G. Isaac and N. Hammonds (eds) (1981) *Pattern of the past*, 413–438. Cambridge University Press.

Ellison, A. (1988) Discussion. In Longworth, Ellison and Rigby (1988), 36–50.

Evans, J. G. (1972) *Land Snails in Archaeology.* Academic Council Press.

Evison, V. and Hill, P. (1996) *Two Anglo-Saxon cemeteries*

at Beckford, Hereford and Worcester. Council for British Archaeology Research Report 103.

Fagan, L., Hurst, D. and Pearson, E. (1994) *Evaluation at Kemerton WRW*. County Archaeological Service, Hereford and Worcester County Council, internal report 225.

Field, D. (2000) *Midsummer Hill Camp: a survey of the earthworks on Midsummer and Hollybush Hills, Eastnor, Herefordshire and Worcestershire*. English Heritage survey report (NMR SO 73 NE 11).

Fleming, A. (1988) *The Dartmoor Reaves: investigating prehistoric land divisions*. Batsford.

Foster, J. (1990) Other Bronze Age artefacts. In Bell (1990), 158–175.

Garwood, P. (2007) Late Neolithic and Early Bronze Age funerary monuments and burial traditions in the West Midlands. In Garwood (ed.) (2007), 134–165.

Garwood, P. (ed.) (2007) *The undiscovered country: The earlier prehistory of the West Midlands*. The Making of the West Midlands 1. Oxbow, Oxford.

Gelfand, A. E. and Smith, A. F. M. (1990) Sampling approaches to calculating marginal densities. *Journal of the American Statistical Association* 85, 398–409.

Gent, H. (1983) Centralised storage in later prehistoric Britain. *Proceedings of the Prehistoric Society* 49, 243–268.

Gilbert, A. S. and Steinfeld, P. (1977) Faunal Remains from Dinkha Tepe, Northwestern Iran. *Journal of Field Archaeology* 4, 329–351.

Gilks, W. R., Richardson, S. and Spiegelhalther, D. J. (1996) *Markov Chain Monte Carlo in practice*. London (Chapman and Hall).

Gingell, C. (1992) *The Marlborough Downs: a later Bronze Age landscape and its origins*. Wiltshire Archaeological and Natural History Society monograph 1. Salisbury.

Grant, A. (1982) The Use of Tooth Wear as a Guide to the Age of Domestic Ungulates. In B. Wilson, C. Grigson, and S. Payne (eds) (1982) *Ageing and Sexing Animal Bones from Archaeological Sites*. British Archaeological Reports (British Series) 109, 92–108. Oxford.

Greig, J. (1986) Great Britain – England. In B. E. Berglund, H. J. B. Birks, M. Ralska-Jasiewiczowa, and H. E. Wright (eds) (1986) *Palaeoecological events during the last 15000 years; regional syntheses of palaeoecological studies of lakes and mires in Europe*, 15–76. Wiley, Chichester.

Greig, J. (1987) *Site VIII: the late prehistoric surroundings of Bidford-upon-Avon, Warwickshire*. English Heritage Ancient Monuments Laboratory Report 170/87.

Greig, J. and Colledge, S. (1988) *The prehistoric and early medieval waterlogged plant remains from multiperiod Beckford sites HWCM 5006 and 5007 (Worcestershire), and what they show of the surroundings then*. English Heritage Ancient Monuments Laboratory Report 54/88.

Greig, J. (1991) The botanical remains. In Needham (1991), 234–261.

Goodburn, D. (1992) Woods and Woodland: Carpenters and Carpentry. In G. Milne (1992) *Timber Building Techniques in London c. 900 – 1400, An Archaeological Study of Waterfront Installations and Related Material*. London and Middlesex Archaeological Society Special Paper 15, 106–130.

Guttmann, E. B. A. (2000) Excavations on the Hatfield Heath to Matching Tye rising main, north-west Essex. *Essex Archaeology and History* 31, 18–32.

Guttmann, E. B. A. and Last, J. (2000) A Late Bronze Age landscape at South Hornchurch, Essex. *Proceedings of the Prehistoric Society* 66, 319–360.

Hall, K. and Seager Smith, R. (2000) Fired clay objects. In Lawson (2000), 178–184.

Harrison, R. J., Jackson, R. and Napthan, M. (1999) A rich Bell Beaker burial from Wellington Quarry, Marden, Herefordshire. *Oxford Journal of Archaeology* 18, 1–16.

Hearne, C. and Heaton, M. (1994) Excavations at a Late Bronze Age settlement in the Upper Thames Valley at Shorncote Quarry, near Cirencester, 1992. *Transactions of the Bristol and Gloucestershire Archaeological Society* 112, 17–57.

Hearne, C. and Adam, N. (1999) Excavations of an extensive Late Bronze Age settlement at Shorncote Quarry, near Cirencester, 1995–6. *Transactions of the Bristol and Gloucestershire Archaeological Society* 117, 35–74.

Hedges, R. E. M., Bronk Ramsey, C. and Housley, R. A. (1989) The Oxford Accelerator Mass Spectrometry facility: technical developments in routine dating. *Archaeometry* 31, 99–113.

Hill, J. D. (1995) *Ritual and rubbish in the Iron Age of Wessex: a study on the formation of a specific archaeological record*. British Archaeological Reports (British Series) 242.

Hillman G. C. (1981) Reconstructing crop processing from charred remains of crops. In R. Mercer (ed.) (1981) *Farming practice in British prehistory*. Edinburgh University Press.

Hillson, S. (1975) Aston Mill Farm, Kemerton, Worcestershire. *West Midlands Archaeological News Sheet* 17 (1974), 46–48.

Hillson, S. (1992) *Mammal bones and teeth: an introductory guide to methods of identification*. Institute of Archaeology, University College London.

Hingley, R. (1988) Whitchurch, Bronze Age, Iron Age and Roman site 300m west of Birchfurlong Cottages. *West Midlands Archaeology* 31, 37.

Hingley, R. (1993) Bronze Age pottery. In Allen *et al* (1993), 28–31.

Hingley, R. (1999) Prehistoric Warwickshire: a review of the evidence. *Transactions of the Birmingham and Warwickshire Archaeological Society* 100, 1–24.

Hodder, M. A. and Barfield, L. H. (1991) *Burnt mounds and hot stone technology: papers from the second international conference 1990*. Sandwell.

Hughes, G. and Crawford, G. (1995) Excavations at Wasperton 1980–1985. Introduction and Part 1: the Neolithic and early Bronze Age. *Transactions of the Birmingham and Warwickshire Archaeological Society* 99, 9–46.

Hughes, G., Leach, P. and Stanford, S. C. (1995) Excavations at Bromfield, Shropshire 1981–91. *Transactions of the Shropshire Archaeological and Historical Society* 70, 26–170.

Hunt, A. M., Shotliff, A. and Woodhouse, J. (1986) A Bronze Age Barrow Cemetery and Iron Age enclosure at Holt. *Transactions of the Worcestershire Archaeological Society* 10, 7–46.

Hurst, D. (1984) Weights from Beckford, Worcestershire. Unpublished typescript.

Jackson, R., Bevan, L., Hurst, D. and de Rouffignac, C. (1996) Archaeology on the Trimpley to Blackstone Aqueduct. *Transactions of the Worcestershire Archaeological Society* (3 ser.) 15, 93–126.

Jeffrey, P. (1991) Burnt mounds, fulling and early textiles. In Hodder and Barfield (1991), 97–107.

Jones, R. T., Locker, A. M., Coy, J. and Maltby, M. (1981) *Ancient Monuments Laboratory Computer Based Osteometry*

Data Capture Computer User Manual. Ancient Monuments Laboratory Report 3342. London.

Kent, D. H. (1992) *List of vascular plants of the British Isles*. Botanical Society of the British Isles. London.

Kerney, M. P. and Cameron, R. A. D. (1979) *A field guide to the land snails of Britain and North-west Europe*. Collins.

Küster, H-J. (1997) The role of farming in the postglacial expansion of beech and hornbeam in the oak woodlands of central Europe. *The Holocene* 7(2), 239–242.

Ladle, L. and Woodward, A. (2003) A Middle Bronze Age house and burnt mound at Bestwall, Wareham, Dorset: an interim report. *Proceedings of the Prehistoric Society* 69, 265–278.

Ladle, L. and Woodward, A. (2009) *Excavations at Bestwall Quarry, Wareham 1992–2005. Volume 1: The Prehistoric Landscape*. Dorset Natural History and Archaeological Society Monograph 18.

Lawson, A. J. (2000) *Potterne 1982–5. Animal husbandry in Later Prehistoric Wiltshire*. Wessex Archaeology monograph 17.

Levitan, B. (1992) Vertebrate remains. In Moore and Jennings (1992), 98–103.

Longworth, I. H. (1984) *Collared Urns of the Bronze Age in Great Britain and Ireland*. Cambridge.

Longworth, I. H., Ellison, A. and Rigby, V. (1988) *Excavations at Grimes Graves Norfolk 1972–76. Fascicule 2: the Neolithic, Bronze Age and later Pottery*. British Museum, London.

Longworth, I. and Varndell, G. (1996) The Neolithic pottery. In Needham and Spence (1996), 100–101.

Loveday, R. (1989) The Barford ritual complex: further excavations (1972) and a regional perspective. In A. Gibson (ed.) (1989) *Midlands Prehistory*. British Archaeological Reports (British Series) 204, 51–84.

Macan, T. T. (1977) *A key to the British fresh and brackish water gastropods*. Freshwater Biological Association.

Mackin, M. L. (1971) Further excavations of the enclosure at Swine Sty, Big Moor, Baslow. *Transactions of the Hunter Archaeological Society* 10(1), 5–13.

Malim, T. (2001) Place and space in the Cambridgeshire Bronze Age. In Brück (2001), 9–22.

Mant, A. K. (1987) Knowledge acquired from post-War exhumations. In A. Boddington, A. N. Garland, and R. C. Janaway (eds) *Death, decay, and reconstruction: Approaches to archaeology and forensic science*, 65–80. Manchester University Press.

McKinley, J. (1989) Cremations: Expectations, Methodologies and Realities. In C. Roberts, F. Lee, and J. Bintliff (eds) (1989) *Burial Archaeology: Current Research, Methods and Developments*. British Archaeological Reports (British Series) 211, 65–76.

McKinley, J. (1994) Spong Hill, Part VIII: The Cremations. *East Anglian Archaeology* 69.

McOmish, D. (1996) East Chisenbury: ritual and rubbish at the British Bronze Age-Iron Age transition. *Antiquity* 267, 68–76.

Mepham, L. (1999) Pottery. In Hearne and Adam (1999), 58–63.

Moffett, L., Robinson, M. A. and Straker, V. (1989) Cereals, fruit and nuts: charred plant remains from Neolithic sites in England and Wales and the Neolithic economy. In A. Miles, D. Williams, and N. Gardner (1989) *The beginnings of agriculture, Symposia of the Association for Environmental Archaeology 8*. British Archaeological Reports (International Series) 496, 243–261.

Mook, W. G. (1986) Business meeting: Recommendations/ Resolutions adopted by the Twelfth International Radiocarbon Conference. *Radiocarbon* 28, 799.

Moore, J. and Jennings, D. (1992) *Reading Business Park: a Bronze Age landscape*. Thames Valley landscapes: the Kennet Valley 1. Oxford.

Moray Williams, A. (1954) Socketed axe and spearhead from Bredon Hill. *Transactions of the Worcestershire Archaeological Society* XXXI, 49–50.

Morris, E. L. (1994) Production and distribution of pottery and salt in Iron Age Britain: a review. *Proceedings of the Prehistoric Society* 60, 371–394.

Morris, E. (1994) Pottery. In Hearne and Heaton (1994), 34–43.

Morris, E. (2004) Later prehistoric pottery. In Brossler, Early and Allen (2004), 58–90.

Mortimer, R. and McFadyen, L. (1999) *Investigation of the archaeological landscape at Broom, Bedfordshire: phase 4*. Cambridge Archaeological Unit Report 320.

Mudd, A. (1995) The excavation of a Late Bronze Age/early Iron Age site at Eight Acre field, Radley. *Oxoniensia* LX (1996), 21–65.

Mudd, A., Williams, R. J. and Lupton, A. (1999) *Excavations alongside Roman Ermine Street, Gloucestershire and Wiltshire. Volume 1: Prehistoric and Roman activity*. Oxford Archaeology Unit.

Myers, A. (2007) The Upper Palaeolithic and Mesolithic archaeology of the West Midlands. In Garwood (ed.) (2007), 23–38.

Napthan, M., Jackson, R., Pearson, E. and Ratkai, S. with contributions by Bayley, J., Greig, J. and Woodward, A. (1997) *Salvage Recording at Huntsman's Quarry Kemerton 1994–6: Post-Excavation Assessment and Updated Project Design*. Hereford and Worcester County Archaeological Service, internal report 449.

Neal, D. (1987) Stanwick. In *Current Archaeology* 106, 334–335.

Needham, S. (1991) *Excavation and salvage at Runnymede Bridge, 1978: the Late Bronze Age waterfront site*. British Museum Press.

Needham, S. (2005) Transforming Beaker culture in north-west Europe; processes of fusion and fission. *Proceedings of the Prehistoric Society* 71, 171–217.

Needham, S. (2007) 800BC, the great divide. In C. Haselgrove and R. Pope (eds) (2007) *The Earlier Iron Age in Britain and the near Continent*, 39–63. Oxford: Oxbow Books.

Needham, S. and Longley, D. (1980) Runnymede Bridge, Egham: a late Bronze Age riverside settlement. In J. C. Barrett and R. Bradley (eds) (1980) *Settlement and society in the British late Bronze Age*. British Archaeological Reports (British Series) 83, 397–436.

Needham, S. and Spence, T. (1996) *Refuse and disposal at Area 16 East Runnymede, Runnymede Bridge Research excavations, Volume 2*. British Museum Press.

Needham, S. and Spence, T. (1997) Refuse and the formation of middens. *Antiquity* 71, 77–90.

Needham, S., Bronk Ramsey, C., Coombs, D., Cartwright, C. and Pettitt, P. (1997) An independent chronology for British Bronze Age metalwork: the results of the Oxford radiocarbon accelerator programme. *Archaeological Journal* 154, 55–107.

Northover, J. P. (1980) The analysis of Welsh Bronze Age metalwork. In H. N. Savory (1980) *Guide catalogue of the Bronze Age collections*, 229–243. National Museum of Wales, Cardiff.

Nowakoski, J. (2001) Leaving home in the Cornish Bronze Age: insights into planned abandonment processes. In Brück (ed.) (2001), 139–148.

O'Connor, T. (1991) Bones from 46–54 Fishergate. *The Archaeology of York* 15/4. York: York Archaeological Trust.

O'Kelly, M. (1956) An ancient method of cooking meat. *Congresos internacionales de ciencias prehistoricas y protohistoricas, actas de la IV sesion,* 615–618.

Oswald, A. (1969) Excavations for the Avon/Severn Research Committee at Barford, Warwickshire. *Transactions of the Birmingham and Warwickshire Archaeological Society* 83 (1966–7), 1–64.

Palmer, S. (2000) Excavations in the Arrow Valley: the A435 Norton Lenchwick Bypass. *Transactions of the Birmingham and Warwickshire Archaeological Society* 103 (1999).

Palmer, S. (2007) Recent work on the Neolithic and Bronze Age in Warwickshire. In Garwood (ed.) (2007), 123–133.

Parker Pearson, M. and Syde, R. E. (1997) Iron Age enclosures, Sutton Common, S Yorkshire. *Proceedings of the Prehistoric Society* 63, 221–259.

Payne, S. (1973) Kill Patterns in Sheep and Goats: The Mandibles from Asvan Kale. *Anatolian Studies* 23, 281–303.

Payne, S. (1985) Morphological distinctions between the mandibular teeth of young sheep, Ovis and goats, Capra. *Journal of Archaeological Science* 12, 139–147.

Payne, S. (1987) Reference codes for wear states in the mandiblar cheek-teeth of sheep and goats. *Journal of Archaeological Science* 14, 609–614.

Payne, S. and Bull, G. (1988) Components of variation in measurements of pig bones and teeth, and the use of measurements to distinguish wild from domestic pig remains. *Archaeozoologia* 3, 27–66.

Peacock, D. P. S. (1968) A petrological study of certain Iron Age pottery from western England. *Proceedings of the Prehistoric Society* 34, 414–426.

Price, R. and Watts, L. (1980) Rescue excavations at Combe Hay, Somerset, 1968–73. *Proceedings of the Somerset Archaeological and Natural History Society* 124, 1–49.

Prummel, W. and Frisch, H-J. (1986) A guide for the distinction of species, sex and body size in bones of sheep and goat. *Journal of Archaeological Science* 13, 567–577.

Pryor, F. (1978) *Excavations at Fengate, the second report.* Royal Ontario Museum monograph V, 226–267.

Pryor, F. (1991) *Flag Fen, prehistoric fenland centre.* English Heritage, Batsford.

Pryor, F. (1998) *Farmers in prehistoric Britain.* Stroud: Tempus.

Richmond, A. (1999) *Preferred economies: the nature of the subsistence base throughout mainland Britain during prehistory.* British Archaeological Reports (British Series) 290.

Richards, V. and Thomas, J. (1984) Ritual activity and structured deposition in later Neolithic Wessex. In R. Bradley and J. Gardiner (eds) (1984) *Neolithic Studies.* British Archaeological Reports (British Series) 133, 189–218.

Robinson, M. (1995) Molluscs and carbonised plant remains. In A. Barclay, H. Glass and C. Parry (1995) Excavations of Neolithic and Bronze Age ring ditches, Shorncote Quarry, Somerford Keynes, Gloucestershire. *Transactions of the Bristol and Gloucestershire Archaeological Society* 113, 21–60.

Roe, F. (1999) The worked stone. In A. Mudd, R. J. Williams and A. Lupton (1999) *Excavations alongside Roman Ermin Street, Gloucestershire and Wiltshire. The archaeology of the A419/417 Swindon to Gloucester Road Scheme. Volume 2: Medieval and post-medieval activity, finds and environmental evidence.* Oxford Archaeological Unit.

Rozanski, K., Stichler, W., Gonfiantini, R., Scott, E. M., Beukens, R. P., Kromer, B. and van der Plicht, J. (1992) The IAEA ^{14}C intercomparison exercise 1990. *Radiocarbon* 34, 506–519.

Sachse, K. H. (nd) History of Kemerton, undated typescript.

Schweingruber, F. H. (1978) *Microscopic wood anatomy.* Swiss Federal Institute of Forestry Research.

Schweingruber, F. H. (1990) *Anatomy of European woods.* Haupt, Berne and Stuttgart.

Scott, E. M., Long, A. and Kra, R. S. (eds) (1990) Proceedings of the international workshop on intercomparison of radiocarbon laboratories. *Radiocarbon* 32, 253–397.

Scott, E. M., Harkness, D. D. and Cook, G. T. (1998) Inter-laboratory comparisons: lessons learned. *Radiocarbon* 40, 331–340.

Schiffer, M. B. (1987) *Formation processes of the archaeological record.* Albuqurque, University of New Mexico Press.

Shipman, P., Foster, G. and Schoeninger, M. (1984) Burnt bones and teeth: an experimental study of color, morphology, crystal structure and shrinkage. *Journal of Archaeological Science* 11, 307–325.

Shotton, F. W. (1978) Archaeological inferences from the study of alluvium in the lower Severn – Avon valleys. In S. Limbrey and J. G. Evans (eds) (1978) *The effect of man on the landscape.* Council for British Archaeology, Research Report 21, 27–32.

Stanford, S. C. (1982) Bromfield Shropshire – Neolithic, Beaker and Bronze Age sites, 1966–79. *Proceedings of the Prehistoric Society* 48, 279–320.

Stuiver, M. and Kra, R. S. (1986) Editorial comment. *Radiocarbon* 28 (2B), ii.

Stuiver, M. and Polach, H. A. (1977) Reporting of ^{14}C data. *Radiocarbon* 19, 355–63.

Stuiver, M. and Reimer, P. J. (1986) A computer program for radiocarbon age calculation. *Radiocarbon* 28, 1022–1030.

Stuiver, M. and Reimer, P. J. (1993) Extended ^{14}C data base and revised CALIB 3.0 ^{14}C age calibration program. *Radiocarbon* 35, 215–230.

Stuiver, M., Reimer, P. J., Bard, E., Beck, J. W., Burr, G. S., Hughen, K. A., Kromer, B., McCormac, F. G., van der Plicht, J. and Spurk, M. (1998) INTCAL98 radiocarbon age calibration, 24,000–0 cal BP. *Radiocarbon* 40, 1041–1084.

Taylor, M. (1995) The worked wood. In Mudd *et al.* (1995), 40–41.

Terrain Archaeology (2001) *Kemerton, Worcestershire. Investigations by the Time Team, September/October 1998.* Terrain Archaeology report 5032.1.

Thomas, J. (1999) *Understanding the Neolithic.* Routledge.

Thomas, N. (1965) A double Beaker burial on Bredon Hill Worcestershire. *Transactions of the Birmingham Archaeological Society (1967)* 82, 58–76.

Thomas, N. (2005) *Conderton Camp, Worcestershire. A small Middle Iron Age hillfort on Bredon Hill.* Council for British Archaeology, Research Report 143.

Timby, J. (2001) The pottery. In M. Leah and C. Young (2001) A Bronze Age burnt mound at Sandy Lane, Charlton Kings, Gloucestershire: excavations in 1971. *Transactions of the Bristol and Gloucestershire Archaeological Society* 119, 59–82.

Timby, J. (2003) The pottery. In A. Thomas, N. Holbrook and

C. Bateman (2003) Later prehistoric and Romano-British burial and settlement at Hucclecote, Gloucestershire. *Bristol and Gloucestershire Archaeological Report* 2, 31–35.

Tylecote, R. F. (1986) *The prehistory of metallurgy in the British Isles*. Institute of Metals, London.

Tyler, K. and Woodward, A. (2009) The pottery. In Best, J. (2009) *A Late Bronze Age Pottery Production Site and Settlement at Tinney's Lane, Sherborne, Dorset.* http://ads.ahds.ac.uk/catalogue/adsdata/arch-910-1/dissemination/pdf/09.09_Tinneys_lane_text_and_bib.pdf (accessed 5 September 2012)

von den Dreisch, A. (1976) A guide to the measurement of animal bones from archaeological sites. *Peabody Museum* 1. Peabody Museum of Archaeology and Ethnology, Harvard University, Cambridge, MA.

von den Driesch, A. and Boessneck, J. (1974) Kritische Anmerkungen zur Widerristh öhenberechnung aus Löngenmassen vor-und froühgeschichtlicher Tierknochen. *Saugetierkundliche Mitteilungen* 22, 325–348.

Waddington, K. E. and Sharples, N. M. (2007) Pins, pixies and thick dark earth. *British Archaeology* 95, 8–33.

Wainwright, G. J. and Longworth, I. H. (1971) *Durrington Walls: Excavations 1966–1968*. Society of Antiquaries Research Report 29. London.

Walker, G., Thomas, A. and Bateman, C. (2004) Bronze Age and Romano-British sites south-east of Tewkesbury: evaluations and excavations 1991–7. *Transactions of the Bristol and Gloucestershire Archaeological Soc* 122 (2004), 29–94.

Wallis, S. and Waughman, M. (1998) *Archaeology and the landscape in the Lower Blackwater Valley*, Chelmsford: East Anglian Archaeology 82.

Ward, G. K. and Wilson, S. R. (1978) Procedures for comparing and combining radiocarbon age determinations: a critique. *Archaeometry* 20, 19–31.

Warren, S. H., Piggott, S., Clark, J. G. D., Burkitt, M. C.,

Godwin, H. and Godwin, M. E. (1936) Archaeology of the submerged land-surface of the Essex coast. *Proceedings of the Prehistoric Society* 2, 178–210.

Whitehead, P. (1988) Lower Palaeolithic artefacts from the lower valley of the Warwickshire Avon. In R. J. MacRae and N. Maloney (eds) (1988) *Non-flint stone tools and the Palaeolithic occupation of Britain*. British Archaeological Reports (British Series) 189, 103–121.

Whittaker, A. (1972) Geology of Bredon Hill. *Bulletin of the geological survey of Great Britain* 42, 1–49.

Wilson, B. (2004) Animal bone. In Brossler, Early and Allen (2004), 105–106.

Wilson, K. and White, D. J. B. (1986) *The anatomy of wood: its diversity and variability*. London: Stobart and Son.

Woodward, A. (1990) The Bronze Age pottery. In Bell (1990), 121–145.

Woodward, A. (2000a) The Late Bronze Age pottery. In Palmer (2000), 38–42.

Woodward, A. (2000b) When did pots become domestic? Special pots and everyday pots in British prehistory. *Medieval Ceramics* 22/3, 3–10.

Woodward, A. (2000c) *British Barrows. A matter of life and death*. Stroud: Tempus.

Woodward, A. (undated) Typescript in Beckford archive.

Worssam, B.C. (1982) *Geology of sheet SO93 with special emphasis on potential sands and gravel resources*. Institute of Geological Sciences.

Wyles, S. F. (2000) Shale and jet. In Lawson (2000), 208.

Yates, D. T. (1999) Bronze Age field systems in the Thames Valley. *Oxford Journal Archaeology* 18, 157–170.

Yates, D. T. (2001) Bronze Age agricultural intensification in the Thames Valley and Estuary. In Brück (ed.) (2001), 65–82.

Yates, D. T. (2007) *Land, Power and Prestige. Bronze Age field systems in Southern England*. Oxford: Oxbow

Appendix 1.
Additional pottery tables and figures

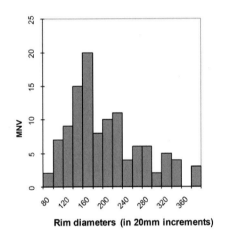

Figure 1: Rim diameters - MNV (whole assemblage)

Table 1: Occurrence of fabrics (whole assemblage)

Fabric	Data	Total	Fabric	Data	Total	Fabric	Data	Total
4	Qty	171	4.9	Qty	297	5.10	Qty	12
	Wt (g)	91		Wt (g)	444		Wt (g)	50
4.7	Qty	241	4.9.1	Qty	404	5.11	Qty	143
	Wt (g)	1208		Wt (g)	3412		Wt (g)	1280
4.8	Qty	47	4.9.2	Qty	716	5.12	Qty	127
	Wt (g)	36		Wt (g)	9137		Wt (g)	687
4.8.1	Qty	234	4.9.3	Qty	136	5.13	Qty	13
	Wt (g)	2242		Wt (g)	1986		Wt (g)	92
4.8.2	Qty	133	4.9.4	Qty	487	5.3	Qty	116
	Wt (g)	1053		Wt (g)	3365		Wt (g)	486
4.8.3	Qty	134	4.10.1	Qty	115	5.7	Qty	95
	Wt (g)	1400		Wt (g)	558		Wt (g)	306
4.8.4	Qty	288	4.10.2	Qty	98	5.8	Qty	47
	Wt (g)	1305		Wt (g)	1308		Wt (g)	237
4.8.5	Qty	12	4.11	Qty	59	5.9	Qty	56
	Wt (g)	79		Wt (g)	524		Wt (g)	301
4.8.6	Qty	88	4.12	Qty	27	97	Qty	23
	Wt (g)	388		Wt (g)	249		Wt (g)	102
						139	Qty	40
							Wt (g)	267

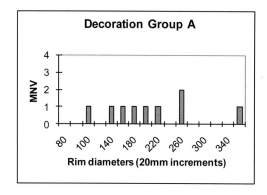

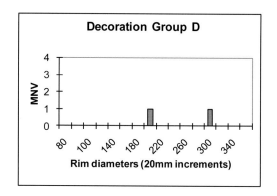

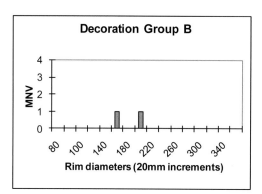

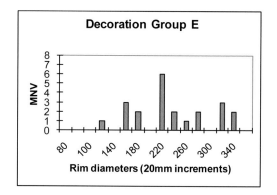

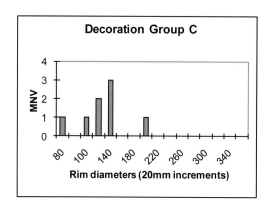

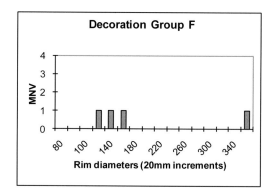

Decoration Group A = D01 and D02

Decoration Group B = D03 and D04

Decoration Group C = D05, D06, D07, D08, D09, D13 and D14

Decoration Group D = D11 and D12

Decoration Group E = D15 and D16

Decoration Group F = D10, D17, D18 and D19

Figure 2: Occurrence of major decoration styles (by rim diameter)

Table 2: Occurrence of fabric groups (whole assemblage)

Fabric group	Data	Total
A	Qty	47
	Wt (g)	237
B	Qty	307
	Wt (g)	1360
C	Qty	40
	Wt (g)	341
D	Qty	222
	Wt (g)	1788
E	Qty	367
	Wt (g)	3295
F	Qty	300
	Wt (g)	1384
G	Qty	404
	Wt (g)	3412
H	Qty	852
	Wt (g)	11123
I	Qty	487
	Wt (g)	3365
J	Qty	241
	Wt (g)	1208
K	Qty	12
	Wt (g)	50
L	Qty	483
	Wt (g)	3833
M	Qty	59
	Wt (g)	524
N	Qty	23
	Wt (g)	102
N/A	Qty	548
	Wt (g)	1021
Total Qty		**4392**
Total Wt (g)		**33043**

Table 3: Occurrence of form (whole assemblage)

Form	Data	Total
B1	Qty	81
	Wt (g)	1242
B2	Qty	129
	Wt (g)	2346
B3	Qty	41
	Wt (g)	853
P3	Qty	15
	Wt (g)	132
P4	Qty	3
	Wt (g)	44
R1	Qty	108
	Wt (g)	1048
R10	Qty	1
	Wt (g)	12
R11	Qty	6
	Wt (g)	48
R12	Qty	2
	Wt (g)	94
R13	Qty	7
	Wt (g)	54
R2	Qty	22
	Wt (g)	79
R3	Qty	1
	Wt (g)	4
R4	Qty	36
	Wt (g)	214
R5	Qty	6
	Wt (g)	32
R6	Qty	49
	Wt (g)	618
R7	Qty	65
	Wt (g)	664
R8	Qty	23
	Wt (g)	232
R9	Qty	7
	Wt (g)	172
Total Qty		**602**
Total Wt (g)		**7888**

Total numbers (whole site)

Bases	251
Profiles	18
Rims	333

Table 4: Occurrence of decoration (whole assemblage)

Decoration	D1	D2	D3	D3/P3	D4	D4/10	D5	D5/D12	D6	D7	D8
Wt (g)	162	46	102	40	128	14	196	28	18	40	125
Qty	12	5	13	5	10	1	19	1	3	11	30

Decoration	D8/13	D8 Dragged	D9	D10	D10/15	D10/16/12	D10/19	D11	D11/16	D12/D15	D13
Wt (g)	26	6	25	802	24	58	82	98	6	6	307
Qty	3	2	9	29	2	1	5	5	3	1	42

Decoration	D13/21	D14	D15	D16	D16/13	D17	D18	D19	D20	P3
Wt (g)	4	42	863	334	42	538	318	1050	40	12
Qty	1	2	82	17	4	23	30	63	3	1

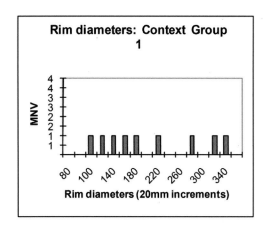

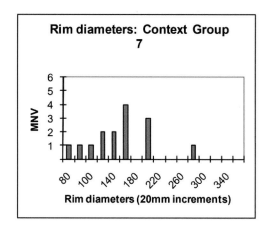

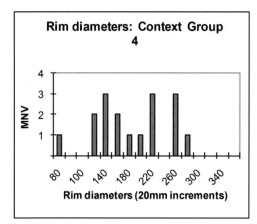

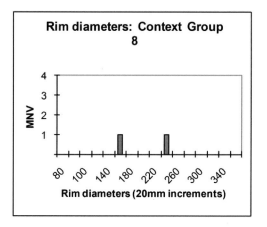

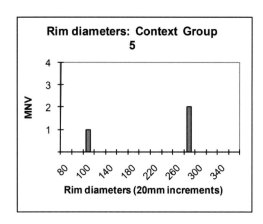

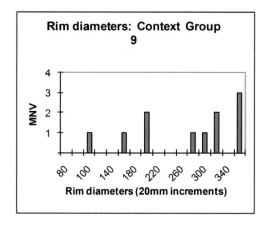

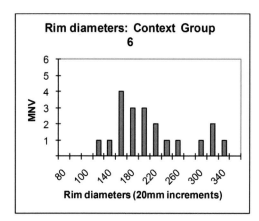

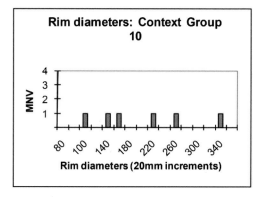

Figure 3: Occurrence of rim diameters in all major Context Groups

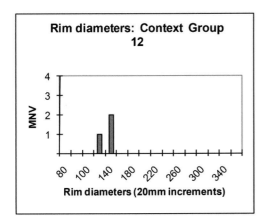

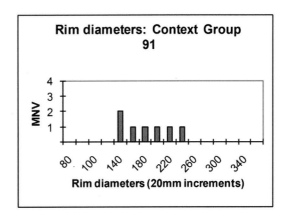

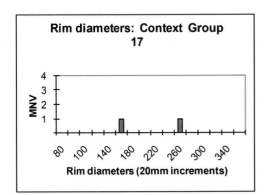

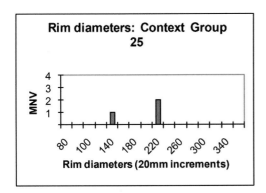

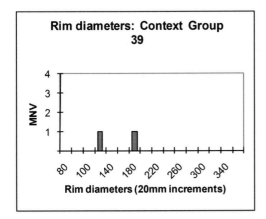

Figure 3: continued

Table 5: Occurrence of form (by fabric group)

Fabric group	Form	B1	B2	B3	P3	P4	R1	R2	R3	R4	R5	R6	R7	R8	R9	R11	R12	R13	R11	Total
B	Qty	16	3	0	0	2	2	9	0	2	0	1	0	1	0	0	0	0	0	36
	Wt (g)	190	116	0	0	22	28	55	0	4	0	4	0	6	0	0	0	0	0	425
C	Qty	0	0	0	0	1	6	0	0	0	0	1	2	0	0	0	0	0	0	10
	Wt (g)	0	0	0	0	22	54	0	0	0	0	4	14	0	0	0	0	0	0	94
D	Qty	13	7	0	0	0	2	0	1	2	0	4	6	0	0	0	0	0	0	35
	Wt (g)	126	44	0	0	0	10	0	4	12	0	32	34	0	0	0	0	0	0	262
E	Qty	5	35	3	0	0	20	0	0	7	0	2	2	0	0	0	0	0	0	74
	Wt (g)	34	630	28	0	0	326	0	0	46	0	52	16	0	0	0	0	0	0	1132
F	Qty	15	5	0	0	0	5	0	0	5	0	4	8	0	0	0	0	0	0	42
	Wt (g)	348	38	0	0	0	20	0	0	14	0	14	50	0	0	0	0	0	0	484
G	Qty	3	15	9	0	0	20	0	0	4	4	9	7	0	0	0	0	5	0	76
	Wt (g)	32	116	114	0	0	114	0	0	28	10	176	52	0	0	0	0	36	0	678
H	Qty	8	36	21	0	0	20	13	0	6	1	4	16	4	4	0	0	0	0	133
	Wt (g)	310	1078	507	0	0	174	24	0	36	4	94	300	90	142	0	0	0	0	2759
I	Qty	3	18	0	0	0	18	0	0	1	0	12	10	5	0	0	0	0	0	67
	Wt (g)	18	210	0	0	0	152	0	0	10	0	142	98	40	0	0	0	0	0	670
J	Qty	1	1	1	15	0	1	0	0	0	0	0	1	13	0	0	0	0	0	33
	Wt (g)	4	28	20	132	0	8	0	0	0	0	0	4	96	0	0	0	0	0	292
K	Qty	4	0	0	0	0	0	0	0	0	0	0	0	0	0	0	0	0	0	4
	Wt (g)	32	0	0	0	0	0	0	0	0	0	0	0	0	0	0	0	0	0	32
L	Qty	9	9	7	0	0	12	0	0	3	1	9	11	0	3	6	2	2	6	74
	Wt (g)	112	86	184	0	0	152	0	0	48	18	88	80	0	30	48	94	18	48	958
M	Qty	4	0	0	0	0	1	0	0	6	0	2	2	0	0	0	0	0	0	15
	Wt (g)	36	0	0	0	0	6	0	0	16	0	2	16	0	0	0	0	0	0	76
Total Qty		81	129	41	15	3	107	22	1	36	6	48	65	23	7	6	2	7	6	602
Total Wt (g)		1242	2346	853	132	44	1044	79	4	214	32	608	664	232	172	48	94	54	48	7888

Table 6: Occurrence of decoration (by fabric group)

Fabric Group	Data	Decoration															
		D1	D2	D3	D3/P3	D4	D4/10	D5	D5/D12	D6	D7	D8	D8/13	D8 Dragged	D9	D10	D10/15
A	Qty	0	0	0	0	0	0	6	0	0	0	0	0	0	0	0	0
	Wt (g)	0	0	0	0	0	0	104	0	0	0	0	0	0	0	0	0
B	Qty	0	0	0	0	0	0	0	0	3	11	30	3	2	9	0	0
	Wt (g)	0	0	0	0	0	0	0	0	18	40	125	26	6	25	0	0
C	Qty	0	0	0	0	0	0	7	0	0	0	0	0	0	0	0	0
	Wt (g)	0	0	0	0	0	0	62	0	0	0	0	0	0	0	0	0
D	Qty	0	0	0	0	0	1	0	0	0	0	0	0	0	0	0	0
	Wt (g)	0	0	0	0	0	14	0	0	0	0	0	0	0	0	0	0
E	Qty	0	0	0	0	0	0	0	0	0	0	0	0	0	0	1	0
	Wt (g)	0	0	0	0	0	0	0	0	0	0	0	0	0	0	12	0
G	Qty	9	1	0	0	0	0	0	0	0	0	0	0	0	0	0	0
	Wt (g)	140	10	0	0	0	0	0	0	0	0	0	0	0	0	0	0
H	Qty	1	0	0	0	0	0	1	1	0	0	0	0	0	0	1	0
	Wt (g)	12	0	0	0	0	0	6	28	0	0	0	0	0	0	6	0
I	Qty	2	0	1	5	0	0	0	0	0	0	0	0	0	0	16	0
	Wt (g)	10	0	8	40	0	0	0	0	0	0	0	0	0	0	600	0
J	Qty	0	1	12	0	10	0	5	0	0	0	0	0	0	0	9	0
	Wt (g)	0	8	94	0	128	0	24	0	0	0	0	0	0	0	134	0
L	Qty	0	3	0	0	0	0	0	0	0	0	0	0	0	0	0	2
	Wt (g)	0	28	0	0	0	0	0	0	0	0	0	0	0	0	0	24
Total Qty		**12**	**5**	**13**	**5**	**10**	**1**	**19**	**1**	**3**	**11**	**30**	**3**	**2**	**9**	**29**	**2**
Total Wt (g)		**162**	**46**	**102**	**40**	**128**	**14**	**196**	**28**	**18**	**40**	**125**	**26**	**6**	**25**	**802**	**24**

Fabric Group	Data	Decoration														
		D10/19	D11	D11/16	D12/D15	D13	D13/21	D14	D15	D16	D16/13	D17	D18	D19	D20	P3
A	Qty	0	0	0	0	0	0	0	0	0	0	0	0	0	3	0
	Wt (g)	0	0	0	0	0	0	0	0	0	0	0	0	0	40	0
B	Qty	0	0	0	0	33	1	0	0	0	0	0	3	1	0	0
	Wt (g)	0	0	0	0	239	4	0	0	0	0	0	22	4	0	0
C	Qty	0	0	0	0	0	0	0	0	2	0	0	0	0	0	0
	Wt (g)	0	0	0	0	0	0	0	0	14	0	0	0	0	0	0
D	Qty	0	0	0	0	2	0	0	1	1	0	0	2	30	0	1
	Wt (g)	0	0	0	0	6	0	0	8	4	0	0	10	434	0	12
E	Qty	0	2	0	0	0	0	0	5	1	4	3	0	0	0	0
	Wt (g)	0	52	0	0	0	0	0	26	8	42	58	0	0	0	0
G	Qty	0	0	0	0	0	0	0	8	0	0	0	0	0	0	0
	Wt (g)	0	0	0	0	0	0	0	59	0	0	0	0	0	0	0
H	Qty	0	0	3	0	0	0	0	3	1	0	1	24	5	0	0
	Wt (g)	0	0	6	0	0	0	0	30	6	0	12	280	78	0	0
I	Qty	5	2	0	1	6	0	2	23	4	0	16	1	26	0	0
	Wt (g)	82	44	0	6	58	0	42	182	142	0	446	6	520	0	0
J	Qty	0	0	0	0	0	0	0	25	4	0	0	0	0	0	0
	Wt (g)	0	0	0	0	0	0	0	280	70	0	0	0	0	0	0
L	Qty	0	1	0	0	0	0	0	0	0	0	3	0	0	0	0
	Wt (g)	0	2	0	0	0	0	0	0	0	0	22	0	0	0	0
M	Qty	0	0	0	0	1	0	0	0	0	0	0	0	0	0	0
	Wt (g)	0	0	0	0	4	0	0	0	0	0	0	0	0	0	0
N	Qty	0	0	0	0	0	0	0	15	4	0	0	0	1	0	0
	Wt (g)	0	0	0	0	0	0	0	268	90	0	0	0	14	0	0
Total Qty		**5**	**5**	**3**	**1**	**42**	**1**	**2**	**82**	**17**	**4**	**23**	**30**	**63**	**3**	**1**
Total Wt (g)		**82**	**98**	**6**	**6**	**307**	**4**	**42**	**863**	**334**	**42**	**538**	**318**	**1050**	**40**	**12**

Table 7: Occurrence of form (by sherd thickness)

Av thick	Data	Form B1	B2	B3	P3	P4	R1	R10	R11	R12	R13	R2	R3	R4	R5	R6	R7	R8	R9	Total
	Nosh	0	2	0	0	0	0	0	0	0	0	0	1	0	0	0	0	1	0	4
	Wt (g)	0	12	0	0	0	0	0	0	0	0	0	4	0	0	0	0	2	0	18
5	Nosh	5	0	0	1	0	5	0	0	0	0	0	0	1	0	3	2	1	0	18
	Wt (g)	44	0	0	2	0	12	0	0	0	0	0	0	2	0	4	6	6	0	76
5/11	Nosh	3	0	0	0	0	0	0	0	0	0	0	0	0	0	0	0	0	0	3
	Wt (g)	204	0	0	0	0	0	0	0	0	0	0	0	0	0	0	0	0	0	204
5/8	Nosh	0	1	0	0	0	0	0	0	0	0	0	0	0	0	0	0	0	0	1
	Wt (g)	0	6	0	0	0	0	0	0	0	0	0	0	0	0	0	0	0	0	6
5/9	Nosh	2	0	0	0	0	0	0	0	0	0	0	0	0	0	0	0	0	0	2
	Wt (g)	52	0	0	0	0	0	0	0	0	0	0	0	0	0	0	0	0	0	52
6	Nosh	1	7	3	1	2	22	1	0	0	6	8	0	9	2	4	11	11	0	88
	Wt (g)	22	30	40	2	22	158	12	0	0	38	43	0	36	8	32	68	84	0	595
6/12	Nosh	1	0	0	0	0	0	0	0	0	0	0	0	0	0	0	0	0	0	1
	Wt (g)	20	0	0	0	0	0	0	0	0	0	0	0	0	0	0	0	0	0	20
6/7	Nosh	3	0	0	0	0	0	0	0	0	0	0	0	0	0	0	0	0	0	3
	Wt (g)	22	0	0	0	0	0	0	0	0	0	0	0	0	0	0	0	0	0	22
6/8	Nosh	6	0	0	0	0	0	0	0	0	0	0	0	0	0	0	0	0	0	6
	Wt (g)	50	0	0	0	0	0	0	0	0	0	0	0	0	0	0	0	0	0	50
7	Nosh	12	10	8	7	0	22	0	6	0	1	1	0	11	0	6	8	0	0	92
	Wt (g)	126	132	114	50	0	228	0	48	0	16	12	0	90	0	46	48	0	0	910
7/10	Nosh	1	0	0	0	0	0	0	0	0	0	0	0	0	0	0	0	0	0	1
	Wt (g)	10	0	0	0	0	0	0	0	0	0	0	0	0	0	0	0	0	0	10
7/11	Nosh	0	3	0	0	0	0	0	0	0	0	0	0	0	0	0	0	0	0	3
	Wt (g)	0	54	0	0	0	0	0	0	0	0	0	0	0	0	0	0	0	0	54
7/5	Nosh	0	1	0	0	0	0	0	0	0	0	0	0	0	0	0	0	0	0	1
	Wt (g)	0	8	0	0	0	0	0	0	0	0	0	0	0	0	0	0	0	0	8
7/7	Nosh	2	0	0	0	0	0	0	0	0	0	0	0	0	0	0	0	0	0	2
	Wt (g)	20	0	0	0	0	0	0	0	0	0	0	0	0	0	0	0	0	0	20
7/9	Nosh	4	4	0	0	0	0	0	0	0	0	0	0	0	0	0	0	0	0	8
	Wt (g)	36	36	0	0	0	0	0	0	0	0	0	0	0	0	0	0	0	0	72
8	Nosh	6	33	7	6	0	26	0	0	2	0	13	0	12	4	15	20	3	0	147
	Wt (g)	46	540	146	78	0	225	0	0	94	0	24	0	72	24	108	166	70	0	1593
8/9	Nosh	0	0	0	0	0	0	0	0	0	0	0	0	0	0	4	0	0	0	4
	Wt (g)	0	0	0	0	0	0	0	0	0	0	0	0	0	0	104	0	0	0	104
8/10	Nosh	0	1	0	0	0	0	0	0	0	0	0	0	0	0	0	0	0	0	1
	Wt (g)	0	14	0	0	0	0	0	0	0	0	0	0	0	0	0	0	0	0	14
9	Nosh	18	12	3	0	0	15	0	0	0	0	0	0	2	0	6	9	1	3	69
	Wt (g)	390	390	90	0	0	189	0	0	0	0	0	0	8	0	130	190	10	30	1427
9/10	Nosh	2	0	0	0	0	0	0	0	0	0	0	0	0	0	0	0	0	0	2
	Wt (g)	26	0	0	0	0	0	0	0	0	0	0	0	0	0	0	0	0	0	26
9/13	Nosh	0	2	0	0	0	0	0	0	0	0	0	0	0	0	0	0	0	0	2
	Wt (g)	0	34	0	0	0	0	0	0	0	0	0	0	0	0	0	0	0	0	34
9/16	Nosh	0	24	0	0	0	0	0	0	0	0	0	0	0	0	0	0	0	0	24
	Wt (g)	0	614	0	0	0	0	0	0	0	0	0	0	0	0	0	0	0	0	614
9/8	Nosh	0	2	0	0	0	0	0	0	0	0	0	0	0	0	0	0	0	0	2
	Wt (g)	0	22	0	0	0	0	0	0	0	0	0	0	0	0	0	0	0	0	22
9/9	Nosh	1	3	0	0	0	0	0	0	0	0	0	0	0	0	0	0	0	0	4
	Wt (g)	8	74	0	0	0	0	0	0	0	0	0	0	0	0	0	0	0	0	82
10	Nosh	6	15	6	0	0	13	0	0	0	0	0	0	0	0	7	13	6	4	70
	Wt (g)	80	278	217	0	0	174	0	0	0	0	0	0	0	0	128	156	60	142	1235
10/10	Nosh	1	0	0	0	0	0	0	0	0	0	0	0	0	0	0	0	0	0	1
	Wt (g)	36	0	0	0	0	0	0	0	0	0	0	0	0	0	0	0	0	0	36
10/11	Nosh	0	0	5	0	0	0	0	0	0	0	0	0	0	0	0	0	0	0	5
	Wt (g)	0	0	108	0	0	0	0	0	0	0	0	0	0	0	0	0	0	0	108
11	Nosh	0	1	0	0	1	5	0	0	0	0	0	0	0	0	1	2	0	0	10
	Wt (g)	0	40	0	0	22	62	0	0	0	0	0	0	0	0	14	30	0	0	168
12	Nosh	0	2	6	0	0	0	0	0	0	0	0	0	1	0	0	0	0	0	9
	Wt (g)	0	10	120	0	0	0	0	0	0	0	0	0	6	0	0	0	0	0	136
13	Nosh	0	1	0	0	0	0	0	0	0	0	0	0	0	0	2	0	0	0	3
	Wt (g)	0	12	0	0	0	0	0	0	0	0	0	0	0	0	48	0	0	0	60
14	Nosh	0	0	0	0	0	0	0	0	0	0	0	0	0	0	1	0	0	0	1
	Wt (g)	0	0	0	0	0	0	0	0	0	0	0	0	0	0	4	0	0	0	4
N/R	Nosh	7	5	3	0	0	0	0	0	0	0	0	0	0	0	0	0	0	0	15
	Wt (g)	50	40	18	0	0	0	0	0	0	0	0	0	0	0	0	0	0	0	108
Total Nosh		81	129	41	15	3	108	1	6	2	7	22	1	36	6	49	65	23	7	602
Total Wt (g)		1242	2346	853	132	44	1048	12	48	94	54	79	4	214	32	618	664	232	172	7888

Table 8: Occurrence of decoration (by sherd thickness)

Dec	Data	4	5	6	7	8	8–9	9	10	11	12	13	15	N/R	Total
D1	Qty			1	1	4	4	2							12
	Wt (g)			6	12	30	104	10							162
D2	Qty		1	2	1				1						5
	Wt (g)		2	26	10				8						46
D3	Qty			11				2							13
	Wt (g)			84				18							102
D3/P3	Qty								5						5
	Wt (g)								40						40
D4	Qty				5	5									10
	Wt (g)				38	90									128
D4/10	Qty				1										1
	Wt (g)				14										14
D5	Qty			1	3	9							6		19
	Wt (g)			2	18	72							104		196
D5/D12	Qty				1										1
	Wt (g)				28										28
D6	Qty				3										3
	Wt (g)				18										18
D7	Qty			3	6			1	1						11
	Wt (g)			8	16			2	14						40
D8	Qty		2	19	2	1		1	1					4	30
	Wt (g)		5	91	14	4		4	4					3	125
D8 Dragged	Qty			2											2
	Wt (g)			6											6
D8/13	Qty			3											3
	Wt (g)			26											26
D9	Qty			3	2			4							9
	Wt (g)			14	3			8							25
D10	Qty			1	2	2		19	5						29
	Wt (g)			66	18	38		504	176						802
D10/15	Qty							2							2
	Wt (g)							24							24
D10/16/12	Qty							1							1
	Wt (g)							58							58
D10/19	Qty								5						5
	Wt (g)								82						82
D11	Qty	1				2		2							5
	Wt (g)	2				44		52							98
D11/16	Qty					3									3
	Wt (g)					6									6
D12/D15	Qty				1										1
	Wt (g)				6										6
D13	Qty	1	1	22	6	4		4	2	1				1	42
	Wt (g)	4	4	128	54	25		22	36	32				2	307
D13/21	Qty			1											1
	Wt (g)			4											4
D14	Qty					2									2
	Wt (g)					42									42
D15	Qty		3	2	10	36		8	18	2	1	2			82
	Wt (g)		8	8	102	287		60	288	20	42	48			863
D16	Qty			3	2	3		3	5		1				17
	Wt (g)			22	10	82		20	144		56				334
D16/13	Qty			4											4
	Wt (g)			42											42
D17	Qty				1	8		11	3						23
	Wt (g)				12	136		312	78						538
D18	Qty			1	6	8		4	11						30
	Wt (g)			4	42	88		86	98						318
D19	Qty				16	11		25	10					1	63
	Wt (g)				152	208		518	168					4	1050
D20	Qty					3									3
	Wt (g)					40									40
P3	Qty				1										1
	Wt (g)				12										12
Total Qty		**2**	**7**	**79**	**69**	**102**	**4**	**89**	**67**	**3**	**2**	**2**	**6**	**6**	**438**
Total Wt (g)		**6**	**19**	**537**	**551**	**1220**	**104**	**1698**	**1136**	**52**	**98**	**48**	**104**	**9**	**5582**

Table 9: Occurrence of internal residues (by form)

Form	Data	Internal residue no	yes	Total
B1	Nosh	52	29	81
	MNV	33	7	40
	Wt (g)	684	558	1242
B2	Nosh	75	54	129
	MNV	37	17	54
	Wt (g)	1324	1022	2346
B3	Nosh	33	8	41
	MNV	17	3	20
	Wt (g)	693	160	853
P3	Nosh	15		15
	MNV	2		2
	Wt (g)	132		132
P4	Nosh	3		3
	MNV	2		2
	Wt (g)	44		44
R1	Nosh	81	27	108
	MNV	50	12	62
	Wt (g)	719	329	1048
R2	Nosh	22		22
	MNV	7		7
	Wt (g)	79		79
R3	Nosh	1		1
	MNV	1		1
	Wt (g)	4		4
R4	Nosh	32	4	36
	MNV	18	4	22
	Wt (g)	168	46	214
R5	Nosh	5	1	6
	MNV	3	1	4
	Wt (g)	14	18	32
R6	Nosh	41	8	49
	MNV	25	3	28
	Wt (g)	404	214	618
R7	Nosh	50	15	65
	MNV	30	8	38
	Wt (g)	510	154	664
R8	Nosh	19	4	23
	MNV	5	3	8
	Wt (g)	142	90	232
R9	Nosh	1	6	7
	MNV	1	2	3
	Wt (g)	28	144	172
R10	Nosh	1		1
	MNV	1		1
	Wt (g)	12		12
R11	Nosh		6	6
	MNV		2	2
	Wt (g)		48	48
R12	Nosh	2		2
	MNV	1		1
	Wt (g)	94		94
R13	Nosh	6	1	7
	MNV	2	1	3
	Wt (g)	38	16	54
Total Nosh		**439**	**163**	**602**
Total MNV		**235**	**63**	**298**
Total Wt (g)		**5089**	**2799**	**7888**

Table 10: Occurrence of fabrics (by major Context Group)

Fabric	Data	Context Group 1	4	5	6	7	8	9	10	11	12	14	17	19	25	39	79	91	92	Total
4	Qty	96	3	8	0	0	36	0	0	0	0	0	0	0	0	0	0	0	24	167
	Wt (g)	64	2	6	0	0	8	0	0	0	0	0	0	0	0	0	0	0	8	88
4.10.1	Qty	39	9	38	3	0	0	7	1	15	0	0	0	0	0	0	0	0	0	112
	Wt (g)	202	76	132	14	0	0	48	8	70	0	0	0	0	0	0	0	0	0	550
4.10.2	Qty	0	5	0	65	9	0	2	14	0	0	0	0	0	1	0	0	0	0	96
	Wt (g)	0	40	0	900	68	0	36	180	0	0	0	0	0	64	0	0	0	0	1288
4.11	Qty	5	2	0	25	5	0	1	4	2	0	0	0	0	0	0	0	0	15	59
	Wt (g)	14	18	0	316	40	0	6	26	24	0	0	0	0	0	0	0	0	80	524
4.12	Qty	1	0	0	26	0	0	0	0	0	0	0	0	0	0	0	0	0	0	27
	Wt (g)	12	0	0	237	0	0	0	0	0	0	0	0	0	0	0	0	0	0	249
4.7	Qty	0	2	0	0	0	0	0	0	0	0	0	0	0	0	0	63	161	0	226
	Wt (g)	0	8	0	0	0	0	0	0	0	0	0	0	0	0	0	109	1067	0	1184
4.8	Qty	0	0	0	0	0	0	47	0	0	0	0	0	0	0	0	0	0	0	47
	Wt (g)	0	0	0	0	0	0	36	0	0	0	0	0	0	0	0	0	0	0	36
4.8.1	Qty	0	22	12	29	10	0	63	0	0	0	18	73	0	0	4	0	3	0	234
	Wt (g)	0	416	62	406	144	0	541	0	0	0	201	432	0	0	28	0	12	0	2242
4.8.2	Qty	0	45	0	19	54	0	5	0	0	0	0	3	0	0	0	0	3	0	129
	Wt (g)	0	306	0	132	389	0	126	0	0	0	0	34	0	0	0	0	32	0	1019
4.8.3	Qty	0	5	13	5	23	1	65	0	0	0	0	3	0	0	0	0	5	0	120
	Wt (g)	0	12	316	40	171	2	746	0	0	0	0	34	0	0	0	0	17	0	1338
4.8.4	Qty	188	37	8	0	1	3	0	7	0	0	0	4	0	0	36	0	3	0	287
	Wt (g)	440	603	37	0	2	20	0	52	0	0	0	9	0	0	131	0	9	0	1303
4.8.5	Qty	0	0	0	0	0	0	0	0	0	0	0	0	0	0	7	0	0	0	7
	Wt (g)	0	0	0	0	0	0	0	0	0	0	0	0	0	0	72	0	0	0	72
4.8.6	Qty	52	8	4	1	4	0	10	0	0	0	1	0	0	0	2	0	0	0	82
	Wt (g)	228	28	12	10	26	0	52	0	0	0	2	0	0	0	8	0	0	0	366
4.9	Qty	0	66	0	27	44	11	80	0	0	0	69	0	0	0	0	0	0	0	297
	Wt (g)	0	144	0	78	86	8	100	0	0	0	28	0	0	0	0	0	0	0	444
4.9.1	Qty	19	43	14	161	36	7	47	2	3	0	26	24	0	1	0	0	1	3	387
	Wt (g)	170	648	92	1109	260	62	512	16	16	0	214	175	0	14	0	0	2	20	3310
4.9.2	Qty	0	195	2	39	288	12	67	0	0	0	8	50	0	8	0	0	34	0	703
	Wt (g)	0	2662	6	972	3508	127	1270	0	0	0	38	215	0	82	0	0	173	0	9053
4.9.3	Qty	12	45	0	1	36	7	3	0	0	0	0	0	0	1	0	0	22	0	127
	Wt (g)	62	770	0	10	529	30	282	0	0	0	0	0	0	6	0	0	149	0	1838
4.9.4	Qty	193	49	5	2	13	2	0	73	35	0	7	35	0	23	17	0	7	0	461
	Wt (g)	1082	869	12	8	72	12	0	424	143	0	25	333	0	77	88	0	42	0	3187
5.10	Qty	0	0	0	0	1	0	0	1	1	0	0	0	0	0	5	0	0	0	8
	Wt (g)	0	0	0	0	4	0	0	2	2	0	0	0	0	0	34	0	0	0	42
5.11	Qty	0	0	0	67	3	0	0	1	0	0	0	0	66	1	0	0	0	0	138
	Wt (g)	0	0	0	911	42	0	0	14	0	0	0	0	294	12	0	0	0	0	1273
5.12	Qty	8	33	17	0	1	0	7	27	1	0	3	0	0	0	0	0	0	8	105
	Wt (g)	41	102	53	0	4	0	54	302	20	0	4	0	0	0	0	0	0	72	652
5.13	Qty	0	13	0	0	0	0	0	0	0	0	0	0	0	0	0	0	0	0	13
	Wt (g)	0	92	0	0	0	0	0	0	0	0	0	0	0	0	0	0	0	0	92
5.3	Qty	5	1	0	0	0	1	0	0	0	63	0	0	0	0	0	0	2	0	72
	Wt (g)	16	6	0	0	0	16	0	0	0	305	0	0	0	0	0	0	10	0	353
5.7	Qty	9	11	0	0	0	0	0	0	0	6	0	4	0	17	19	1	0	0	67
	Wt (g)	22	60	0	0	0	0	0	0	0	64	0	12	0	58	48	4	0	0	268
5.9	Qty	0	0	0	0	0	12	0	0	0	0	0	0	0	0	4	13	0	0	29
	Wt (g)	0	0	0	0	0	32	0	0	0	0	0	0	0	0	20	72	0	0	124
97	Qty	0	3	0	0	0	0	0	0	0	0	0	0	0	0	0	20	0	0	23
	Wt (g)	0	40	0	0	0	0	0	0	0	0	0	0	0	0	0	62	0	0	102
139	Qty	0	0	0	0	0	0	0	0	0	39	0	0	0	0	0	0	0	0	39
	Wt (g)	0	0	0	0	0	0	0	0	0	263	0	0	0	0	0	0	0	0	263
Total Qty		627	597	121	470	528	92	404	130	57	108	132	196	66	52	94	97	241	50	4062
Total Wt (g)		2353	6902	728	5143	5345	317	3809	1024	275	632	512	1244	294	313	429	247	1513	180	31260

Table 11: Occurrence of fabric groups (by major Context Group)

Fabric group	Data	Context Group																		Total
		1	4	5	6	7	8	9	10	11	12	14	17	19	25	39	79	91	92	
B	Qty	14	12	0	0	0	13	0	0	0	108	0	4	0	17	23	14	2	0	207
	Wt (g)	38	66	0	0	0	48	0	0	0	632	0	12	0	58	68	76	10	0	1008
C	Qty	1	13	0	26	0	0	0	0	0	0	0	0	0	0	0	0	0	0	40
	Wt (g)	12	92	0	237	0	0	0	0	0	0	0	0	0	0	0	0	0	0	341
D	Qty	52	13	17	6	27	1	75	0	0	0	1	3	0	0	2	0	5	0	202
	Wt (g)	228	40	328	50	197	2	798	0	0	0	2	34	0	0	8	0	17	0	1704
E	Qty	0	67	12	48	64	0	68	0	0	0	18	76	0	0	4	0	6	0	363
	Wt (g)	0	722	62	538	533	0	667	0	0	0	201	466	0	0	28	0	44	0	3261
F	Qty	188	37	8	0	1	3	0	7	0	0	0	4	0	0	43	0	3	0	294
	Wt (g)	440	603	37	0	2	20	0	52	0	0	0	9	0	0	203	0	9	0	1375
G	Qty	19	43	14	161	36	7	47	2	3	0	26	24	0	1	0	0	1	3	387
	Wt (g)	170	648	92	1109	260	62	512	16	16	0	214	175	0	14	0	0	2	20	3310
H	Qty	12	240	2	40	324	19	70	0	0	0	8	50	0	9	0	0	56	0	830
	Wt (g)	62	3432	6	982	4037	157	1552	0	0	0	38	215	0	88	0	0	322	0	10891
I	Qty	193	49	5	2	13	2	0	73	35	0	7	35	0	23	17	0	7	0	461
	Wt (g)	1082	869	12	8	72	12	0	424	143	0	25	333	0	77	88	0	42	0	3187
J	Qty	0	2	0	0	0	0	0	0	0	0	0	0	0	0	0	63	161	0	226
	Wt (g)	0	8	0	0	0	0	0	0	0	0	0	0	0	0	0	109	1067	0	1184
K	Qty	0	0	0	0	1	0	0	1	1	0	0	0	0	0	5	0	0	0	8
	Wt (g)	0	0	0	0	4	0	0	2	2	0	0	0	0	0	34	0	0	0	42
L	Qty	47	47	55	135	13	0	16	43	16	0	3	0	66	2	0	0	0	8	451
	Wt (g)	243	218	185	1825	114	0	138	504	90	0	4	0	294	76	0	0	0	72	3763
M	Qty	5	2	0	25	5	0	1	4	2	0	0	0	0	0	0	0	0	15	59
	Wt (g)	14	18	0	316	40	0	6	26	24	0	0	0	0	0	0	0	0	80	524
N	Qty	0	3	0	0	0	0	0	0	0	0	0	0	0	0	0	20	2	0	25
	Wt (g)	0	40	0	0	0	0	0	0	0	0	0	0	0	0	0	62	16	0	118
N/A	Qty	96	70	8	29	44	47	127	0	1	0	69	2	0	0	0	0	0	24	517
	Wt (g)	64	152	6	88	86	16	136	0	62	0	28	14	0	0	0	0	0	8	660
Total Qty		627	598	121	472	528	92	404	130	58	108	132	198	66	52	94	97	243	50	4070
Total Wt (g)		2353	6908	728	5153	5345	317	3809	1024	337	632	512	1258	294	313	429	247	1529	180	31368

Table 12: Occurrence of forms (by major Context Group)

CG	Data	B1	B2	B3	P3	P4	R1	R2	R3	R4	R5	R6	R7	R8	R9	R10	R11	R12	R13	Total	Form	Qty
1	Qty	3	26				5			5		16	13							68	Bases	29
	Wt (g)	26	162				26			14		158	84							470	Rims	39
4	Qty	15	26	4			25				1	7	13	4						95	Bases	45
	Wt (g)	394	596	220			215				4	180	136	68						1813	Rims	50
5	Qty		4				2			3	3		3							15	Bases	4
	Wt (g)		36				6			6	6		14							68	Rims	11
6	Qty	4	30	16		1	16			3		3	14		4			2	7	100	Bases	50
	Wt (g)	64	676	298		22	106			26		50	112		142			94	54	1644	Rims	50
7	Qty	15	20	7			14		1	4		3	4	1						69	Bases	42
	Wt (g)	140	414	138			115		4	26		62	38	28						965	Rims	27
8	Qty	2	1				2			1			2							8	Bases	3
	Wt (g)	24	40				24			4			18							110	Rims	5
9	Qty	5	6	2			19			4			9							45	Bases	13
	Wt (g)	222	102	54			328			52			212							970	Rims	32
10	Qty	3	3				5			3	1	7	1		3		6			32	Bases	6
	Wt (g)	18	56				22			18	18	48	6		30		48			264	Bases	24
11	Qty	6					1					1								8	Bases	6
	Wt (g)	50					10					4								64	Bases	2
12	Qty	14						7												21	Rims	14
	Wt (g)	162						41												203	Bases	7
14	Qty		3				1													4	Bases	3
	Wt (g)		54				4													58	Rims	1
17	Qty	3	3	1				12		6		1								26	Bases	7
	Wt (g)	4	36	12				16		40		10								118	Rims	19
19	Qty											1								1	Bases	
	Wt (g)											2								2	Rims	1
25	Qty		1				1			1		5								8	Bases	1
	Wt (g)		12				64			12		10								98	Rims	7
39	Qty	4		2								1	3							10	Bases	6
	Wt (g)	32		16								4	22							74	Rims	4
79	Qty						1													1	Bases	
	Wt (g)						26													26	Rims	1
91	Qty	1	2	5	14		3	1		2	1			12		1				42	Bases	8
	Wt (g)	22	36	59	130		16	8		4	4			94		12				385	Rims	20
92	Qty	1					7													8	Bases	1
	Wt (g)	12					66													78	Rims	7
Total Qty		**76**	**125**	**37**	**14**	**1**	**102**	**20**	**1**	**32**	**6**	**45**	**62**	**17**	**7**	**1**	**6**	**2**	**7**	**561**	**Bases**	**238**
Total Wt (g)		**1170**	**2220**	**797**	**130**	**22**	**1028**	**65**	**4**	**202**	**32**	**528**	**642**	**190**	**172**	**12**	**48**	**94**	**54**	**7410**	**Rims**	**308**

Table 13: Occurrence of decoration (by major Context Group)

Decoration	Data	1	4	5	6	7	8	9	10	12	14	17	25	39	79	91	92	Total
D1	Qty	2	4		1			4	1									12
	Wt (g)	10	104		12			30	6									162
D2	Qty		1		1	1										1		4
	Wt (g)		10		16	10										8		44
D3	Qty		1													12		13
	Wt (g)		8													94		102
D4	Qty															10		10
	Wt (g)															128		128
D4/10	Qty	1																1
	Wt (g)	14																14
D5	Qty		7			1										5		13
	Wt (g)		62			6										24		92
D5/D12	Qty					1												1
	Wt (g)					28												28
D6	Qty									3								3
	Wt (g)									18								18
D7	Qty									9								9
	Wt (g)									24								24
D8	Qty									21								21
	Wt (g)									96								96
Dragged D8	Qty									2								2
	Wt (g)									6								6
D8/13	Qty									3								3
	Wt (g)									26								26
D9	Qty									2								2
	Wt (g)									12								12
D10	Qty		7			10			11									28
	Wt (g)		250			302			184									736
D10/15	Qty								2									2
	Wt (g)								24									24
D10/16/12	Qty		1															1
	Wt (g)		58															58
D10/19	Qty		5															5
	Wt (g)		82															82
D11	Qty					2		2										4
	Wt (g)					52		44										96
D11/16	Qty			3														3
	Wt (g)			6														6
D12/D15	Qty		1															1
	Wt (g)		6															6
D13	Qty	1	2			6				24					1			34
	Wt (g)	2	36			30				170					26			264
D13/21	Qty									1								1
	Wt (g)									4								4
D14	Qty		2															2
	Wt (g)		42															42
D15	Qty	19	14	1	7	1	1	1	4			17	5	2		1	5	78
	Wt (g)	211	178	16	150	8	4	28	44			46	10	26		4	64	789
D16	Qty	2			9			1	2		1		1					16
	Wt (g)	60			182			8	10		6		64					330
D16/13	Qty							4										4
	Wt (g)							42										42
D17	Qty		11			5	1	2					1			3		23
	Wt (g)		220			128	12	132					24			22		538
D18	Qty	11	5			1		13										30
	Wt (g)	98	32			6		182										318
D19	Qty		3			12		45										60
	Wt (g)		110			118		804										1032
P3	Qty	1																1
	Wt (g)	12																12
Total Qty		37	64	4	18	40	2	72	20	65	1	17	7	2	1	32	5	387
Total Wt (g)		407	1198	22	360	688	16	1270	268	356	6	46	98	26	26	280	64	5131

Table 14: Occurrence of abrasion (by major Context Group)

	Abrasion					
Context Group	**1**	**2**	**2/3**	**3**	**N/R**	**Total**
1	53	419	0	41	114	627
4	6	546	2	44	0	598
5	0	86	0	35	0	121
6	6	428	2	36	0	472
7	22	471	0	35	0	528
8	14	20	1	44	13	92
9	0	252	136	16	0	404
10	0	98	0	13	19	130
11	0	12	9	37	0	58
12	0	98	1	9	0	108
14	0	51	0	81	0	132
17	35	115	0	48	0	198
19	0	2	0	64	0	66
25/47	10	27	0	15	0	52
39	3	76	0	15	0	94
79	1	54	0	42	0	97
91	5	195	0	43	0	243
92	0	26	0	24	0	50
Total	**155**	**2976**	**151**	**642**	**146**	**4070**

Appendix 2.
Pottery fabrics (Derek Hurst and Robin Jackson)

The following are pottery fabrics defined during Kemerton post-excavation analysis with the addition of a few fabrics previously defined at Aston Mill but not fully published in that report. All the latter were present on the Kemerton site. The definition of the Kemerton fabrics was undertaken through consultation between Derek Hurst, Robin Jackson and Ann Woodward. The descriptions have been compiled as part of the County fabric series (Hurst and Rees 1991; Hurst 1994 (as amended)), and follow guidelines drawn up by the Prehistoric Ceramics Research Group (1995).

Fabric 4.7 Fossil shell and grog

Manufacture	Handmade
Firing	Fairly hard; dark grey outer surface and core (10YR 4/1) inner surface greyish brown (10YR 5/2)
Texture	Soapy
Surface treatment	Wiped
Thickness	8–11mm
Inclusions	Frequent inclusions of shell (< 2mm) scattered throughout the clay matrix, together with a little sparry calcite indicating that the shell is fossiliferous, some shelly limestone, a few quartz grains under 0.05mm in size, flecks of mica, iron ore and some pieces of angular grog (< 2mm) which contain small pieces of shell and limestone
Source	Unknown – ?local
Period	Bronze Age

Description based on petrological report (Aston Mill)

Fabric 4.8 Limestone

Manufacture	Handmade
Firing	Soft. Pinkish red to dark brown outer surface and variably coloured inner surface with a grey core
Texture	Soapy
Surface treatment	Both surfaces occasionally burnished
Thickness	4–14mm
Inclusions	Very common fossilised shelly limestone which is poorly sorted, angular and generally less than 5mm in size; rare quartz sand which is rounded and of 0.25–0.5mm
Source	Unknown – ?Malverns/May Hill area
Period	Bronze Age

Fabric 4.9 Shell

Manufacture	Handmade
Firing	Soft. The inner and outer surfaces are red or brown (inner surface occasionally black), and the core is medium grey
Texture	Soapy
Surface treatment	Wiped surface inside
Thickness	4–14mm
Inclusions	Common shell which is poorly sorted, and less than 6mm in size.
Source	Unknown – ?local
Period	Bronze Age

Fabric 4.10 Limestone and quartzite tempered ware

Manufacture	Handmade
Firing	Fairly hard. The surfaces are reddish buff and the core can be oxidised or reduced red throughout
Texture	Rough
Surface treatment	None represented
Thickness	4–11mm
Inclusions	Common to moderate, subangular fossiliferous limestone which is poorly sorted, and less than 8mm in size
Source	Unknown – ?local
Period	Bronze Age

Fabric 4.11 Shell and quartzite

Manufacture	Handmade
Firing	Soft. The external surface is red while inner surfaces are oxidised or reduced; the core is grey
Texture	Soapy
Surface treatment	None represented
Thickness	7–10mm
Inclusions	Common fossil shell which is poorly sorted, and less than 8 mm; rare white, angular ?quartzite which is well sorted and less than 2mm in size
Source	Unknown – ?local
Period	Bronze Age

Fabric 4.12 Shell

Manufacture	Handmade
Firing	Pale buff surfaces and margins, except for pale red external surface. There is a grey core
Texture	Soapy or smooth
Surface treatment	None represented
Thickness	6–12mm
Inclusions	Moderate plate shell which is poorly sorted and less than 2mm; rare rounded quartz which is 0.1–0.5mm in size
Source	Unknown – ?Local
Period	Bronze Age

Fabric 5.3 Coarse quartz (and ?grog)

Manufacture	Handmade
Firing	Soft. Oxidised red throughout
Texture	Rough
Surface treatment	None represented
Thickness	5–10mm

Inclusions	Abundant medium (<0.5mm) sub-rounded to sub-angular quartz; moderate coarse quartz/quartzite; sparse-moderate clay pellets/mudstone (,2.5mm)
Source	Unknown – ?local
Period	Beaker

Fabric 5.7 Quartz and limestone

Manufacture	Handmade
Firing	Hard, shades of dark grey (5YR 4/1) throughout
Texture	Rough
Surface treatment	May be wiped
Thickness	5–13mm
Inclusions	Clean matrix containing sub-rectangular quartz grains up to 0.60mm in size together with small fragments of limestone, iron ore, a little calcite and some largish pieces of grog containing small pieces of limestone
Source	Unknown – ?Local
Period	Beaker

Description based on petrological report (Aston Mill)

Fabric 5.8 Quartzite

Manufacture	Handmade
Firing	Soft. Generally brown surfaces and margins and a grey core
Texture	Smooth or rough
Surface treatment	Smoothed inside surface
Thickness	7–15mm
Inclusions	Very common angular white ?quartzite which is well sorted and generally less than 5mm
Source	Unknown – ?local
Period	Neolithic

Fabric 5.9 Quartz

Manufacture	Handmade
Firing	Soft. Surfaces and margins are brown, except for red to pale brown external surface. The core is dark grey
Texture	Rough
Surface treatment	Inside surface possibly smoothed
Thickness	5–10mm
Inclusions	Common rounded quartz which is 0.25–1.00mm in size and generally well sorted; rare, rounded, red iron rich ?silty pellets which have a dark surface and which are moderately sorted. Mica is also present

Source   Unknown – ?local
Period   Beaker

Fabric 5.10 Fine quartz

Manufacture   Handmade
Firing   Soft. Dark grey surfaces and a
                          brown core
Texture   Smooth
Surface treatment   None represented
Thickness   4–10mm
Inclusions   Common rounded quartz which is
                          poorly sorted and mainly 0.1mm,
                          but occasionally 1.0mm in size;
                          common fine mica which is well
                          sorted
Source   Unknown – ?local
Period   Bronze Age

Fabric 5.11 Quartz, quartzite, and limestone

Manufacture   Handmade
Firing   Soft. Red surfaces and a grey core
Texture   Rough
Surface treatment   None represented
Thickness   5–15mm
Inclusions   Very common rounded quartz sand
                          which is well sorted and 0.25–
                          0.50mm in size; white angular
                          quartzite which is rare and less than
                          5mm in size; rare limestone which
                          is well sorted and 0.1–0.25mm in
                          size
Source   Unknown – ?local
Period   Bronze Age

Fabric 5.12 Quartz and limestone

Manufacture   Handmade
Firing   Soft. Oxidised throughout to buff
                          or red, or reduced on the inside
Texture   Rough

Surface treatment   None represented
Thickness   6–13mm
Inclusions   Common rounded quartz sand
                          which is well sorted and 0.1–0.25
                          in size; moderate sub-rounded
                          limestone which is poorly sorted
                          and less than 6mm in size
Source   Unknown – ?local
Period   Bronze Age

Fabric 5.13 Quartz

Manufacture   Handmade
Firing   Soft. Brown throughout except for
                          orange external surface
Texture   Rough
Surface treatment   None represented
Thickness   6–10mm
Inclusions   Abundant rounded quartz sand
                          which is well sorted and 0.1–
                          0.5mm in size
Source   Unknown – ?local
Period   Bronze Age

Fabric 139 Grog (?), quartz and limestone

Manufacture   Handmade
Firing   Soft. Buff external surface and dark
                          grey inside surface with a dark grey
                          core
Texture   Soapy
Surface treatment   None represented
Thickness   6–8mm
Inclusions   Rare subrounded clay pellets
                          (?grog) which are less than 8mm
                          in size; rare rounded quartz sand
                          which is well sorted and 0.1–0.25
                          in size; rare limestone which is
                          well sorted and *c.* 0.25mm in size
Source   Unknown – ?local
Period   Beaker

Index

Figures in italics denote pages with illustrations. Excavated features and structures are presumed to be Late Bronze Age unless otherwise stated